The Battle for Hunger Hill

Other books by Dan Bolger

Dragons at War: 2-34th Infantry in the Mojave
Americans at War, 1975-1986: An Era of Violent Peace
Feast of Bones
Scenes from an Unfinished War
Savage Peace: Americans at War in the 1990s

The Battle for Hunger Hill

The 1st Battalion, 327th Infantry Regiment
at the Joint Readiness Training Center

Daniel P. Bolger

★
PRESIDIO

Copyright © 1997 by Daniel P. Bolger

Published by Presidio Press
505 B San Marin Drive, Suite 300
Novato, CA 94945-1340

Library of Congress Cataloging-in-Publication Data

Bolger, Daniel P., 1957–
    The Battle for Hunger Hill : the 1st Battalion, 327th Infantry
Regiment at the Joint Readiness Training Center/Daniel P. Bolger.
        p.   cm.
    Includes index.
    ISBN 0-89141-453-3 (hardcover)
    1. United States. Army. Infantry Regiment, 327. Battalion, 1st.
2. United States. Dept. of the Army. Joint Readiness Training
Center. 3. Fort Polk (La.) I. Title.
UA29 327th.B65   1997
356'.113'0973—dc21   96-47564
                                                        CIP

All photographs courtesy of the Department of the Army.
Printed in the United States of America

For Cmd. Sgt. Maj. Mark S. Ripka and all the other soldiers of the 1st Battalion, 327th Infantry Regiment, June 1994 to June 1996 . . . "Above the Rest"

Contents

Preface

A dozen years ago, I wrote a book called *Dragons at War*. It reflected my experiences as a company commander at the National Training Center in Fort Irwin, California. To tell that story, it became useful to try to explain the battalion's operations as a whole, although my role necessarily skewed my views. Anyway, I did the research and wrote the book, all a very pleasant learning experience for me, and hopefully for some readers, too. In the certitude typical of young captains of infantry, I made some pretty tough judgments about the performance of my superiors, especially my battalion commander, an officer still serving at that time but since retired. To read *Dragons at War* you might wonder how such an average senior officer had been entrusted with an infantry battalion. Surely any of us could do better.

Well, I have had my chance, as recorded in this book. To paraphrase Mark Twain, when I was a punk captain my battalion commander was so ignorant I could hardly stand to have him around. But when I got to be a battalion commander myself, I was astonished at how much the old man had learned. Command of troops in training calls for a soldier's full commitment. Command of troops in combat, I am sure, will demand even more, perhaps even the last full measure of devotion, so easy to talk about and so hard to do. In retrospect, I now know just how much my former commander gave to all of us in the long-defunct 2d Battalion (Mechanized), 34th Infantry. Some of it lived on in the 1st Battalion, 327th Infantry Regiment.

Many wonderful people made this book possible. A good number of the great men of the 1st of the 327th are named in these pages, but it would take a library to record all of their fine deeds in defense of America. The chain of command in the 101st Airborne Division (Air Assault) gave 1-327th Infantry an opportunity to train at the Joint

Readiness Training Center, and then let us go back and try to get it right. A few outside of the "Above the Rest" battalion deserve special note: Lt. Gen. Jack Keane, Maj. Gen. Buck Kernan, Maj. Gen. Michael B. Sherfield, Brig. Gen. Sam Thompson, Brig. Gen. Jim Donald, Col. Jack Donovan, Col. Mark T. Kimmitt, Col. Mike Barbero, Maj. Mark Martins, and Lt. Col. Kenneth Mason "Mace" Crowe. Thanks also to the greatest editor ever, E. J. McCarthy, a model of tolerance and endless source of good advice. Finally, none of this could have been done without the love and trust of my wife Joy, son Philip, and daughter Carolyn. It was all fun, every bit of it.

Prologue
Tigerland

"The liberal society has no use or need for legions—as its prophets have long proclaimed. Except that in this world there are tigers."

—T. R. Fehrenbach
This Kind of War

They rushed through the moonless night like a black wind, tearing across the sleeping countryside just above the trees, flying almost too swiftly to be heard, but low enough to be felt. Disturbed air rippled from their path like the wake of a great ocean liner, rattling screen doors, raising dust, swirling scraps and twigs, and tossing the higher treetops to expose the silvery undersides of the leaves. The racing dark presence awoke none, but it crossed through the sleep of those most sensitive to night terrors. Cattle lowed in their musty stalls, chickens fussed and shifted on their shelves, and small children moaned and fidgeted under their coverlets. A few little ones instinctively hid their heads, sensing the uncomfortably near passage of some shapeless, dark Angel of Death.

This death angel, though, had not come from heaven or hell, but from the northeast at an altitude of 450 feet, in the form of eighteen UH-60L Blackhawk helicopters, each loaded with nineteen United States Army soldiers. Ahead of them prowled two pairs of heavily armed AH-64A Apache gunships, and in their wake wallowed six ungainly twin-rotor CH-47D Chinook heavy-lift choppers, each dangling a load from its slab of a belly: trucks, howitzers, and supplies bound for battle. To the north and above, a solitary Blackhawk circled, its radio voices speaking for the commander and his staff overseeing this aerial armada. To the east and below, two more Blackhawks orbited, along with another Chinook, waiting patiently to retrieve the dead and wounded certain to result from this night's violent escapade. More than thirty Army aircraft raced to their places or marked time, all striving to make certain that 342 men landed together deep in enemy territory. Everybody had important roles, but this mission would succeed or fail based on what happened to those eighteen Blackhawks.

Any Vietnam veteran, indeed any adult American who had seen a Vietnam movie, would have recognized the Blackhawk's pedigree as pure Huey, the latest incarnation of the seemingly immortal UH-1 Iroquois that came to symbolize the heartbreaking American war in Southeast Asia. This one was bigger, leaner, racier, like a Huey that had embraced Soloflex, a sensible diet, and marathon running. Tadpole-shaped, its main rotor mast rising between twin jet engines, the craft sported a large, almost cartoonish, black landing wheel on either flank rather than the Vietnam-era skids. The powerful Hawk wore a flat, green-black coating of paint that contrasted with the lighter, olive shades of the older Huey type. Coloring reflected purpose. While a Huey flew and fought in the sun, this muscular new UH-60L was a night creature, a hunter in the dark, designed to streak across roofs and hedges when most honest citizens had long since rolled over into slumber.

There was no sleep and damn little comfort for the nineteen air assault troopers sandwiched in together on the unforgiving corrugated gray metal of each airframe's floor. The men crouched, squirmed, and sprawled, jostling constantly as their choppers hurtled along at two miles a minute. With rifles and machine guns gripped in sweaty hands, ungainly black night-vision goggles protruding from under dome-shaped Kevlar helmets, and faces painted into greens and blacks that melted into the crowded darkness, the soldiers waited for their moment of truth, eyes wide, mouths dry. Most saw the back of the man in front of them, if that. But they felt more—booted feet, rifle butts, wandering radio antennas, and shifting bodies, an endless human kaleidoscope of discomfort.

For those facing that way, toward the nose of each UH-60L, a soft green glow outlined the dim shapes of the two pilots, spacemen goggled and helmeted and encased in fire-resistant Nomex suits. Between the fliers and their tightly packed riders, just forward of the rectangular side cargo doors with their big rectangular windows that showed trees and dark sky, in random alternation, two flight-suited figures squatted on little outward-facing jump seats. These crew chiefs looked right and left respectively through their narrow open windows. When on the ground, the two soldiers serviced their helicopter. Up here, they acted as lookouts and gunners, each using a long, wicked-looking M60D aerial machine gun that swung on a pintle mount on the windowsill. With the crew chief portals open, screaming jet engines and roaring slipstream made it impossible to carry on a conversation aboard the UH-60L. The aviators had complete radio/intercom systems built into their helmets and, in true laconic flyboy tradition, exchanged brief messages, mainly involved with verifying the selected route way-points and keeping track of the other flying machines in near proximity.

The guys in back heard none of this pilot talk. True, the key leaders had radios on their backs or on the backs of one of their nearby men, and every radio featured a little black plastic handset, shaped like a traditional telephone (hear on top, talk on the bottom) but only six inches long, and hooked to the main transceiver by a thick black spiral cord. You could clip a handset to a helmet chin strap in a way that placed the earpiece and mouthpiece in the right places, and everyone did so, although the sound quality even at full volume only allowed for snatches of information to filter through the aircraft din. In theory, each Blackhawk included sophsticated headsets to allow the senior man in back to listen and talk during flight. In practice, the aviators monopolized the onboard sets trying to get all of the tricky night flying stuff straight; the headsets seldom worked; and nobody wanted to be tangled up in a Blackhawk phone cord when the doors flew open on a landing zone (LZ) hot with enemy firing. So officers and sergeants in back continued to use their own field radios. Those in charge strained to hear updates from higher headquarters, then the men shouted and beat on each other to pass the word. Given that the only important decision—to abort or not—was made by the full colonel in the circling command bird, it was just as well. Big changes in plans could not really happen en route. Once aboard for an air assault, the riflemen were as committed as bullets shot out of a gun.

They were going to take a runway. Insurgents might own the roads, but those gomers did not own the night skies. No, Uncle Sam's Blackhawks and Apaches dominated that realm, and they and their well-armed passengers were en route to open an airhead right in the guerrillas' backyard. The task force rehearsals and final shakedowns had ended hours before. Now came what the boys did best: execution, actions on the objective.

The more experienced riflemen knew they were close to landing when the door gunners charged their weapons and the leaders held up their index fingers, mouthing "one minute" into the gale roaring through the open gun ports forward of the troop compartments. One minute! Men shifted on bent, throbbing legs, checked their bobbing black night-vision goggles, and instinctively glanced out the rectangular gray-black troop windows, the lower third marred by a blur of passing treetops as the aircraft slid gradually toward the ground. In eighteen Hawks the same sequence played out, the end of this particular act marked by the death angels arriving.

Now the left crew chief held his thumb and forefinger in a C—30 seconds left—then turned back to his machine gun, fingering the long ammunition belt that waved in the angry night air, his right hand tightening on the M60D's butt-mounted spade grips. "Thirty seconds!" echoed the cry, thin in the screaming wind, and next, in each Blackhawk, the riflemen chorused almost as one, an inchoate chanting, deep from their guts: "Huh! Huh! Huh!" It seemed senseless, primeval, a war cry without words that washed over the huddled, tense soldiers. And then the deck tilted upward, the door gun on the right flashed out a burst, and the left door cracked open a sliver. Left door exit, boys! The thought passed like chain lightning around the cabin. The big wheels bumped onto the waving grass.

Now the left door slammed back into its stops, gaping, and the men spilled out. "Go! Go! Go!" they said, urging each other into the night, muscling heavy weapons and radio backpacks onto unhappy shoulders. Men burdened by huge rucksacks rolled off the lip of the chopper doorway, staggering forward. Tightened muscles gave way, uneven ground played men false, and the heavy weight of all of those "must have" items, the curse of the so-called "light" infantry, pushed helmets in front of eyes and tripped men up. So the squads stumbled and swayed away from the helicopters, weaving like bands of drunks as the UH-60Ls slowly began to lift off.

The men listened for firing, looked for muzzle flashes or explosive bursts, but all they heard was unrelenting rotor noise, and all they saw were flying debris, strings of blacked-out aircraft departing, indistinct clots of troops forming up into squads, and a treeline of tall pines two hundred yards ahead, due west. The dirt airstrip was to their backs. Clear out the fringe of forest and the runway would be theirs. That was the scheme.

And as the Blackhawks veered away into the starlit sky, the rotorwash faded in volume and began to echo, and the dust began to settle. The book said you could spend up to a half hour assembling on the LZ, and the boys looked like they would need every tick of that.[1] Some of the birds had touched down out of order; some of the troops had exited the right door. Now, using their night goggles and infrared Cyalume light sticks, the unit leaders struggled to account for their people and equipment before moving off the field. It all seemed to proceed in slow motion. Five minutes stretched to ten, then fifteen. Well, the Chinook follow-on lifts weren't due for another twenty-five minutes, and the enemy wasn't here, was he?

Right on cue, the western treeline erupted into unholy life. One very loud machine gun began hammering, followed by a growing spatter of rifle shots, yellow sparks against the blue-black curtain of foliage. The enemy, very much present, intended to fight for the airstrip, starting here and now, with 342 Americans struggling through an open meadow. An air assault force is most vulnerable on the LZ. The unfortunate soldiers now scrambling around out there under fire, out of breath and confused, would certainly agree.

The first shots drove the assembling formations down into the swaying weeds, splitting up machine gun teams, separating leaders from the led, reducing the view of reality to a few inches of prairie grass. Pinned under the weight of heavy rucksacks, eyes stinging with sweat, the men waited for someone to tell them what to do. A few, very few, returned fire. Most were not sure where to find their sergeants or lieutenants. The Apaches and the naval gunfire should have killed any enemy in the treeline as part of the preassault bombardment. So everyone had agreed during the rehearsal. In the practice session they had all linked up in no time and advanced through the woodline. But the dry run had been done without full packs, in daylight, on the broad, neatly trimmed lawns of a regional airport. The rehearsal bore little resemblance to this incoherent disintegration before a deadly, rapid-fire ambush.

Somebody had to take charge, and somebody did, the typically agressive corporals and sergeants and young officers assigned to light infantry forces. The battalion commander, nominally the overall chieftain of these Americans, had landed almost on the edge of the flight strip at the eastern end of the grassy field. He had designed the scheme of attack and picked the landing zone. The riflemen out there could only do so much to remedy some bad choices made days ago.

So the lieutenant colonel tried to do what officers of that grade did best. His pistol would not make a difference, but his mind might. He crawled to his brace of radio operators, trying to get some help, trying to get something going. *We need fires on that treeline,* he thought. The fire support officer usually did that kind of thing without prompting, but he was conspicuously absent at the moment. That worthy artillery captain and the rest of the tactical command post team, the S3 (operations officer), S2 (intelligence officer), ALO (air liaison officer), the ANGLICO (Air-Naval Gunfire Liaison Company) element, the communications team, the bodyguards, and all the rest were somewhere out in that field, getting lashed by hostile fires. Like many of the rifle platoons, the tactical command post had gotten separated in the darkness. So now it would be up to the lieutenant colonel and his radiomen. The enemy shooting continued, and in the field, his men were trying to get moving. A stray thought from his daughter's favorite movie slipped through his head: It's dangerous out on the meadow, Bambi. Amen, Walt Disney.

"Frontline 6, this is Braveheart 6, over," he said. No response came.

"Frontline 6, this is Braveheart 6, over." Nothing.

"Any Frontline station, this is Braveheart 6, over." The radio handset chattered merrily with flight crews checking in and out with the aerial Frontline commander, who controlled the Apaches, the artillery, the naval gunfire, and all the rest. But for some reason, the battalion commander could only receive, not send. He reached for his other radio handset, hoping for better luck with that one.

"It's dead, sir. It got stepped on," whispered the private first class.

"Put his handmike on yours and let's try that." The soldiers scuttled together and got to work. More minutes were going by. The Chinooks were inbound, the battalion commander could not raise the Apaches, even though he could see one through his green-tinted night-vision goggles, hovering well to the north. He hoped the S3 or someone was talking to the company commanders.

Just as the radioman handed back the mike, the lieutenant colonel heard the whistle of incoming mortar rounds. One, two, three, four, five, six sharp, ragged bursts out in the long grass, squarely among his troops huddled out there. "Switch me to battalion command," he spat, and the soldier twisted the knob.

". . . ah, roger that, Charlie Rock. Can you see the dishka?"

"Affirmative, Braveheart 3," came a breathless answer. "But I can't get to it. I have at least two-zero men down, maybe more. We're still taking mortar fire. It's bad, over."

Another six 82mm mortar rounds impacted to emphasize that point.

The battalion commander knew that the captain commanding Company C was in trouble, as were his mates and, indeed, everyone here tonight. A "dishka," a DShK 12.7mm Russian-made heavy machine gun, would shred the ungainly Chinook heavy lifters.[2] It was dismembering Company C at the moment, keeping them pinned while the opposing mortar-men dropped high-explosive shells on the impotent Americans. With no aid available from higher, the battalion had to fight it out for itself.

"Charlie Rock 6, this is Braveheart 6," said the commander. "I'm going to try to push Buffalo 6 around to your south. Try to keep the bad guys focused on you. Can your company mortars fire, over?"

"Negative, Braveheart. They're down. All I have are rifles, over."

The lieutenant colonel shook his head. Maybe Buffalo was in better shape.

"Buffalo 6, Braveheart 6. Can you maneuver to Charlie Rock's south flank and take out that dishka, over?"

No response came. The commander tried again, and then again. The handset remained mute. Six additional high-explosive projectiles smashed into the LZ.

"Braveheart 6, Braveheart 3," said the S3 wearily. "Buffalo is not up on comms, even on his internal net, over."

The lead Chinook, an ambulance swinging from its cargo hook, was just cresting the trees to the south. Another cargo bird was a minute behind the first. Enemy fire swelled. Great, just terrific! This was going to be very ugly. *Time to try something else,* thought the lieutenant colonel. But the options were really very few indeed.

"Axeman 6, Braveheart 6, over."

"This is Axeman 5 Romeo," came an unfamiliar voice. "Axeman 6 is wounded, over." It was the Company A radio operator. The captain was out of the fight, and his executive officer had the controls.

"Put 5 actual on, over," directed the battalion commander.

"He's not here, over," came the answer. Whatever the lieutenant now acting as company commander did right, he surely made a bad choice in separating himself from his radio. But that act could not be undone quickly in the middle of a night firefight.

"Axeman 5 Romeo, this is Braveheart 6. Get your 5 up on this net now, over." The order urged speed, but the battalion commander held no illusions.

"Roger, over," came the uncertain reply.

The net went silent, not that it mattered. Unable to contact his key leaders, incapable of talking to his commander overhead, and without any means to influence the procession of slow, defenseless Chinooks now at hand, the frustrated lieutenant colonel stared like a spectator powerless to stop an inevitable train wreck. The commander knew exactly what would happen next. It did.

Steady as a Greyhound bus, and about as nimble, the lead CH-47D cargo chopper motored majestically across the congested LZ, then flared to drop its slingload. Enemy fires immediately converged on this big, fat, twin-rotored target, rattling and pounding away with immediate effects.

A flurry of bright yellow flashes lighting its dull green skin, the hovering Chinook took one hit, then another, and finally a clutch of blows, one or more of these fatal. Stricken, the great craft pancaked into the center of the LZ, bouncing once. The strobe-like amber glare coming from the downed aircraft lit up several crouched figures. Then, just for good measure, another half-dozen mortar shots peppered the place. Hostile small-arms fire continued unabated. The bad guys had scored big.

Disgusted, mainly at himself, the battalion commander checked his watch. It had been forty-two minutes since touchdown, and still more than three hours until sunrise, with possession of the airstrip obviously in doubt. Hell, the battalion did not even control its own LZ. It promised to be a very long, painful night. It was.

By noon the next day, the lieutenants, sergeants, and air assault troopers had retrieved something from the awful first hour. They gradually gained control over the treeline, and most of the runway. Americans killed four and wounded eleven guerrillas, although the DShK and mortar tube and their crews escaped. It all cost most of Company C, along with raw strips gouged out of the rest of the battalion: 41 dead and 107 wounded, many of them key leaders, the heart of the organization.

In theory, things should have gone much better, like a well-organized tiger hunt to corner and kill a dangerous but outgunned foe. But battles—and tiger hunts—occur in messy reality, not in a classroom. Sometimes, like this time, the tigers won. That happened a lot down in this place. After all, this was Tigerland.

Tigerland was better known as Fort Polk, Louisiana. It gained its nickname during the Vietnam era, when young men went to the post to learn how to hunt the human tigers of Southeast Asia, the un-yielding People's Army of Vietnam and their guerrilla associates of the National Liberation Front, all known colloquially as Charlie Cong. More than a quarter of a million United States Army recruits learned their brutal trade in the pinewoods, sand flats, streambeds, and swamps that make up the 198,000-acre post, roughly five times the size of the District of Columbia.[3] Located in the soggy, sparsely-populated interior of Louisiana, Polk's empty forests allow soldiers to blaze away without fear of bothering anyone or anything of consequence.

Thanks to its location, Fort Polk allowed a pretty good introduction to Southeast Asia. The subtropical climate offers the requisite insects, reptiles, and numbing, draining wet heat. Temperatures hover around the 100-degree mark for much of the late spring, summer, and early autumn, an oppressive, smothering blanket of stale hot air relieved now and then, typically in the late afternoon, by violent, monsoon-caliber thunderstorms. Polk's lateritic soil sucks up moisture rapidly and dries just as quickly, creating a passable substitute for Vietnamese mud and dust. All this heat and water compounds the effects of careless land clearing and lots of marshy streams, producing massive thickets in all the low-lying wetlands. Sticker bushes of various types and all three kinds of poison plants— ivy, oak, and sumac—grow in annoying profusion.[4] Men bound for Vietnam could get used to suffering at Fort Polk.

Today, the Vietnam War is a distant memory, but Fort Polk still metes out big doses of misery to all in attendance, amply replicating the unhealthy Third World scenes that host the majority of contemporary American overseas operations. Accordingly, Fort Polk serves as the home of the U.S. Army's Joint Readiness Training Center (JRTC), one of the Army's three Combat Training Centers (CTCs). Activated at Fort Chaffee, Arkansas, in 1987 and moved to the more ample pine-covered wetlands of Fort Polk in 1993, JRTC focuses on training light forces: paratroopers, Rangers, heliborne infantry, and walking infantry, plus all their affiliated combat, support, and service support elements. Thanks to its unforgiving environment, the reservation known to Vietnam veterans as Tigerland makes a perfect locale for the JRTC.

The JRTC was the second of the Army's realistic unit training venues created during the defense buildup of the 1980s. Like the third center—the smaller-scale Combat Maneuver Training Center (CMTC) in Hohenfels, Germany—Polk's JRTC builds upon lessons learned by the first and, in many ways, still the greatest among the CTCs. Polk and Hohenfels owe their essence to the pioneering work done out among the scrubby creosote bushes that dot the sprawling desert complex at Fort Irwin, California.

From its opening in 1981, Fort Irwin's National Training Center concentrated on armored warfare against the Soviet Army, and recreated battles involving hundreds of tanks, high-performance jets, and even nuclear explosions, all waged in the high desert of southeast California. Building upon the successes of the U.S. Navy Top Gun and U.S. Air Force Red Flag aerial combat exercises, Irwin introduced the three basic components of the CTC experience: an un-cooperative opposing force (OPFOR), uncompromising observer/controllers, and a state-of-the-art force-on-force battle resolution process.

Just as Navy and Air Force fliers found it challenging to practice dogfights against pilots schooled to ape Soviet tactics in Soviet-style airplanes, so U.S. soldiers gained insights by battling a mock Soviet motorized rifle regiment bristling with the latest USSR war technology and indoctrinated with the speed, shock, and firepower methods that characterized Moscow's forces in the 1980s. The NTC OPFOR not only faithfully reproduced a hostile military that operated differently than any U.S. Army contingent, but Irwin's motor-rifle legion proved to be a very demanding foe. In the sham fights in Irwin's dusty valleys and sharp, jumbled hills, the OPFOR usually prevailed. Visiting soldiers learned by getting "killed," then had the chance to try again and again during successive two-week stints at the NTC. Irwin's armored OPFOR administered many hard lessons over the years.[5]

Getting the crap beat out of you sends its own crude message: "Don't do this again; you lost." To learn how to win, to make sense out of the often overwhelming defeats inflicted by the Irwin motor-rifle people, the NTC assigned observer/controllers (O/Cs) to every platoon, company, staff section, and attached element. These officers and sergeants, exhaustively educated in the details of the Army's voluminous, confusing, and contradictory doctrinal literature, served as subject matter experts in explaining what happened to player units. Presiding over comprehensive after-action reviews (AARs) that resembled nothing so much as classic Maoist self-criticism sessions, the O/Cs led the visiting units through self-discovery of their strengths and weaknesses. Even in a lost engagement many things often went right, and no victory was ever perfect. The NTC O/Cs insisted on taking time to discuss what happened, why, and how to fix things for the next round. Accordingly, every major episode of mock combat concluded with several hours for AARs at all levels.[6]

Learning doctrinal concepts and who shot John all helped the learning process, but Regular Army soldiers, especially the leaders, tend to thirst for the bottom line, the score, the results. Just as in war, how many good and bad guys were "killed" largely determines mission success at NTC. To provide this vital feedback, Fort Irwin employs an elaborate simulation process to depict who wins and loses its desert clashes. Built around the Multiple Integrated Laser Engagement System (MILES), every soldier, firearm, tank, fighting vehicle, and aircraft features a receiver and a transmitter to simulate shooting and being shot. The coded light pulses mimic the effectiveness of each weapon and each target. A tank can kill another tank or blow away a rifleman, but a rifleman or machine gunner cannot damage a metal monster. Just for added pain, friendlies can, and do, shoot each other, tragedies neatly recorded by computers and replayed at AARs. Artillery, land mines, air strikes, and even nerve gas factor into this concocted combat, although here O/C judgment and radio-dispatched marking teams supplement the far cleaner direct fires reproduced by MILES.[7] It all amounts to the world's largest laser-tag match, but in this league, with the O/Cs taking notes, all the players are deadly serious.

OPFOR, O/Cs, and MILES make Irwin what it is today and has been for more than a decade. The NTC did a superb job training heavy forces for the war they fought successfully in 1990–91 against the Soviet-style Iraqi armored forces. Indeed, many commanders in the Gulf War specifically mentioned their National Training Center rotations as excellent preparation for their clashes with Saddam Hussein's Republican Guard mechanized divisions.[8] Today the facility continues to train American armored forces to fight an intense desert war against a mythical Soviet Union surrogate known as the Krasnovians. Therein lies the rub.

Why do we persist in fighting our Cold War enemies? Mainly, we do it because the Army cannot think of any tougher kind of foe for conventional warfare. The fact that the USSR and its army no longer exist renders this whole setup a bit strange, and leads one to consider the old cliché about generals always refighting their last war. Perhaps it will all make sense if there is another round with the Iraqis, or the Russians go haywire. But for now, it surely appears to be a monument to ages past.

And yet, the logical flaw within the Irwin scenario is not new. Even at the height of the Cold War, many thinking soldiers noticed a disconnect between the straightforward, blitzkrieg nature of the Army's premier unit training event at Fort Irwin and the muddled, frustrating character of the unremitting succession of confused, dirty little operations that kept occupying Americans between 1945 and the fall of the Soviet Union. America has endured more than fifty years of painful guerrilla fighting, peacekeeping, noncombatant evacuations, and unbidden interventions into areas not unlike Fort Polk, and only four days of Irwin-variety tank battles. The world the U.S. Army lived and fought in, the real world, demanded forces that could deal with the ghosts of the failed crusade in Vietnam. Americans and their Army tend to have a lot more trouble with what Korean War veteran T. R. Fehrenbach so astutely labeled "this kind of war."

Fort Irwin was not much help in solving that problem. The National Training Center approach wished away the mess that marked Vietnam and all the other small wars, hearkening back instead to an idealized vision of Gen. George S. Patton's Third Army campaigns in France, clean panzer fights between uniformed opponents. While certainly challenging and professionally rewarding, the NTC has never reflected the most likely battles the U.S. Army has fought and will fight. Like it or not, the Army must confront and master the issues that typify interventions in the developing world, especially insurgent/terrorist enemies and native populations. Fort Irwin has been kept sterile, free of these "impediments."[9] Out there, it's always high noon at Kasserine Pass.

A pretty big segment of the Army leadership recognized that deficiency and corrected it at JRTC. To re-create dirty wars, grappling with guerrillas—tiger hunts—the Army adds a fourth element to the NTC triad of OPFOR, O/Cs, and MILES. From the start, JRTC has insisted on cluttering the landscape with things soldiers would rather not experience, all related to civilians on the battlefield. Thus, role-players re-create small hamlets, farmers in the fields, hunters, news media folks, United Nations and private relief groups, and a cast of other third and fourth parties, all with their own agendas, most unsure whether to support or oppose the gringo interlopers. This Maoist stew typifies JRTC and, lately, CMTC, which has been made over from a little NTC into Danubia, a rather depressingly accurate analogue of the former Yugoslavia.[10]

Of the two, JRTC has clearly taken the lead in re-creating the nasty Third Word environs typical of U.S. interventions. Once you inter-ject even sixty or so civilian role-players (and there are seldom more in action at Polk) the whole complexion of operations changes from the conventional to the unconventional, from good, clean, manly "war" as the Army defines it to murky "operations other than war" full of unguided, uncooperative civilians.[11] These folks explain why the basic scenario at Polk looks so different from the Irwin game plan.

When American forces like the Bravehearts enter JRTC, they supposedly land on the island of Aragon, a mythical place out in the Caribbean. Aragon features three countries: weak, pro-American Cortina, heavily armed Marxist Atlantica, and neutral Victoria. Sometimes, a breakaway group of Acadians foments civil war in Cortina. In general, though, Aragon seethes with standard lesser-developed-country woes: poverty, pestilence, and pathos. Atlantica stirs the pot by backing the Cortinian Liberation Front (CLF), which alternately torments and woos Cortinian villagers and wages unceasing insurgency against the local government and their American allies. Every rotation places U.S. troops among sullen peasants, crafty rebels, and wandering free agents like the press, missionaries, and private charity providers. Just to complicate matters, about halfway through each twelve-day training rotation, the Atlantican OPFOR usually launches a cross-border invasion spearheaded by tanks, heavy artillery barrages, poison gas, and attack helicopters, a spectacle worthy of NTC's Krasnovians, but layered atop the unruly civilians and undaunted CLF. Added to MILES combat resolution procedures and watched by well-schooled O/Cs, it all makes for a very challenging arena, often too challenging for the visitors.

This helps explain why the tigers ate the Braveheart battalion. What happened to this unfortunate battalion could, and does, happen to others, including the elite ranks of the 75th Ranger Regiment, the 82d Airborne, and the 101st Airborne. A flashy reputation means nothing to Polk's denizens. Indeed, puncturing overinflated unit pride has become a specialty at the Joint Readiness Training Center. To understand that, you have to understand why Fort Polk's tigers win. You have to understand the nature of the best insurgent force on Earth: the Cortinian Liberation Front, the arrogant, talented, and seemingly unstoppable CLF.

Notes

The epigraph is from T. R. Fehrenbach, *This Kind of War* (New York: The Macmillan Company, 1966), 428.

1. U.S., Department of the Army, *ARTEP 7-20-MTP Mission Training Plan for the Infantry Battalion* (Washington, D.C.: U.S. Govt. Printing Office, 1988), 5–76.

2. Ian V. Hogg, ed., *Jane's Infantry Weapons* (Alexandria, Va.: Jane's Information Group, Inc., 1992), 298. The DShK (V. A. Degtyarev/ G. S. Shpagin/ M. T. Kalashnikov) 12.7mm heavy machine gun reflects a cooperative effort by three Soviet-era weapons designers.

3. James R. Ebert, *A Life in a Year* (Novato, Calif.: Presidio Press, 1993), 45.

4. "U.S. Army Posts and Installations," *Army* (October 1994), 225; U.S., Department of the Army, Headquarters, 1st Brigade, 101st Airborne Division (Air Assault), "JRTC Climatology and Terrain Analysis" in *Road to War* (Ft. Campbell, Ky.: Headquarters, 1st Brigade, 101st Airborne Division [Air Assault], 1994), 8–19.

5. Sfc. Edward L. Crum, USA, "History of the Opposing Force at NTC," *Red Thrust Star* (October 1994), 4–7; Gen. Gordon R. Sullivan, "Flexibility Sets the Pace at Combat Training Centers," *Army* (July 1993), 31–33.

6. U.S., Department of the Army, TC 25-20 *A Leader's Guide to After-Action Reviews* (Washington, D.C.: U.S. Govt. Printing Office, 1993), A-1.

7. U.S., Department of the Army, *ARTEP 7-20-MTP*, A-1 to A-32.

8. Dr. Susan Canedy, *TRADOC Pam 525-100-1 Leadership and Command on the Battlefield* (Ft. Monroe, Va.: U.S. Army Training and Doctrine Command, 1992), 36.

9. Dr. Lawrence A. Yates, "Political Factors," in *Combined Arms in Battle Since 1939,* ed. Roger J. Spiller, (Ft. Leavenworth, Kans.: U.S. Army Command and General Staff College, 1992), 209. For the differences between the training centers, see Sullivan, "Flexibility Sets the Pace at Combat Training Centers," 30–34. In his article, General Sullivan describes at some length the "dirty," civilian-clogged battle-

fields that characterize JRTC (Polk) and CMTC (Hohenfels). The discussion of NTC, interestingly, focuses on weapons technology.

10. U.S., Department of the Army, *CTC Trends: Combat Maneuver Training Center, 1st and 2d Quarter, FY 95* (Ft. Leavenworth, Kans.: Center for Army Lessons Learned, 1995), II-2, II-11, II-19.

11. U.S., Department of the Army, *FM 100-5 Operations* (Washington, D.C.: U.S. Govt. Printing Office, 1993), 2-1 to 2-3, 13-1 to 13-15.

Learning
JRTC 94-10
September 1994

"If the actions of these rude campaigns are of less dignity, the adventures in them are more interesting to the heart, and more amusing to the imagination, than the events of a regular war."

—Col. Henry Bouquet, Esq.

Chapter 1

Them

Enemy advances, we retreat.
Enemy halts, we harass.
Enemy tires, we attack.
Enemy retreats, we pursue.

—Mao Zedong

Americans hate to fight guerrillas. For a country born in the crucible of a revolutionary war, this is a rather strange development, but it is true nevertheless. One wonders just how much of a Revolutionary War our founding fathers might have waged had they heeded George Washington, who so longed to form and lead a proper army in the British, French, and Prussian style.[1] Instead, Washington's hapless, restive Continentals proved utterly inferior to their highly disciplined counterparts from Europe, and the homespun militia had more sense than to stand shoulder-to-shoulder and trade musket balls with red-coated professionals. It is not surprising that French regulars on land and sea decided the issue, and the war, at Yorktown in 1781. The small Continental corps and their fair-weather militia auxiliaries won largely by surviving, a most unimpressive effort for an aspiring conventional army.

Yet the British who surrendered at Yorktown would never have ended up cornered on the Chesapeake coast had it not been for the relentless campaigns of American guerrillas, men who embraced by necessity a style of fighting that Washington so heartily disdained and condemned. Led by shrewd southerners like Francis Marion ("the Swamp Fox"), Thomas Sumter ("the Carolina Gamecock"), and Andrew Pickens, all orchestrated by Nathanael Greene, a Quaker from Rhode Island with a flair for partisan combat, small irregular bands harassed and attrited British columns floundering through the hot, overgrown Carolina piedmont. Greene never actually "won" a battle, but Mao Zedong or Vo Nguyen Giap would have approved of Greene's methods: "We fight, get beat, rise and fight again." That constant pressure, always with an eye toward swaying the watching American populace, did the job. As Professor Russell F. Weigley, one of the deans of American military history, put it so well: "Greene wrecked enemy armies."[2]

One might expect that the new country might gleefully insist on a military establishment built to wage a people's war. After all, that ugly stuff had worked when the doctrinaire Continentals so often stumbled. Yet in the decades after the humiliated British regiments laid down their Tower muskets to the tune of "The World Turned Upside Down," Washington's more conventional views gradually prevailed. America's military structure rapidly turned right side up, and the armies that marched into Canada in 1812, into Mexico in 1847, into Cuba in 1898, into France in 1917, into Europe in 1944, and into Korea, Vietnam, and Iraq were "proper" bodies of soldiery, trained and equipped to fight face-to-face against similar uniformed foes. About all that was left of the heritage of Greene and the Swamp Fox amounted to a few thousand overtasked special forces and an ongoing insistence on some form of popular militia, epitomized to this day by the numerous, politically powerful National Guard.

When America's opponents obliged and granted a relatively fair fight in the European style, American troops almost always prevailed, running up a pretty impressive score in more than two centuries worth of battles. Things went less well against enemies who chose, or were forced into, guerrilla warfare. Adversaries as diverse as the Seminoles, Confederate partisan rangers, Filipino *insurrectos*, Nicaraguan rebels, the Vietnamese Communists, and more recently, Somali warlords have found protracted warfare to be quite useful against the Yankee colossus. Like Nathanael Greene, they, too, have wrecked some armies, great and small, in their time.

For today's generation of U.S. soldiers, however, there can be little doubt that the greatest stain on the prowess of American arms occurred in Southeast Asia, inflicted by the People's Army of Vietnam and their Viet Cong associates. With a few exceptions, U.S. Army commanders never really figured out how to defeat the guerrilla tactics employed in Vietnam. Oh, they killed the Viets by the gross, with shot, shell, and napalm, but like Lord Cornwallis en route to York-town, somehow all of these "victories" added up to a debacle.[3]

It is a tribute to the U.S. Army that an influential segment of its generals did not want to forget what happened to them as lieutenants and captains in a hundred hot landing zones. The easy thing would have been to keep ignoring the problem, but the realities imposed by a steady diet of American Third World interventions warned against such thinking. So when it came time to create a premier train-ing environment for American light forces, the senior leadership elected to re-create an American soldier's worst nightmare, coun-terinsurgency in rugged terrain amid a volatile local population. What the JRTC is, in truth, is Vietnam revisited. And not surprisingly, its version of the Viet guerrillas is very good indeed.

The Cortinian Liberation Front, the CLF, Tigerland's tigers, are the best guerrilla force in the world. They control the countryside of Cortina, including its tiny villages. The Republic of Cortina's in-effectual National Gendarmerie cannot do much about the insur-gents, and keeps requesting U.S. help. So about once a month Americans arrive, determined to beat the CLF. Instead, in homage to Nathanael Greene, the outnumbered, outgunned CLF almost al-ways wrecks the visiting U.S. brigade.

The CLF were never intended to be so deadly to rotational units. They are not the only opposing force (OPFOR, in generic Army-speak) furnished at JRTC. In fact, in JRTC's mythical construct of Cortina, the CLF are merely trailblazers for the armored legions of the Atlantican People's Revolutionary Army (PRA), passable ana-logues of the Soviet clones that rule the deserts of Fort Irwin. The CLF are just a "low-intensity" threat, the tankers of the People's Democratic Republic of Atlantican (PDRA) the more dangerous force. That's the theory, at least.

Truth is something else, of course. Few objective students of the U.S. Army would be surprised to hear that the brigades in training usually dispatch the conventionally armed and trained PRA rather efficiently, beating back armored columns and shredding fortified battle positions with methodical success, although sometimes at excessive cost. Fighting the utterly unconventional CLF rarely proceeds as well. Nobody looks forward to tangling with them.

Who are the CLF, these baddest of bad guys? In reality, they are paratroopers assigned to the 1st Battalion, 509th Parachute Infantry Regiment, a nondeployable organization built specifically to fight at JRTC. In their CLF role, the 509th soldiers portray the 91st Assault Battalion, a main force insurgent outfit assigned to the 24th District of the Red River Rural Command. The 91st typically organizes in two assault companies (rifle infantry), the 54th Heavy Weapons Company of antiaircraft guns and mortars, an element of sappers amply supplied with various kinds of land mines, the 64th Reconnaissance Company, and a very small headquarters; all in all about 300 men.[4] This relatively small amount of opposition usually cripples the far more numerous ranks of the rotational brigade.

On paper, the CLF units reflect simplicity itself. Each assault company, for example, includes three rifle platoons of twenty-six men, usually broken into three squads of eight soldiers each and a two-man headquarters. Each squad has six American-made Colt M16A2 5.56mm rifles and two Belgian-designed 5.56mm M249 Squad Automatic Weapons (SAWs—small one-man machine guns). A pair of Russian-model 82mm mortars responds directly to the company commander, as do three SA-14 teams, pairs of men carrying a shoulder-fired surface-to-air missile launcher and its reloads, each round about the size of a length of four-inch wide plastic plumbing pipe. The assault company arranges its fights via old, short-range American-made AN/PRC-77 FM radios, the first solid-state models, built with 1960s technology. They lack cryptographic scramblers or frequency-jumping technology. The assault company makes do with about eighteen light-intensifying night sights, equivalent to Vietnam-era "starlight scopes"—no thermal imaging heat trackers or laser range finders for these guys. This CLF unit owns no vehicles, not even a pickup truck to cart its mortars around.

Nothing about this pedestrian suite of arms gives pause. The CLF mortars range out to 3000 meters; the SA-14s can go to 5000, and the small arms can do damage out to about 800 meters, tops, with effective use limited to about 300 to 400 meters.[5] How can this lightly armed bunch so damage visiting American units?

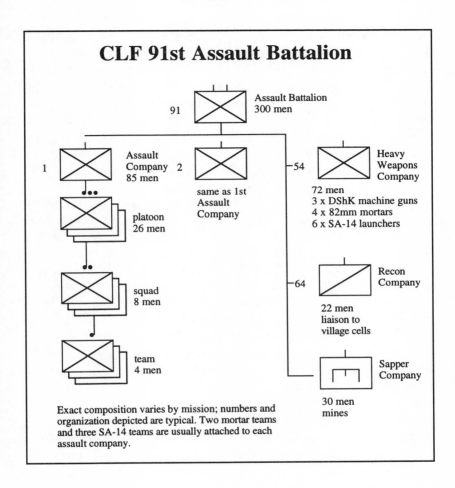

CLF 91st Assault Battalion

91 — Assault Battalion 300 men

1 — Assault Company 85 men

2 — same as 1st Assault Company

platoon 26 men

squad 8 men

team 4 men

54 — Heavy Weapons Company
72 men
3 x DShK machine guns
4 x 82mm mortars
6 x SA-14 launchers

64 — Recon Company
22 men
liaison to village cells

Sapper Company
30 men
mines

Exact composition varies by mission; numbers and organization depicted are typical. Two mortar teams and three SA-14 teams are usually attached to each assault company.

As with actual guerrillas, the answer lies in "how" not "what." Lacking sophisticated toys, the CLF emulates the wily Viet Cong. In answer to Yankee firepower, the JRTC insurgents rely on a suite of approaches that, in the aggregate, amount to a great advantage for Tigerland's home team.

First, each CLF rifleman and SAW-gunner is a crack shot, schooled in the vagaries of MILES marksmanship, and hence able to kill out to 250 meters with the Army's laser-tag device. This takes daily practice, a luxury not afforded rotational U.S. units, who cannot always train with MILES and must, of course, also learn to shoot real bullets. Because the 1st of the 509th fights only at JRTC, this allows its CLF men to become true MILES sharpshooters and maintain those skills. Most CLF soldiers have customized telescopic sights zeroed to their weapons. In a firefight, a CLF soldier will almost always take out three Americans before falling to return fire. Kill ratios of ten to one or more are not unheard of, with six to one about the norm.[6] The CLF loves a daylight direct firefight, head-to-head, without benefit of night-vision wizardry or supporting U.S. artillery and aerial firepower.

Not surprisingly, CLF tactics emphasize creating opportunities for such stand-up gunfights. The guerrillas prefer to work in four-man teams, rarely congregating into larger, less supple squads or platoons. These CLF quartets, headed by a corporal or young sergeant, have only three basic battle drills: break contact, the "box" ambush, and the baited ambush.[7] Each method relies on two men holding the U.S. "nose" with accurate rifle or SAW fire (read that as taking down one to six Americans) while the other two execute the chosen maneuver. The visitors play right into this by tending to plod along in endless, overburdened files, a weaving string of sweating green forms smashing through the piney woods and tangled underbrush, focused exclusively to the front. It's as if the point man wears a neon sign saying "Shoot me first." The CLF oblige.

In the break contact drill, one CLF pair shoots while their partners run. The engaged CLF duo dumps CS (O-chlorobenzylidene malanonitrile) tear gas grenades to discourage pursuit and compound any casualties already inflicted. Then, while one fires, the first backs away. Once he is in position to provide covering fire, his buddy moves back out of U.S. small arms range, followed, after a parting shot or two, by the final guerrilla. This deadly brand of leapfrog can be played all day long as lithe opposing force fire teams play hit-and-run on larger American columns.

If the CLF wants to hang in for a better clash and add to the score, the box technique is used. Once the first two insurgents engage, the trail pair split up. While their comrades shoot at the lead U.S. element, the unengaged men circle around the flanks of the U.S. formation, then turn in to pick it apart from both sides. When done at running speed—and the CLF trains for that—this drill can cause Americans to start blazing away at each other. It usually ends with the CLF breaking contact.

For the really big kill, the guerrilla leaders prefer the baited ambush. This works particularly well when a CLF team has been stalking a Yankee column for hours, especially as snipers, booby traps, heat, humidity, mosquitoes, and frustration take their tolls on the lumbering visitors. In this technique, the CLF leader chooses a good

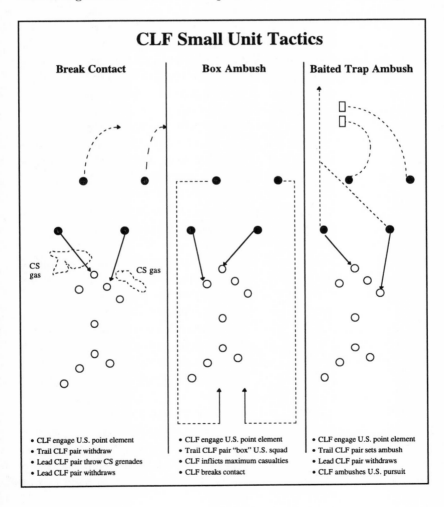

CLF Small Unit Tactics

Break Contact

- CLF engage U.S. point element
- Trail CLF pair withdraw
- Lead CLF pair throw CS grenades
- Lead CLF pair withdraws

Box Ambush

- CLF engage U.S. point element
- Trail CLF pair "box" U.S. squad
- CLF inflicts maximum casualties
- CLF breaks contact

Baited Trap Ambush

- CLF engage U.S. point element
- Trail CLF pair sets ambush
- Lead CLF pair withdraws
- CLF ambushes U.S. pursuit

kill zone not far off the evident U.S. route. The four insurgents then divide, with the trail team setting up behind good cover and concealment, overlooking the designated ambush site. The other CLF twosome hits the U.S. force, drawing fire and attention, but not necessarily hitting anyone. These two then withdraw through the chosen kill zone, and the overanxious Americans usually try to follow. The results are often pretty one-sided. Four JRTC opposing force riflemen can destroy an entire rifle company using this method.

The three drills can be, and are, run in combinations, and just to increase the bag, the bad guys often employ 82mm mortar fires on an American platoon struggling to evacuate casualties, or shoot SA-14 missiles to blast inbound medical evacuation choppers. There are ways to defeat this damnable CLF three-step, but U.S. forces prove amazingly obstinate in not using them. Hence, six-to-one or ten-to-one exchanges have become the rule.

To make the most of their hunting tactics, the Cortinian Liberation Front spreads out. They divide the JRTC battlefield into areas of roughly twenty-five square kilometers, allowing elbow room to each well-trained team. This allows every insurgent NCO to be lord of his own turf, akin to a great tiger stalking through the Sumatran jungle. As each assault company includes at least eighteen of these potent little elements, and more when sappers, recon men, and heavy weaponeers join in, the two rifle companies in the 91st Assault Battalion can influence more than 900 square kilometers simultaneously. Remember, the whole post covers only 801 square kilometers. To the Americans, it seems as if the CLF is everywhere.

The CLF strengthens its deadly omnipresence by shrewdly resorting to land-mine warfare, the poor man's answer to Uncle Sam's arsenal of fires. Dirt roads crisscross JRTC's mythical Cortina, and both truck-happy American forces and innocent Cortinian citizens insist on driving everywhere, day and night. With these fat targets in mind, the CLF is adept at selecting blind turns, stream crossings, and overgrown stretches. Clever sappers emplace all manner of evil explosives: brick-like antitank mines, fruit-can-size bouncing betty types designed to spurt upward and shred a man's loins, homely wooden boxes undetectable by metal-sensitive minesweeping gear, and even deep-buried magnetic influence mines that cannot be found until

you drive across them.[8] Thankfully, MILES lasers do not fully repro-
duce the horrific results of these items, but the simulation system
does reflect their insidious effects. Every road must be cleared to be
used, and every minefield is a guaranteed target of killing rifle fires
and mortar barrages, the same grimly efficient CLF three-step run
ad infinitum on stalled convoys and unlucky singletons. Most U.S.
units suffer loss after loss, often to the same minefield; the guerrillas always reseed a swept field. Those senior officers who wanted to
re-create the frustrations of Vietnam have certainly done the job in
this regard.

Mortars add to the travail inflicted by riflemen and mines. Popping a few rounds and then running to preselected ammunition
caches and hides, the 82mm crews maintain a healthy respect for the
terrible speed and precision of American counterbattery fires.
Guided by an AN/TPQ36 Firefinder radar capable of tracking mortar rounds in flight and then determining their origin, U.S. artillery
can have shells en route to the calculated source within two minutes.[9]
The observer/controllers at JRTC play this radar game pretty fairly.
If the radar could have seen real rounds in the air, then the O/Cs
provide pinpoint data to U.S. gunners, revealing the exact insurgent
firing site.

The CLF know all about the Q36 radar. So they hide behind reverse slopes where radars cannot easily see and, more importantly,
they shoot and scoot. The mortar gunners haunt the same areas, running well-rehearsed racetracks from hides to ammunition dumps,
shooting whenever an observer can see a worthy target. Most U.S.
artillery and mortar missions hit nothing. The CLF shoots far less often, but rarely misses.[10] Their roving mortars are brutally effective.

With the CLF all too capable in the infantry battle, battered
Americans turn to their uniquely versatile technology to save them.
As in Southeast Asia, Uncle Sam's boys look up and listen for the
"whop-whop" that signals the imminent arrival of Army helicopters,
harbingers of salvation from above. An embattled rifle platoon can
call on heavy metal aboard AH-64A Apache gunships to try to destroy
CLF shadowers and ambush teams. With the insurgents pinned
down, the U.S. soldiers dare to vector in choppers to extract casualties, bring in ammunition, or even land reinforcements. This all

tends to happen after the initial *mano-a-mano* gunfight, after the Americans have begun to get beaten up in the usual style.

Well aware of their foe's tactics, the CLF anticipates this all too predictable sequence. They "hug" the American infantry to confuse and confound the Apache gunners, whose 70mm rockets and 30mm cannon shots are anything but precise, especially when spewed by bucking aircraft whose crews can barely make out anything under the tossing tree canopy. The suffering Americans cry for help, the CLF stays in tight plinking away, and, more often than not, somebody in an Apache makes a mistake and blows away a good number of unfortunate friendlies.[11]

Flying medics and "slick" troop and supply utility birds cannot be faked out. These must be killed. Here, the CLF employs SA-14 missile launchers. As a ground firefight develops, these hostile gunners set up on high ground overlooking likely landing zones and flight routes.[12] In their haste to intervene, inbound U.S. aviators often neglect to take adequate precautions, and the SA-14 folks are there to exact payment. Once a helicopter goes down, what was a "situation" or an "incident" turns into a bona fide crisis as the U.S. command realizes that there will be no quick, cheap rescue from the sky.

As if lethal fire teams, mines, mortars, and SAM shooters were not enough, the Americans pretty quickly figure out that the CLF enjoys a transparent battlefield, while the gringos blunder about, seeing through a glass darkly—if at all. As with the Viet Cong, the CLF lives at Polk and moves with ease. Sure of the plant-choked swamp bottoms and undulating red-dirt folds and runoff ditches, the rebels move rapidly across the area. The opposing forces at Polk know where to hide their tiny patrol bases, usually nothing more than four rucksacks and some water stashed in a godforsaken mud hole. Having watched brigade after brigade come to JRTC, the CLF knows where the Americans will likely go; the airstrip, the major roads, and the towns always figure in the scheme. And while the U.S. comes with hundreds of trucks and tents and bundles and boxes, the lightly armed enemy hangs silent on the fringes, watching the fixed base clusters grow while clumsy U.S. fighting companies and platoons stumble around.

Stumble they do, for along with continuous observation and expert use of civilian sympathizers, the CLF hides its own small signatures quite well. Radio transmissions are rare and feature a constantly changing series of double-talk codes and key words. Most communication is by dead drop in true John Le Carré style, with coded notes hidden in rotting logs or under stones in the dead of night. Training and discipline allow the CLF's leadership to pass dead drop information quite rapidly, with twelve hours from initiation to receipt fairly typical.[13] This process is nearly undetectable and almost impossible to interdict.

Interfering with CLF resupply is equally unrewarding. Perhaps because so many U.S. brigades have problems establishing and safeguarding their own supply lines, their officers assume that their opponents have the same problem. These men try to grasp the CLF will-o'-the-wisp by what they hope is its vulnerable tail. As with so many other surefire solutions, this one does not work.

Cortina's insurgency does have a logistics system of sorts, with battalion, company, and platoon stockpiles of ammunition, food, water, and medicine.[14] Much of this is well camouflaged, even buried. Frankly, little of it is truly needed. Like the Vietnamese Communists, the CLF can and do live off captured ammunition and supplies. Local civilians retrieve guerrilla dead, aid the wounded, and contribute food and water to the revolution, services provided willingly or at gunpoint. Moreover, the standard JRTC scenario envisions a massive Atlantican invasion within five days of the U.S. arrival, so long-term guerrilla survival does not depend on securing any network of buried caches. This obvious point is routinely missed by rotational forces, who often expend a lot of energy and simulated blood unearthing and fighting for supply sites that the CLF does not really need. It all makes it that much easier for CLF leaders to outguess likely American moves and smack them with the favorite hammers: the three battle drills, the mines, the mortars, and the SAMs.

Unfettered by conventional logistics, drawing on captured stuff and civilian largess, guerrillas travel light, with a butt-pack of bare essentials on their fighting harness of food, water, and ammunition. They do not wear heavy helmets or carry rucksacks. Because of this, they can literally outrun heavily laden U.S. soldiers. Additionally, whereas most visiting infantry moves with all the elegance of sundazed wildebeests, CLF men glide confidently through the familiar woods, well spread out, always looking and listening. They are good at finding the Americans. Just as their Viet Cong predecessors did, the CLF initiates almost 90 percent of all contacts.[15]

Insurgent assault companies also benefit from the habitual strength of any true revolutionary army: the support of the people. The CLF guarantees this by two means. First, the guerrillas pay due respect to the villagers and farmers, helping them and protecting them in ways that would make Mao proud. Responsive CLF propaganda sections take advantage of every U.S. blunder and oversight to sway the citizenry firmly in favor of the rebellion. When the Americans do not screw up, the CLF will sometimes mount operations strictly to foment Yankee overreactions, all good grist for the agitation mills. The CLF never forgets that popular support must underwrite any successful insurgency.

Along with positive incentives, just to make sure, the CLF's paramilitary infrastructure, the Leesville Urban Group (LUG), places its cadres among the populace. These men and women scout targets, transport guerrilla supplies in civilian vehicles, arrange the recovery of CLF dead and wounded, and in some cases, commit acts of terror directed against U.S. and Cortinian government forces. The usual JRTC scenario features about sixty or so civilians grouped into two towns and two hamlets, with a few hunters and farmers on the loose. Of that number, perhaps six will be true LUGs.[16]

This handful can orchestrate a great deal of mayhem if left unchecked. While an occasional truck bombing certainly gains notice, the real benefit of these village infrastructure teams involves their unfettered access to the entire battlefield, not to mention their uncanny ability to garner useful insights from innocent citizens traveling through the region. Almost all visiting forces ignore the civilians, but the favor is not repaid. Instead, the LUGs, aided by their unwitting accomplices, carefully chart and pinpoint all manner of U.S. activities, to include command post locations, main supply routes, and unit positions. This information acts to focus the CLF's shooters as surely as the countermortar radar can direct the fires of an American howitzer battery. One JRTC OPFOR commander noted that the civilians, when guided by alert urban cadres, provide more than 60 percent of all intelligence gathered by the CLF.[17]

In this way, much like the population of a real country in turmoil,

Fort Polk's civilian role-players end up serving the goals of a revolution. The seventy-odd civilians that populate Cortina do not come from the 1st Battalion of the 509th Parachute Infantry Regiment. About half really are civilians, actors employed by the BDM Corporation, a contractor that runs much of the JRTC for the U.S. Army. The other half consists of soldiers on detail from the post sending the rotational units. If the soldiers in training hail from 1st Brigade, perhaps the 2d Brigade will send the civilian augmentees, along with other sundry odds and sods to assist in making sure the rotation runs smoothly. The BDM people train their military fillers while the rotational forces move into the Fort Polk area and prepare to begin operations.

Fort Polk's civilians live in ramshackle towns that just happen to dominate key routes around the maneuver box. The two larger villages, with about twenty souls apiece, are Carnis, overlooking the pivotal Fullerton flight landing strip, and Jetertown, squarely athwart the major north-south dirt thoroughfare heading away from the Fullerton airstrip. Haynes Settlement, right alongside the Peason Ridge flight landing strip, houses about a dozen people. Smith Villa, Rancho 45, and Maddox Homestead comprise family manors of the hacienda variety, with servants and tenants living near the great house. From six to twelve people may be at each of these locales.[18]

Each little cluster of buildings has a mix of private homes, storage sheds, and animal pens. Carnis and Jetertown add a church (the Cortinians favor Catholicism), a few stores, a medical clinic, and a town hall. With these settings come the expected casts. The role-players include farmers, farm families, a few shopkeepers, and a smattering of merchants and elected officials like mayors and constables. The farmers actually till the local fields. Dingy general stores sell food, drink, housewares, and trinkets to citizens and others, including the CLF and Americans. The medical teams treat the wounded; the priests minister to all. The built-up areas bustle with activity, but the Cortinians do not stay at home all the time. There are a few cars and trucks, and the people travel among the various villages, carrying on business, looking for relatives, or just driving around.

Freely moving civilians certainly complicate matters, especially as Americans quickly figure out that the CLF's urban elements wear civilian dress, and sorting out the bad guys gets pretty tough. Many of the locals own their own weapons and hunt for food, presenting a tough dilemma for U.S. patrols: Is that guy looking for dinner or looking for us? You cannot simply shoot everyone carrying a rifle in Cortina. Any one of them, however, can shoot you.

Intermixed with the citizenry, the chaff among the wheat, one finds a LUG or two in each settlement, posing as a solid member of the community. The other civilians can be manipulated and, at a minimum, pumped for information by these CLF men and women. Yes, the CLF employs women in their infrastructure, finding that a young thing in a halter top can often slip through even the most forbidding Airborne Ranger checkpoint, nineteen-year-old riflemen still being human. Within hours of the U.S. intervention, the CLF knows everything, or almost everything, needed to take action against the invaders. Its civilian friends see and hear it all. What has been found will be hit.

Finding the enemy is the central problem for the visiting side at JRTC, but this much can be stated: there are some CLF in every hamlet. Amazingly, most U.S. units never do anything about this. And so the CLF owns the civilians, thus owning the countryside and the towns. The Americans must strive mightily merely to own the ground where they stand.

The lopsided contest with the CLF engenders Vietnam at its toughest, with a brutal climate, an unseen enemy, a constant attrition of Americans, a sullen and uncooperative civilian presence in league with the bad guys, and a sense that the forces of darkness call every tune. This "low-intensity" phase often inflicts greater casualties on U.S. brigades than the conventional phase that follows. After going up against the CLF, fighting the regulars of the People's Democratic Republic of Atlantica amounts to a relief. They, thank God, represent the sort of uniformed military the United States Army was custom-built to thrash.

Atlantica's People's Revolutionary Army plays the second half of most JRTC scenarios, arriving like a summer thunderstorm boiling up out of the Gulf of Mexico, smashing in with a big armored invasion, then defending gains against the inevitable (it's on the training schedule, after all) American counterattack. The PRA is just a runt cousin of the National Training Center's vaunted OPFOR of Soviet-style motor-rifle troops, in the same way that Fidel Castro's Cubans resemble their Russian big brothers. The PRA motorized infantry regiment is smaller and less well armed than the NTC's OPFOR. But, like the CLF, it is schooled to fight and win in the Polk environment. Along with fillers from Fort Polk's tenant 2d Cavalry Regiment, the PRA ranks incorporate the same 1st of the 509th men who also play the CLF, and that alone makes the PRA an enemy worthy of respect.[19]

In the mythos of the JRTC world, the PRA forms the primary striking component of the People's Revolutionary Armed Forces of Atlantica. Supported by a small naval force and a rather impressive little air arm, the PRA fields three army groups, with the Central Army Group directly opposed to the U.S. intervention forces. The Central Army Group's order of battle includes two motorized divisions (the 5th and 6th), two infantry divisions (10th and 25th), the 32d Independent Tank Regiment, the 51st Artillery Brigade (with heavy guns and rocket launchers), and the 52d Air Defense Brigade. Often, the PRA dips into its strategic reserves to attach a special operations brigade to the Central Army Group.[20] While all of these contingents, plus the People's Revolutionary Air Force, make their presence felt on the Fort Polk battlefield, the motorized infantry regiment and the special operations forces comprise the PRA manifestations most often seen by visiting U.S. Army brigades.

The motorized infantry regiment, one of three in a PRA motorized division, composes a powerful combined arms force equipped largely with the cast-off armaments of the late "evil empire." Two of its three battalions ride in Soviet-era ZIL-157 4½ ton trucks, portrayed at JRTC by standard American 5-tons. Armed with the same weapons as the CLF, these battalions range up to 620 strong, with three line companies and a weapons company. The latter formation includes six 82mm mortars. The truck battalions usually fight on foot.[21] Although they have no more night-fighting toys than the CLF, these infantrymen prefer to move under cover of darkness, seeking gaps in U.S. positions or flanks of moving American companies. Often, entire PRA battalions infiltrate undetected right through an

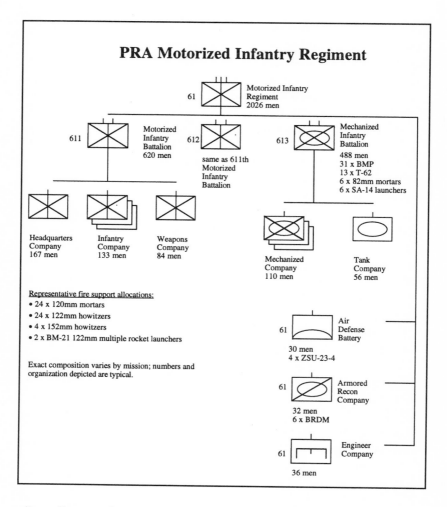

allegedly stout American defense in depth. They stake out key terrain and hold it to the death, shred unguarded obstacles, and destroy unwary U.S. units, all to open the way for their armored brothers.

The third battalion, a true mechanized battalion, fights from old Soviet Army BMP infantry fighting vehicles, which JRTC re-creates by dressing up the venerable M113A2, a track-laying aluminum shoe-box that can carry 10 to 12 men in its cargo compartment. The PRA's particular BMP variant sports a small cupola with a DShK

12.7mm heavy machine gun, for which JRTC substitutes the similar U.S. M2HB .50-caliber weapon. A real Russian-made BMP would carry a 73mm low-velocity gun or a 30mm automatic cannon, but as with actual Third World armies, the PRA has made a few local fixes on their foreign-made equipment.[22] The BMP battalion attempts to fight mounted as long as it can, filing through holes found or made by the dismounted truck infantry.

The motorized infantry regiment usually receives significant help from its parent division, including tanks, massive fire support, and helicopters. Units in the offense can expect more assistance, in keeping with the PRA's emphasis on maintaining the initiative. But even going against a PRA defensive effort in a secondary area, Americans can expect to see more than just a few guys with rifles. The PRA likes to fight a combined arms battle.

Tanks are surely the rifleman's worst nightmare, and as the U.S. Army Rangers learned at Cisterna in 1944, elite training and hardcore spirit count for little against churning treads and a hail of machine-gun bullets.[23] Up to a battalion of T-62 medium tanks, thirty-one at full strength, can be attached to the PRA motorized rifle regiment. At a minimum, a company of thirteen tanks participates. To depict this older Russian-made tank, JRTC employs the same M551 light tank chassis used out at Fort Irwin to play the contemporary T-80. As at NTC, Polk doctors up the old M551 with a bulky round turret skirt and a long fake cannon, in this case simulating the T-62's 115mm main gun. Pitted against today's U.S. Army M1A1 Abrams tanks, the T-62's primitive optics and lack of thermal sights, thin armor, and smaller gun all spell doom.[24] Against U.S. light infantry forces, however, even a T-62 is all too often more than a match.

While tanks terrify, modern artillery is the real killer, inflicting the bulk of ground casualties in most warfare since 1914. Accordingly, the PRA looks to liberal use of fire support to pave the way to success. Working from the old Soviet Army reliance on massive preattack bombardments, where there was no such thing as too much, the PRA employs mortars, 122mm howitzers, 152mm howitzers, and BM-21 multiple rocket launchers in great volume. Targeted by CLF observers already in zone and stealthy regimental reconnaissance teams, the PRA gunners endeavor to evaporate entire grid squares with intense barrages. These fires can penetrate even thick bunker roofs, thus fixing dug-in U.S. forces up to battalion size as surely as beetles pinned to a piece of shingle. Once nailed down, the trapped light-fighters can be pummeled apart, bypassed, or overrun at the convenience of the regimental commander. Just to add a diabolical twist, the PRA often flavors its preassault fires with nerve gas, a little touch guaranteed to get the defenders up out of their gas-filled holes.[25]

PRA forces can also rely on an aggressive aerial fleet, to include attack-and-assault lift helicopters and capable fixed-wing assets. To some extent, JRTC uses the real thing: actual Mi-2, Mi-8, Mi-24 choppers procured by various means, plus an An-2 light cargo plane, all the original Soviet-made versions. These authentic bad guy (or at least former bad guy) aircraft are supplemented by a souped-up UH-1 Huey gunship. In addition, Air Force F-16C Fighting Falcons act as the Atlantican jet armada and prove unnervingly good at low-level bombing runs, typically aimed at vulnerable U.S. fuel and ammunition dumps. The PRA's helicopters can all deliver troops as well as fires—even the Mi-24 Gorbach attack bird carries a squad or so, a heritage of its design as a multipurpose KGB Border Guards aircraft built to patrol the long, dangerous border between the former USSR and China. Thus, the helicopters speed the PRA attack by inserting platoons drawn from the truck-borne battalions; these raiding parties grab key bridges and fords, assail U.S. reserves or command posts, or simply raise hell behind the American lines. As a final threat, the An-2 can drop ten paratroopers to add to the mayhem from the air.[26]

Assembling all of this fighting strength, supplemented by air defense, engineers, supply teams, and the like, the PRA motorized rifle regiment poses a substantial challenge. And yet, while it wins enough engagements, the PRA has never achieved the reputation of the wily CLF. Compared to the guerrillas, the PRA plays by familiar rules, fights by timetables, employs big formations, and uses things like tanks, artillery, and helicopters. In short, this enemy fights fair, like real soldiers, like . . . well, like Americans. And so the Americans can beat these folks. If the PRA wins, the U.S. brigades can usually point to the mistake that lost the battle, and fix it. When the CLF wins, as usual, all the Americans can do is scratch their heads and wait for the PRA to show up and level the playing field.

Sometimes the JRTC scenario writers refuse to give rotational units any relief. Rather than the good old motorized rifle regiment, the JRTC staffers throw an extra curve ball into the mix by injecting a PRA element that fights almost as unconventionally as the CLF. The Special Operations Forces live to destroy U.S. brigades, and they are good at it. Dressed in ominous black uniforms and equipped with a variety of strange, one-of-a-kind weaponry, these enemy paratroopers favor the same decentralized tactics that make the CLF so dangerous. But rather than bearing hand-me-down arms, these teams carry far more deadly items. These include the Egyptian-built as-Saqr long-range portable multiple rocket launcher, capable of raining accurate death from outside the effective range of American tube artillery. Even more sobering for the aviation-happy U.S. Army, the black-suiters use the Swedish-made RBS70, far more capable than the tail-chasing SA-14 heat-seeker carried by the rest of the PRA and the CLF. The RBS70, with its six-kilometer range, is a laser-guided surface-to-air killer that can track its prey from any angle and cannot be spoofed by flares.[27] In addition, the PRA's special operators employ special long-range radios to direct air strikes and heliborne raids, not to mention skillfully using the usual array of mortars and small arms. A company of these people can easily break a U.S. brigade.

Together, the CLF and the PRA offer visiting forces a twelve-day glimpse into an externally supported insurgency, clearly one of the messiest and least forgiving kinds of battlefields that might confront American soldiers. When you look at situations like Somalia, Haiti, and Bosnia, though, you understand why the JRTC gurus and godfathers insist on this unholy mix, and especially on the resident tigers of Tigerland, the CLF. The enemy is supposed to be tough, and the scenarios are meant to be realistic and hard. To a lot of highly motivated paratroopers and air assault commanders who train there, it looks a lot like a no-win situation. To such a complaint, the JRTC observer/controllers smile and tell U.S. commanders that "learning is winning." Thanks to an unforgiving enemy, rotational units do a lot of the former and not much of the latter.

Notes

The section epigraph is found in Robert B. Asprey, *War in the Shadows* (New York: William Morrow and Co., 1994), 57. Colonel Bouquet led British regulars and colonial forces against the Ohio Indians in the 1760s.

The epigraph is from Mao Zedong, *Strategic Problems of China's Revolutionary War* (Beijing, China: Foreign Languages Press, 1954).

1. Geoffrey Perret, *A Country Made by War* (New York: Random House, 1989), 22–26.

2. Russell F. Weigley, *The American Way of War* (Bloomington, Ind.: Indiana University Press, 1977), 36.

3. Col. Harry G. Summers, Jr., USA, *On Strategy: A Critical Analysis of the Vietnam War* (Novato, Calif., 1982), 1.

4. U.S., Department of the Army, Headquarters, 1st Brigade, 101st Airborne Division (Air Assault), "Insurgent Organizations," in *Road to War* (Ft. Campbell, Ky.: Headquarters, 1st Brigade, 101st Airborne Division [Air Assault], 1994), 36–39; U.S., Department of the Army, Headquarters, 1st Brigade, 101st Airborne Division [Air Assault], *JRTC Handbook* (Ft. Campbell, Ky.: Headquarters, 1st Brigade, 101st Airborne Division [Air Assault], 1995), 14. U.S., Department of the Army, Headquarters, 1st Battalion, 509th Infantry, *JRTC OPFOR Briefing* (Ft. Polk, La.: Headquarters, 1-509th Infantry, 1993), 18, 24; U.S., Department of the Army, "JRTC OPFOR," in *JRTC Update Briefing* (Ft. Polk, La.: Headquarters, Joint Readiness Training Center, 10 November 1993), 9. As of November 1993, the Army allocated to the 1st of the 509th a total of 479 men, organized into a headquarters and headquarters company, two rifle companies, and ground cavalry troops. Reinforcements usually included a 340-man light cavalry squadron, plus engineers and, occasionally, an augmentee rifle company drawn from an off-post division.

5. David C. Isby, *Weapons and Tactics of the Soviet Army* (New York: Jane's Publishing Inc., 1988), 250, 364; U.S., Department of the Army, *FM 7-8 Infantry Platoon and Squad* (Washington, D.C.: U.S. Govt. Printing Office, 1992), B-1.

6. Lt. Col. Lloyd W. Mills, USA, "JRTC 94-07: A Commander's Perspective" (Ft. Campbell, Ky.: Headquarters, 3d Battalion, 327th Infantry, 24 June 1994), 1; HQ. 1-509th Infantry, *JRTC OPFOR Briefing*, 4.

7. Lt. Col. Daniel French, USA, "JRTC OPFOR Observations," *CALL News from the Front* (January/February 1995), 1; 1st Brigade, 101st Airborne Division, *JRTC Handbook*, 15–16; Capt. Steve Young, USA, "Dissecting a Firefight," *Combat Training Centers Bulletin 95-1* (February 1995), 16.

8. Capt. John K. Leighow, USA, "Route Clearance Operations," *Infantry* (September/October 1995), 16–22; HQ, JRTC, "Mobility /Countermobility Trends" in *JRTC Update*, 26.

9. U.S., Department of the Army, Headquarters, Division Artillery, 101st Airborne Division (Air Assault), *Fire Support Handbook* (Ft. Campbell, Ky.: Headquarters, Division Artillery, 101st Airborne Division [Air Assault], 1995), 2–21; U.S., Department of the Army, Headquarters, Joint Readiness Training Center, "JRTC Client Update Letter" (Ft. Polk, La.: Headquarters, Joint Readiness Training Center, 1995), 33.

10. Young, "Dissecting a Firefight," 17–18; 1st Brigade, 101st Airborne Division, *JRTC Handbook*, 18; HQ, JRTC, "JRTC Client Update Letter," 32–33.

11. HQ, JRTC, "JRTC Client Update Letter," 30–31.

12. 1st Brigade, 101st Airborne Division, *JRTC Handbook*, 19.

13. Lt. Col. Steven M. Sittnick, USA, "OPFOR Capabilities Briefing." Oral presentation at Ft. Polk, La., 21 March 1995. Lieutenant Colonel Sittnick commanded the 1st Battalion, 509th Parachute Infantry Regiment, the JRTC opposing force unit.

14. U.S., Department of the Army, 1st Brigade, 101st Airborne Division (Air Assault), "Methods of Resupply," in *Road to War* (Ft. Campbell, Ky.: Headquarters, 1st Brigade, 101st Airborne Division [Air Assault], 1994), 48–49; French, "JRTC OPFOR Observations," 1; HQ, 1-509th Infantry, *JRTC OPFOR Briefing*, 20.

15. Lt. Col. Andrew J. Krepinevich, USA, *The Army and Vietnam* (Baltimore, Md.: Johns Hopkins University Press, 1986),188. Department of Defense studies in 1967 stated that the Vietnamese Communist forces initiated 88% of contacts.

16. U.S., Department of the Army, Headquarters, Joint Readiness Training Center, "Civilians on the Battlefield" in *JRTC 95-07 Scenario* (Ft. Polk, La.: Headquarters, JRTC, March 1995), 42.

17. French, "JRTC OPFOR Observations," 2.

18. 1st Brigade, 101st Airborne Division, "Terrain and Weather" in *Road to War*, 16–17.

19. U.S., Department of the Army, Headquarters, Joint Readiness Training Center, "Task Organization (Attack)" in *JRTC 94-10 OPFOR Laydown* (Ft. Polk, La.: Headquarters, JRTC, August 1994), 3. Although a famous tank outfit in the Persian Gulf War, the 2d Cavalry Regiment has become a "light" formation, having traded in its heavy armored vehicles for HMMWV gun trucks and related variants. Many of these trucks should have been replaced by versions of the XM-8 Armored Gun System, a light tank with a 105mm gun designed to add punch for U.S. Army light infantry divisions. Unfortunately, constrained by a shrinking budget, the Army leadership canceled the entire XM-8 program early in 1996. It was just as well, given how slowly the Army expected to field the ill-fated light tank. (For details on the glacial production schedule envisioned prior to outright cancellation, see Scott R. Gourley, "M8 Armored Gun System," *Army* [January 1996], 36–39). There has been talk of reintroducing tanks and tracked fighting vehicles, converting the 2d Cavalry back to its previous configuration, a twin of the 3d Armored Cavalry Regiment, presently the only example left of three similar organizations that once spearheaded Cold War ground forces. For now, Polk's cavalrymen bring armor and cavalry expertise to the PRA OPFOR mission.

20. 1st Brigade, 101st Airborne Division, "National Military Structure" in *Road to War*, 30.

21. Ibid., 32; 1st Brigade, 101st Airborne Division, *JRTC Handbook*, 28–30.

22. 1st Brigade, 101st Airborne Division, *JRTC Handbook*, 34. The Russians derisively refer to their stripped-down export vehicles as "monkey models," shorn of high-technology night sights and first-rate weaponry. JRTC's BMPs are definitely monkey models.

23. Dr. Michael J. King, *Rangers: Selected Combat Operations in World War II* (Ft. Leavenworth, Kans.: Combat Studies Institute, June 1985), 29–41. The Rangers lost all but six of 767 men who attacked at Cisterna. Most were captured.

24. Isby, *Weapons and Tactics of the Soviet Army*, 130–38.

25. U.S., Department of the Army, Headquarters, Joint Readiness Training Center, "Fires (Attack)" in *JRTC 94-10 OPFOR Laydown* (Ft. Polk, La.: Headquarters, JRTC, August 1994), 16–17.

26. 1st Brigade, 101st Airborne Division, *JRTC Handbook*, 37–41; HQ, JRTC, "OPFOR Aircraft Fleet," *JRTC Update*, 10.

27. Anthony H. Cordesman and Abraham R. Wagner, *The Lessons of Modern War*, vol. 2, *The Iran-Iraq War* (Boulder, Colo.: Westview Press, 1990), 344; 1st Brigade, 101st Airborne Division, *JRTC Handbook*, 32.

Chapter 2

Us

"They have no time for glory in the infantry."
—Frank Loesser
"The Ballad of Rodger Young"

It should not surprise anyone that visiting brigades often stumble in the face of the JRTC's hostile Cortinian Liberation Front. Figuring out how to defeat an insurgency has never been easy for any conventional military, and the very nature of today's United States defense establishment only complicates an already difficult problem. At the close of the twentieth century, the American way of war, built around our industrial might and mastery of high technology, always suggests the same solution, whether to World War III, Iraqi armored divisions, guerrilla wars, terrorism, peacekeeping, or anything else ugly that goes bump in the international night. The standard U.S. answer can best be summarized by a blunt Regular Army formula: "Send a bullet, not a man."[1]

Expend things, not people. That is exactly the approach one might expect from the children of Thomas Edison and Henry Ford, and it has become holy writ for the contemporary leadership of the U.S. armed forces. Such a view undergirded the great precision aerial bombardment campaign against Nazi Germany in 1943–45, the deadly B-29 fire raids against imperial Japan that culminated in the 1945 atomic bombings, the artillery-dominated meat grinder tactics used in Korea during 1951–53, and all aspects of the Indochina War, from the laser-bomb bridge strikes up north to the find 'em and pile on Niagara of firepower unleashed on hapless enemy formations.[2] The concept reached its full fruition in the Yankee blitzkrieg unleashed against the Iraqi Republican Guards and their odious supreme leader. We have all grown familiar with CNN's stark imagery of American prowess—a laser-guided bomb zinging down the chimney, barreling right through the main hatch of a hostile command bunker, an unerring thunderbolt incredibly precise and brutally destructive at the same time. That is the way Americans prefer to fight their twentieth-century wars.

And yet, only a few wars, and few enemies, succumb to such direct, neatly engineered methods. Fighting guerrilla wars and the other common strains of political violence, even backed by all the wonders of the American arsenal, still requires men on the ground. Good guns, even great guns, will not by themselves kill tigers. To kill tigers, you need beaters with the guts to raise the deadly prey, trackers bold enough to follow the beasts to their lairs, hunters willing to pull the triggers with their enemies' hot breath blowing warm on their faces. America's most likely opponents, the ones that Fort Polk's CLF pretend to be, know all about those keen-eyed bombs and deadly accurate missiles. Desiring to be more than bloodied targets, they choose to oppose us by guile and deceit, by ambush in cluttered battlegrounds rife with cowering civilians, not open arenas suitable for panzer battles and carrier air strikes. To win against the Yankee juggernaut, smart enemies try to force us to fight against our grain— to send men, not bullets.

A century ago our uniformed leaders would have known exactly what to do with bad actors like the CLF. Led by whipcord-tough old sergeants and clever young colonels, U.S. frontier regulars—volunteers all, just like our present force—waged the kind of relentless political/military campaigns necessary to find, harass, and weary to death those who stood against the will of an expansion-minded America. It took many long years, cost plenty of lives, and was never pretty, not in the American West, the Philippine Islands, or Latin America.[3] But it worked.

That preindustrial military had all the right things to fight and win against rebellious bands: gunboats and Marine landing parties; cavalry who threw away their sabers and fought on foot with carbines; native scouts and spies; gunners who stood alongside their dismounted brothers; and especially infantry, the men who walked and carried long arms, the men who settled the issue sooner or later. Yes, to find, outsmart, and outfight hostile guerrillas, to win the allegiance of endangered populations, to comb hillsides, hedgerows, haystacks, and hovels, requires skilled men on the ground, the exhausted, grimy Regular riflemen who "live rough," who do the most dying, and not very much killing, in any war. That is especially true in little wars that sputter on year after year.

Depending on riflemen was clearly the correct answer a century ago, and it is just as important now, but it is not what Americans want to hear today. The idea of young men dying in the dust, gut-shot, their slack mouths bubbling bloody pink foam as they cry for their mothers—well, it's antiquated, unseemly, even obscene. We're beyond all of that now, aren't we? After all, if we can land men on the moon, build a computer the size of a magazine, cure leprosy, and so forth, we can surely do better than putting our boys face-to-face with some garlic-smelling gutter fighter in an African back alley.[4] Thus goes the thought among the majority of the *cognoscenti*, whose sole knowledge of the military appears to come from Hollywood. They want dazzling Tomcat fighter ace Tom Cruise kicking high-tech ass in *Top Gun*, not stinking, sweat-stained grunt Tom Cruise getting his low-tech sergeant's ass shot off in *Born on the Fourth of July*. So what if circumstances cry out far more often for Sergeant Cruise and his Marines than Lieutenant Cruise and his supersonic gizmos?

In a national exercise in self-denial, then, we simply ignore the demands of reality, and insist on trying to pound annoying Third World screws with high-speed, high-technology hammers. We hope to avoid casualties by avoiding the use of infantry, and so go through all sorts of mental gymnastics and logical cheetah flips trying to avoid sending men with rifles, or, alternatively, convincing ourselves that when we do commit our infantry, we are not really involved in war.[5] This sort of business manages to entertain the CNN audience, at least until the first blood debt comes due. Then we witness scenes like the Marine barracks blown apart in Beirut, fliers dragged through the dirt byways of Mogadishu, young men shredded by mines near Tuzla, and the horror washes over us. We long for brother Cruise and the whisper jet, or better, a cruise missile shot from an ocean away, to "solve" these situations. Anything but a gory infantry fight, say many.

Just to make sure we do not misuse and kill our precious riflemen, we elect not to have very many. With 1.4 million people in uniform, America fields 95 battalions of Regular infantry, about a third of them Marines, for a total of less than 70,000 men.[6] In other words, one in twenty of those in service comes face-to-face on the ground with Mr. Wrong. Everybody else does something else, the "bullets, not men" kind of stuff.

But, oh, those bullets can, and do, make all the difference! It is the other stuff, not the rather unimpressive 95 battalions of grunts, that makes the United States of America the globe's sole military superpower. Today, we field the strongest armed forces on Earth. Other countries have more numerous militaries, but none possess the concentrated firepower, all-seeing reconnaissance, guaranteed resupply of largess, and unprecedented mobility that characterize the American way of war.[7] Because we can send bullets, not men, no conventional power dares to rise against us.

At sea, the United States Navy dominates with some 443 combatant and auxiliary ships, not to mention its own formidable air arm numbering some 2,995 aircraft, many carrier-based. The Navy even has its own "army," the tough U.S. Marine Corps, 174,000 strong, with more than 328 fighter/attack airplanes and numerous helicopters of its own. The Navy exists to control the sea lanes and to shoot things ashore, mainly bombs and missiles, but occasionally a battalion or so of Marines.[8] No country has seriously threatened American prowess on the oceans since the Japanese defeat at Leyte Gulf in 1944. Accordingly, American shipping goes where it will around the world.

In the air, the United States Air Force ranges at will, and even posts its unsleeping electronic sentries in outer space. No service better epitomizes the American fascination, bordering on worship, with the products of science and engineering. With 4,745 fighting aircraft, the progeny of Billy Mitchell and Curtis LeMay can deliver death from above in quantity and on target, choosing from a kit bag that spans the gamut from 20mm cannon rounds through laser-guided bombs to thermonuclear city-killers.[9] Since 1944, no other state has been able to stop the U.S. Air Force. Air supremacy allows workhorse jet transports to span the planet, delivering everything from fighting men and munitions to medicine and food bundles.

The Army, our smallest component relative to its likely competitors, relies explicitly on the sea services and the Air Force to get it to battle, sustain it overseas, and provide additional weight of hot metal. Even in America's land-power contingent, the infantry is hardly the dominant arm. Some 88 of 100 Regular Army soldiers do something other than infantry duties, reflecting the long-term trend toward sending bullets, not men. Used to fighting far from home and outnumbered, the American Army focuses firepower, its killing bullets, like no other. From the TOT (Time on Target) artillery barrages that stunned the Germans in Normandy to the "mad minutes" of Vietnam and the "steel rain" of the Gulf War, the U.S. Army has become above all a fire-intensive force, with everything built to find targets or serve the hungry guns, be they in tank turrets, artillery batteries, rocket pods, or aboard helicopter gunships. This style of war demands more than two thousand helicopters, some five thousand armored fighting vehicles, and seventy thousand–odd trucks of all descriptions, so few should be surprised that the bulk of the Army's enlisted soldiers and officers necessarily serve in logistics organizations, keeping everything flying and rolling, getting those deadly bullets to the front, maintaining and fueling the sophisticated launchers, and the like. The clerks, mechanics, and drivers far outnumber the riflemen.[10] This sort of sophisticated combined arms force guarantees rapid, decisive victory, at a low cost in lives, against any conventional army.

But how to use this devastating firepower, this omnipotent air armada, this preeminent naval strength against the wily CLF and their insidious kin? How to fight an enemy who has only infantry, and who mixes with innocent, or at least noncombatant, local citizenry? Therein lies the real problem, the one JRTC was built to explore, the one the American military failed so miserably to master in Vietnam. Not surprisingly, as in Southeast Asia, as on the Great Plains, as in all nasty little skirmishes, the burden of sorting this all out falls squarely on the heads of infantrymen. The grunts have every incentive to choose correctly. If they get it wrong, they pay with their lives.

Not paying with blood is why the Army invented JRTC and similar combat training centers, to learn lessons without terminal results.

Of the ninety-five infantry battalions that represent America's boots on the ground around the world, the JRTC principally concerns itself with the forty-two normally called U.S. Army "light forces." This is not to say that the Army's twenty-six mechanized infantry battalions and the twenty-seven Marine battalions never come to Fort Polk. They do, but they also have their own dedicated training centers, Irwin and Hohenfels for the Army, and Lejeune, Twenty-Nine Palms, and Okinawa, among others, for the Marine Corps. But in general, Polk caters to Army light infantry and their usual combined arms comrades.

The forty-two Regular Army light battalions divide into four categories: Rangers, parachute (often called "airborne"), air assault, and light infantry. By past standards, all four types represent elite forces, specially selected, highly trained, well-led, and extremely motivated. Given the Army's persistent individual assignment policies, there is much interchange between these various battalions. The same officers and NCOs often serve in all four varieties of light battalions; this creates a degree of standardization across the force, which clearly has far more in common than not. This does not preclude some pretty fierce rivalries among the four Army light communities.

There are differences, mainly related to capabilities. The three Ranger battalions, all assigned to the 75th Ranger Regiment, work for the Joint Special Operations Command, performing direct action missions in immediate support of national objectives. All Rangers are paratroopers, and all but the newest junior rankers have graduated from the grueling Ranger Course, even the few cooks and clerks allocated to these lean battalions. In line with their motto, "Rangers Lead the Way," the Black Berets spearheaded parachute assaults into Grenada and Panama, and had a prominent role in the awful street fighting in Somalia in 1993.[11] The Rangers stand a cut above, and everyone knows it, except for the CLF, of course.

The parachute battalions, nine from Fort Bragg's "All-American" 82d Airborne Division, one from Italy, and one from Alaska, see themselves as next in the pecking order after the Rangers. Every man has completed Airborne School, the very tough three-week Basic Parachutist Course at Fort Benning, Georgia, and thereby earned the right to wear the coveted silver jump wings. Built around their ability to load aircraft at home station and then jump anywhere accessible to the U.S. Air Force, the Maroon Berets epitomize instant readiness. Along with the Rangers (and Marine battalions afloat), American paratroopers have also participated in every fracas: Grenada, Panama, the Gulf War, Kurdistan, Rwanda, and Bosnia. Their ranks heavily salted with Ranger-qualified sergeants, led almost exclusively by Ranger-trained officers, the paratroopers bring to their work the same élan and discipline that characterizes airborne forces around the world.[12] The CLF draws on the 1st of the 509th Parachute Infantry to gain these same benefits, which makes for an interesting clash of elites whenever visiting parachute brigades show up at Fort Polk.

The air assault battalions, nine with the "Screaming Eagles" of the 101st Airborne Division (Air Assault) and two in Korea, specialize in heliborne insertions. While the units in Korea, the Rangers, 82d Airborne, light infantry, and the Marines all use helicopters, none employ them with the skill, or on the scale, of the 101st Airborne's battalions. As with the parachute infantry, the air assault forces include a high proportion of Ranger-schooled NCOs and officers. Many of the men are airborne-trained, and four-fifths wear air assault wings, awarded for finishing Fort Campbell, Kentucky's Air Assault School, known informally as "the ten toughest days in the Army." Unlike the paratroop units, the air assault battalions come in intact, unscattered by wind or air transport dispersion. Of all the light forces, this ability to mass, integrated with the all-weather fires of far-ranging AH-64A Apache attack helicopters, makes the air assault troops valuable even against conventional armies; their rapid mobility and capacity for vertical envelopment ensures them key roles in lesser fights, too. Screaming Eagles leapt to the Euphrates River, and the doorstep of Baghdad, in a matter of hours during the Gulf War, a brilliant exploitation of the air assault concept in a major conflict. Five years later, they formed the core of the U.S. forces covering the extraction from Haiti, again by virtue of their unique skills.[13] Trained to fight at night and land in force, the heliborne infantry has taken up the mantle of the World War II glider troops, the other half of the airborne concept, the part that lands as formed units, not as individuals. This is why, like the 82d, the 101st still proudly carries the title "airborne." The "real" airborne troopers of the CLF are not impressed.

The seventeen battalions of pure light infantry, split between the "Tropic Lightning" 25th Infantry Division and the 10th Mountain Division, complement the forced entry capabilities emphasized by the Rangers, paratroopers, and air assault battalions. If you want sustained ground operations, you look to these people. Trained to conduct heliborne assaults, adept in night fighting, led by the same Ranger cadre of officers and sergeants as the other light battalions, the light infantry prides itself on its ability to live and fight in harsh terrain for extended periods, all on foot. Light infantry performed well in Somalia and Haiti, providing skilled patrols and ready reac-

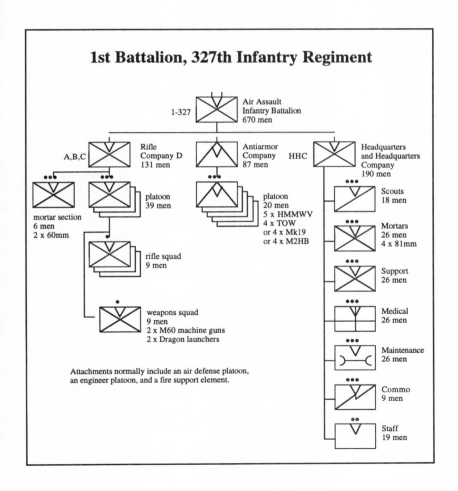

1st Battalion, 327th Infantry Regiment

1-327 — Air Assault Infantry Battalion 670 men

A,B,C — Rifle Company D 131 men

Antiarmor Company 87 men — HHC

Headquarters and Headquarters Company 190 men

mortar section 6 men 2 x 60mm

platoon 39 men

platoon 20 men 5 x HMMWV 4 x TOW or 4 x Mk19 or 4 x M2HB

Scouts 18 men

rifle squad 9 men

Mortars 26 men 4 x 81mm

weapons squad 9 men 2 x M60 machine guns 2 x Dragon launchers

Support 26 men

Medical 26 men

Maintenance 26 men

Commo 9 men

Staff 19 men

Attachments normally include an air defense platoon, an engineer platoon, and a fire support element.

tion forces to support U.S. and United Nations operations in these countries.[14] Less specialized than the Rangers, 82d, or 101st, these skilled battalions were custom-built to deal with the likes of the CLF. Or, at least, that's the idea.

While there are variations in exact organization, any one of these light battalions pretty well resembles its brother units. All feature the same mixture of rifle companies, heavy weapons and other specialty platoons, and a small headquarters, in proportions that would be comfortable to any American infantryman of this century. The 1st Battalion, 327th Infantry Regiment, an air assault infantry battalion assigned to the 1st Brigade, 101st Airborne Division, allows as good a basis for examination as any.

Three identical rifle companies, lettered A (Alpha), B (Bravo), and C (Charlie), form the heart of the battalion. On paper, each consists of 5 officers and 126 enlisted men, split into three rifle platoons, a 60mm mortar section, and a company headquarters. Served by six men, the twin mortars are handy hip-pocket artillery on tap, able to pump high explosives, burning white phosphorus smoke, and illuminant flares out to thirty-five hundred meters. The company headquarters entails a young captain, a younger lieutenant executive officer, and an experienced first sergeant, along with five others to handle supplies and radio watch.

The rifle platoons mirror the company composition, with three subordinate rifle squads and a weapons squad, plus a three-man headquarters with a lieutenant, a platoon sergeant, and a radiotelephone operator (RTO). If the rifle companies make up the battalion's primary fighting strength, then the twenty-seven rifle squads form the true cutting edge. When you speak of infantry, you are talking about these young men.

Each rifle squad in the 1st of the 327th should have nine men: a staff sergeant squad leader and two four-man fire teams, led by buck sergeants. The fire teams build around the M249 Squad Automatic Weapon (SAW), a fragile, sixteen-pound Belgian-designed light machine gun on a somewhat flimsy bipod, able to spit an eye-popping eight hundred 5.56mm rounds a minute out to eight hundred meters with good effect. All others carry the nine-pound M16A2 5.56mm rifle, an upgrade of the somewhat infamous Vietnam-era model, with a stronger barrel, better sights, and the ever-popular full automatic "rock 'n' roll" setting replaced by a more conservative three-round burst option. It can also hit out to eight hundred meters, but in truth, for even well-trained infantry, anything past three hundred meters is gravy. Finally, one of the men carries an M203 40mm grenade launcher on his rifle, capable of plunking egg-size shells out to 350 meters. These grim little items come in a few useful types, including illumination, buckshot, CS riot gas, unquenchable white phosphorus incendiary, and good old high explosive. All of these weapons have impressive night sights, and even better, can carry a cigarette-pack-size AN/PAQ4 laser designator that, when zeroed to the weapon, permits a soldier with night-vision goggles to hit exactly where his laser illuminates, regardless of how the firearm is aimed.[15] In other words, with a PAQ4, you can shoot from the hip, over the shoulder, or even around corners, and make it count.

Along with its three rifle squads, each platoon also has a weapons squad, led by a staff sergeant. Two of the men carry M60 machine guns, the Vietnam War's ungainly twenty-three-pound "Pig" capable of shooting its 7.62mm slugs out to eleven hundred meters from a sturdy bipod or tripod. (The tripod also makes a great club in its own right.) Two others carry the M47 Dragon antitank missile, an awkward sixty-nine pound behemoth outranged by the M60 machine gun and, unfortunately, by most of the tanks it is designed to destroy.[16] Along with rifles for self-defense, the other four men in the weapons squad carry ammunition and ancillary equipment, like the machine gun spare barrels, night sights, and tripods. The pair lugging the massive Dragon rounds are particularly burdened.

The rifle companies allow the 1-327th Infantry to contact and destroy hostile forces and to control areas by saturation patrolling and, if necessary, dug-in defense. Strong as they are, together they amount to only about a quarter of the battalion's firepower strength. Half of that fire potential lies in Company D, the antiarmor company, a type of unit found only in the parachute and air assault battalions, not in the Rangers or purely light battalions.

Company D (Delta) is designed as a mounted force, with seven officers, eighty enlisted men, and twenty-seven HMMWVs (High Mobility Multipurpose Wheeled Vehicles—Hummers or, more usually,

Humvees), twenty of these converted to gunships with small central rooftop firing hatches and hard-shelled Kevlar armor. Four gunships and a cargo truck make up a platoon, and five such platoons comprise the company. Delta offers a multiple threat. Its armed Humvees can carry M220A2 TOW (Tube-launched Optically tracked Wire-guided) antitank guided missile launchers, a superb, battle-proven armor-slayer that ranges out to 3,750 meters. Alternatively, they can mount the Mark-19 40mm automatic grenade launcher, no less than a grenade machine gun spewing 375 M203-style grenades per minute out to 2,100 meters, with predictably pulverizing results. Or, for a well-tested blast from the past, the Delta gunners can select the venerable, World War II M2HB .50-caliber (12.7mm) machine gun, shooting wicked thumb-size bullets out past 1,800 meters.[17] The Delta soldiers supplement these top-of-the-line infantry weapons with rifles and SAWs, although the company cannot dismount very many men and still man its potent weaponry.

Company D's arsenal can be mixed and matched aboard the Humvees, subject only to the limitations of ammunition and the fact that only one type of gun can be up at any one time. Along with its firepower, this wheeled company permits its dismounted parent battalion the luxury of a rapid reaction force, a blocking element in the attack, a mobile reserve in the defense. Using Company D wisely can make the difference between success and failure for an air assault infantry battalion.

The other company in the battalion is Headquarters and Headquarters Company (HHC), an eight-headed hydra going in as many directions at once, with 19 officers and 171 enlisted. Along with a small company headquarters that runs the battalion's service support efforts, the other seven principal parts include two fighting platoons, three logistics platoons, and two elements that together make up the actual battalion headquarters.[18]

The HHC fighting platoons, the eighteen-man Scout Platoon and the twenty-six-man Mortar Platoon, work directly for the battalion commander in the field. The Scouts provide the battalion with its focused reconnaissance capability, and also furnish three sniper teams for good measure. With four 81mm mortar tubes, the Mortars contribute a quarter of the battalion's total firepower, and their potent rounds reach out to 5,600 meters.[19]

The service support platoons of the company work directly for its commander, usually back in some relatively secure training area that serves as a staging base for all aspects of logistics. Central to this effort, the Support Platoon moves food, ammunition, water, fuel, and spare parts forward by helicopter sling-load or, when necessary, ground convoy. The Maintenance Platoon repairs the battalion's fleet of trucks, almost all assorted kinds of Humvees, as well as a vital handful of five-ton cargo trucks held by the Support Platoon. Finally, the Medical Platoon detaches aid teams to the four fighting companies while retaining an aid station and ambulance section under battalion control.[20] Typically, about a third of these service support troops go forward with the letter companies to form a combat train and furnish immediately responsive logistics.

The last segment of HHC is the battalion headquarters proper, with the Communications Platoon on hand to ensure radio and telephone connections higher, lower, and to adjacent units. Including the lieutenant colonel and command sergeant major, the headquarters has thirteen officers and thirty enlisted troops. Responsive to a major serving as battalion XO, four primary sections make up the staff: S1 (Personnel), S2 (Intelligence), S3 (Operations), and S4 (Logistics). These sections divide up into a main command post (also called the TOC, for Tactical Operations Center), a tactical command post (the Tac) well forward, and, running the combat trains, a rear command post (often called the ALOC, Administrative/Logistics Center).[21] All of this exists solely to serve the commander. Sometimes, as the staff gets busy setting up command posts and briefing each other, one can lose sight of that.

The battalion never fights "pure," but always brings in help from the rest of the Army, the 88 percent that is not wearing the crossed rifles of the infantry. Several distinct sorts of combined arms reinforcements routinely go to outfits like 1st of the 327th, a process so standardized that these elements deserve consideration in an enumeration of the structure of an air assault battalion, making it what the Army prefers to call a task force, a purpose-built grouping of nonorganic units under one commander, created to carry out a certain operation.[22]

Two platoons almost always accompanied the 1-327th Infantry. The 1st Platoon, Battery A, 2nd Battalion, 44th Air Defense Artillery, brought Stinger air defense missile teams and early warning to the task force. The Stinger teams carried their long, pipe-shaped launchers and, guided by a sophisticated air surveillance network tied into orbiting Air Force radar planes, engaged hostile jets and choppers. For dealing with land mines or emplacing the same, the task force relied on the sappers of 1st Platoon, Company A, 326th Engineers.[23] It was hard to conceive of committing 1st of the 327th without these men alongside.

Often, other small teams would be attached too. These might be military intelligence prisoner interrogators, sensor and ground radar sections, psychological operations loudspeaker squads, civil affairs liaison parties, or even foreign military or police guides and assistants. This bunch was a bit more amorphous, and a lot less familiar, than the engineers or air defenders. Sometimes the task force got them. Sometimes it did not.

One other attachment was as certain as sunrise, though. The task force consistently deployed with its Fire Support Section, a platoon's worth of forward observers (FOs) that hailed from the 2d Battalion, 320th Field Artillery. These artillerymen covered down on every fighting company and platoon. Although they carried rifles, these men really fought by means of long-range radios, always looking to shake down the thunder when required. Along with coordinating the fires of their own artillery unit, the fire support teams could also plan, call for, and adjust mortar fires, air strikes, and even naval gunfire. Often, the fire supporters were augmented by U.S. Air Force forward air controllers and Air/Naval Gunfire Liaison Company (ANGLICO) personnel.[24] Here, indeed, was the physical manifestation of sending bullets, not men. These few FOs represented more firepower than ten air assault infantry battalions put together.

Even a single air assault battalion, however, had a unique claim on the rotary-wing fleet that characterized the modern 101st Airborne Division (Air Assault). The 1st of the 327th could expect to go in and pull out by air, as a battalion, borne aloft in the dead of night by swift UH-60L Blackhawks, with Delta gun Humvees and ambulances following along, swaying under twin-rotored CH-47D Chinooks. Casualties could be pulled out by Blackhawk medevac birds; resupply would arrive regularly thanks to dedicated log birds. Finally, any squad in contact could anticipate aerial fires from AH-64A Apaches, overhead day and night to administer the kill, whether to rampaging tanks or insurgent tigers.[25] Indeed, no infantry battalion, not even the mechanized forces, could call on more rapid, more flexible, or more potent support than those lucky enough to be part of the Screaming Eagles. That is, when it worked as advertised.

This, then, is the construct known as the 1st Battalion, 327th Infantry Regiment, a U.S. Army air assault infantry battalion task force and its habitual associates. On paper, in theory, this battalion can do all of those things the Army expected: deploy to war, air assault, attack, and defend. But there is the book and there is real life, and as has always been true, the battalion is only as good as its men. These men, most of them young, breathed life into the 1st Battalion, 327th Infantry Regiment, and made it often more, and sometimes less, than the sum of its sterile structural parts and equipment.

Once you get past the line and block diagrams and the weapons characteristics, you always come down to the men. The men that comprised the 1st of the 327th in the late summer of 1994, the men who would undergo JRTC Rotation 94-10, exhibited the same fundamental nature as most of the other light infantry battalions in the Army and Marine Corps. The mechanized folks, wedded to their twenty-seven-ton M2A2 Bradley Fighting Vehicles, clearly belonged to a different breed, as did the other seven-eighths of the Army, the ones who drew the same pay but never lived or fought like grunts. But the 1-327th Infantry offers as good a study subject as any if you want to know the state of elite U.S. riflemen at the close of the American Century.

Before discussing quality, the more important discriminator, it is worth our while to consider quantity. As the old Soviets liked to say, at a certain level, quantity has a quality all its own.[26] Johnny Rambo may be able to function as a one-man army, but actual infantrymen prefer the comfort of numbers, at least something resembling the table of organizational strength. It allows a margin for friction and mayhem.

Like most U.S. Army battalions of this period, or indeed any period, the 1st of the 327th constantly limped along somewhat understrength and undergrade. The stable, fully manned battalion starring in Army field manuals has yet to be found out in the line units. As anyone on the frontier a century ago would tell you, that's the Army, and nobody seriously expects it to be completely up to establishment. The Screaming Eagles in general, and 1-327th Infantry in particular, were not, even though they were much closer than a lot of outfits. As it prepared to head for Fort Polk, the battalion was running more than 200 men short of its authorized 670.

Four factors generated this shortage. First, the battalion lacked about twenty men of its full complement, largely the result of early discharges granted as the end of the fiscal year approached on 30 September, a policy designed to save money in a stretch of constrained service budgets. Second, another sixty or so were assigned, but off in various NCO schools, dealing with intractable family crises or baby births, or recovering from injuries or surgery too severe to permit field duty. Third, another twenty represented the battalion's share of the Fort Campbell overhead, the soldiers skimmed off for special duty running firing ranges, gymnasiums, auto registration, post cleanup crews, and a variety of other ash and trash functions that the Department of the Army chose not to fund civilians or contract labor to carry out on behalf of the twenty-three thousand or so soldiers (and almost twice as many dependents) living in and around Fort Campbell, Kentucky.[27] These diversions really could not be avoided, although there could have been significant clamping down in that middle category had the chain of command gotten serious about it. After all, injured men could answer telephones and count equipment in rear areas, and they could help in the rear echelon at Fort Polk. But nobody in 1-327th thought that way in August of 1994.

Finally, and most significantly, the battalion, like any other similar unit in the U.S. Army, rotated its soldiers as individuals, to the tune of a 15 percent turnover on a monthly basis. The individual replacement system, disparaged in World War II as ineffective, immoral, and inhumane, has been adopted since 1945 as the standard approach, supposedly because it offers some type of efficiency and cost savings, and meshes nicely with individual recruiting contracts. In one sense, it does replicate the turmoil generated by combat losses, for whatever that may be worth. Commonwealth armies, like the British, the Canadians, and the Australians, wedded to solid regimental structures that see officers and men serving repeatedly in the same battalions, look in horror as their Yank counterparts transfer merrily from battalion to battalion every two years (or less). Every attempt to alter the current American system, and there have been several, has been subverted and defeated by bureaucrats every bit as insidious, and entrenched, as the Department of War bureau chiefs of the nineteenth century who repeatedly refused to issue repeating rifles to hard-pressed frontier regulars.[28]

So the 1st of the 327th, like its brother battalions, endures some hundred men a month "coming and going and never really arriving," as they used to say in World War II.[29] Every one of these men required time to get oriented upon arrival and get cleared upon departure, with all the attendant handling of records, medical examinations, transfers of field equipment, waiting around for clerks, and the like. Added to the other hundred people not present or off on other Army business, this translates into missing rifle squads, Delta gunships with only two of three crewmen, mortar sections without ammunition bearers, absent medics, officers not on hand, and sergeants bumped up to serve a grade or two above their heads. In the summer of 1994, for example, all nine rifle platoons manned only two rifle squads, and averaged about twenty-five men in struggling to do that.

Working at two-thirds strength, every man counted. Quality had to stretch to make up for the open spaces on the manning roster, and this started right at the lowest level. In a light fighter unit, there are no "cannon fodder" privates or unimportant supernumeraries. Accordingly, a lot depended on the junior soldiers, the privates and specialists carrying the SAWs and rifles. Based upon stereotypes dating back to the draftee Army (and not true then, either), most American civilians see riflemen as some sort of half-witted losers, stuck toting a shooting iron because they lack the brains or connections to do anything else.

Those days, if they ever really existed, are definitely over. Far from being ignorant rednecks or sullen urban gangbangers, today's infantryman, military occupational specialty 11B10, is a healthy, drug-free high school graduate, above average in height and strength, with a clean police record. Some 81 percent score in the top mental categories in Army entrance testing, compared to 50 percent of the populace at large.[30] Many have some college, and each company boasts at least a few graduates in its ranks. Given its reputation, priority in the U.S. Army, and known insistence on high standards, 101st Airborne tends to skim off the top layer of the overall infantry gene pool.

And yet, one should not overstate the case. The rankers in 1-327th were good men, but they shared a certain sameness in their origins and aspirations, not exactly Ivy Leaguers or the children of privilege. If you wonder who volunteers to be an 11B10 in the Screaming Eagles, you need to look among the sons of the lower middle class, the products of small towns and tract suburbs, teens who made up the faceless middle in a high school with three thousand students, young men who sometimes preferred the couch or the video game console to the basketball court or wrestling mat. Some hailed from broken or mixed-up homes, and wanted a sense of stability and order. A great many knew a father or an uncle who had served proudly in Vietnam. Almost to a man, these men volunteered for the Army, the infantry, and the Screaming Eagles because they wanted adventure and challenge, not just college money or three squares—you could get that shuffling folders as a file clerk in some six-story Air Force office building. These people wanted, indeed demanded, discipline, shared hardship, and inspiration, and with it would go anywhere or do anything. In short, they had joined the Army for all the right reasons, bringing a hunger, not to mention a tolerance for disappointment, that America's so-called best and brightest would never bring.[31] Those sort of folks went on to Wall Street to make millions. These other young men, the Army's men, cut their hair and went into uniform, hoping to make war.

Staying in, naturally, was not as easy as joining up. The ones who lacked physical stamina, the fat boys, the sickly, usually were culled at Fort Benning during One Station Unit Training, what Hollywood would label "boot camp." Still, some slipped through to the 1st of the 327th, miserable youngsters wheezing along on five-mile runs and suffering through shin splints and sprains. They got a good look at Army socialized medicine in all its "hurry-up-and-wait" glory before they finally quit and went home, or were sent home by a chain of command that had given up on them.

There was another notable drag on the performance of a number of the newer soldiers, spawned by the fact that the majority of the 1st of the 327th troops married young. Many moved into the trailer parks and ramshackle apartment complexes spreading like cancer cells all around Fort Campbell's periphery. Here, the slogan "You'll never get rich in the Army" imposed its own grim logic. Believe it or not, Army on-post housing policies still reflect the draft era, when most of the lower ranks lived in the barracks. Officers and NCOs get on-post quarters, one of the few perquisites for those who made rank. Married privates, however, do not get on-post quarters, even though they make substantially less than their sergeants and captains. While Fort Campbell has consistently led the way in creating on-post housing for junior married soldiers, not to mention putting the heat on local developers to build decent, affordable commercial housing, the ubiquitous trailer parks continue to do a booming business. Encouraged by these squalid surroundings, wife abuse, battered children, drinking problems, marital infidelity, petty crimes, and even suicide all come into the equation. Private soldiers married to other soldiers, especially with babies involved, do not help the recipe. As surely as a man who cannot run or march, a soldier whose family life goes south will not complete his enlistment. The NCOs and officers at Fort Campbell had more than enough of these sad cases.

As a rule, then, from a tenth to a quarter of each month's crop of new troops developed physical complaints, acute family problems, or a variety of other sorts of emotional maladjustments severe enough to warrant separation from the service.[32] As the 1-327th Infantry prepared to go to JRTC, it had its share of these unhappy people hanging around, largely due to a lack of command emphasis within the battalion on either resolving their problems or making them civilians. The majority of the previous chain of command, determined to keep strength high for a six-month peacekeeping rotation in the Sinai in the latter months of 1993, tended to be optimistic about troubled soldiers. Hoping for the best over time, they determined to help, or make, these frustrated young men fulfill their enlistment obligations. That mentality created a lack of urgency. Coupled with unfamiliarity with how to handle the mountain of paperwork affiliated with such cases, not much got done. This issue hampered the battalion's readiness in the summer of 1994.

These unfortunates, though, were a clear minority, atypical and out of place. The much greater proportion of the nineteen- and twenty-year-olds in the battalion made infantry soldiers as good as any in history, well suited to displaying initiative, to fighting in small units at night, the way air assault forces did their business. As Robert E. Lee asserted on the eve of Gettysburg; good soldiers would surely do their part, if well-led. "But there is the difficulty," he lamented. "Proper commanders—where can they be obtained?"[33]

Proper commanders, leadership in the officer and NCO ranks, was indeed the key variable. Units reflect their leaders. Of all the things the battalion could do to get ready for JRTC, or indeed actual combat, the most important effort involved getting the right men in charge, and teaching them what they needed to know. As the typically high summer changeover subsided, the battalion's chain of command, impersonally delivered by the revolving-door assignment system and inherited from previous regimes, readied itself for JRTC 94-10. Although undergrade in spots, some tough cuts had been made to get it into this condition. More were due in the months to come. Yet the overall soundness of the lineup said volumes about the high quality of the 101st Airborne and the U.S. Army in 1994.

Each of the three rifle companies showed a distinictive style. Company A (radio call sign Abu[34]) worked for Capt. Drew Felix, a Ranger-qualified Officer Candidate School (OCS) graduate with previous service in the 4th Infantry Division (Mechanized). A man of few words, very tough, Drew was well-complemented by 1st Sgt. Scott D. Craig, a Ranger with recent experience in one of the air assault battalions in Korea. The two of them could go hours without saying anything to each other, yet they knew what each wanted, being very much kindred souls. All three of the Abu rifle platoons were led by Rangers, but only the 1st Platoon had a lieutenant to complement its veteran platoon sergeant. The Abus had a reputation as a hard-nosed company, tough on their men and unforgiving about standards.

Company B (radio call sign Bushmaster) was the best rifle company, responding to the strong personality of Capt. Alfredo Mycue, a Ranger West Pointer with experience in Germany's defunct 8th Infantry Division (Mechanized). Talkative, demanding, tireless, and very much "hands-on," Alfredo was one of those rare officers who preferred to do everything himself and could get away with it. His quiet Ranger right hand, 1st Sgt. Gerald S. Eubank, provided a calming influence in Alfredo's wide wake. With one brand-new Ranger lieutenant in the 1st Platoon, Alfredo depended on his three superb platoon sergeants, just as strong as the Abu trio. The Bushmasters traditionally led the battalion in all areas involving training and operations. If you wanted something done right, you gave it to these guys.

You certainly did not give it to Company C (radio call sign Cold Steel), not unless you did not care about what happened. Capt. Chris Forbes, an able ROTC Ranger from the University of South Carolina, earned the Combat Infantryman Badge in the Gulf War with the 3d Armored Division. Unfortunately for him, he inherited an absolute mess when he assumed command of his company in late March 1994. The previous commander, a very mixed-up young man, had run the unit for twenty-nine months as some sort of social club, with everybody on a first-name basis and rampant indiscipline, all abetted by a weak-willed first sergeant counting the days until his retirement. Chris had been cleaning house with a fire hose, literally promoting and installing any NCO who would take charge, almost up to the hour of deployment to JRTC. With the old first sergeant headed home, the company had no real "first shirt," instead borrowing a signal NCO, Sfc. Dino LaRocca, from Company D, simply to help with administration. Squads were led by specialists, platoons by whoever Captain Forbes and the battalion could find. As a result of all of this turbulence, his 1st Platoon was led by a bucked-up squad leader, but an undoubtedly good man, a Ranger who was not afraid to lead. The 2nd Platoon, which had been completely overhauled in July, had a very able new Ranger lieutenant with a just-arrived 82d Airborne staff sergeant to help him. The 3d Platoon had not been fixed. It essentially had no one in charge, its sole senior NCO being extremely weak. Chris Forbes, and the battalion as a whole, knew that Cold Steel lacked cohesion, proficiency, and drive. It was present for duty, and that was about it.

Company D (radio call sign Maddog), the powerful antiarmor force with its twenty Humvee gun wagons, coalesced around the battalion's best commander, Capt. Willie T. Utroska. Willie offered an "only in America" life story: a Polish-American father, a Puerto Rican mother, raised and schooled on the island as an electrical engineer, and like Alfredo Mycue, trained with the 8th Infantry Division (Mechanized) as a lieutenant. A charismatic leader with a ready smile and a coaching style all his own, Willie exuded an enthusiasm and competence that infected his entire command. Captain Utroska formed a great tandem with his gaunt, chain-smoking, perceptive senior NCO, 1st Sgt. Ronald D. Morgan, who had been with the battalion for almost five years and knew how to get things done. Blessed with five great platoon sergeants, exhibiting tremendous skill with all their various weaponry, the Maddogs epitomized the teamwork and family feeling of a great company. They would have to live up to their reputation for the battalion to succeed at Fort Polk.

Headquarters and Headquarters Company (radio call sign Headhunter), less its Scouts, Mortars, and command post elements, ran the battalion's service support trains. Captain Ronz L. Sarvis, a graduate of South Carolina State ROTC and, like Chris Forbes, a Gulf War combat veteran from the 3d Armored Division, was the senior company commander in the battalion. With more than three years in the 101st Airborne, including a May 1994 stint at JRTC as a battalion S1, Ronz knew all the ropes, especially in the arcane worlds of personnel administration, medical support, and resupply. He exuded calm and good humor, useful qualities in the often hectic world of the trains. Ronz worked closely with 1st Sgt. Jordan L. Jeffcoat, a tough old NCO who had served with the 101st Airborne Division in Vietnam and the Gulf and who, when asked by a fresh-faced lieutenant at a social function which high school he attended, responded with the laconic growl of a real old Army sergeant: "G.E.D. [general equivalency diploma]." The Support and Maintenance platoons certainly knew how to execute their difficult tasks, the Medical Platoon less so. By themselves, the Headhunters in the trains could not win battles. But without their capable contributions, the battalion would not win any either.

Along with the five companies, much rode on the quality of the leadership in the five independent platoons. None had a tougher job than the Scouts (radio call sign Tiger[35]). These eighteen young men would be asked to find the enemy on their own, alone in the Great Gulp. Led by a clever, sarcastic senior Ranger lieutenant named Mark Lawry, ably assisted by Ranger S/Sgt. Kirk A. Mayfield, the Scouts were about halfway through a transition from battalion pretty-boys to a true battalion reconnaissance team, skilled in all aspects of field-craft. By nature independent, and daily becoming more so, the platoon had ample opportunity to show initiative at JRTC.

The Mortar Platoon (radio call sign Baseplate) could expect similar chances to shine. By rights, like the Scouts, it should have been one of the strongest platoons in the battalion. Instead, this group displayed consistent mediocrity. The leadership at the top rarely got excited about anything, good or bad. The Mortars looked to be non-players at JRTC, a disturbing development, as a quarter of the battalion's firepower resided in this unimpressive platoon.

As average as the Mortars appeared, the air defenders (radio call sign Big Dog) gave evidence of being anything but that. Driven by a strong-willed, smart lieutenant named Freddie Mack, disciplined by Sfc. Joe Edgar, the Stinger gunners trained hard to seek out, and take out, all varieties of enemy air. If this platoon displayed any weakness, it might be said to show too much initiative, getting out and about without reference to other ongoing operations, and thus exposing itself to hostile action or friendly fire.

With regard to the engineers (radio call sign Sapper), their contribution relied on their abilities to dispose of and lay mines. In all operations, the sappers would be expected to clear CLF minefields and breach wire entanglements. In the defense in particular, the engineer platoon would carry a tremendous load, as the battalion had no hope of stopping enemy armor without a tremendous obstacle-building and mine-laying effort, with the sappers at center stage. Although the platoon's leadership seemed willing enough, they lacked the determined focus, the take-charge spirit, of someone like 2/Lt. Freddie Mack. This bunch of sappers would wait for guidance, and in the lack of same, or in the face of adversity, might just do nothing. So it would be up to the battalion to make certain these men received clear and timely instructions.

The same applied to the platoon-strength fire support section, responsible for bringing together the mighty hammers of mortars, artillery, and close air support where and when the battalion needed these equalizers. The FOs with each platoon knew their jobs, as did their NCOs at company level and in the battalion TOC. But while enlisted men plan and call in fires for a living, and have the schooling and experience to do so, fire support officers tend to be assigned after all important duties in a firing battalion have been filled. The fire support officers too often came from the ranks of the new, the inexperienced, and, frankly, the suspect. Captain Mike Temple, an OCS man like Drew Felix, fit the usual stereotype. A Gulf War veteran, Mike's wartime service had been with a technologically advanced long-range rocket launcher battery supporting the 1st Cavalry Division. While fascinating and professionally rewarding, it did little to prepare him for arranging and adjusting the fires of the 105mm towed howitzers found in air assault field artillery, tubes not all that different from the standard U.S. field pieces used in World War II. Mike's slow Southern drawl reminded many who knew him of Forrest Gump, and at times the captain seemed just as slow as his speech, although he had heart enough for twenty men. In league with his rookie company-level lieutenants, and suffering from the fact that the battalion task force's home-station artillery/infantry integration had been largely ignored, Mike and his fire supporters faced an uphill climb at JRTC, especially against the fleeting CLF.

That oversight was one among several that would haunt the battalion headquarters proper (radio call sign Bulldog): the staff officers and NCOs who acted as the battalion's brain in consonance with the commander. The nervous system, the Communications Platoon, could be counted on to get the word out. Thinking up the word, and making certain it made sense for the situation, fell to the staff, which divided naturally into the operators (S2, S3, S5) and the service supporters (S1, S4). The staff reported to the commander through the

XO, Maj. Jim Laufenburg, a Ranger-qualified ROTC graduate of Ripon College and the Army's prestigious Command and General Staff College at Fort Leavenworth, Kansas. In the 1980s, as a captain, Jim commanded a rifle company in the neighboring 3-327th Infantry. A few months prior to JRTC 94-10, following the Sinai peacekeeping mission, had moved up from the battalion S3 position. Representative of the high-quality men who came to the 101st Airborne Division, Jim Laufenburg stood at the very front of the Army's pack of majors—indeed, the Army chose him for lieutenant colonel just prior to his departure for JRTC, Jim's second below-the-zone (early) promotion. With experience working directly for the U.S. Army Chief of Staff, destined to command his own battalion, Jim could easily have taken the reins himself at any time, the hallmark of a good XO. By the book, Jim acted as the second-in-command, the chief of staff, the overseer of logistics, the king of the TOC, and the all-round "go to" guy.

The other major, the S3, happened to be one of Jim Laufenburg's oldest Army acquaintances, another OCS graduate, Leavenworth man, Ranger, and former 3-327th company commander named Bill Phelps. Every bit a southern gentleman in the martial tradition of Robert E. Lee, Bill experienced the tail end of the Gulf conflict as an advisor to a Saudi infantry brigade, a sobering episode that reinforced his convictions about the importance of strict discipline and high training standards. As the S3, Bill exercised staff supervision over all aspects of tactical planning, integration of attachments, unit training, the internal functionings of the TOC, and the execution of field operations. The Army manuals encourage the S3 to be well forward, and Bill's naturally aggressive bent and crack shooting ability allowed him to follow that advice with alacrity.

The soldiers working for Major Phelps included some of the top talent in the battalion. It made sense that an air assault unit, dependent on its links to Army aviation, placed one of its best men in the S3 Air slot. Here, 1-327th Infantry turned to 1st Lt. Dave Bair, a West Pointer, a Ranger, and the longest-serving lieutenant in the battalion. Possessed of an incredible tolerance for hard work, Dave produced the calculations and tables necessary to get the battalion task force to battle by air, then supervised the conduct of those operations. Dave Bair surely lived up to another aspect of the airborne tradition; if there was a job that needed doing, Dave grabbed hold of it and accomplished the mission without waiting for help, guidance, or the next phase of the moon.

Along with the S3 Air, Bill's chief deputies included the S2 and S5. The S2 handled intelligence functions, designing collection schemes and analyzing the results to account for terrain and weather and, when things went correctly, to predict enemy behavior in as much detail as possible. Captain Dirk Blackdeer, yet another OCS officer, a former infantryman transferred into military intelligence, served as the S2. Physically imposing and as brilliant as he was tough, Dirk hailed from an American Indian family with long traditions of military service, not all of it with the bluecoats, either. He had a real nose for the bad guys, and unlike most intelligence types, had no fears about going out on a limb. He almost always guessed right.

Although not authorized by the formal table of organization, the new battalion commander, soon after his arrival in June 1994, had seen fit to designate an S5 responsible for interaction with the civilian population.[36] This cost the organization a quality platoon leader "out of hide," but in light of the nature of current U.S. conflicts, the commander judged the gain to be worth the pain. Based on some good recommendations, the job fell to 1st Lt. Matt Bounds, a smart, energetic young Ranger bubbling with imagination. The battalion commander could offer only a few skimpy, generic U.S. Army doctrinal materials to help Matt get started in his unfamiliar assignment, and nobody could get too excited about that stuff. Instead, the lieutenant colonel steered Matt Bounds toward two sources of much greater value: the U.S. Marine Corps *Small Wars Manual* (circa 1940) and Jean Larteguy's masterful novel of French paratroopers in Vietnam and Algeria, *The Centurions*. So equipped, and despite some initial misgivings about the whole concept, Matt soon saw the importance of his role in light of the likely trouble spots that might call for the 1st of the 327th's attention, and that included dealing with the confusing civil-military scene in JRTC's Cortinian countryside. The choice turned out to be exactly correct, and both by his personal presence and by the practical training he provided to the riflemen, Matt Bounds probably contributed more than any single individual to the battalion's fortunes while interacting with civilian role-players at Fort Polk. Having an S5, especially this particular S5, turned out to be the right call.

The other two primary staff officers, the S1 and S4, hung out at the ALOC in the combat trains, and reported directly to the battalion XO, Major Laufenburg. The S1, the adjutant, dealt with personnel issues, mainly strength accounting, tracking evacuees, and requesting replacements. The battalion's S1 would have preferred to be an office aide-de-camp rather than a field soldier, and this diffident lieutenant had volunteered for his job in hope of avoiding tough duty. That may have worked for the earlier battalion commander, but it did not wash with the fellow taking the outfit to JRTC 94-10, who had no need for a "dog robber" and high expectations for a front-line, hands-on adjutant.

The S4, who oversaw logistics and actually ran the combat trains, gave no such cause for concern. You could not ask for a more thorough, dedicated officer than Capt. Ted Donnelly, a Ranger and ROTC graduate from the University of Virginia who had done his lieutenancy in Germany. Ted had the patience, and the native intelligence, to slog through the sometimes unresponsive service support bureaucracies and get his battalion what it needed. More importantly, Ted Donnelly understood that you cannot do any infantry job, even S4, from behind a desk. This captain made the rounds and looked problems in the face, then solved them. He would soon take over Company B, but for now, he soldiered on in the thankless S4 arena, providing the front-end direction for the supplies pushed from Capt. Ronz Sarvis's field trains.

No, you could not find men any better than Ted Donnelly, or Dirk Blackdeer in S2, or Maj. Bill Phelps, for that matter. Good as they were as individuals, the battalion staff as a group suffered from one overall weakness—it was organized for routine garrison training activities, not intense combat. Part of this came from Army doctrinal literature and practice, which has never really sorted out exactly what you do with all of those damn command posts recommended by Leavenworth experts: Tac, TOC, ALOC, and, God help us, an alternate command post. In other words, the Army proposed one command post per fighting company in an air assault battalion. Just for fun, the literature left confusion concerning the role of the Tac versus the TOC versus the ALOC, the ALOC versus the HHC commander, the activation and composition of the alternate CP, the XO running the TOC yet responsible for the service support functions controlled by the ALOC, the S3 who trained and manned the TOC but supposedly ran his war from the Tac well forward, and the idea that everybody was supposed to generate brilliant, highly detailed orders and yet still run the current battle.[37] It all allowed for swell reading, and many of the pieces made a lot of sense. But taken as a whole, the voluminous book solutions crisscrossed too much, and just did not get the job done. The battalion headquarters needed a practical, streamlined structure that actually worked.

The staff and the battalion commander would have known that if they had ever really trained under pressure, and not just burned up endless hours playing around with map exercises and canned computer war games. Like most battalions, 1-327th Infantry spent the bulk of its training time teaching squads, platoons, and sometimes companies. That's what the Army said to do: Train the folks one level down, evaluate two levels down.[38] The staff knew exactly how to plan, resource, and run platoon live-fire-ranges, company air assault exercises, and squad force-on-force sham battles. Through it all, the staff could sit atop this activity like the gods on Olympus, above the fray, the unmoved movers. But these training support and monitoring functions, though crucial to creating excellent squads and platoons, certainly did not teach the headquarters officers and NCOs how to fight as a staff.

To figure out that the book recommendations for battle staffs were a cock-up if you tried all of them, you simply needed a good dose of common sense and imagination. Nobody really applied that dose in the 1st of the 327th. Instead, lulled by the results of some command post exercises and the quality of the staff, the new commander and his headquarters team spouted the textbook bromides and attempted to do things the way almost every other staff did them. And like almost every other staff, when this bunch got to Fort Polk, several of the wheels came off.

That they did was certainly not the fault of the battalion's senior enlisted man, who left the internal TOC regimen to others. He stood outside the formal staff, reporting directly to the battalion commander. By definition, a battalion command sergeant major must be an outstanding soldier, the exemplar of the NCO corps, fulfilling the same senior noncommissioned counterpart role to the lieutenant colonel as the platoon sergeants and first sergeants did for their lieutenants and captains respectively. Without a doubt, Cmd. Sgt. Maj. Mark S. Ripka met those criteria and then some. Ranger-qualified, a combat veteran from the Panama incursion, former first sergeant of two companies, holder of a master's degree, once designated the U.S. Army's Drill Sergeant of the Year, Mark Ripka had been promoted more rapidly than almost any other sergeant major in the infantry. He stood first in every Army school he had ever attended, including the Ranger course, and even placed number one as a visiting student at the U.S. Air Force Senior NCO Course. With a fine sense of propriety, the U.S. Army personnel mavens had chosen even better than they could have known. In 1975, Private Ripka had been a mortar man in Company D, 1st Battalion, 327th Infantry Regiment. Now, on the eve of departing for JRTC, Cmd. Sgt. Maj. Ripka returned to his roots as the battalion's new top soldier.

In assuming his new posting, Mark Ripka staked out his own role. As a platoon sergeant, he was the designated second-in-command, mentoring young lieutenant platoon leaders. As a company first sergeant, he was not the official second-in-charge—an officer XO, a lieutenant, held that portfolio—but he was clearly the ramrod, the standard-bearer and enforcer, the savvy foreman of the crew. Now at the battalion level, the duties were potentially much more nebulous, and many of Mark Ripka's counterparts, even in the infantry, settled into a sinecure of semiretirement, fretting over the state of the unit's lawns or the details of close-order drill. After all, it was so hard to keep up with the nineteen-year-olds, to stay current with the new radios and night sights, to sweat and stink out there with the line troops. Mark Ripka did not see it that way.

This command sergeant major chose instead to focus on individual and small-unit training, and so concentrate on the soldier discipline and NCO leader development that form the foundation for that training. Troops grew accustomed to seeing this sergeant major laying next to them on the machine gun range, marching with them on long humps through the bush, always teaching, coaching, and accepting nothing but the proper standards. Through all of this, because of all of this, everything else got done, too, the promotion boards, the barracks checks, the NCO classes, even the lawns and the close-order drill. If any soldier in the command, from private to lieutenant colonel, wanted to know what to do, what "right" looked like, he had only to look at Command Sergeant Major Ripka.

Nobody appreciated that example more than the battalion's new commander, Lt. Col. Daniel P. Bolger, who had taken command on 17 June 1994. Like his senior enlisted advisor, Dan Bolger believed in leading by example. He might be a battalion commander, but he was a soldier first. He carried his own radio, and knew how to set up and use the complex frequency-hopping SINCGARS system. He also carried a rifle and a bayonet, and knew how to use them, too. The new commander did not believe in briefings and meetings, but in getting out there, out front, on the ground, and taking charge.

Given Dan Bolger's background, this was all pretty unlikely. This one seemed more like an academic than a soldier, especially an infantry soldier, let alone a commander in the 101st Airborne. By rights, he probably should have been a history professor at the Tweed Jacket College of Liberal Arts, given his schooling and interest in writing. Dan Bolger had never been in combat. In a profession that requires Ranger School as a rite of passage, he had not attended. The man spent two years in a civilian graduate school and three years on the faculty of the U.S. Military Academy at West Point, New York. His assignment prior to assuming command had been in the Pentagon, working for the U.S. Army Chief of Staff as a speechwriter, for God's sake. The guy's pedigree screamed "geek," all right.

And yet there was that rifle, and the intensity that it represented. There had been those five years in the same mechanized outfit at Fort Stewart, Georgia, going from butter-bar lieutenant to captain and rifle company commander. There had been that year in Korea as a battalion S3, with three-and-a-half months on the Demilitarized Zone, many nights on patrol with a loaded M16A2 in hand, trying to set the example. There had been two years in the 101st Airborne Division's G3 section, running the command posts and attempting to learn the air assault process from the top down. Yes, he liked to write, but his work always focused on his vocation, which was also his avocation and his only passion: the military. While Dan Bolger's academic record might create some questions about his priorities, his professional credentials suggested otherwise. He saw himself as an infantryman, first, foremost, and always. In the end, that probably mattered the most.

Now this same Lt. Col. Dan Bolger, erstwhile geek and would-be combat infantry commander, led the 1st Battalion, 327th Infantry Regiment, one of the premier organizations in the U.S. Army. As a student of military history, Dan Bolger knew well the battalion's heritage of glory, and it humbled him. Formed for World War I, the colors that Dan Bolger saw in his office every day bore campaign streamers for the St.-Mihiel and Meuse-Argonne offensives. There were other streamers too. As a glider force, the battalion fought in Normandy, joined the great airborne landing in Holland known as Operation Market-Garden, and stood like steel in the surrounded Belgian city of Bastogne, earning a Presidential Unit Citation. There, the battalion earned its nickname, "Bastogne Bulldogs," still echoed in the unit radio call sign. In Vietnam, as paratroopers, the battalion coined its motto, "Above the Rest." The men lived up to that reputation under the leadership of colorful figures like Lt. Col. Elliot "Bud" Sydnor and then-Maj. David H. Hackworth. Cited for gallantry on several occasions as a unit, including a second Presidential Unit Citation, the battalion also benefited from the example of leaders like 1st Lt. Jim Gardner and SSgt. John Gertsch, both posthumous Medal of Honor winners. In the Gulf War, following the aggressive Lt. Col. Frank Hancock, the battalion fought one of the largest pitched battles of that brief campaign, earning another Valorous Unit Award to go with the one earned in Vietnam.[39] Just before Dan Bolger arrived, the battalion had set records in performance in its peacekeeping mission as part of the Sinai peninsula's Multinational Force and Observers. Now it was up to the latest "old man" to add to the luster of the battalion, to keep achieving "Above the Rest."

This he fully intended to do. Like their commander, the young grenadiers and corporals in the ranks, the sergeants and the lieutenants, the medics and the riflemen, all learned that in this battalion, there were high expectations. Every time they marched when other units rode, stayed in uniform when certain units did not, sweated and trained when counterparts went home early, the men of the "Above the Rest" task force knew that they were not just in any battalion, but part of an outfit with a story to tell, a story that now included them. They would need to draw every last ounce of inspiration and pride they could from that proud heritage, and each other, to get through the ordeal they were about to encounter, and inflict on themselves, during JRTC 94-10.

Notes

The epigraph comes from "The Ballad of Rodger Young," by Frank Loesser, a poem quoted in Robert A. Heinlein, *Starship Troopers* (New York: Ace Books, 1987), 208. Pvt. Rodger W. Young, 148th Infantry Regiment, died in a one-man attack against a Japanese machine-gun bunker on the island of New Georgia in 1943. He won the Medal of Honor.

1. Lt. Col. Andrew F. Krepinevich, USA, *The Army and Vietnam* (Baltimore, Md.: Johns Hopkins University Press, 1986), 6. He offers the axiom in this format: "It is better to send a bullet than a man."

2. The best treatment of this entire idea is by Russell F. Weigley, in *The American Way of War* (Bloomington, Ind.: Indiana University Press, 1977), with pp. xvii–xxiii laying out the thesis. A description of the "Army Concept" in full flower during the Vietnam War can be found in Krepinevich, *The Army and Vietnam*, especially on pp. 4–6. The emphasis upon material solutions and firepower in Southeast Asia cost America some 8,500 aircraft lost in combat from 1964 to 1975, a number greater than the current active duty inventory of all Army, Navy, Marine Corps, and Air Force fixed-wing and rotary-wing assets. For authoritative loss figures, see Malcolm McConnell and Theodore Schweitzer, *Inside Hanoi's Secret Archives* (New York, NY: Simon and Schuster, 1995), 31. One wartime CIA estimate noted that the bombing cost America ten times as much as the damage inflicted, a comment found in John Morocco et al., *The Vietnam Experience: Rain of Fire, Air War, 1969–73* (Boston: Boston Publishing Co., 1985), 179–80.

3. For a description of the practical, and decidedly nontraditional, methods used with success against the Plains Indians, see Robert M. Utley, *Frontier Regulars* (New York: The Macmillan Company, 1973), 45–59. Larry Cable, *A Conflict of Myths: The Development of American Counterinsurgency Doctrine and the Vietnam War* (New York: New York University Press, 1986) shows the continuities and disconnects as Americans attempted to draw on their ambiguous military heritage to confront the challenges of the Vietnamese Communists.

4. Harvey M. Sapolsky, *War Without Killing* (Boston: Massachusetts Institute of Technology, September 1992), 1–3, 11–15.

5. U.S., Department of the Army, *FM 100-5: Operations* (U.S. Govt. Printing Office, 1993), 2-1 to 2-3. The United States Army, and the Department of Defense in general, applies the name "operations other than war" to small conflicts and otherwise unconventional interventions.

6. Col. David M. White, USA, *Office of Infantry Proponency Overview* (Fort Benning, Ga.: Office of Infantry Proponency, 1994), 4.

7. According to the authoritative International Institute for Strategic Studies, American active duty armed forces (1.4 million) stand third in the world, behind the conscript masses of China (3 million) and Russia (2.7 million). This data is excerpted in Robert Famighetti, 1995, ed. *The World Almanac 1995,* (Mahwah, N.J.: Funk and Wagnalls Corp., 1994), 161. Interestingly, the present U.S. Army is outnumbered by the armies of several countries, including China, Russia, India, Vietnam, North Korea, South Korea, Iraq, and probably Pakistan. See Peter G. Tsouras, *Changing Orders* (New York: Facts on File, 1994), 307–14, 323.

8. Floyd D. Kennedy, Jr., "U.S. Naval Aircraft and Weapon Development in Review," *U.S. Naval Institute Proceedings* (May 1995), 157; "Major Weapons Systems and Combat Forces" in *Defense 93: Almanac* (Washington, D.C.: U.S. Govt. Printing Ofice, 1993), 40–41.

9. Tamar A. Mehuron, ed., "Aircraft Type and Total and Primary Aircraft Authorized," *Air Force* (May 1995), 51.

10. Regular Army strength in aircraft and armor can be extrapolated from figures in Tom Clancy, *Armored Cav* (New York: Berkeley Books, 1994), 37, and from White, *Office of Infantry Proponency Overview,* 14, 35A, 39A. The exact numbers change from year to year, but some recent figures are illuminating. In 1994, the U.S. Army included 67,249 infantrymen (not all in battalions by any means). That same year, there were some 134,000 supply, transportation, and maintenance personnel on active duty, not to mention 56,000 administrative troops handling personnel affairs, legal matters, and financial concerns. The Infantry Branch reported some 7,000 officers on its rolls; the various Army medical services (Medical Corps, Medical Service Corps, Dental Corps, Nurse Corps, Veterinary Corps) totaled 17,000.

11. Joel Nadel with J. R. Wright, *Special Men and Special Missions* (London: Greenhill Books, 1994), 121–25, 183–6; Mark Lloyd, *Special Forces* (London: Arms and Armour Press, 1995), 139–40, 228.

12. Hans Halberstadt, *Airborne* (Novato, Calif.: Presidio Press, 1988), 61–79.

13. Patrick H. F. Allen, *Screaming Eagles* (London: The Hamlyn Publishing Group, 1990), 9–37; Thomas Taylor, *Lightning in the Storm* (New York: Hippocrene Books, 1994), 12–18; Michael R. Gordon and Lt. Gen. Bernard E. Trainor, USMC, ret., *The Generals' War* (Boston: Little, Brown, and Co., 1995), 405–06, 422–24.

14. For insights on a light infantry battalion in Somalia, see Lt. Col. William C. David, USA, "Preparing a Battalion for Combat: Marksmanship," *Infantry* (July–August 1995), 30. For similar views of a light infantry force in Haiti, see Maj. Christopher Hughes, USA, and Maj. Thomas G. Ziek, USA, "Cordon and Search," *Infantry* (July–August 1995), 8.

15. U.S., Department of the Army, *FM 7-8 Infantry Rifle Platoon and Squad* (Washington, D.C.: U.S. Govt. Printing Office, 1992), A-4, B-1.

16. Ibid., B-1; Halberstadt, *Airborne,* 126–28. See also Clancy, *Armored Cav,* 155–59.

17. U.S., Department of the Army, *FM 7-20 The Infantry Battalion* (Washington, D.C.: U.S. Govt. Printing Office, 6 April 1992), 7-29 to 7-31.

18. U.S., Department of the Army, Headquarters, Forces Command, *MTOE 07055LFC21* (Ft. MacPherson, Ga.: Headquarters, Forces Command, 1994), 6–9. The acronym MTOE refers to "Modified Table of Organization and Equipment."

19. Army, *FM 7-20,* 7-5.

20. Ibid., 8-7.

21. HQ, Forces Command, *MTOE 07055LFC21,* 6–7.

22. U.S., Department of the Army, *FM 101-5-1 Operational Terms and Graphics* (Washington, DC: U.S. Govt. Printing Office, October 1985), 1-10, 1-71.

23. Army, *FM 7-20,* 7-15, 7-18.

24. Ibid., 7-2; U.S. Army, Headquarters, Division Artillery, 101st Airborne Division (Air Assault), *Fire Support Handbook* (Ft. Campbell, Ky.: Headquarters, Division Artillery, 1995), 7-11.

25. U.S., Department of the Army, Headquarters, 101st Airborne

Division (Air Assault), *The Air Assault School Handbook* (Ft. Campbell, Ky.: Headquarters, 101st Airborne Division [Air Assault], 1990), 1-2 to 1-8, 1-36 to 1-41.

26. This is not only a Soviet Army view. In the closing months of World War II, Gen. Joseph W. Stillwell, Commander, Army Ground Forces, made almost exactly the same point to General of the Army George C. Marshall, the U.S. Army Chief of Staff. Stillwell believed that the Americans had too little infantry to complete the contemplated fight for the Japanese home islands. Marshall's staff replied, on behalf of their chief, that America did not need a lot of men in the infantry, because this country trusted in "the great masses of armor and airplanes that prepare the way for the final assault of the foot soldier, with the resultant saving of human life." Stillwell remained unconvinced, having seen enough combat to form his own opinion. For this exchange, see Kent Roberts Greenfield, Robert R. Palmer, and Bell I. Wiley, *The Organization of Ground Combat Troops* (Washington, D.C.: U.S. Govt. Printing Office, 1947), 255.

27. U.S., Department of the Army, Headquarters, 101st Airborne Division (Air Assault) and Ft. Campbell, "Current Post Population," 30 September 1994.

28. Russell F. Weigley, *History of the United States Army* (Bloomington, Ind.: Indiana University Press, 1984), 268–69.

29. The present individual replacement system dates from the 1941 to 1945 era. A description of its drawbacks can be found in Eli Ginzberg, et al., *The Ineffective Soldier*, vol. 2, *Breakdown and Recovery*, (New York: Columbia University Press, 1959) 53. Ginzberg noted that, in assessing which men would break in combat, "the worst problems were encountered by soldiers trained as individual loss replacements, who were sent overseas as casuals, and who were distributed to understrength units." The authors continue: "Although the Army became aware of the special emotional stress to which the individual replacement was exposed, it never fully solved the problem of training, transporting, and assigning them in groups." As of the 1990s, this remains an unsolved issue.

30. White, *Office of Infantry Proponency Overview*, 29.

31. For a wonderful description of today's young soldiers in training and in their first battalion, see George C. Wilson, *Mud Soldiers*

(New York: Charles Scribner's Sons, 1989), 43–66. Wilson has grasped the essential nature of our Army's current crop of infantrymen.

32. The situation at Ft. Campbell in 1994–95 was not unique. Rear Adm. Roberta L. Hazard, USN, ret., who investigated the quality of life for all junior enlisted troops, reported to the Department of Defense that she was "stunned by the number of people hurting." She went on: "We have an inherently flawed housing system in all its dimensions." "The bill to get well," she concluded, "is shocking." For her remarks, and other commentary, see Tom Philpott, "Quality of Life Indictment," *U.S. Naval Institute Proceedings* (December 1995), 90. See also John T. Correll, "The Quality of Life," *Air Force* (January 1996), 2. Correll notes that military pay lags 12.6% or more behind comparable civil employment (where applicable), and that housing allowances fall 22% below the actual costs of living off-post. The U.S. Air Force, traditionally the best of the services at providing for its people, can meet only 53% of day-care requirements, leaving the uniformed parents of some 8,000 toddlers to fend for themselves.

33. Edwin B. Coddington, *The Gettysburg Campaign: A Study in Command* (New York: Charles Scribner's Sons, 1984), 12.

34. *Abu* is a term with quite a history, reflective of the sense of tradition found in Regular Army units. Orginally, during the Korean War, the word was *Ibu*. In 1952 paratroopers in Company I of the 187th Airborne Regimental Combat Team were trying to find an animal as a unit symbol, subject only to the idea that the creature's name must start with the company's letter. Others chose the alligator (A), the bear (B), and so forth, but the men of Company I could only come up with the ibis, a rather inoffensive waterbird. That did not work for hard-charging airborne troops, so they invented a mythical beast, the Ibu. With the body of an ape, the head of a lion, the tail of an alligator, and the antlers of a moose, the Ibu became the patron animal of Company I. In the late 1950s, Company I, 3d Battalion, 187th Infantry Regiment became Company A, 1st Battalion, 327th Infantry, and the Ibu became Abu. The 3-187th Infantry is back in the force structure, too, and it also has an Abu company. See Col. David H. Hackworth, USA, ret., *About Face* (New York: Simon and Schuster, 1989), 519–21.

35. Ibid., 485.

36. The S5's duties are not even covered in the current (6 April 1992) doctrinal manual for infantry battalions, an interesting omission in view of contemporary U.S. Army missions. For a reference to the S5, see the previous edition of infantry battalion doctrine, U.S., Department of the Army, *FM 7-72: Light Infantry Battalion* (Washington, D.C.: U.S. Govt. Printing Office, March 1987), 2-9. This manual states that the S5 is "not normally assigned to the battalion," but does address his role and responsibilities.

37. For an example of these and other issues, see U.S., Department of the Army, Battle Command Battle Laboratory, *Battle Command Techniques and Procedures (First Coordinating Draft)* (Ft. Leavenworth, Kans.: Battle Command Battle Laboratory, 21 April 1995). This thick book is full of the latest doctrinally approved methods for the command and control of fighting forces.

38. U.S., Department of the Army, *FM 25-101: Battle Focused Training* (Washington, D.C.: U.S. Govt. Printing Office, September 1990), 5-3.

39. James A. Sawicki, *Infantry Regiments of the U.S. Army* (Dumfries, Va.: Wyvern Publications, 1981), 471–72; Hackworth, *About Face*, 475. Lieutenant Colonel Bud Sydnor commanded the ground forces during the raid on the Son Tay prison camp in North Vietnam.

Chapter 3

Noncombatant Evacuation Operation (NEO)

"Airmobility, dig it, you weren't going anywhere. It made you feel safe, it made you feel Omni, but it was only a stunt, technology. Mobility was just mobility, it saved lives or took them all the time (saved mine I don't know how many times, maybe dozens, maybe none), what you really needed was a flexibility far greater than anything the technology could provide, some generous, spontaneous gift for accepting surprises, and I didn't have it."

—Michael Herr
Dispatches

The 1st Battalion, 327th Infantry Regiment, deployed from Fort Campbell, Kentucky, to the environs of Fort Polk, Louisiana during the Labor Day weekend of 1994, ostensibly to intervene in the perennially unhappy Caribbean island country of Cortina. A few hundred miles to the east and northeast, their brothers in the 82d Airborne Division at Fort Bragg, North Carolina, and the 10th Mountain Division at Fort Drum, New York, readied for their own deployment, aimed at some unfinished U.S. business in the restive Caribbean island state of Haiti. Of course, the former mission was an exercise, a mock war, and any blood spilled would be by accident. Any resemblance to what the boys from Bragg and Drum stood ready to launch was, as the legal disclaimer puts it, "strictly coincidental."

Although the call went to the 10th and 82d this time, it might just as well have gone to the 101st Airborne, and about a year from JRTC 94-10, unbidden and unexpected, it would. After all, many of the All-American paratroopers and Mountaineer light fighters gearing up to enter Port-au-Prince and Cap Haitien had certainly been to Cortina and done that awkward MILES three-step with the CLF

tigers. Everything seemed very familiar, tactical life imitating training art. This time, the civilians would not be role-players. The bad
guys would not be shooting eye-safe laser tag pulses, either. But all
those hard JRTC lessons surely applied. When the big U.S. Air Force
jets came to pick up the 10th and 82d riflemen, and their combined
arms teammates in tow, all would be off to war, or at least what passes
for it in this closing decade of the American Century.

No Air Force C-141B Starlifters or C-5B Galaxies came for the 1st
of the 327th. Destined at present for the practice ground, not the
true arena, they headed into Cajun country ignominiously, their men
packed into chartered tour buses for a fourteen-hour jaunt through
some of the poorest counties in America, their trucks and cargo
lashed to rust-streaked river barges and pushed down the Mississippi
by indifferent tug crews. While the majority looked forward to the
challenges sure to come, and almost everyone appreciated the
change of scenery from the overly familiar "back forty" at Campbell,
the deployment necessarily lacked the electricity, the edge of the real
thing. The Polk bunch could re-create just about everything but that,
and the bus and barge caravan reminded everyone that this was, indeed, just another big drill.

And yet—well, things were at stake here. Not lives, thank God, nor
the fate of nations, but smaller things, more personal matters, and
anyone affiliated with the U.S. Army in 1994–95 knew about that. A
JRTC rotation clearly offers the best training a light force can undergo short of actual battle. Army leaders know that, and draw the
appropriate conclusions. A rotation is, in essence, the final exhibi-
tion game, and like all contests of that sort, more of a test than anything else. Just how ready is this particular unit? More to the point,
how good is this chain of command, in particular the battalion commander?

In an Army that now fights and deploys by battalions, the chance
to get into the fray, to contribute, might well ride on performance
in this version of a military preseason, the only experience common
to all Army light battalions save the pair in Korea. The regulations
denied it, the senior chain of command denied it, the O/Cs denied
it, but the more they did so, the more obvious and even necessary it
all seemed to become.[1] Performance on the demanding JRTC mis-

sions offered a definite yardstick, both for units and for individuals. The track record might not identify the next battalion to win the Presidential Unit Citation or the next George S. Patton, Jr., but it would certainly be a strong indicator. Conversely, a debacle at Polk pretty well marked the perpetrators as also-rans, weak sisters, the "needs improvement" crowd, not the steady, steely-eyed types to be sent to some crude little two-battalion flare-up in the bowels of Africa. That was the unwritten truth about JRTC Rotation 94-10, and all those there, at Hohenfels, and at Irwin, and it always had been so.

Few grasped that unsaid reality more firmly than Dan Bolger. He had commanded a rifle company during one of the very early runs out at Fort Irwin's NTC. Out in the high desert of California, jousting with the OPFOR motorized rifle regiment, Bolger and his peers learned a great deal. Everybody made mistakes.[2] Those who made the least mistakes, and did some smart or lucky things to boot, now had the chance to try again at the lieutenant colonel level. Of the many good men in his old battalion, Captain Bolger turned out to be the only company commander fortunate enough to advance, a dozen years later, to this next round. Somebody, some bunch of senior somebodies, must have liked what they saw. They judged him a winner.

What constituted winning at JRTC, where the scenario appeared so laden with fatal pitfalls for the visiting units? Several definitions applied. Winning units posted a favorable kill ratio, albeit a strangely skewed variant of favorable. Against JRTC's slanted odds, anything better than losing three friendlies for each OPFOR casualty amounted to victory. From 4:1 to 6:1 spelled a draw. Worse than that and you were getting powdered.[3] This objective criterion, one of the few in the slippery world of judging force-on-force skills, the hoary old body count that poisoned a generation of soldiers in Vietnam, forms the primary measure of success at JRTC. There, unlike in Southeast Asia, omniscient O/Cs verify every kill. The numbers mean something.

Though the body count matters most, other criteria also apply. Ranking right behind the kill/loss figures, a unit must accomplish its assigned missions: seizing ground, destroying a certain enemy element, holding a position, and the like. Of course, if you lose the battalion doing so, it is not a noteworthy triumph. It could be said that the kills reflect efficiency, but completing the missions shows effectiveness. If you cannot do the former well, you had better try to do the latter.

Next, for those who get creamed and blow their tasks, too, one can reach for the moral victories, the JRTC equivalencies of Antietam, Bataan, and St. Vith. In these cases, the chain of command hangs in there, plugging away as the heavens crash in, giving evidence of at least a game spirit. If you have to fail at Fort Polk, this is the way to do it. By going down swinging, the organization will keep some shred of self-respect intact, and might well rebound on the next mission.

Finally, in those not uncommon situations of total meltdown, when the CLF is doing the happy dance on the TOC and the force has disintegrated, one can resort to the standard O/C tag line that "learning is winning." The line troops, never at a loss for the fitting sentiment, snort that "losing is learning," a far more accurate appraisal of what has transpired by this point. Everybody learns at JRTC. That's why it exists, to teach bloodless lessons. In general, whenever sergeants or officers talk only about how much they learned at JRTC, and never get specific about kill numbers or missions, you can bet that they suffered through a rough rotation.

As 1-327th Infantry would soon learn, the JRTC leadership could adjust the intensity of the scenario to match the capabilities of the inbound brigade. Like skilled medieval torturers, the Polk O/Cs and planners knew how to turn the screws just tight enough to bring outfits to the breaking point without pushing them into the abyss. All kinds of variables abounded: number of hostiles, number of civilians, attitude of civilians, degree of mine warfare activity, and aggressiveness of the OPFOR, to name the more obvious adjustments. Other, more subtle variations could be used too. These included more or less planning time for major operations, using more favorable terrain, speeding up the logistics and personnel replacement flows from the simulated divisional rear, or limiting the size and scope of missions. A rotating brigade's commanding general established these boundaries before the deployment. The JRTC staff, in company with the U.S. brigade's division leadership, looked at conditions daily in light of the evolving scenario in the maneuver box, fine-tuning and, at times, making radical shifts as the exercise proceeded.[4] Nobody racked up easy wins under this system.

The O/Cs did not much care if the visitors ever won, given that even a smashing victory might see three times as many U.S. casualties as CLF killed and wounded. As doctrinal experts and designated coaches and teachers, the O/Cs truly desired the rotational forces, especially the NCOs and officers, to learn from their experiences. That education took root best along the narrow precipice of high stress and physical discomfort, a trick borrowed from Ranger School to substitute for the absent fear of death that plagues men in actual combat. Fear of failure counted for something, all right.

It is worth noting that, among the performance criteria at JRTC, conforming to prevailing doctrine did not rate particularly high, playing like background music behind all four of the usual measurements (kills, mission attainment, drive, and learning). Army doctrine merely generated a common language, a professional jargon, for discussion of why things went wrong. Following or not following doctrine, the form, really did not much matter. The substance, how things turned out and why, mattered a lot more than abstract doctrinal constructs. This only made sense, because Army doctrine pretty much defies rigid adherence.

Talking about the Army's written doctrine, how our ground forces claim to fight, may lead the casual observer of military affairs to think that an agreed-upon scheme truly exists, and that tactics may be judged based upon how they do or do not conform to some body of shared prescriptive beliefs, dogma set down by the great kahunas of Fort Benning, Fort Leavenworth, and the Pentagon. Nothing could be farther from reality. Formal U.S. Army doctrine, in the sense of telling you what to do under certain circumstances, does not really exist. And given the unpredictable and brutal nature of war, that is a good thing.

You can find doctrinal literature by the hundredweight, of course. In fact, the myriad of manuals, pamphlets, regulations, circulars, articles, lessons learned, and memoranda that apply to an air assault infantry battalion would fill a good-size living room from floor to ceiling. Perhaps Carl von Clausewitz could digest this gray mass of dead trees, and make some sense out of its earnest descriptions of what everybody already knows, its vague exhortations, its major and minor contradictions, its maddening ellipses, and its outright errors. As if to compound matters, every manual appears to be in constant revision, forever in draft, or sporting "change 1," testimony to a plethora of printing presses at various Army schools, if nothing else. Fortunately, because all of these items tend to be descriptive in nature, not prescriptive, this Everest of dull material seldom gets read. This is just as well. Riflemen, athletic, type-A young men, do not go in for reading all that much.

Some armies, the old Soviet model for example, actually try to fight "by the book," in a final acknowledgment that you simply cannot trust men to make their own decisions. Fearful that the boys will screw up, Big Brother tells all exactly how to suck every egg, a feature that meshes nicely with the gray conformity expected by the denizens of a totalitarian state. Soviet doctrine featured plenty of prescriptive techniques, from how to deploy a motorized rifle regiment from march into the attack to how many howitzer shells to shoot on a battalion river-crossing operation. The Russian Communists even tried to reduce battlefield choices to a series of nifty either/or algorithms, a computer flowchart you could carry with you under fire, strapped to your wrist like an NFL quarterback's list of audible plays. ("Let's see. I'm under fire from my right front. My choices are attack right, flank to the left, call for an airstrike—oops, now where's that continuation card?") Year after year, the Soviets practiced and drilled their great lockstep formations, even as their Arab surrogates got pounded to bits, their Asian allies chose other paths (but kept the weaponry), and their own troops in Afghanistan rapidly discarded their algorithms and geometric arrays in favor of choosing the most perceptive leaders and following their own unique methods.[5] The Soviet Army books may still be read, a monument to faith in doctrine. But the Soviet Army is no more.

The U.S. Army, although sometimes reduced to similar mass-production techniques in the great mobilizations of the Civil War and the World Wars, never really embraced such an approach—the American character would not allow for it, even if our professional soldiery sometimes thought it useful. Hailing from an anti-intellectual society of insistent individualists, impatient tinkerers, and inveterate do-it-yourselfers, people who do not read instruction manuals, American commanders throughout history consistently ignored published doctrine, if they even knew of it. General Ulysses S. Grant spoke for all of them when he said: "I don't understate the value of military knowledge, but if men make war in slavish obedience to rules, they will fail."[6] One could find similar sentiments in the writings of William T. Sherman, George Crook, Douglas MacArthur, George Patton, and Matthew Ridgway, all of whom improvised, innovated, took risks, and won.

Even General of the Army George C. Marshall, considered by so many to be the great guru of the Army school system, supposedly the prince of formal doctrine, decried that same structure. Writing to the commandant at Fort Leavenworth in 1933, then-Colonel Marshall spared nothing.

> In the corps area maneuvers, the mistakes were so numerous, and often so gross, that a critique was extremely difficult to handle with tact. Staff officers of brilliant reputation in the Army, graduates of Leavenworth and the War College, former instructors at those schools, committed errors so remarkable that it plainly indicated that our school system had failed to make clear the real difficulties to be anticipated and surmounted in a war of movement. The individual sank in a sea of paper, maps, tables, and elaborate technique. Or, if he attempted to shorten the working method he confused everything because of lack of training in the more difficult—the simpler—methods. I insist we must get down to the essentials, make clear the real difficulties, and expunge the bunk, complications, and ponderosities; we must concentrate on registering in men's minds certain vital considerations, instead of a mass of less important details. We must develop a technique and method so simple and so brief that the citizen soldier of good common sense can readily grasp the idea.[7]

Despite his firmly held and often stated convictions, and his eventual rise to a position to implement them as U.S. Army Chief of Staff in World War II, Marshall did not achieve complete success. Even during his tenure at Benning's Infantry School, he admitted that "we never got to the point of teaching tactics" realistically, and that "most of our supposed tactical instruction fell into the domain of technique."[8] That devotion to approved lines of thought, to map exercises and the school solution, to form over substance, lives on at Leavenworth, Benning, and the other branch schools, and spills forth routinely among the ocean of literature unloaded on the busy leaders of field units. Some buy it. Like Marshall's "staff officers of brilliant reputation," more than a few in line battalions try mightily to apply book answers to real events, with about the same results as in 1933.

Most of the Army, though, follows a doctrine that George C. Marshall would understand and applaud. This is a practical, situational doctrine, the actual American way of war. Its negative, constricting tactical manifestion—send a bullet, not a man—has already been identified, and is woven throughout the infantry-poor, technology-rich U.S. force structure. Its other component, the positive aspect, may be called situational command, the trust in the man on the scene to solve the problem his own way. "Do not tell people how to do things," said General Patton. "Tell them what to do, and they will amaze you with their ingenuity."[9] That is true, as long as they expend things, not troops. These two simple yet subtle, long-standing beliefs, not a vast morass of piled paperwork, summarize true Army doctrine, the doctrine of tradition.

That simple approach offers little comfort to those groping for that mythical *coup d'oeil*, taking it all in at a glance, that "grip" on the interrelations between us, them, terrain, and time, which allows a man to make the right call under pressure.[10] This art can be developed, but like hitting a curve ball, it takes a bit of innate talent, too. One day, if you have it, you look at a situation and you get the picture. Some folks, even very senior officers, never get it. These men, often very bright, insist upon learning all the proper buzz words, and chant them repeatedly, as if saying them enough would somehow impart understanding. Despite Benning, Leavenworth, and all the books, such people never quite bridge the gap between theory and practice. They look, but do not see.

As for those, and they are the majority, who understand their trade, the practical doctrine comes as second nature, and the formal doctrine offers a reference library, a smorgasbord from which to pick and choose, rather than a rote checklist. In this, American soldiers resemble Roman Catholics, who also pick and choose, grabbing at half-understood Biblical verses in order to justify a daily faith principally founded on tradition. You can search both testaments of the Bible from stem to stern and you will not find a pope, saints, rosary beads, or seven sacraments rattling around, and yet Catholics think these conventions are in there, and even contrive to find them when they look. In the same way, practical doctrine people, who rarely crack the cover of an FM, often choose to talk about the latest attack in terms of the principle of surprise or the tenet of agility or some other such touchstone. As with the Church, it lends an air of official credibility to ongoing activities.

In so many ways, indeed by design, JRTC emphasized learning by doing, not the dead hand of textbooks. The Bastogne Bulldogs fully expected to converse about doctrine, to try certain recommended methods and discard others, to send bullets not men, and to give that *coup d'oeil* stuff a shot. In this valley of shadow, however, results counted. Learning was good. Winning was better.

The 1st of the 327th did not go alone. Just as the battalion usually accepted attachments and reinforcing elements to become a purpose-built task force, so the Bulldogs formed just one portion of a larger entity, the 1st Brigade of the 101st Airborne Division (Air Assault). Commanded for almost two years by Col. James E. Donald, a Gulf War battalion commander with the Screaming Eagles, the Always First Brigade disposed a powerful team of teams. The brigade, as organized for 94-10, grouped command, combat, support, and service elements into a fairly cohesive team of seven battalions and several smaller outfits. Except for the infantry battalions, most of the rest had just completed JRTC 94-07 in May. They did not win every fight, but all in all, the brigade acquitted itself pretty well.[11]

The brigade headquarters numbered many officers and NCOs with experience on the May rotation. As could be expected for any good staff, this bunch took after their commander, mirroring Colonel Donald's sunny disposition. Congenitally optimistic and positive, the brigade commander inherited his position much earlier than programmed due to the relieving of his predecessor. That officer cracked under the strain of his duties, but in his final months he had ravaged camaraderie and professional regard throughout the brigade and its attached units. When Jim Donald succeeded this foul-tempered bully, he faced a major rebuilding effort. The colonel emphasized teamwork and cooperation, and would not tolerate any sort of squabbling or backbiting. A positive command climate and a string of successes followed, culminating in JRTC 94-07.

Now Jim Donald and his brigade staff faced an unexpected, unprogrammed trip to Fort Polk. The average battalion or brigade commander holds his posting for two years, and in that stretch can anticipate one trip to the appropriate training center, Irwin, Polk, or Hohenfels. With JRTC 93-03 (an icy ball-buster at old Fort Chaffee, Arkansas) and 94-07 under his belt, the last thing Colonel Donald expected was another JRTC rotation. But the 82d Airborne, with an urgent appointment down in Haiti, backed out. The 101st Airborne backed in. And so, on about eleven weeks notice, rather than the usual year or so, Jim Donald prepared for round three against the CLF and friends.

The brigade team formed for this one followed the age-old wedding formula: some old, some new, some borrowed, and some blue, the traditional heraldic color of U.S. Army infantry. Old reliables included Donald's own staff, the direct support artillery battalion, the assault aviation battalion task force (Blackhawks and Chinooks), the forward support battalion (FSB, which handled logistics), the air defense battery, the engineer company, the military intelligence company, the signal element, and the military police platoon. Allowing for four months of the usual 10–15 percent personnel turnover, these units remained from just under half to two-thirds intact from the May deployment, with a good chunk of JRTC-experienced leadership and soldiers. At least you could say they had been in the Fort Polk maneuver box recently. These folks had seen the Monkey Show. They had met the CLF.

Not so the newcomers, it must be admitted. These included a new assault aviation battalion commander, several officers and NCOs in subordinate positions in all organizations, and, of course, Dan Bolger and almost all of his eager Bulldogs. Oh yes, the 1st of the 327th went on that frozen test of manhood back in January of 1993, but the steady encroachments of turnover winnowed out JRTC 93-03 veterans month by month, leaving but a handful with any personal memory of the brutal exercise. Still, somebody in the 1-327th knew what could happen, which eased the rawness just a bit.

Some parts of the brigade, platoons here and there, certain staff sections, could not even draw on that much recent JRTC experience. Prominent among the complete rookies, the attack pilots of the 3d Battalion, 101st Aviation Regiment, brought eighteen mighty AH-64A Apaches to the table. Last time the 1st Brigade went, the Apache drivers were off at mandatory gunnery training, and so the 101st Airborne's divisional air cavalry stood in. Good as the air cav proved, they flew obsolescent AH-1F Cobra gunships, once the hottest thing in the skies of Vietnam, but now an undergunned, day-only relic. The CLF enjoyed that substitution. But now the mighty Apaches loomed, with Hellfire missiles, rockets, and cannons at the ready day and night. Using these wonder weapons properly might make a big difference. Properly—now there is an adverb fraught with portent, especially considering the 101st Airborne Apache fleet's JRTC track record. On a 2d Brigade mission earlier in 1994, 3-101st's sister battalion shot the hell out of Polk's opposition on a few big nights. Unfortunately, on several other occasions, they shredded an uncomfortably large number of unlucky friendly elements.[12] The Always First Brigade staff and the Apache fliers intended to arrive at a workable way to tie together the aerial firepower and the ground fight, to make the Apache a sword that cut only one way.

Complicating this effort, Jim Donald found himself with two borrowed infantry battalions to complement Bolger's largely untried bunch. Normally, 1st Brigade controlled the 1st, 2d, and 3d battalions of the 327th Infantry Regiment, and the last JRTC trip featured the latter pair of outfits. This time, those veteran formations and their skilled, JRTC-veteran commanders stayed home. Instead, Jim Donald inherited the 3d Battalion, 187th Infantry Regiment (Iron Rakkasans) from 3d Brigade. That battalion should have gone to NTC during 1994, but schedules shifted, and now the commander and his men would not get any chance at a training center

deployment that year unless 3-187th tagged onto Jim Donald's un-
planned JRTC 94-10 excursion. So it happened. To add to this challenge, the division leadership also directed another 3d Brigade unit,
1-187th Infantry, to send its commander and his staff to play a computer war game that would run concurrently with the 94-10 MILES
force-on-force exercise. This group would also come under Colonel
Donald's direction, and insist upon their share of brigade's attention to assist their plans and clashes of electrons.

A final ground combat force, also borrowed but not infantry blue,
came from the 82d Airborne Division, the last reminder of the original owners of rotation 94-10. Equipped with fourteen M551 Sheridan light tanks (the same speedy model used by the OPFOR to play
vehicles of Russian manufacture), Company D of the 3d Battalion,
73d Armor offered a unique hybrid of paratroopers and tankers. The
little Sheridans packed a wallop, thanks to their unusual 152mm
main gun/missile tube, and their light construction and aluminum
armor allowed them to be air-dropped under huge nylon cargo
canopies.[13] Of course, nobody wanted to drop in any Sheridans at
JRTC. Rather, the company trained to clear mined roads, attack particularly tough objectives, and act as a mobile reserve. Those who
knew better preferred a standard mechanized/armor company
team, with M1A1 Abrams main battle tanks and M2A2 Bradley infantry fighting vehicles, complete with mounted rifle squads and armored engineers. This light tank outfit packed a lot less firepower,
and possessed three small truckloads of engineers, but no infantry.
Some air assault rifle platoons could expect to work closely with these
Sheridan crews from Fort Bragg. A few of the paratrooper/tankers
knew something from previous trips to Polk. None of them knew anything about the inner workings of the 1st Brigade, 101st Airborne
Division (Air Assault).

All of this placed 1st Brigade in an awkward posture. To the good,
Colonel Donald and many of his surbordinates knew how to win at
JRTC, that is to say, really win, in both the body stacking and mission
accomplishment categories. To the bad, the brigade's centerpiece
force to chase down the CLF, its infantry, could not have been more
polyglot, with the Bulldogs rusty from their Sinai peacekeeping mission and under an unseasoned commander, and worse, this unfa-

miliar Iron Rakkasan battalion on loan from 3d Brigade, where things often proceeded differently than in Jim Donald's realm. The command post exercise (CPX) battalion and these Sheridan guys from the 82d Airborne only increased the friction. Well, this is why full colonels command brigades, and why Col. Jim Donald would eventually become a general. He pulled his boys together, applied the sunshine, and made it work.

Field training, shared stress, could homogenize this lumpy mixture, but the calendar did not allow for much of that for the brigade as a whole. In the 101st Airborne, as in all Army divisions, resources like firing ranges, practice ammunition, and money do not permit all outfits to do everything all of the time. To rationalize use of the fine but limited facilities at Fort Campbell, the brigades take turns doing intensive unit training, standing alert for deployment (and doing small-unit and individual skills work), and doing post details and individual training. This schedule is established more than a year in advance, with land, ranges, ammunition, and helicopter support aligned accordingly. Trying to unplug two-thirds of 3d Brigade and glue them into one-third of 1st Brigade, while still allowing the other pair of 327th battalions to do all of their operations, as the rest of 3d Brigade scrambled to cover for absent brothers, all on less than ninety days notice, promised a truly massive scheduling trainwreck. Therefore, 1st Brigade never got to hold preliminary maneuvers, and division counted on Jim Donald to pull everything together anyway, mainly by force of his personality.

He did what he could, focusing his chain of command on the key piece parts needed to triumph at Fort Polk. Leaders attended noontime "brown bag" seminars on tactics and techniques, taught by JRTC veterans. The commanders and staffs diddled with issuing orders, conducting map exercises, and running through the ever-popular computer games, which simulated the wily CLF not at all. In between everything else, including the summer airshow and National Guard assistance taskings, the Bulldogs and 3-187th each went out for two weeks, with 1-327th doing their stuff all at once, and the Iron Rakkasans splitting it into three smaller segments. Both battalions did night air assaults, allowed their rifle platoons to fire live bullets in mock attacks, and worked on rudiments of tactics from squad through battalion levels. Other than on the night air assaults, the brigade combined arms team did not really play. Classroom discussions, blathering about map overlays, and goosing computers substituted for actual brigade force-on-force training. It would all have to come together in the box, under pressure, under the guns of the CLF.

Dan Bolger knew from his own NTC experience that his battalion required the right training to be ready for the CLF. More would be better, but by using time well from 17 June to 14 September, he guessed that the men had done enough. Or so he thought, prior to a rather harsh reeducation at Fort Polk.

An objective observer would certainly have given Bolger's Bulldogs credit for trying to eat the entire pizza in one big gulp: battalion-scale air assault landings, platoon night live fires, urban warfare training, staff drills, foot marching, restructuring the chain of command, and adjusting soldier load, among a thousand other initiatives typical of an energetic commander and command sergeant major, both just arrived. As generic air assault infantry training, it hit the mark. Because Dan Bolger and Mark Ripka insisted upon discipline and doing things to Army standards, orders reinforced by their constant presence and example, a lot of good came of all of this. If nothing else, the battalion began to show a keen edge of determination and discipline that would serve it well in any combat, MILES or real.

Good intentions, and even the start of good execution, could not make up for what wasn't there. Nobody, from Dan Bolger down to the greenest rifleman, understood these CLF characters. Whatever the battalion knew about defeating conventional enemies, they did not know how to fight and defeat JRTC's guerrillas. Rather than focus on a few skills that would beat the CLF, the Bulldogs dabbled in far too many secondary matters. Their predeployment training, like the Platte River, turned out to be a mile wide and an inch deep.[14]

Preparations in one critical area, however, went into sufficient depth, and this paid off. Thanks to their lieutenant colonel's inclinations about the nature of likely operations, the battalion knew how to handle civilians, a prerequisite for winning a people's war. Most JRTC rotations see civilians either ignored by harried soldiers or slaughtered by aggravated grunts, without much middle ground. Only the CLF benefits from those two approaches.

To carry out warfare amid a populace, aroused or inert, requires drastic fire discipline, unless you intend to commit genocide. Americans don't go in for that. Instead, we constrain ourselves by rules of engagement (ROE), politically inspired wraps on weapons and tactics that have always been part of combat. During the Cold War, ROE emerged in their present incarnation, gaining particular notoriety in the Southeast Asian air campaign of 1964–73, but also affecting every contingency operation since 1945, from the Formosa Straits and Lebanon in the 1950s to Somalia and Bosnia in the 1990s. Almost always, ROE limited the conflict and protected innocent civilians. Protecting populations with strict ROE also extended to our own people, in that our commanders had to avoid employing armaments (like subkiloton-yield nuclear shells) and methods (invading Red China) that might bring down thermonuclear retribution on the folks at home.

Contemporary ROE work against the old "bullets, not men" thesis, in that few arms discriminate much when they impact or explode, and while that may make the grunts happy, it plays poorly on *60 Minutes*. Whereas close is good enough against a uniformed foe, it equals dead children when U.S. weapons hit populated locales. And dead children turn the native peoples against Uncle Sam, encourage the insurgents, and create a hell of a backlash in the living rooms of Peoria. So when Dan Bolger and his leaders used the usual American fire-intensive methodology, they had to do so very carefully, a big change from the Vietnam years. Despite all the hand-wringing about the ROE strictures supposedly hamstringing our military in the Vietnam War, you must remember that North Vietnam absorbed several times the aerial tonnage delivered in all of World War II, and became the second most heavily bombed country in history. South Vietnam, no longer an independent country, holds the number one slot.[15] There is a lesson there that has not been lost on our military since 1975.

Today, U.S. soldiers know all about ROE. These often lengthy, intricate regulations flow from the fertile minds of military lawyers, one of whom accompanies any brigade-level unit into battle to help translate political guidance and legal codes into orders. Just for fun, smart guys from the White House on down interject their ideas into this legal stew. The military and civilian lawyers cross-check each other, and the commanders brief each other to distraction, but rarely does anyone check with the privates and corporals who will have to apply these overlong, nitpicky laundry lists of things not to do when wandering through somebody else's village shooting rebels. Rifle squads keep running into situations not on the instruction sheet. Dead soldiers and dead civilians come of this.

The JRTC imposed ROE to allow visiting brigades to gain experience dealing with civilians under these measures. Acting as a notional Joint Task Force (JTF) Cortina, the Polk exercise staff issued an all too typical sixteen-point manifesto on a little card designed to be carried by every man.[16] Lawyers, and the CLF, must have loved it.

The Fort Polk ROE featured all the favorite weasel words and nebulous phraseology that have consistently enraged rifle platoon sergeants throughout the U.S. Army. Try this one: "Avoid harming civilians unless necessary to save U.S. lives." Well, why the hell else would we shoot at civilians? Presumably, the ones we kill must be armed and dangerous, and hence combatants. Either that, or we're slaying innocents, and therefore in league with 1st Lt. William Calley and the Nazi SS *Einsatzgruppen*. What if, as usual, the CLF intermixed? Shoot or not? Who could tell?

Here is another: "Avoid harming civilian property unless necessary to save U.S. lives." What does *necessary* mean? Is it okay to kick down a door to get a sniper in a house? How about just to find the CLF? To find an arms cache? To find the light switch? It makes your teeth grind just saying it.

In a last lawyerly hand-wave, the JRTC ROE ends with the reminder that "Annex P of the OPLAN (operations plan) provides more detail. Conflicts between card and OPLAN should be resolved in favor of the OPLAN." Of course, only the brigade headquarters even sees the OPLAN, a document about a half-inch thick. The troops must get by with their cards and their best guesses.

Dan Bolger knew ROE could be trouble. Thanks to an enterprising military attorney named Mark Martins, an alternative existed. Major Martins, a West Pointer, Rhodes scholar, airborne Ranger, and former infantry officer, knew Bolger from their mutual service on the division staff, and when this attorney spoke, the battalion commander listened. Mark rejected the legal model of ROE and argued, in an award-winning paper written for the Staff Judge Advocate Advanced Course, that ROE should be taught to soldiers using the same simple terms used to teach marksmanship and squad tactics.[17] Mark's paper offered plenty of sound advice, all placing a trigger-puller's spin on the issue. ROE were too important to be left to attorneys.

JRTC Rules of Engagement
Tactical Rules of Engagement (TACROE)
(Joint Task Force Cortina)

All enemy military personnel and vehicles transporting the enemy or their supplies may be engaged subject to the following restrictions:

A. Armed civilians will only be engaged in self-defense.

B. Civilian aircraft will not be engaged without approval from division commander unless it is in self-defense.

C. Avoid harming civilians unless necessary to save U.S. lives; if possible, evacuate prior to any U.S. attack.

D. If civilians are in the area, only targets positively observed and identified as hostile will be engaged. These may only be engaged with small arms; however, other weapons systems may be authorized on a mission-by-mission basis by the local ground commander, lt. col. or above.

E. Approval by the Area Coordination Center (ACC) is required prior to firing indirect fire on targets within villages and urban areas.

F. The use of incendiary munitions will be positively controled at all echelons to preclude unnecessary destruction of civilian property, equipment, or crops.

G. If civilians are in the area, close air support (CAS) and incendiary weapons are prohibited without division approval.

H. Public works such as power stations, water treatment plants, dams, and/or other utilities may not be engaged without division commander's approval, except in self-defense.

I. Hospitals, churches, shrines, schools, museums, and any

other historical or cultural site will not be engaged except in self-defense.

J. All indirect fire and air attacks must be observed, except when unit is in contact and in serious danger of being overrun or target area is sparsely inhabited and deemed essential by the tactical unit commander directing the fire.

K. Pilots must be briefed for each mission on the locations of civilians and friendly forces.

L. Booby traps, mines, and minefields will be recorded, marked, and must be recovered.

M. Avoid harming civilian property unless necessary to save U.S. lives.

N. Treat all civilians and their property with respect and dignity. Before using privately owned property, check to see if any publicly owned property can substitute. No requisitioning of civilian property without permission of a company-level commander and without giving a receipt. If an ordering officer can contract for the property, then do not requisition it. Do not sleep in their houses. If you must sleep in privately owned buildings, have an ordering officer contract for it.

O. Treat all prisoners humanely and with respect and dignity.

P. Annex P of the OPLAN provides more detail. Conflicts between card and OPLAN should be resolved in favor of the OPLAN.

Dan Bolger agreed. Impressed by Mark Martins's work, the lieutenant colonel seized upon a concept that this bright attorney called "RAMP," a baseline ROE tool. Similar to other Army mnemonic keywords, RAMP jogged a tired mind to recall the only four things a rifleman really needs to apply ROE in battle. Once you knew RAMP, 95 percent of the likely situations suddenly made sense, with no lawyering necessary. To shoot or not to shoot? RAMP prods a soldier to make the right choice.

The R told men to "Return fire with well-aimed fire." If somebody shoots at you, shoot back. Using well-aimed fire, not just a spasmodic mad minute, precluded overreactions that could harm interspersed civilians. This technique also conserved ammunition, no small matter for walking infantrymen who must carry every round into battle.

Did R mean you must eat the first hostile shot? Not at all, said A, because it stood for "Anticipate attack." Here, Major Martins's system urged soldiers to use the same target evaluation skills schooled since induction training. Shooters should check the size, activity, location, uniform, time available, and equipment, with special scrutiny of the potential target's hands. Policemen know this method very well. Just because a guy holds an AK-47 does not necessarily make him a badnik. It all depends on what he's doing with the item. Here is discipline distilled to its essence—to shoot or not to shoot, with each individual rifleman calling his shot. So much for Frederick the Great's army of automatons.

RAMP (Task Force 1-327 Infantry)

Return fire with well-aimed fire.
Anticipate attack. (Hand SALUTE)
    Hand: What is in his hands?
    Size: How many?
    Activity: What are they doing?
    Location: Within range?
    Uniform: Are they in uniform?
    Time: How soon before they are upon you?
    Equipment: If armed, with what?
Measure the amount of force you use. (VEWPRIK)
    Verbal warning
    Exhibit weapon
    Warning shot
    Pepper spray
    Rifle buttstroke
    Injure with bayonet
    Kill with fire

Protect with deadly force only **human life** and **property designated** by the commander.

Employing violence proportionate to the threat came next. Soldiers had to "Measure the amount of force." Unlike Vietnam, nobody should call for B-52 ARCLIGHT deluges in response to a few sniper slugs, nor should the troops resort to killing to solve every confrontation. Local civilians rarely cooperated with big green men who only speak English. How do you make them do what you want without zapping them? Major Martins offered a menu of responses to help a man under pressure, accessed by the memorable soldier-friendly acronym VEWPRIK. These suggestions, ranging from a shout to a shot, applied only when trying to control civilians or a crowd that had not yet turned ugly. If the jokers fired or got ready to fire, then R and A applied.

With these three simple self-defense rules in hand, one more made the method complete by extending its umbrella over others. The final letter, P, said "Protect with deadly force only human life and property designated by the commander." Taking out a sniper about to kill a nearby farmer was okay. Capping casual looters was not. The property designated by the commander meant U.S. weaponry, the TOC, the aid station, the embassy, and so on. It did not mean hubcaps.

Soldiers in the 1st of the 327th learned RAMP from 1st Lt. Matt Bounds, the battalion's unauthorized but wholly essential S5. Matt concocted a sequence of shoot/don't shoot vignettes set in Fort Campbell's ramshackle city combat training site, replete with civilian role players and sneaky terrorists and gunmen. The RAMP concept worked very well, and within a few hours of hearing about it, soldiers could reliably kill hostiles and not civilians. The trick involved a simple formula learned by doing, rather than lengthy verbiage imparted by briefing. That same sort of scheme could have met the battalion's tactical needs too, but Dan Bolger's thinking did not crystallize enough to devise such a framework. So RAMP occupied a unique place in the battalion's predeployment preparations. When Cortina's civilians showed up, the Bulldogs would know what to do.

Civilians turned out to be the objective for 1-327th Infantry's first mission during JRTC 94-10. The locals surely weren't going anywhere, but as in actual underdeveloped countries, Fort Polk's Cortina played host to a number of Americans conducting official business, carrying out unofficial business, and just plain wandering around loose. Before the Bulldogs or anybody in 1st Brigade could go after the wily and elusive CLF, or trade blows with Atlantican regulars, somebody had to get about thirty U.S. citizens out of beleagured Jetertown, out of the line of fire. Screwing up this kind of tricky sideshow would not go over well in the White House or on Main Street USA, which is exactly why JRTC wanted the rotational troops to try it. Until now, only Ranger battalions had attempted such a mission at Fort Polk. So the 101st Airborne would be breaking new ground on this one.

The civilian extraction only raised the curtain and, to a small extent, cleaned off the battlefield. Defeating the CLF remained the main event, and as with all JRTC rotations, as in Grenada in 1983 and Panama in 1989, the Americans needed a guaranteed doorway into unhappy Cortina. The Always First Brigade would start the war with a brigade-scale night air assault to take a flight landing strip (FLS), in this case, the one in the Fullerton region of Fort Polk. All subsequent operations would launch from this foothold.

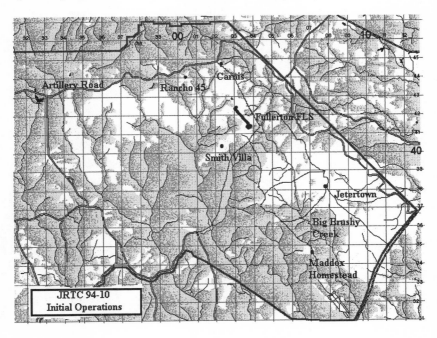

Normally, Colonel Donald could have used his entire brigade to take the dirt runway, as he had in his previous visits to JRTC. But because it was his third rotation, his second in four months, and because he and much of his team already knew how to outfox the basic scenario, the JRTC scriptwriters elected to insert a curveball. Hence, along with the landing strip and the damnable CLF lurking in the swamps, Donald inherited those thirty Yankee souls at Jetertown, desperate to get out. The FLS seizure worked best with a pair of infantry battalions, but Jetertown demanded another. Jim Donald only had two.

Splitting the effort at the outset made nobody happy, except perhaps the devilish JRTC O/Cs and planners, who created this Hobson's choice. To force the issue, JRTC mandated that the brigade could not attack before nightfall on 14 September, must have the runway secured by 1000 on 15 September, and needed to pull out all American civilians by noon that same day. The brigade's third infantry battalion, 1-187th, offered no help, as they only had a staff and computer gamers to support their command post exercise, a notional escapade supposedly unfolding off 1st Brigade's eastern flank, on turf in reality not even owned by the U.S. government. Assigning combat power and sequencing it into the real fighting box, with three battalions' worth of work and two battalions' worth of rifle troops— well, here was a chance for the Always First folks to earn their pay.

They did the best they could. Based on uncertainty about the capabilities of the attached Iron Rakkasan battalion to handle Jetertown, and some trust in Dan Bolger's strong-willed S5 and that clever RAMP stuff, Col. Jim Donald handed the dicey extraction task to the 1-327th Infantry. The 3-187th Rakkasans inherited the big FLS, along with its CLF defenders. The brigade cooked up a two-phase show, with two days and nights of preliminary reconnaissance and attack aviation sweeps, followed by a massive brigade insertion commencing at 2300 on the night of 14 September. The 3-187th would hit first, grabbing the 4400-foot Fullerton airstrip. At 0120, brigade planned a second wave to bring the 1-327th Bulldogs to Jetertown, capping off the heliborne operations by picking up the U.S. citizenry about 0600, as dawn broke. Of course, the scheme did not truly resolve which task took priority, the runway or the civilians.

While the brigade staff could, and would, agonize over which battalion really constituted the main effort, Bolger's Bulldogs simply got
to work. The book called 1-327th's evolution a noncombatant evacuation operation (NEO), although the applicable written Army doctrine on hand in September 1994 would not have sufficed to wipe
your nose. A very wonderful NEO manual, *FM 90-29*, waited in draft,
destined for eventual publication. Had it been available, Dan Bolger
and his men might have read it. The O/Cs owned a copy.[18]

As for the Bulldogs, they resorted to common sense and a few
guidelines found in a locally produced 101st Airborne Division NEO

Task Force 1-327 Infantry
14 September 1994

Company A(-)	Company B	Company C
HQ/FIST	HQ/FIST	HQ/FIST
Mortars (2 x 60mm)	Mortars (2 x 60mm)	Mortars (2 x 60mm)
2d Platoon/A	1st Platoon/B	1st Platoon/C
3d Platoon/A	2d Platoon/B	2d Platoon/C
5th Platoon/D	3d Platoon/B	3d Platoon/C
FCT 3	Stinger Team 2	Section/4th Platoon/D
Stinger Team 1	Team Golf	FCT 1
	ATLS Team	Stinger Team 3

Task Force Control

Mortar Platoon (4 x 81mm)
Main CP/Combat Trains
Field Trains

Detachments

Company D (-) to TF 3-187 Infantry
Scout Platoon to 3-101st Aviation
1st Platoon/A to 3-101st Aviation
3d Platoon/D to Team Tank

Strengths (with attachments)		*Key to Abbreviations/Terms*
Company A:	62	ATLS: Advanced Trauma Lifesaving Team
Company B:	109	CP: command post
Company C:	94	FCT: Fire Control Team (Navy/Marine)
Mortar Platoon:	27	FIST: Fire Support Team (Army)
Main CP/Combat Trains:	52	HQ: Headquarters
Field Trains	44	Team Golf: S5, civil affairs team,
		loudspeaker team, and
		counterintelligence agent
TF 1-327 Infantry Total	388	

handbook. The battalion commander envisioned an NEO as a raid to snatch prisoners, only this time, the prisoners were friendly. Get in, get 'em, and get 'em out, before the CLF could intervene.

Getting in meant dropping out of the night sky, securing Jetertown, and holding an extraction pickup zone. Two rifle companies, Cold Steel and Abu, planned to isolate the villages to the north and south respectively. Alfredo Mycue's Bushmasters, Bolger's best company, prepared to go into the little town and get the Americans out. A map survey, coupled with recent aerial photographs, led Bulldog S3 Air Dave Bair to recommend four likely landing zones, with the noncombatants coming out from LZ Blackbird, nestled just west of the center of the hamlet. To the northwest, LZ Cardinal served Cold Steel, and in the south Abu planned for LZ Albatross. The Bushmasters looked toward LZ Bluebird, a location bound to get confused with nearby LZ Blackbird. Bluebird lay just northeast of the ten-building "J" that passed for Jetertown. With nineteen UH-60L Blackhawks flying with seats out, each crammed with nineteen soldiers, it looked like the battalion could pump all three companies into their three main LZs within a few minutes, grabbing Jetertown in a single *coup de main.*[19]

Getting the civilians, the main effort for 1-327th, fell to Company B, 109 strong. Most of the interaction looked like a job for 1st Lt. Matt Bounds, the S5. Augmented by a civil affairs duo, a counter-intelligence interrogator to screen for hostile agents, and a loudspeaker team ready to broadcast reassuring messages, Matt linked up with Captain Mycue's Company B Bushmasters for the assault. To run the helicopter pickup when ready to get the Americans out, Mycue also received 1st Lt. Dave Bair and his S3 Air NCO, SSgt. James Phelps. The Bushmasters readied themselves to go from house to house to find confused civilians, and also took in the battalion surgeon, just in case. The boys did not expect to do a hostage rescue; that sort of "takedown" belonged to the ninja-suited Delta Force types. The Bushmaster riflemen did anticipate that the CLF would come into Jetertown if the operation slowed down or fell apart. Once rounded up, Dave Bair intended to call in the extraction birds and clear LZ Blackbird.

In the calm tents and blocky buildings of JRTC's secure Interme-diate Staging Base (ISB) at England Air Park (formerly England Air Force Base), seventy-three kilometers by air from the exercise box, it all looked pretty straightforward. The ISB tent city replicated the sort of in-theater facility that any heliborne force needed to stage for action; only paratroopers like the 82d Airborne or the Rangers could go right into battle from their stateside posts. Those people were busy lining up to invade Haiti. And at England Air Park, Bol-ger and his men rehearsed to invade Cortina.

The Haiti occupation went off like clockwork. Thanks to the CLF, darkness, and things that just plain go wrong, the Bulldogs' entry into Cortina proved a little tougher.

"The aviators can only get us to our NEO extraction LZ, Blackbird. Albatross, Bluebird, and Cardinal are all out," said an aggravated Dave Bair. Twilight beckoned on 14 September, a few hours shy of the 2300 kickoff. Bolger and Phelps, laden with backpack radios, am-munition, MILES harnesses, their night-vision goggles dangling around their necks, looked at each other and, simultaneously, swore. It was a bad ending to a bad 48 hours.

One law of war always applies, that being Mr. Murphy's observa-tion that what can go wrong will go wrong. Carl von Clausewitz la-beled it friction, but he meant the same thing. In a complex human endeavor, with thousands of men trying to cooperate while hundreds try to thwart them, fear, fatigue, the unknown, and "countless minor incidents—the kind you can never really foresee—combine to lower the general level of performance, so that one always falls short of the intended goal."[20] So it had gone for the Bulldogs.

The great reconnaissance effort foundered, with both infantry bat-talion scout platoons inserted two nights ago, then largely destroyed snooping around near the proposed landing zones, and thereby ef-fectively telegraphing the coming punches. An attempt to put in some military intelligence voice-intercept people and an attack avi-ation tactical command post up near the Fullerton FLS turned into a disaster, with all but a single female lieutenant killed and the en-tire brigade operation order handed over to the CLF for their amusement.[21] Indeed, the score amounted to about forty-odd U.S. casualties versus less than five for the bad guys, with the main event still pending.

The scout debacle returned nothing useful for the investment. Most of what Bolger knew about Jetertown came from his meeting with the Deputy Chief of Mission from the U.S. Embassy, a Mr. James K. Williams.[22] Everything else remained guesswork, supplemented by a few fleeting contacts by patrolling Apache sections. The 1-327th troops possessed maps of Jetertown, with the buildings numbered one through ten. They carried lists of the Americans waiting in the community center, building #7. But as for pinpointing the CLF in the area, all the battalion S2 could say for certain was that Mark Lawry's battalion scouts no longer answered on the satellite link when the battalion called.

Matters around Jetertown, therefore, seemed unclear. Around the Fullerton runway, the questions had been answered, rather violently. The attack aviators sent to deal with the ghostly guerrillas counted few kills. This boded ill for 3-187th's chances as it landed around the airstrip, a target as obvious as it could be.

Reluctantly, Colonel Donald beefed up the Rakkasans at the expense of the Bulldogs. The brigade commander ordered Bolger to turn over three of his five Company D platoons, two to the 3-187th Infantry and one to the Sheridan force, Team Tank destined to drive in for ground link-up with the Rakkasans. Given that the bulk of the company was gone, Bolger sent Capt. Willie Utroska with his pair of detached platoons, as much to help the 3-187th as to ensure that this contingent returned at the end of the air assault, as scheduled. So Dan Bolger and his S3, Bill Phelps, spread out the remaining two Company D platoons. Two gunships went to the Abus, and another pair to Cold Steel, to aid in their blocking tasks. Four more gunships remained with Capt. Ronz Sarvis and his trains, preparing to move into the box by ground convoy, following Team Tank and the Rakkasan trains once the initial landings ended.

With the scouts blown away and the Maddogs of Company D gravely reduced to aid the neighbors, the Bulldogs waited to enter the fray at a little less than two-thirds strength. Here, every personnel issue not cleared up at Campbell, every weakling still on the rolls, every soldier back at home station solving personal issues and not contributing in the field, all of these buzzards came home to roost. This degradation came in addition to the loss of a rifle platoon from Company A. To assist the aviators in dealing with downed aircrews, Bolger gave up his best group of riflemen, 1st Lt. Matt Moore's 1st Platoon of the Abus, leaving Drew Felix with a rump company of two platoons, some sixty men. Each deduction made sense, but in the aggregate, they added up to trouble.

And now the fliers denied all three of the primary LZs, citing safety concerns. So much for a simultaneous landing, a perimeter slammed around the hamlet while Alfredo Mycue and Matt Bounds sorted things out in the buildings. That was not to be. Instead, the companies would feed directly into little Jetertown, one after another: Chris Forbes and ninety-three others in Cold Steel, then the Bushmasters with the battalion Tac CP, and finally, the shrunken Abus. Just to add to the bitter stew, some obscure flight regulation prohibited passengers from coming in with the gun, ambulance, mortar, and communications Humvee trucks slinging in. These loads would land unmanned, and their drivers and crews would have to find them in the postmidnight gloom out on Blackbird.

Yet at the brigade level, as the minutes counted down, orchestrating the insertion of an artillery battery, the brigade Tac CP, the Rakkasans, and, finally, the Bulldogs took on the atmosphere of a gigantic mass transit system at work, plucking men and cargo from the crumbling England Air Park taxiways and placing them, probably under fire, into several landing zones unmarked by pathfinders and unseen by most of the flight crews. To make all these interlocked moves, timing was everything, and diddling with the schedule a matter for Colonel Donald's personal attention. Bolger and others often cursed their aviator counterparts, but in a sober assessment, the intricate ballet of some eighty aircraft in pitch blackness, zipping at high speeds over unfamiliar flight routes, required some pretty damned fine flying.[23] Simply dreaming up grandiose ground schemes and willing pilots in night goggles to execute them begged for disaster, real flames and deaths, not MILES game play. When the pilots nixed Albatross, Bluebird, and Cardinal, Bolger, Bair, and Phelps accepted it, and realigned forces.

The CLF realigned the air assault at 2310, as the Bulldogs lay in quiet rows on the pickup zone, waiting for their turn to go in. Bolger, Phelps, and the S2, Dirk Blackdeer, heard the brigade radio net erupt with chatter as the third Rakkasan company landed. Ironically, Capt. Art Bair, Dave's older brother, commanded this bunch, caught in a crushing crossfire right on their landing zone. Within minutes, dozens went down, including the engineer teams designated to clear mines and barbed wire off the dirt FLS.[24] This engagement rapidly balled up the carefully calculated air schedule.

Along with the radio reports, another sure indicator of trouble began to develop. Aircraft customarily flew in four- to six-ship formations. Now, as the Rakkasan landings came unglued, the Bulldog soldiers looked up to see individual Blackhawks and Chinooks staggering in. Only one UH-60L went down, but many more went awry.

By 0100, when 1-327th should have been boarding its share of UH-60Ls, the pickup zone lay silent and pristine, empty of aircraft. Bolger asked Colonel Donald what was going on, and got told to stand by. Finally, meandering in by twos and threes, the Blackhawks wafted in. The carefully cross-checked flight schedule unraveled. Soldiers loaded quickly, and by 0130, Cold Steel took off, destination: Jetertown. At uneven intervals, in five- and four-chopper groups, the rest of the battalion followed.

The ride was, unfortunately, the usual: sweating men clogged like stacked corpses in the dark, bucking helicopters. Outside, sleeping Louisiana flashed by, then stygian blackness at last as the birds clipped over the Fort Polk reservation. A long, slow left bank, and then rolling upright, nose beginning to flare, a glimpse of Jetertown out the right side; the impressions flowed and then stopped abruptly. Each UH-60L thumped down, the doors rasped back on their tracks, and the boys tumbled out into the warm orange mud, the dull yellow lights of Jetertown glowing ahead of them.

Or behind them, or beside them, or right next to them—the aviators had interpreted LZ Blackbird rather broadly, and casually deposited Bulldog soldiers everywhere.[25] Viewed from above, the 1-327th landing pattern looked very much as if God shook up the squads and platoons like puzzle pieces and then dumped the whole

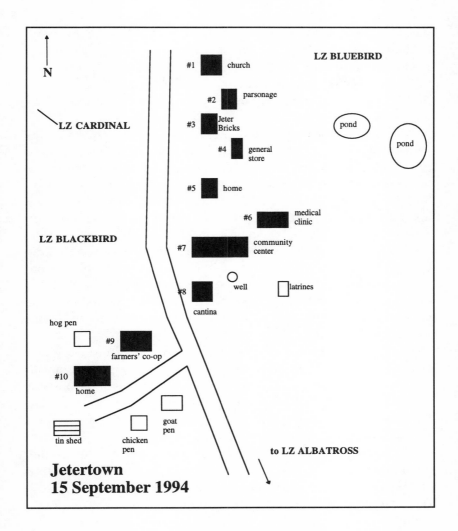

damn box. Amazingly, more than half of the loads landed in LZ Bluebird, allegedly unsafe for use.

As luck would have it, Dan Bolger and his Tac team popped down right in the southwest corner of Bluebird, within hand grenade range of the town's church and parsonage. Bolger's men moved to a vantage point in a thicket just east of building #3, the brick factory, and gained good communications with all subordinates and brigade. No shooting could be heard, although the sounds of heavy firing came from the direction of the FLS, seven kilometers by road to the north. Obviously, the Rakkasans were in trouble. A half hour after the lead 1-327th squads set down, the rotorblades whopped away into the distance, and the Bulldogs milled in the night, unscrewing themselves. Jetertown waited.

Not all waited quietly, though. The mayor and constable appeared, attracted by the turbine engine noise, blowing dust, and groups of men rushing around their houses.[26] They confronted a rifle squad led by SSgt. Stephen Young of Company C, who landed not far from his battalion commander's party. Young and his five charges intended to move north and establish a roadblock when two Cortinian males approached them near the church. One, the constable, carried a sidearm. Young took no chances. He told his men to grab both and disarmed the policeman. It wasn't exactly neighborly, but it beat a bullet in the head, and in the dark, few could dispute that call. The RAMP method had just passed its first test. Within minutes, the two shaken but wiser natives returned to their village to announce the arrival of some decidedly brusque Yankees.

The scrambled landing plan made hash of Alfredo Mycue's ground scheme of maneuver. Part of his 2d Platoon mixed in with the Abus; the rest of it ended up with Captain Forbes and Company C. The Bushmaster 3d Platoon also got entangled with the Abus. Matt Bounds and his S5 crew, known as Team Golf, ended up well off course, over in the far northeast. It took them a while to work south. In true airborne fashion, knowing the key mission demanding action, it fell to the one man who did get to the Community Center to take charge. Grabbing up some Bushmaster riflemen for security, 1st Lt. Dave Bair entered building #7, the community center, at 0240, about eighteen minutes after the last UH-60L departed.

Bair found plenty to do. The scene inside looked like a potluck dinner in Hades: screaming women, angry men, and two bodies bleeding on the floor, with everybody yelling at once. The lieutenant motioned for quiet and, identifying the Jetertown mayor in the crowd, explained why the Bulldogs had come knocking this fine night. As Dave Bair calmed the frightened townspeople and Americans, SSgt. Phelps motioned in medical personnel to treat the wounded and sick. One U.S. citizen looked pretty bad, suffering from the effects of a land mine explosion. Another bled from a gunshot injury, courtesy of the CLF. (And where were those nasties?) By the time Matt Bounds and his men finally arrived at 0313, processing of the Americans for evacuation was under way. Dave Bair, relieved of his thirty civilians, went outside to set up LZ Blackbird to receive the extraction lift of Chinooks, due by 0600 or so. As he exited, he heard the loudspeaker team blaring away: "We are American soldiers. We are here to help you. . . ." *Thank God the Cortinians speak English,* he thought. *Oh, well. We lucked out that way in Grenada, so it isn't all that far-fetched.*

While Bair and his NCO marked the LZ, the village hummed with activity. That portion of Company B not involved in assisting Matt Bounds and Team Golf began, with the constable, a house-to-house search of Jetertown. Ostensibly, they looked for separated, uninformed Americans. In reality, Alfredo Mycue's Bushmasters hunted for evidence of CLF sympathizers and hidden gunmen who might disrupt the inbound freedom birds. All good done so far would collapse with one lucky SA-14 hit on a chopper stuffed with U.S. civilians. The search duties fell to 1st Platoon and those men of 2d and 3d that had turned up.

On the perimeter, companies A and C slowly set in their blocking positions without incident. Chris Forbes's men found a cache of rucksacks and water cans just off the east side of the main Fullerton Road, a wide dirt trail running up toward the FLS. They also reported mines in the roadway, the first of all too many similar reports. To the south and east, Drew Felix slowly worked his 2d and 3d Platoons out to their blocking positions. Nobody sighted any guerrillas.

One alarming development involved the trucks, plopped crewless hither and yon over the various cleared patches around Jetertown. The drivers and crews could not figure out where their Humvees had finally alighted. The mortar squads, ambulance team, command trucks, and Maddog gunships all remained out of action, their seething owners unable to find these misplaced vehicles. First light might help the men search for their equipment, but for now, the battalion went without everything it had slung in, a substantial risk.

That pretty much summed up operations so far. Dan Bolger knew that he had dodged a very big bullet by not finding the CLF in town, especially given the disjointed style of landing that the battalion exhibited. The O/Cs later criticized brigade's decision to do the NEO concurrent with the FLS takedown at Fullerton, but Bolger thought otherwise. Landing at night confounded both sides, and if the Bulldogs happened to get unscrewed first, so much the better. Evidently the CLF, too, could not do everything all of the time.

This reprieve, though, would not last forever. Before it ended, the Bulldogs had to get rid of their thirty Americans, starting with those in rough shape. Attempts to bring in a medevac chopper to pull out the wounded citizens bore no fruit. Brigade committed all assets to the bloodbath, now over two hundred casualties, in that awful hot LZ near the Fullerton airstrip. Although the battalion surgeon and his corpsman did what they could, two Americans eventually died of wounds waiting for aerial ambulances that never came. Another American, fed up with the slow pace of the withdrawal, elected to stay in Jeterown, and signed a waiver to that effect. Believe or not, processing such waivers is part of the NEO drill, as is interviewing evacuees to detect potential enemy agents. Fortunately, Matt Bounds and his Team Golf soldiers came to Jetertown ready to play.

Indeed, although Matt's people briefed and marshalled all U.S. civilians for departure by 0600, brigade could only spare a single Chinook to pull them out, and that after it extracted some more Rakkasan casualties first. The first load finally left at 0730; the next, and last, at 0829. It had taken more than six hours, but the NEO was complete, and successful.

Ominously, just before the second CH-47D lift, four 82mm mortar rounds impacted on the fringe of LZ Blackbird, killing one of Captain Mycue's men, the only loss inflicted during the entire mission.[27] The CLF had finally shown their hand. Obviously, an enemy observer could see the NEO in progress, and had called in fire.

Bolger expected as much. *Now the American noncombatants are gone. We can unplug from Jetertown and plunge west*, thought the lieutenant colonel, *pushing into the Big Brushy Creek watershed, a wilderness certain to contain guerrilla lairs.* The battalion commander guessed that the insurgents did not expect his battalion to move quickly after the NEO wrapped up. Well, the CLF guessed wrong.

So did Lt. Col. Dan Bolger.

Notes

The epigraph is from Michael Herr, *Dispatches* (New York: Avon Books, 1978), 13.

1. U.S., Department of the Army, Headquarters, Forces Command, *FORSCOM Regulation 350-50-2: Training at the Joint Readiness Training Center* (Ft. McPherson, Ga.: Headquarters, Forces Command, 1 June 1994), 3.

2. For an account of this experience, see Daniel P. Bolger, *Dragons at War: 2-34th Infantry in the Mojave* (Novato, Calif.: Presidio Press, 1986).

3. Lt. Col. Lloyd W. Mills, USA, *JRTC 94-07: A Commander's Perspective* (Ft. Campbell, Ky.: Headquarters, 3d Battalion, 327th Infantry Regiment, 24 June 1994), 1.

4. For an example of a scenario tailored to particular brigades, see U.S., Department of the Army, Headquarters, Joint Readiness Training Center, *Scenario Laydown Briefing, JRTC 95-07* (Ft. Polk, La.: Headquarters, JRTC, 30 March 1995), which addressed the 1st Brigade, 101st Airborne Division. Contrast this demanding plan, with numerous complex and simultaneous operations, a strong opposing force, and plenty of loose civilian role-players, with the relatively simple battlefield presented to the 53d Infantry Brigade, a National Guard outfit, found in U.S., Department of the Army, Headquarters, Joint Readiness Training Center, *Scenario Laydown Briefing, JRTC 95-08* (Ft. Polk, La.: Headquarters, JRTC, 13 June 1995).

5. Lt. Col. William P. Baxter, USA, ret., *Soviet Air-Land Battle Tactics* (Novato, Calif.: Presidio Press, 1986), 94–95; David C. Isby, *Weapons and Tactics of the Soviet Army* (New York: Jane's Publishing Inc., 1988), 11–14.

6. William Conant Church, *Ulysses S. Grant* (New York: Church Co., 1897), 188–89.

7. Marshall as found in Gen. Paul F. Gorman, USA, ret., *The Secret of Future Victories* (Ft. Leavenworth, Kans.: Combat Studies Institute, 1992), I-24.

8. Ibid.

9. Gen. George S. Patton, Jr., USA, *War As I Knew It* (New York: Pyramid Books, 1970), 308.

10. Carl von Clausewitz, *On War*, ed. and trans. by Michael Howard and Peter Paret (Princeton, N.J.: Princeton University Press, 1976), 102.

11. Mills, *JRTC 94-07: A Commander's Perspective*, 1–6.

12. U.S., Department of the Army, Headquarters, 1st Battalion, 502d Infantry Regiment, *Joint 1-502nd IN and 1-101st AVN Information Memorandum* (Ft. Campbell, Ky.: Headquarters, 1st Battalion, 502nd Infantry Regiment, 29 August 1994), 1-2.

13. Hans Halberstadt, *Airborne* (Novato, Calif.: Presidio Press, 1988), 99. The M-551 Sheridan is officially known as an ARAAV, an armored reconnaissance airborne assault vehicle. Everybody calls it a light tank. The aborted XM-8 Armored Gun System would have eventually replaced the 82d Airborne's Vietnam-era Sheridans, but the Army canceled that program early in 1996. Now it looks as if the 3d Battalion, 73d Armor itself will be canceled, deactivated as its elderly Sheridans succumb to age and lack of spare parts. The All-Americans will have to look elsewhere for antitank firepower.

14. This echoes the infamous slam at William Jennings Bryan, the "Boy Orator of the Platte," and a distinguished American political figure at the close of the nineteenth century.

15. Thomas C. Thayer, *War Without Fronts* (Boulder, Colo.: Westview Press, 1985), 57, 79.

16. Capt. Kevin Dougherty, USA, "Tactical Rules of Engagement," *Army Trainer* (Spring 1992), 11. This brief article includes a full transcript of the JRTC ROE.

17. Maj. Mark S. Martins, USA, "Rules of Engagement for Land Forces: A Matter of Training, Not Lawyering," *Military Law Review* (Winter 1994).

18. U.S., Department of the Army, Headquarters, Joint Readiness Training Center, "Marshalling Force Operations" in *1-327 IN Rotation 94-10 LIC AAR* (Ft. Polk, La.: Headquarters, JRTC, 20 September 1994), 19. The term LIC means low-intensity conflict, the counterinsurgency phase of a JRTC rotation. At one time, LIC was part of Army doctrine that divided warfare into low, middle, and high in-

tensities. Since enemies never cooperated with this taxonomy, and men under fire considered themselves at the high end regardless of what the doctrine writers said, this structure has been discarded. It lives on, however, at JRTC. The Atlantican invasion is sometimes called the MIC (mid-intensity conflict) phase.

19. U.S., Department of the Army, Headquarters, 1st Battalion, 327th Infantry Regiment, *OPORD 94-10-1 NEO* (England Air Park, La.: Headquarters, 1st Battalion, 327th Infantry Regiment, 12 September 1994), 1, 2, A-1.

20. Clausewitz, *On War,* 119.

21. U.S., Department of the Army, Headquarters, Joint Readiness Training Center, "Captured Documents and Intel Gained" in *1st Brigade, 101st Airborne Division (AASLT) Rotation 94-10 First AAR* (Ft. Polk, La.: Headquarters, JRTC, 16 September 1994), 2-3.

22. A truly exquisite addition to realism, Mr. Williams was a BDM Corporation employee who played his diplomatic role to the hilt. Arriving at the England Air Park staging base, he insisted upon talking to Lt. Col. Bolger to impress upon him the ambassador's views on the upcoming NEO. In return, Bolger offered an overview of the extraction plan, carefully avoiding specifics that might compromise the plan if Mr. Williams talked too much to reporters later that day.

23. HQ, JRTC, "Air Assault Operations," *1st Brigade, 101st Airborne Division (AASLT) Rotation 94-10 First AAR,* 8-9. The entire night entailed 102 UH-60L and CH-47D sorties, plus almost fifty attack aviation, medevac, command and control, and search and rescue flights.

24. By daybreak, Task Force 3-187 Infantry suffered 72 killed and 153 wounded. Company B had been almost wiped out. HQ, JRTC, "BluFor BDA by Type Wpn Systems (sic)," *1st Brigade, 101st Airborne Division (AASLT) Rotation 94-10 First AAR,* 37.

25. HQ, JRTC, "Jetertown NEO Ops 15 Sep 94" in *1-327 IN Rotation 94-10 LIC AAR,* 5A.

26. HQ, JRTC, "Civil Affairs—NEO Timeline," *Speaker Notes for 1st Brigade, 101st Airborne Division (AASLT) Rotation 94-10 First AAR,* 6-8.

27. HQ, JRTC, "BluFor BDA by Type Wpn Systems (sic)," *1st Brigade, 101st Airborne Division (AASLT) Rotation 94-10 First AAR,* 37.

Chapter 4
Search and Attack (I)

"Have you ever been experienced? I have."
—Jimi Hendrix

Like any real disaster, everything started off very well. That must be said. Indeed, a good start makes for a really spectacular four-star fiasco, because it encourages decision makers to keep right on gambling, throwing good money after bad, all in a misbegotten attempt to restore the bright prospects promised at the outset. The 1st of the 327th began the game aggressively, and with victories, as the battalion turned from the harrowing of Jetertown to its war against the Cortinian Liberation Front.

By 0840 on the overcast morning of 15 September, all three rifle companies disengaged from their tasks around Jetertown and formed for a parallel advance toward Big Brushy Creek, a tangled morass of the type favored by guerrillas in need of hidden bases. Dirk Blackdeer and his commander agreed that the CLF must have hidden something at the junction of the stream and the dirt road heading southwest from Jetertown. It might be a command post or a supply site, perhaps the main underground storage, the battalion supply point (BSP) for the entire 91st Assault Battalion. Brigade S2 thought so too.[1] If true, then the entire watery conduit north of that important logistics area might be full of goodies: enemy squad and team campsites, ammunition caches full of 82mm mortar rounds and SA-14 missile reloads, or even one or two of the boxy little three-wheel all-terrain vehicles favored by the rebel resupply teams.

In heading west, Dan Bolger took heed of advice given him by the voice of experience, Col. Jim Dubik. A few years before, Dubik led his 5th Battalion, 14th Infantry Regiment from Hawaii into Fort Chaffee, Arkansas, for a JRTC rotation. Jim Dubik, shrewd and innova-

116

tive, reasoned that to beat an OPFOR like the CLF, you had to take away his food and water. The bad guys typically stashed this all down in a deep, dark, stinking swamp, hoping the American infantry lacked the stomach to go hunting in such thick, difficult ground. Dubik and 5th of the 14th went right into the muck, overran the CLF supply caches, and slowly starved out the desperate guerrillas. The resulting ambushes and counterambushes resulted in about three U.S. dead and wounded for every CLF casualty, and it all paralyzed the enemy. Hence, Dubik's approach won. Even as Bolger prepared to emulate it, Col. Jim Dubik's 2d Brigade of the 10th Mountain Division landed near Cap Haitien, Haiti, endeavoring to try out JRTC techniques on real foes.

Dubik's answer to defeating the CLF found a ringing endorsement from Col. Jim Donald, who employed similar tactics in JRTC 94-07 just a few months ago. That time, in an attempt to establish an offset artillery firebase to cover the main brigade objective near the dirt runway, Donald inserted the 3-327th Infantry smack atop the BSP, then held on as the CLF went crazy. The U.S. battalion ran up an impressive kill ratio below the usual 3:1 (U.S./CLF), wrecking a guerrilla company in a tremendously successful operation. Interestingly, Task Force 3-327 won its violent series of firefights under the leadership of Lt. Col. Lloyd Mills, who had been Jim Dubik's XO as a major back in 5-14th Infantry.[2] And just to cement the validity of Dubik's advice to dominate the enemy supply network, his old S3, Mace Crowe, now wore the silver leaves of a lieutenant colonel and served as Bolger's senior O/C. With all of this incentive, not to mention Jetertown's proximity to a very likely target area, was there any doubt that the Bulldogs would go after what they assumed to be the CLF's jugular, the rebel supply system?

Another option involved killing the enemy without regard to his supplies. You could argue, rather persuasively, that the Dubik/Donald/Mills experiences really boiled down to using the CLF logistics structure as bait to bring about fights and run up the score. Of course, that necessitated platoons and squads capable of beating the JRTC's dreaded CLF three-step, outboxing the boxers, so to speak. If you subscribed to this idea, finding a BSP became step one, stirring up the varmints. Step two required destroying them. For some reason, perhaps the hope for a key to easy victory, Bolger's Bulldogs acted as if simply finding the holy grail of the BSP equaled final triumph in itself.

Army doctrine, predictably, encouraged both seizing supplies and zapping badniks, leaving it up to the commander to choose what to chase. The book concentrated a lot more on how to do it, how to search and attack, the current parlance for the discredited Vietnam term *search and destroy*. The battalion field manual suggested a need for three distinct forces: one to find, one to fix the enemy in place, and the third to finish; kind of handy for an outfit with three rifle companies. Search and attack tactics squatted in the middle of a discussion on conventional attacks, the kind aimed at seizing Pork Chop Hill, as if the Army hierarchy knew they needed to address this counterguerrilla stuff, but hoped nobody would ever have to try it.[3] The controlling powers at JRTC, with an eye on the awful realities of today's world, evidently thought otherwise.

The 101st Airborne Division senior leadership agreed with JRTC. Unconvinced by the brief, generic descriptions of search and attack tactics in the doctrinal literature, the Screaming Eagles commissioned a local publication, Air Assault Battle Note #18, "Search and Attack Operations." This ten-page document laid out in great detail just how an air assault battalion would search and attack. As the text put it, when hunting the elusive insurgent, "his CSS (combat service support) network offers the most predictable and identifiable target for attack." Once taken by American forces, the loss of vital enemy supplies "may spark him to risk a stand-up battle against superior U.S. firepower."[4] In other words, locate his stash, snag his stash, then send a bullet, not a man. Its author was a major in G3 named Dan Bolger. For some reason, Bolger recalled the exhortation to target guerrilla stores, but forgot the part about killing the rebels who objected to such actions.

Truthfully, with the battalion's undermanned two-squad rifle platoons unskilled in basics like all-around security and rapid actions on contact, Bolger's willing riflemen stood to get kicked around tangling with the supple CLF. That wasn't unusual at JRTC, nor had it been unusual in Polk's real-life prototype, the Vietnam War. In Nam, and at JRTC, U.S. forces rarely did the find, fix, finish cycle to standard. British historian Paddy Griffith tartly stated that matters "became a case of finding, being fixed, and fighting a desperate battle to regain freedom of action."[5] So it went in Southeast Asia. So it went for Bolger and his men.

But not at first—that kind of situation took a while to ripen. The CLF evidently expected 1st of the 327th to hang around Jetertown waiting for their ground convoy, the combat trains, TOC, and supplies to allow for sustained operations. Bolger thought differently, and prodded his commanders to move out and find the enemy supply caches. They did.

Task Force 1-327 Infantry
16 September 1994

Company A(-)	Company B	Company C
HQ/FIST	HQ/FIST	HQ/FIST
Mortars (2 x 60mm)	Mortars (2 x 60mm)	Mortars (2 x 60mm)
2d Platoon/A	1st Platoon/B	1st Platoon/C
3d Platoon/A	2d Platoon/B	2d Platoon/C
Scout Platoon	3d Platoon/B	3d Platoon/C
FCT 3	Stinger Team 2	FCT 1
Stinger Team 1		Stinger Team 3

Task Force Control
Mortar Platoon (4 x 81mm)
Main CP/Combat Trains
    ATLS
    Sec/4th Platoon/D
    Team Golf
Field Trains

Detachments
Company D (-) to TF 3-187 Infantry
1st Platoon/A to 3-101st Aviation
3d Platoon/D to Team Tank
2d Platoon/A to Live Fire (17–18 September)
3d Platoon/C to Live Fire (19–20 September)

Strengths (with attachments)

Company A:	59
Company B:	101
Company C:	89
Mortar Platoon:	27
Main CP/Combat Trains:	68
Field Trains:	44

Key to Abbreviations/Terms
ATLS: Advanced Trauma Lifesaving Team
CP: command post
FCT: Fire Control Team (Navy/Marine)
FIST: Fire Support Team (Army)
HQ: Headquarters
Team Golf: S5, civil affairs team,
    loudspeaker team, and
    counterintelligence agent

TF 1-327 Infantry Total   388

Starting strengths; casualties not included

To the north, Company C pushed due west, hurrying to the creekbed in a column of platoons. The southern prong, under Drew Felix, found the two-platoon Abu Company marching to find any remaining scouts, and the enemy logistics infrastructure, in the vicinity of the road-stream junction southwest of Jetertown. Alfredo Mycue's Bushmasters, again at center stage, focused on the most likely enemy base location, on a small slope about five hundred meters north of Abu's goal, the trail-stream junction. If it was the BSP, or a CLF company supply point (CSP), or the transhipment yard called a supply transfer point (STP), Mycue's men expected to see evidence of a lot of foot, truck, and all-terrain vehicle traffic crossing the muddy creek bottom.

Within a short time, by the gray, humid noon hour, the big push west caught two CLF elements by surprise. In the center, about halfway down to Big Brushy Creek, the Bushmasters smashed into about a dozen guerrillas dozing near a circle of rucksacks. Led by Sfc. Charles W. Lipke and 2nd Platoon, Mycue's column of men startled the enemy, who tried to escape by splitting up into two-man teams. The aggressive U.S. riflemen knocked down ten of the foe, losing eight to return fire. A quick search of the abandoned equipment and the CLF casualties confirmed that this had been a platoon command post. One of the wounded OPFOR shook his head, saying, "We never expected to see you so soon." Nor did the CLF routinely lose more men than they took out. The victorious Bushmasters halted near a small open area to await aerial medevac of their own wounded.

The skirmish in the south turned out less well. Here, the understrength Abus struck a belligerent CLF foursome within two hundred meters of the south end of Jetertown, a few steps beyond the previous night's NEO blocking positions. Within minutes Americans started to fall, and the unharmed hostiles began their patented box drill to chew up the lead platoon. A rebel peeled off to each flank as the forward pair kept popping away, methodically slaying 1st Lt. Ken Leeds's 2d Platoon, Company A. Effectively pinned down, with five casualties to care for and another inflicted almost every minute, Capt. Drew Felix committed his company mortar section and his 3d Platoon.

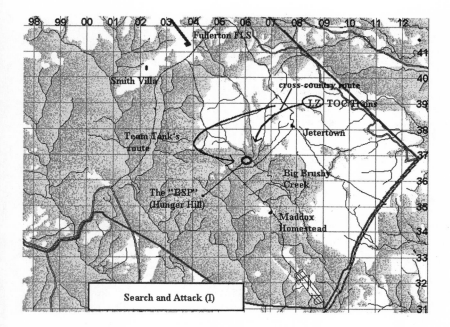

Here, a technique developed back at Fort Campbell paid off. With his gunners carrying their tubes on shoulder slings, mortar section leader SSgt. J. Anthony Angone directed them to fire directly at the CLF duo to the front. The 60mm mortar can be carried with a round in the barrel and fired by a trigger, although it is usually used by dropping finned projectiles down the muzzle. In this case, both gunners braced their weapons on the red clay and loosed simulated white phosphorus shells straight at the stationary, prone guerrillas. In reality, these horrific shots would have incinerated both OPFOR troopers in twin blasts of searing white brilliance, leaving behind some ashes, hot metal rifle parts, and a good-size grass fire. At Polk, an O/C raised his pistol-like controller gun (the "God gun," as the troops called it), and calmly tagged both CLF men.

While Staff Sergeant Angone's mortars finished off the CLF point team, the trailing element, SSgt. Mark A. Gerkin's 3d Platoon, swung into action to stop the two side men. On the run, weaving tree to tree among the slash pines, the platoon brought up both rasping M60 machine guns in an attempt to fix at least one of the enemy soldiers to the flank. Unaccustomed to firing and moving in tandem, a squad crossed in front of its counterpart, and a team leader went down, shot by his own buddies. In the confused exchange of friendly fire that ensued, one of Gerkin's men, Spec. Alfred Rebara, coolly stepped out of formation. Leaning behind a tree, he knelt down and squeezed off a blank round. Crack! One CLF flanker stopped, wounded. Rebara moved, by himself and without covering fire, to the next big tree, and looked in the opposite direction. Crack! The second OPFOR box-out man sat down and removed his floppy boonie hat, dead by a hundred-meter MILES shot. This ended the engagement, with the score standing at fifteen Abus killed or wounded in return for four CLF eliminated. Like Alfredo Mycue's Bushmasters, Drew Felix's company settled down to await helicopter medevac.

Those birds never came. For whatever reason, brigade's carefully crafted aerial evacuation system went to hell that afternoon of 15 September. It had not started raining yet, although not for lack of trying—seldom has a sky looked darker and more forbidding than the banked nimbostratus deck hanging over Fort Polk like a massive anvil. Even so, meteorology permitted flight. Combat did not. Multiple ongoing bloodbaths around the Fullerton FLS claimed brigade's immediate attention. Also, with only intermittent communications from the Jetertown vicinity to brigade, higher headquarters really did not know that the Bulldogs were beginning to accumulate casualties. So the wounded languished in Abu and Bushmaster landing zones, several "dying" as their allotted evacuation windows expired. If the 1-327th possessed a ground evacuation capability, that might have solved the problem. But the battalion truck convoy still struggled along many hours away, clogged behind Team Tank way up north along CLF-infested Artillery Road.

What about the batch of trucks that landed during the NEO? Putting them in without crews probably eased the minds of pilots worried about overstressing their UH-60L airframes and turbine engines. But unmanned trucks dumped hither and yon prove hard to find, especially with the CLF joining in the hunt. By about 1500 on 15 September, the battalion retained four of nine vehicles inserted: the artillery fire support section's cargo truck, chock-full of high-powered radios; a communications Humvee carrying two more radios; and two 81mm mortar carriers crammed with four tubes, 118 rounds, radios, fire direction devices, and the personal gear for nineteen men. With the former two Humvees playing battalion TOC and the latter pair moving to establish a mortar position, the Bulldogs lacked any trucks to spare for a surface medevac attempt.

The CLF saw to that. Using mines and ambushes near Jetertown, insurgents destroyed a medical cargo Humvee and two Maddog gunship trucks, then captured another pair of Company D armed Humvees, each bearing a potent Mark-19 40mm automatic grenade launcher. Among the dozen or so casualties inflicted in these one-sided encounters, the battalion lost its S5, 1st Lt. Matt Bounds, hit and judged badly wounded in a minefield just south of Jetertown. Like the rest of the 1-327th wounded, like the CLF injured now in U.S. hands, Matt waited that gloomy afternoon for a pickup that would not come.

Hours spun on, and the dark afternoon slid into a black, humid night, pregnant with a Louisiana cloudburst. The rifle companies marked time, dozing fitfully in three loose perimeters, with unmolested Cold Steel in the north, the triumphant Bushmasters in the center, and the battered Abus in the south, each about halfway to Big Brushy Creek proper. In the morning, no doubt after a very wet time tonight, the advance would continue, with the casualties (mostly dead of wounds now) left behind with security teams, still waiting for choppers, trucks, or some other way out.

On the battalion's radio net, Capt. Mike Delgado, Maj. Bill Phelps's earnest assistant, reported on the progress of his thirty-four Humvee ground convoy. The painful trek proceeded south from the ambush alley of Artillery Road, along the fire-swept dirt thoroughfare cutting through CLF-held Carnis Village, and then into minefield after minefield. The captain groped through the inky night, feeling for the linkup point in the woods a kilometer northeast of Jetertown.

In this, Capt. Delgado was not helped by the Bulldogs' choice of location for their TOC/combat trains base area. Bill Phelps and his tough S2, Dirk Blackdeer, intentionally chose a nondescript, gently sloping stand of tall hardwoods and stunted pine trees just south of a very large open field. This made it hard for any prospective CLF mortar observers to target the site. Looking too much like every other grid square at Polk, this spot simply could not be pinpointed on a map. Getting to the major Jetertown-Carnis dirt trail was easy, and getting out to the nearby natural LZ worked well too. It made the location ideal for congregating trucks, tents, and supplies without attracting unwelcome attention.

But for Mike Delgado, carrying wounded, exhausted from hours on the road, his ammunition low, and his truck count down by five due to pressure mines, finding this TOC area hidden among sameness simply did not happen. After several hours of radio coaxing, punctuated by more mine damage and casualties in the truck column, Delgado's vehicles neared Jetertown. The leaders halted to check bearings.

Had their captain been a bit more sure of himself, he could have moved onto a firebreak just east of his stopping place, and driven directly into the big LZ at the doorstep of Lieutenant Colonel Bolger's temporary TOC. Instead, discarding advice from the burly, smart S3 NCO, MSgt. Edward Bauerle, Delgado elected to keep heading south on what passed for the main road, toward some weak lights on the horizon. Contacting the battalion headquarters, the young officer announced his intention to go one more kilometer south, and then turn east, into what he guessed might be the TOC/trains area. Over the radio, Bill Phelps and Dan Bolger okayed their subordinate's plan, but warned him to stay out of Jetertown, ceded back to the locals, and so the CLF, following the departure of the last Americans civilians. Just to add to the fun, heavens finally made their views known, and a hard, cold rain began pelting down.

The next few hours went about as badly as they could go. Confused and uncertain, Delgado pushed straight into Jetertown, losing a precious Maddog gun Humvee to a minefield just north of the church. In the ensuing turnabout, with rain-slick trucks backing and filling to get reversed, somebody, maybe not even CLF, opened fire. Two more wounded resulted. It finally took 1st Lt. Dave Bair, the S3 Air, to work his way to the road and walk the convoy in with a hand literally on Capt. Delgado's mud-spattered command truck.

Beaten up, exhausted, soaked, and disoriented, the men who

came in by convoy swelled the TOC/trains force to upward of fifty men. Their safe if belated arrival promised tentage, radios, and full-strength TOC relief shifts for the S3 and battalion commander and their hard-pressed tactical command post team. Among the passengers, Maj. Jim Laufenburg, the battalion XO, ranked as the most important. He and his picked headquarters men had controlled the Chinook pickup zone for the entire brigade the other night. Now, sleepless and bedraggled, Jim joined the search and attack operation underway in the wilderness near Jetertown. Wisely, Bolger put him and the others to sleep in the cold rain. Setup and proper vehicle dispersal could wait until morning. Hopefully, the CLF would accommodate.

The vehicle column left two dozen men and six trucks in their wake, with only the Maddog gunship near Jetertown in any range to be picked up. Even so, Mike Delgado's flotilla swelled the perimeter immensely, with extra communications trucks, maintenance and repair parts carriers, ambulances, more mortar vehicles, the six TOC trucks, the commander, XO, and S3 Humvees, and 1st Lt. Jimmy Williams's supply vehicles stocked with water, food, and ammunition. One cargo carrier, picked up by happenstance at a roadblock, turned out to be filled with exactly the right demolitions needed to blow land mines—but no detonators, and so were useless. More comforting, despite the fighting en route, Mike Delgado brought in three of the four precious Company D armed escort trucks.[6] With bad weather and iffy aviation support, this trio of trucks could soon expect to lead every ground foray to support the rifle companies.

By the next morning, the rain slackened to a steady drizzle, and the Bulldogs resumed full-scale action. The TOC and combat trains spread out and opened for business in their designated patches of generic piney woods. Energetic 1st Lt. Jimmy Williams, with Maddog gun vehicles in tow, blazed a path down to Company B and extracted the casualties back to the battalion LZ. He made several more runs with water and ammunition, avoiding the main road to Jetertown as if it were the third rail of a subway.

As the 1-327th Infantry shook itself out that wet morning, the brigade commander, Colonel Donald, flew in for a short visit. He expressed satisfaction that the Bulldogs were doing well, especially in relation to the tough, expensive fighting up around the FLS. Bolger knew that things could be better, but by comparison, his battalion was having a much better time of it. The brigade colonel promised more aviation support, and even loaned his command bird to aid in a medevac down in the Abu area. As he departed, he directed Bolger to go to an early afternoon After-Action Review up north, at Rancho 45. "I may have something interesting for you by then," he said with a trademark grin. Bolger saluted. His brigade commander climbed aboard his Blackhawk and clattered away, back to the seething mess around the Fullerton landing strip.

By noon, the battalion's advance slowed. Supplies, ammunition and especially water, were running very short in the rifle companies. It certainly seemed odd to be thirsty in the midst of a steady rain shower, but drinking local water, even from the sky, was not permitted by the medical authorities. With nothing detected in the north, Bolger shifted Capt. Chris Forbes's Company C to follow and support Company B's move into the most likely CLF base camp site, down near the creek-road junction. Moving carefully in thick foliage, Company B expected to get into the suspected area by late afternoon.

Company A, under Drew Felix, continued to endure hard luck. In the midmorning, the Abus came upon twelve bodies from the battalion's scout platoon. The CLF had killed them the morning after the NEO, as 1st Lt. Mark Lawry tried to assemble his surviving men and await linkup with Company A. With six other scouts lost somewhere unknown, and only the scout platoon sergeant, SSgt. Kirk Mayfield, still alive, the Abus faced a sizable challenge in moving and evacuating these unfortunates. Naturally, the scouts lay nowhere near a useful LZ or roadway, but were sprawled in among thick undergrowth. In combat you could cut a new landing zone, or blow down trees with explosives. But the environmental laws in Louisiana prohibited that. The dead scouts, with their massive hundred-pound rucksacks, would have to be carried out by muscle power.

But first, they had to be secured. As Staff Sergeant Gerkin's men picked through the prostrate forms dotting the scout assembly area, a CLF quartet opened fire, wounding two Company A riflemen immediately. Once again Captain Felix committed his trail platoon and his 60mm mortars as direct-fire weapons. This time the infantry and mortar-men hit only two of the bad guys, unfortunately topping this success by killing Gerkin's hapless radioman.[7] The other two rebels escaped. A few minutes later, 82mm rounds, or at least the JRTC simulators thereof, whistled in. The Abus suffered another six men killed and wounded. As one of the "dead" scouts said, "It hardly seems worth it, does it?"

And therein the Abus discovered one of the great teaching points of JRTC. In the 1990s American regulars, especially elite troopers like the 101st Airborne, do not leave their wounded or dead behind. In Mogadishu, Somalia, in 1993, a Ranger and light infantry task force took dozens of casualties to secure and extract their fallen comrades, and that is the way we expect it to be.[8] In the Polk training ground, to reinforce that same point, no casualty can be replaced until properly evacuated. Even when done as rapidly as possible, this turnaround takes about half a day. A unit that cannot clean the battlefield, account for its losses, and get them out quickly, will fight short. A force that leaves its men strewn all over the battlefield, unaccounted for and unclaimed, never gets any replacements. Given that the OPFOR kills at least three for every one they lose, it does not take long to run a visiting battalion down to nothing unless they can evacuate their wounded and dead. Thus far the Bulldogs had failed at this basic task. Only the fact of their few number of contacts saved them so far. But like a cancer, the problem was growing.

Bolger went to his AAR that afternoon, given safe passage by the O/Cs to get to Rancho 45. There he heard for the first time of the Iron Rakkasan's agony at a place called LZ Hawk, where Dave Bair's brother Art, his company, a sapper company, and many others became meat for the CLF's grinder. The contested runway had not opened until midday on 15 September, hours behind schedule. The O/Cs mercilessly dissected the air assault debacle near the FLS, offering few comments about the Jetertown NEO.[9] As Bolger would learn, that meant the NEO had been judged a success.

Along with some gauge of the hundreds of dead and wounded absorbed by the reeling 3-187th Infantry, Bolger saw how insignificant his fifty or so casualties seemed by comparison. So this explained why brigade paid him no mind. The battalion would be on its own for a while as the Rakkasans rebuilt, and all of the brigade trains and supplies straggled into the FLS area.

There was other news, not at all good. Captain Willie Utroska and the bulk of Company D would not return soon. En route to Rancho 45, Bolger had already seen Maddog gunships laying abandoned on the road to Carnis, trailing the yellow tape strips that meant "destroyed." He counted six trucks marked with the 1st of the 327th's distinctive insignia, a playing card club painted in sand tone on the rear quarter panel of each Humvee. What caused this? As the AAR proceeded, Bolger learned that Willie and his men had been immolated in the general disaster, shredded by enemy gunners and impaled by a string of minefields.[10] Recovering them and getting them back into the fight might take days.

Still, when the AAR ended, Bolger knew that his battalion was doing pretty well. It had even stopped raining, and the sky yellowed as the late afternoon sun fought through the thinning clouds. As Bolger left the AAR building, a captain from the brigade staff ran up to him: "Your men have found something down at the creek. We think it's the BSP!" The battalion supply point, the CLF's main stockpile of food, water, and ammunition, amounted to the heart of the entire guerrilla sustenance network. Hadn't Lloyd Mills won in JRTC 94-07 by taking the same? Hadn't Jim Dubik said to go for the insurgency's supplies? Bolger smiled. Well, now, this would do. This would do nicely.

With a wave, Col. Jim Donald motioned Dan Bolger and the other commanders over to the hood of the brigade commander's Humvee. Spreading out a map, the colonel nodded his head. "It sounds like we're on 'em, Dan. Press that fight. If we take his BSP, we win this phase."

"We'll get it, sir."

The colonel pointed to Maddox Homestead, four kilometers south and a bit west of Jetertown. "We've gotten orders to raid Maddox tomorrow night, to destroy a logistics facility in this building. With your hooks already in the BSP, this may be all he's got left. Maddox will be your mission; the Rakkasans don't have the combat power. It will take a company-plus, and we know that your Company C hasn't even had a contact yet. With your B and A companies handling that likely BSP, you can fly C down to Maddox, raid, and withdraw. We'll give you five Blackhawks, Apache cover, the usual. The brigade S3 will cover the details."

He did, and he handed Bolger a copy of a map overlay and a brief one-page order. Bolger nodded. *We'll do this too. But first, what about that BSP?*

As Bolger drove back under O/C escort, he again passed the vacant Humvees drooped with yellow tape, the remnants of Willie Utroska's Company D. *Well, we've got the CLF by the short hairs without the Maddogs to help. Stomp on that BSP, take out Maddox, and maybe this great war on the CLF will be all but over.*

The Bulldog TOC crackled with excitement as the commander returned. Bill Phelps, who had given the actual order to Capt. Alfredo Mycue to push across Big Brushy Creek and hit the enemy facility, recounted how it happened. All afternoon the Bushmasters had pressed through the underbrush in a company Ranger file, one man behind the other, swatting flies as the rain decreased and the heat rose. And then the point man found a hidden trail, black mud, full of fresh tire tracks, hundreds of footprints, broken vegetation, all of it leading to a creek crossing. Next they heard motors, generators or trucks, running on the other side of the water. And, with the commander still gone at the AAR, Bill Phelps gave the order, the same aggressive order that Bolger himself would surely have given. Without hesitation Mycue's men deployed, forded the muddy creek, and plunged into the fight.

The shooting went on for two hours, into the early evening. As Bolger and a revived Jim Laufenburg listened on the radios at the TOC, and Bill Phelps crafted a plan to raid Maddox, Alfredo Mycue and his Bushmasters worked their way through the BSP site. The battle went very well, an impression confirmed by Capt. Chris Forbes of Company C, who waited on the east side of the creekbed to assist in carrying out casualties.

It was a straight-on knife-fight, with very little subtlety. The rifle company achieved complete surprise. Led by Sergeant First Class Lipke, another veteran of Jim Dubik's 5-14th Infantry, Mycue's 2d Platoon broke out of the bushes along the water and laid down a base of fire. Then 3d Platoon, under Sfc. David A. Anderson, swung wide right and flanked the ragged CLF defense line. It took some time, but the outcome was never in question.

In the direct-fire exchange, the Bushmasters took out twelve hostiles. Although the vehicles got away, Company B captured three lightly wounded guerrillas who confirmed that, indeed, the Americans had found the rebel BSP. Enemy rifle shots claimed a few Bushmasters, with ten more wounded and killed as they tried to search the overgrown area and struck booby traps and mines. Even in the gloom, despite the trip wires and live mines, Alfredo Mycue's NCOs identified plenty of supplies: ammunition crates, water jugs, meals, all neatly stacked under camouflaging leaves and branches. A typical BSP contains hundreds of cases of meals ready to eat (MREs), hundreds of 82mm rounds, hundreds of mines, and lots more, most of it underground.[11] By daybreak, a better sweep could be made to dig around and find all of this stuff. There was no rush, was there? The company had done enough for one day already. Cleaning up casualties came first.

In a more open area, the battalion may have sent in choppers to bring out those wounded and killed. This area lacked clearings, and contained too many big trees to allow for cutting; the environmentalists might object. So any movement went overland, and by foot, as even small trucks could not pass freely over the creek. To reach Company B from the east, to deliver supplies or remove the injured, the only real option involved walking. That should have raised some neck hairs, especially if something happened to prohibit the bulk of Mycue's force from walking back to the near shore. Something like mass casualties, for example—which promised to get ugly. But nobody conjured such hideous thoughts on that night of glory and triumph.

Company C spent the rest of the night carrying Bushmaster casualties, and the three guerrilla prisoners, across the sloppy Big Brushy ford.[12] The only comfort in this backbreaking labor came from knowing that the next night Cold Steel would get a chance to take out the CLF site at Maddox Homestead. After hours of struggling, the men finally quit carrying their partners away, leaving a few dead with Company B across the water, to be picked up by Jimmy Williams's Support Platoon supply run the next day.

At first light on 17 September, Chris Forbes's Company C began walking east, heading for the battalion landing zone to stage for the

Maddox raid. They were about a third of the way when the ob-
server/controllers froze all action across the mythical land of
Cortina. They called this "Pausex," a pause in the exercise, a chance
to do some quick AARs for the squads and platoons before sleep loss,
rain, and sweat blurred all the experiences together. It marked the
middle of the search and attack phase of JRTC 94-10. By all measures,
the Bulldogs were winning.

The great Chinese commander and military sage Sun-tzu wrote:

> Know the enemy and know yourself; in a hundred battles you
> will never be in peril. When you are ignorant of the enemy but
> know yourself, your chances of winning and losing are equal.
> If ignorant of both the enemy and yourself, you are certain in
> every battle to be in peril. Such people are called "mad bandits."
> What can they expect if not defeat? [13]

Dan Bolger knew the words of Sun-tzu, and respected them. If the
battalion commander could be said to have particular regard for any
military theorist, it would be Master Sun. Like his western equivalent,
the Prussian Carl von Clausewitz, Sun-tzu offers explanation, not simple description, and, thankfully, almost no prescription. As with his
Prussian counterpart, Sun-tzu also drew on plenty of practical experience to underscore his writings. All that having been said, even
as they appeared to be marching to triumph, Bolger and his Bulldogs were again proving the wisdom of Sun-tzu's pithy and justly
famed observation. They did not really know themselves. They did
not really know the enemy. And consequently, this game but ignorant bunch of "mad bandits" faced peril indeed.

The misapprehension of self manifested itself in three areas: security all around, service support, and strength for combat, in that
order. Each of these placed a crippling burden on the battalion.
None could be blamed on anyone but Dan Bolger and his chain of
command. You could offer valid reasons why each problem existed,
but in the end, these were but excuses, and weak ones to boot.

Security meant keeping watch in all directions, and frankly,
whether mounted or dismounted, the Bulldogs did not do this.[14] To
move tactically, you must place out-point, flank, and rear guards, with

radios to give early warning and weapons to hold off marauders. Instead, 1-327th forces plodded in strict columns, all eyes fixed to the front. Often the men lapsed into a Ranger file, one man behind the other, literally looking like baby ducks following the mama. Perhaps the great Fort Campbell live-fire ranges encouraged this frontal fixation, since all live rounds had to go into the downrange impact area, and turning around to shoot a target would get pretty hairy. Maybe the emphasis on air assaults into the teeth of an objective, as in the Jetertown NEO, discouraged work on long ground movements. In any case, the Bulldogs proved lethal within their formation's frontal 60-degree arc, and in real trouble around the other 300 degrees, the portion favored by the well-drilled CLF.

This same weakness hurt the platoons as they tried to maneuver under fire. The men lacked true battle drills to act on contact.[15] Again, home station training, heavily laden with live-fire exercises, exacerbated this tendency. On the range one could merely leapfrog along, with one group shooting while neighbors alongside inched forward. The fixed targets always obediently remained to the front.

Real enemies do not so oblige. A big bold flank cures that. When you make contact, the team hit shoots back, and the rest move out on a 90-degree turn that compels a bad guy to fight two ways at once. If tangling with the CLF, your bold flankers might hit a hostile team trying to do likewise. Yet, conditioned by the one-way shooting of the live-fire ranges, the Bulldogs did not understand or apply these simple tactics. Instead, they fought straight ahead, advancing fire teams and squads side by side. The guerrillas merely sidestepped, slipped down the flanks, and tore into the immobilized U.S. column.

If not stopped by cavorting CLF gunmen, columns also ground down due to nonexistent service support. A finger pointed toward aviation—briefed well at an operation order—but the fact remained that an air assault infantry battalion owned exactly zero helicopters, and should never count solely on help from above. Medical evacuation and resupply both needed a lot of work. Neither functioned in any meaningful sense.

In the battalion area, medevac failed, with some 50 percent of wounded dying before removal.[16] Even the dead did not leave—units lost track of bodies, as in the mined vehicles, and the overmatched

S1 officer had nary a clue as to what the actual status of each unit might be. It seemed like administrative clutter, but that clutter built up like sludge in the gearbox, and with each unreplaced loss, the battalion moved closer to ineffectiveness and extinction.

Resupply collapsed also, largely because, like medevac, no ground measures really worked. Without any mine-clearing capacity (still lots of demolitions on hand but no fuses), the major roads belonged to the CLF. The battalion might clear a route, but that would require a battalion-scale effort, and probably a lot of engineer plows and line-charge projectors that were not available. Considering all of Polk's swamps and creeks, some main roads had to be used, and the Bull-dogs could not break the mine barriers at these choke points. For example, the battalion dared not move a ground column north to the brigade trains, and Capt. Ronz Sarvis's supply site, without risking major losses to mines.

None of this had been forecast, so remedies had not been developed or rehearsed.[17] True, the battalion had plenty of vehicles—a good thing, given the gruesome attrition rate. Nobody figured out how best to use them, or how to move them with the principal road arteries denied. The pre-JRTC plan rested on Company D, but with that outfit mostly a memory, the battalion resorted to hoping 1st Lt. Jimmy Williams could crash cross-country to find beleaguered platoons and companies. Still, it seemed every time a truck rolled, it hit a minefield. Worse, because minefields often went unreported, and tracking minefields was not a priority in the battalion TOC, the same minefields claimed multiple victims.[18]

The resupply breakdown weighed especially hard on the troops in the rifle squads, because Dan Bolger insisted on stripping them down to bare essentials. This went against the usual light-fighter ethos, often seen in Vietnam, of a heavy rucksack. Bolger knew, as S.L.A. Marshall showed five decades earlier, that a heavily laden soldier may be a good porter, but he is no rifleman.[19] So most of Bolger's line forces carried only their fighting harness and weapons, a slim load indeed, with ammunition enough to get through a single firefight and a meager two quarts of water. Supposedly, the supply trains would keep the lean troopers refurbished.

As a slight hedge, and to carry a few other items like soap, shaving gear, night sights, cleaning kits, and more water, one more bag was permitted. Drawing again on Dubik's 5-14th Infantry model, the Bulldogs carried a single light backpack per four-man fire team, a so-called "team ruck." Men intended to trade this off at routine intervals, sharing the pain. This sounded like a fine idea.

In fact, as they do with any bag provided, the soldiers filled the team rucksacks to the brim with "must have" items. The team rucks thus slowed every formation as much as if every man had a bulging backpack, since no fire team could afford to outrun its extra ammunition, water, batteries, and night sights, not to mention outrunning a panting, overheated buddy. Team rucks seemed to be a good solution, but in fact offered a cure as bad as the original malady.

When the air resupply avenue never opened, the far-flung rifle squads soon found themselves nibbling one MRE a day and, contrary to orders, drinking local water with iodine purifier tablets. Many Bulldog soldiers, especially the sergeants, cursed their smart-ass battalion commander for imposing team rucks. "Big enough to slow us down but too small to keep us supplied," said Sergeant First Class Lipke, who had not liked them in Dubik's battalion either.

The losses caused by poor security and compounded by weak logistics, especially the lack of reliable transportation, fell very heavily on the battalion. Understrength at Campbell, overly generous in excusing troubled soldiers from the deployment, hounded by significant brigade-imposed detachments, the battalion endured one more hurtful cut, this one caused by the JRTC live-fire program. The Polk O/Cs ran a fine platoon-level live-fire scenario, obviously separate from the ongoing MILES war. But to carry out these nifty iterations, platoons had to depart the game box and go to distant shooting ranges, about a two-day distraction. As the schedule panned out, 1st of the 327th sent four platoons through these tough lanes. One, from Company B, occurred while the battalion waited at England Air Park, concluding days prior to the NEO. But the other three runs came now, while the battalion scraped for every trigger-puller it could find. Shrunken Company A gave up its 2d Platoon, accompanied by the battalion 81mm mortar platoon. Company C would cough up its 3d Platoon two days later, then its 1st platoon two days after that. Dan Bolger enjoyed the option to have done all four of these live fires

Soldier's Load—A Comparison

Typical JRTC Rotational Unit		TF 1-327 Infantry JRTC 94-10		TF 1-327 Infantry JRTC 95-07		CLF Guerrilla	
Fighting Load		**Fighting Load**		**Fighting Load**		**Fighting Load**	
uniform/boots	7.1	uniform/boots	7.1	uniform/boots	7.1	uniform/boots	7.1
helmet	3.4	helmet	3.4	helmet	3.4	boonie cap	0.5
rifle	8.0	rifle	8.0	rifle	8.0	rifle	8.0
bayonet	1.3	bayonet	1.3	bayonet	1.3	bayonet	1.3
web gear	1.6	web gear	1.6	web gear	1.6	web gear	1.6
canteen 1qt. (2)	5.6	canteen 1qt. (2)	5.6	canteen 1qt. (2)	5.6	canteen 1qt. (2)	5.6
ammunition	7.0	ammunition	7.0	ammunition	7.0	ammunition	7.0
grenades (2)	2.0	grenades (2)	2.0	grenades (2)	2.0	grenades (2)	2.0
MILES	5.0	MILES	5.0	MILES	5.0	MILES	5.0
gas mask	3.0	E-tool	2.5	E-tool/NVG	2.5		
TOTAL	**44.0**	**TOTAL**	**43.5**	**TOTAL**	**43.5**	**TOTAL**	**38.1**
Rucksack		**Team Ruck**		**Buttpack**		**Buttpack**	
pack/frame	6.3	pack/frame	6.3	pack	0.8	pack	0.8
ponchos (2)	1.3	ponchos (2)	1.3	poncho	1.3	poncho	1.3
liner, poncho	1.6	liner, pch. (2)	3.2	liner, pch.	1.6	liner, pch.	1.6
canteen, 2 qt.	4.8	canteen, 2 qt.	4.8				
MRE (2)	2.6	MRE (4)	5.2	MRE	1.3	MRE	1.3
toilet kit	1.0	toilet kit (4)	4.0	toilet kit	1.0	toilet kit	1.0
towel	0.2	towel (4)	0.8	towel	0.2	towel	0.2
weapon kit	1.1	weapon kit (2)	2.2	weapon kit	1.1	weapon kit	1.1
socks (4)	0.8	socks (8)	1.6	socks (2)	0.4	socks (2)	0.4
NVG	2.5	NVG (2)	5.0				
E-tool	2.5	binoculars	4.5				
ammunition	5.0						
claymore	3.5						
smoke gren. (2)	2.6						
flares (2)	3.0						
T-shirt	0.1						
rain gear	2.5						
galoshes	2.0						
TOTAL	**43.4**	**TOTAL**	**38.9**	**TOTAL**	**7.7**	**TOTAL**	**7.7**
LOAD	**87.4**	**LOAD**	**82.4**	**LOAD**	**51.2**	**TOTAL**	**45.8**

Terms: boonie cap: a floppy bush hat; E-tool: entrenching tool, a little collapsible shovel; gren.: grenade; MRE: meal ready-to-eat, a U.S. Army field ration; NVG: night-vision goggles; qt.: quart, canteen sizes include one- and two-quart types; web gear: the shoulder harness and pistol belt used to carry canteens, ammunition magazines, and other items.

1. All weights are shown in pounds. The soldier depicted is a rifleman. For other duty positions, consider these weights: M16A2 rifle with M203 grenade launcher, 8.9 pounds; M-49 squad automatic weapon, 16.9 pounds; M60 machine gun, 23 pounds; AN/PRC-119 radio, 22 pounds.
2. Team rucks carry items for four men. Only one in four carries this weight, which can be traded off to share the burden.
3. During rotation 95-07, soldiers carried either the E-tool or NVGs, not both.

before the force-on-force MILES war. He chose to stick with whatever brigade and JRTC proposed. Thus the battalion would fight without a few platoons during the second half of search and attack operations.[20] It probably wouldn't matter, thought Bolger smugly. Of course it would, and did.

Bad as all of this self-inflicted damage could be, the inability to grasp the CLF's nature eventually cost the battalion much more heavily. The search and attack fight above all revolves around finding an opponent who declines to be found. Cortinian civilian role-players in Jetertown knew where the CLF hid; some were, in truth, CLF agents from the Leesville Urban Group. But Bolger and his boys abandoned this one certain intelligence source and elected to go hunting instead, looking for folks who usually get found when they want to be seen. Most of the 1st of the 327th's finding so far had been by making contact and getting killed, with each scrape drawing the increasingly weaker U.S. force closer and closer to the CLF's creek bottom hideout.

The battalion found no CLF mortars or SA-14s, and only scattered shooters. If the BSP was really so important, would the enemy surrender it so easily? That question should have been asked. It was not.

Instead, slaves to a preconceived idea of where to go, the Bulldogs descended to a pretty obvious place to look for what they believed should have been there. Mesmerized by what Alfredo Mycue ruefully called "the Easter egg hunt" for the BSP and its similar, lesser analogues (CSP, STP, guerrilla battalion CP), Bolger and company forgot that the CLF does not really need its supplies or fixed sites. After all, the People's Democratic Republic of Atlantica stood poised to invade within days of the initial U.S. entry. True, Jim Dubik and Lloyd Mills had triumphed by hitting CLF supply bases—or so they thought. In truth, they had succeeded by killing CLF soldiers. The logistics caches just happened to be where the fights occurred.

Was the battalion ready for those fights? No. To watch Company B, it looked like simply finding the BSP equaled victory. After all, Company C pulled out, heading to the next mission. The whole BSP needed only a mop-up, some demolition work, and then on to other issues.

And if the CLF behaved otherwise, well, without sound security techniques or decent battle drills, Dan Bolger's willing but ill-prepared rifle platoons could not count on winning the big infantry firefights they might bring on. Worse, the 1-327th's suspect logistics system ensured that losses endured in the struggle might never be replaced. In all the flurry to get ready to raid Maddox, the TOC staff neglected to finish the work at the BSP.

Had Bolger truly respected the CLF, he might not have been so cavalier about matters. But so far, the bad guys had not been so tough. They did not even show a consistent capacity to create the usual kill ratio of three U.S. casualties to every dead guerrilla. The 82mm mortars played little part. And now the enemy had been surprised—again—in his own central service support location. Maybe these Tigerland tigers were not all that great after all.

Perhaps it was the lack of sleep, or the heat, or the water shortages that lightened this commander's head. But in all the talk of the great discovery of the BSP, neither Dan Bolger, nor Bill Phelps, nor Dirk Blackdeer in the TOC, nor the smart men up at brigade S2, nor Alfredo Mycue and his Bushmasters on the ground, remarked on a curious fact. Every single cache found so far had been booby-trapped.

Why would insurgents booby-trap their own precious supplies?

The destruction of Company B took about ninety minutes. It began with rifle fire as the Pausex concluded at 1000, and ended with a dozen 82mm mortar rounds stitching across the overrun perimeter that once contained a viable rifle company.[21] The Bushmasters under Alfredo Mycue overstayed their welcome in the BSP, and as usual in this U.S. battalion, neglected to post any security or run any local patrols. So the OPFOR simply drew a noose and, when the cease-fire lifted, pulled hard.

This time enemy troops saw no need to play about with tricky four-man box tactics or baited ambushes. Instead, the CLF swarmed to the kill, closing with three platoons, the whole of the 2d Company, 91st Assault Battalion, all hungry for blood. One of the three hostile platoons actually came up from Maddox Homestead aboard captured 1-327th Humvees. It all happened very fast, according to a well-crafted, well-rehearsed sequence.[22]

The enemy rapidly posted snipers and machine guns on a spit of useful high ground to the south of the engaged Bushmaster circle. The key height looked down on the embattled Company B. Had

Mycue or his men been thinking about elementary security, they would have long ago grabbed that critical overlook. Of course, had they been thinking like that, they would also have done something other than bunch up on a former enemy position and battle site on the wrong side of a nearly impassable waterway. The CLF soldiers grinned wolfishly and prepared to administer a harsh reeducation. Behind the crucial hill, which the Americans soon called "OPFOR Ridge," enemy mortar crews unlimbered, stockpiling rounds for a big shoot.

Within minutes, guerrilla infantry closed tight against the shocked American rifle squads, moving too close to allow easy use of U.S. fire support. When a stunned Alfredo Mycue reported his situation to the TOC, he referred to "wave attacks," and asked for artillery, Apaches, and ground reinforcements. "We have thirty men down," Mycue radioed. "You'd better hurry or don't bother coming."

The battalion commander and Capt. Mike Temple, the fire support officer, shifted priority on all fires to Mycue. Brigade responded quickly, ordering attack aircraft to head south. Naval gunfire and 105mm howitzers began pounding OPFOR Ridge, shooting "danger close," within six hundred meters of the melting Bushmaster perimeter. "Pour it on," ordered the company commander. Around him, his men fell one by one, in the relentless calculus of a JRTC direct-fire contest gone sour: seven Americans for every CLF guerrilla.

A pair of orbiting Apaches streaked toward the surrounded Bushmasters, slowing to bank above the firefight below. The pilots caught one of the empty trucks headed back to Maddox and, with help from a swooping A-10A Thunderbolt II attack jet, destroyed the stolen Humvee. Another A-10A "Warthog" swung in, following an Apache flier's sighting, to chase a white pickup truck into CLF-held Jetertown. The white vehicle carried a mortar; the Apache crew saw it pack up. But the Warthog driver could not shoot into Jetertown for fear of killing civilians. Apaches shot MILES here and there, killing two SA-14 teams and, eventually, an 82mm mortar crew and tube. But all this happened on the periphery, beyond the immediate scene of Company B's crucifixion.

In that main event, the Apaches spun uselessly overhead, unable to distinguish friend from foe in the trees beneath. Mycue called, but the fight had fallen to him and his infantry. Here the company felt the lash of pain, stripe after stripe delivered by a relentless foe. The lack of good security, the careless bunching up, the mistake of all congregating atop the famous BSP, the battalion's error of letting Company B wander out across that damned creek, the battalion commander's mistake of withdrawing Company C for some raid to Maddox (fat chance of that now), the battalion-level carelessness of scheduling at this time a live fire for a Company A platoon and the 81mm mortars (Oh, how they could have helped), the training not done, the common sense not applied—oh, the gall was bitter indeed that hot noon, under a cornflower blue Louisiana sky.

Bolger moved what he could to support the crushed company. He called on Drew Felix for help. The Abu commander responded with dejection. With only a single platoon left and a seeming mountain of leftover casualties, the scouts and his own, and only a one-man jungle trail to move them out to a truck pickup site, Drew Felix would be lucky to avoid Mycue's fate. No joy there. In fact, another slaughter loomed if the CLF figured out how weak Company A had become with the loss of its 2d Platoon to the JRTC Live Fire Branch.

With the Maddox mission certainly down the hole, Bolger turned to what he had left. He countermarched Chris Forbes and his tired, unbloodied Cold Steel men back toward the fatal creek. By pushing hard, unmolested by the CLF who were too busy killing the Bushmasters, Forbes brought his men up by nightfall. An OPFOR squad barred the way, trading gunfire in the dusk. When Company C tried to employ its mortars as the Abus had done, the gunners mistook friends for foes, and killed two and wounded three in a mistaken series of engagements.[23] Forbes backed off.

Only one man survived the destruction of Company B. Somehow, by hiding among the "dead" and then crawling away at twilight, Alfredo Mycue found his way down to the water, across, and into the Cold Steel soldiers' nervous lines. He borrowed Chris Forbes's radio handset to make his report to Bolger and the TOC. As he did, he turned to his fellow company commander. Both of them were sweat-drenched, brush-cut, dust-streaked, and punchy with fatigue.

"We lost it all, man," said Mycue to Forbes. "Over eighty dead and wounded up there. We'll never get them out."

"Battalion will think of something," offered Forbes.

But right now, battalion, in the person of Dan Bolger, could think of only one thing. This round, the search and attack phase, had been irretrievably lost. One smart CLF move, a baited ambush in the best Vo Nguyen Giap style, did the job in less time than it takes to eat a decent lunch. Two rifle companies lay wrecked, one totally blown away. The antiarmor company was gone, save for an overworked trio of gunships. Only Company C, the most fragile of the three rifle units, stood ready to act, and they were physically at their limit after days and nights of trudging back and forth across the swamps and forested hillsides.

With a goodly majority of the battalion dead or missing, Dan Bolger would have to salvage what he could from this one. Do that, or the outfit faced additional failures in the upcoming conventional phases of rotation 94-10. The JRTC would not retrieve the 1-327th Infantry dead, strewn so thick amongst that booby-trapped BSP. No, if they wanted enough strength for the next fight, the Bulldogs must recover their own dead. Given how little the battalion had left to use, Bolger needed to guess right on the first attempt. There would not be another.

The stark truth did not come out until the AAR on 20 September, when the CLF commander proudly described his grand scheme. The 1st of the 327th paid a huge blood debt for nothing. A fake BSP, an absolute phony built strictly for show, lured in and ate Company B, exacting the carnage intended when the guerrilla chieftains cooked it up. The real BSP lay far to the north, in Rakkasan turf. What the Bulldogs banged into looked like a BSP, but turned out to be a snare.

Much later, Bolger saw the OPFOR planning documents that described the ploy. "Brigade commander (Colonel Donald) feels that the BSP is our center of gravity" wrote the CLF staffers weeks before the Always First Brigade arrived in the play box.[24] The colonel wanted to find a BSP. So the bad guys gave him one. Urged on by Jim Donald, the stories of Jim Dubik, and his own desire for a quick, easy win, Dan Bolger fell for it.

The CLF hoped to trap and destroy a company or more in this false BSP. That they did, rather handily, although not without cost. The Bulldogs might be gullible, and tactically inept, but in a head-to-head shootout, their aim proved true enough. Some forty CLF went down executing the mass attack on Company B. On top of previous damage, that about knocked the 2d Company of the 91st Assault Battalion out of the fight. Perhaps two squads, plus an SA-14 team and a single mortar (still aboard that sneaky white pickup in Jetertown), remained in zone.

Momentum, however, once seemingly with the American battalion, now shifted to the Cortinian Liberation Force. Dirk Blackdeer, the S2, foresaw that isolated little Abu Company merited the next CLF blow. "We hurt the enemy badly today," Blackdeer summarized, "but by late tomorrow, and certainly by the nineteenth of September, he will have reinforced." The Bulldogs appeared to have about twenty-four hours to draw themselves together.

Hearing this in the darkened battalion TOC, Dan Bolger gave the orders for the next day. All focus went to recovering the dead waiting in the deception BSP. But getting that done took several preliminary steps, each important. Extract Company C back to the trains (again). Assemble all vehicles in the trains for a run to the south at first light under Capt. Ted Donnelly, the S4, with the purpose of getting as close as possible to Abu's pile of dead to allow for withdrawal. Extract Company A to the trains. Pump all bodies back to brigade for replacements. Await the return of the Company A live-fire platoon; luckily, the Company C element did not have to leave until late on 19 September. Resupply all. Get rest. Make a plan. And hit like a sledgehammer on 19 September, not halting until Alfredo Mycue's abandoned men were redeemed. Perhaps brigade would loan Team Tank to the battalion to strengthen the push.

Nobody really slept much on the muggy night of 17–18 September, not that anyone had slept much before that. In the TOC, feverish plans went forward, looking toward a dawn attack on 19 September. The orderly shift schedule broke down as officers and NCOs of both the day and night groups tried to plan and follow ongoing resupply and ambush activities. The commander slept some each day, but not more than a few hours. Dan Bolger's mind fuzzed somewhat, and he enjoyed lots of company in that department.

In the south, the Abus continued the slow, tortured portage of their dead to the vehicle pickup point to their north. One by one, on poncho litters, over shoulders, or dragged on makeshift travois,

Drew Felix and 1st Sgt. Scott Craig pulled the bodies up through the gnarled, unforgiving underbrush. Nobody dared stop, although all reeled from exhaustion. It is easy to talk about being tough, elite, and "hard," but hardness personified itself that night among the thin ranks of Company A. Without food, out of water, out of everything but discipline and guts, the Abus saved their own.[25] By daybreak, they awaited pickup.

Just north of them, Company C crashed exhausted along the forest trails created by 1st Lt. Jimmy Williams and his drivers over the previous days. At dawn, the Cold Steel men expected to protect the departure of Company A. Then they would leave, once Abu made its pickup time. Like Company A, Chris Forbes and his men were short on water. But they had lots of ammunition, having fired but a few rounds in anger, and a good percentage of those at each other.

Across Big Brushy, the dead were talking, a luxury afforded those killed by MILES and liable to game-play resurrection. In the JRTC universe, dead men left by their unit stayed where they fell, given a single MRE a day and enough water to survive. For a day, that worked, and even seemed a respite after the harsh pace of the previous few days. After two or three or four days, though, the gnawing emptiness, the thirst, and the monotony of laying there waiting and waiting all grew on the men, made them curse their sergeants, their officers, and all the idiots who led them into this infantry Cuisinart, capped by that idiot battalion commander, that Bolger. By the time the Bushmasters finally came out, those who had waited for days thought up a new name for the deception BSP locale. They called it "Hunger Hill."

The next day passed quietly, at least by JRTC standards. The withdrawals happened as decreed, although two precious vehicles fell prey to ambushes on the side trails, and another strayed into mines on the main Jetertown road. This fracas stripped out the S4, Captain Donnelly, killed by rebel gunfire and left behind on the final extraction run. But in general, everything that could get out did get out.

The live-fire platoon came back, and late that night, so did many of the Company A and Scout Platoon casualties, and even the S5, 1st

Lt. Matt Bounds, and his Team Golf specialists. That evening, all the senior leadership gathered in the stifling TOC tents for an order, the aim clear to all: retrieve the Bushmaster dead.

Bolger himself designed the plan, simple in the extreme. Commencing 0615, advancing from key terrain to key terrain with two companies abreast, the battalion endeavored to clear the road to Jetertown, then continue down the route and cross the Big Brushy Creek road bridge, which the map showed as the only certain place to bring vehicles across the stream. Mycue, Forbes, and Felix believed, and convoy master 1st Lt. Jimmy Williams concurred, that Humvees stood no chance of transiting the creekbed where the Bushmaster infantry originally stepped through into Never Never Land. So, this time, the battalion wanted the bridge, the sure bet to get over the obstacle and then secure the dead piled in the false BSP.

The main effort featured Cold Steel (three platoons) to the north and west, and Abu (two platoons plus a handful of scouts) in support to the south and east. A preplanned artillery barrage would clean off each piece of high ground as the battalion advanced. This time, Dan Bolger and his Tac CP readied themselves to go every step of the way, rifles in hand. Just that morning the S3, Bill Phelps, capped a cheeky CLF sniper outside the TOC. The road to Jetertown offered ample chance for more of the same.

Behind the rifle companies and the battalion commander's party, Captain Mycue intended to move a truck group, scraped together from the trains and command post, and equipped with the huge load of demolitions brought in with the ground convoy on that rainy night—brigade having finally flown in some detonators. This column included fourteen Bushmasters, men lucky enough to have been killed at the initial discovery of the BSP, pulled out by Company C the first night, and churned through the replacement cycle. These folks received a crash course in blowing up mines, and prepared to function as ersatz sappers to clear the roadway down to their buddies languishing on Hunger Hill.

If brigade furnished tanks, continuous Apache cover, and real engineers, this kind of pile-driver approach might have succeeded. Brigade chose not to offer tanks, Apaches, or anything else. This meant that the battalion relied exclusively on a frontal attack by foot infantry. It suggested all the finesse and innovation of Pickett's Charge, and turned out about the same way.

Things kicked off on time, with Bolger and his Tac team accompanying Capt. Chris Forbes. Company C marched to the north of the small trail and Company A to the south.[26] Both headed west, focused on the mined intersection of the road to Jetertown. That was the first stop on the long, contested way to Hunger Hill and the salvation of the lost Bushmaster soldiers. Preparatory U.S. artillery pummeled the high ground overlooking the first road barrier, dull booms crashing unseen on the distant hummocks.

Moving like zombies, the Cold Steel rifle platoons slogged on toward where the shells impacted. It took an hour to move some eight hundred meters through a small tree stand and then across an open meadow. Soldiers strung out in a long, listless Ranger file, looking like patrons waiting to see the Grateful Dead. Of course, these riflemen would soon become the dead, and not at all grateful, if they persisted in crossing field and stream in that nonformation, that row of shuffling ducks. One CLF sniper, or a few mortar rounds, and Company C flirted with crippling losses.

Watching this, Bolger grew hot under the collar, and accosted Chris Forbes. As dazed as his men, the captain turned to meet his commander. Bolger noticed that the Cold Steel leader still wore his night-vision goggles, although the sun had been up for an hour or so. The lieutenant colonel, not all that much more coherent himself, shook Chris Forbes by the shoulders and got right in his face. "Get these people spread out now," snarled the older officer. Forbes nodded, and began to issue guidance over the company radio net. Slowly, painfully, the company shook out into a looser column.

Then small arms fire started, echoing from the south. Drew Felix called Bolger, reporting casualties. Bolger barely acknowledged the call before he heard Company C report identifying the first minefield, right at the Jetertown road junction. As Chris Forbes moved to secure the area and bring up Mycue's amateur engineers for road clearance, the Abus began taking an 82mm pounding. Felix called for friendly artillery on suspected enemy lookouts in the distance. It came promptly, but the men struck turned out to be a misoriented group of Marine Corps naval gunfire forward observers.[27] The whole clash cost Company A three dead and thirteen wounded. In return, two CLF fell, an awful exchange rate.

Meanwhile, as Captain Felix and 1st Sgt. Craig executed yet another strenuous medevac process with Company A, Captain Mycue urged forward his ground convoy. His small bunch of Bushmasters dismounted to begin priming the mines strewn about on the brown dirt road. At the same time, a rusty brown sedan rolled up from the north, halting at the edge of the minefield. Three civilians got out, one of them the mayor of Jetertown. He obviously picked a hell of a morning to go for a drive.

A shrewd CLF observer chose this point to unleash six 82mm mortar rounds squarely on the intersection. The unlucky mayor died instantly, as did four other Cold Steel troops. Another three lay wounded. Everyone went to ground, and nobody wanted to chance another hail of mortar shells by returning to the roadway to play with the explosive packages. At only 0939, the CLF effectively stalled the Bulldog attack before it even got started.

Chris Forbes hesitated, uncertain. One of his squad leaders, SSgt. Darren Lewis, did not. He and his squad lay in an erosion ditch just off the roadside, not far from Dan Bolger and the tactical command post men. Unable to see the hostile outpost directing the mortar fire, Lewis made a quick survey of likely terrain. A bald hill to the immediate south offered the likely vantage point. "He's up there," Lewis told Bolger. "Go get him," replied the lieutenant colonel.

This took about twenty minutes, while Abu continued to backhaul casualties and the rest of Company C did the same, or crouched and sprawled in a sloppy perimeter around the minefield. The resumption of the battalion advance waited on Staff Sergeant Lewis. That NCO and his squad reached their intended mark. They found nothing, but their smart maneuver drove off the CLF. With this key terrain held, Chris Forbes waved up Mycue's men to again begin placing demolitions.

This went on for about fifteen minutes. Then, unannounced, three nonmilitary vehicles rolled up slowly from the north, lights on. With a tan civilian ambulance in the lead, a beat-up silver van behind, and a gray stake-and-platform truck bringing up the rear, the group crowded up, bumper to bumper, and braked. Horns sounded.

This drew the attention of SSgt. Jorge Cabacar of Company B, whose pickup team ensured local security for the men trying to string explosives atop the constellation of land mines adorning the uneven dirt thoroughfare. Cabacar went to the ambulance and heard an angry and distractingly attractive young blond woman announce that this was a World Vision humanitarian relief shipment destined for Jetertown. Told that the way was not clear, the woman insisted on proceeding anyway. The two men on the back of the stake-and-platform truck began gesticulating wildly. The blond woman gunned her ambulance's engine and shifted forward. Cabacar's riflemen and SAW gunners leveled their weapons.

Crack! Crack! Two shots rang out. Bolger, who had watched and heard all of this transpire from the shelter of a nearby thicket, figured his men had just killed a civilian. He should have had more faith in all of that RAMP training.

Cabacar's partner shot all right, but not at any human. Rather he popped holes through the front pair of ambulance tires, a wonderfully precise reaction that prevented forward motion and yet did not slay innocents. The O/Cs played the technique as if it really happened, and the civilians screamed and cursed but remained in place. Upon hearing the gunfire, 1st Lt. Matt Bounds and his Team Golf civil affairs troops ran up to the road.[28] After some testy negotiation, the three trucks backed away and headed north, out of zone. Though the rest of the operation steadily accumulated all manner of pain and friction, this part went right.

The departure of the World Vision folks spurred Captain Mycue's men to complete fusing their simulated C4 explosive packs. At 1030 they blew the minefield. For the first time since the Bulldogs arrived in the area, this part of the way to Jetertown stood free of mines. Of course, nobody from Cold Steel or Abu located the mine cache likely to be within three hundred meters of the road, but that would surely come, sooner or later. At this rate of clearance, though, the battalion's arrival at Hunger Hill could well take weeks.

As it turned out, even the long-awaited explosive sweep did not do the job. When Mycue pushed his lead Maddog gunship through the cleared lane, it blew up anyway, as did two cargo Humvees just behind, with two dead and one wounded thrown in as well. When

Bolger, Forbes, Mycue, Cabacar, and all others protested, the O/C gave a Cheshire cat grin and said: "It was a deep-buried magnetic incidence mine."[29] *God help us,* thought Bolger. *How can we find those damn things?*

It took three more hours to clear a lane by pushing wreckage, which sprung another of those magic deep-buried items. During this period, Capt. Chris Forbes and his men fanned out to find the hidden mine stockpile, wandering all over in the heat of another beautifully clear day. The searches miscarried. During the effort, Forbes lost communications with his ineffectual 3d Platoon. When the road finally seemed open, Bolger ordered the company to proceed south. Having seen enough fratricide already, still slowly evacuating his own casualties and wrecked trucks, Forbes showed no enthusiasm to renew the attack. He asked for another half hour.

That did it for the battalion commander. The clock read 1332, most of the day was gone, and the force was not even in Jetertown, that happy hellhole merely the midpoint of this grim sojourn. Just then a sniper opened up on one of the meandering Cold Steel squads. Now they might never move. With Company C hopelessly stymied, largely through the unit's own dearth of drive, Bolger angrily crossed the road under fire to join with the remaining Abu force. "Abu is now the main effort," directed Bolger with pique. Thus Drew Felix and his thrity or so effectives became the spearhead for the continuing grind to the south.

At this point, Bolger might have weighed his dwindling manpower and elected to declare "enough." So far, the battalion still could evacuate its present casualties, and had done so. Without finding the hidden mine cache serving the barrier at the intersection, Bolger knew that the CLF waited to reseed that lethal field. To plunge south without finishing business here begged trouble. Frustrated, Bolger went anyway.

Matt Bounds warned that the CLF owned Jetertown, and so the afternoon became even more bloody, stupidly so. The Abus met death near the village hog pen, after a gruesome house-to-house fight that accomplished nothing and left another pocket of abandoned dead out of reach of the 1st of the 327th Infantry. Twenty wounded bled to death unattended. The wreckage of Abu disengaged and returned to the battalion trains. Drew Felix and his boys were finished. They killed two more CLF, for all that mattered.

As for Company C, the opponent's remaining 82mm mortar, plunking away from the southern outskirts of Jetertown, took out the blundering 3d Platoon, plus part of 2d and the company mortars. Chris Forbes and his men lost another forty bodies without slaying a single hostile. Dumped just northwest of the church in a hollow, these unfortunates, too, remained behind when the wretched pieces of Company C withdrew back to the vicinity of the battalion trains. Jetertown groaned under firm CLF authority. The road south stayed closed.

Bolger experienced every bit of this in person, M16A2 barking while he and the Tac officers fought as riflemen, jumping and rolling to save their own skins. Bolger himself killed two OPFOR by vectoring in an Apache helicopter, the only one that appeared that day. Ominously, the CLF twosome had already staked out the same minefield breached at such cost earlier that day. Thanks to the Apache, the shards of the battalion task force escaped further punishment. With his Tac buddies, Dan Bolger escorted in a few Bushmaster walking wounded. The commander himself braced Sgt. Thomas Hitchens, assessed as enduring a leg wound. When Bolger got back to the TOC, the sun was just going down. With it slipped away the battalion's last opportunity to reclaim matters in zone.

To make a final mockery of the entire futile escapade, the CLF had long before dismantled the bridge that allowed vehicular traffic from Jetertown to pass over Big Brushy Creek. Even if, by sheer dumb luck, the 1st of the 327th made it that far, they could never have brought their Humvees any closer than the east side of the muddy stream. Jimmy Williams was doing that much days ago. So it goes when you rely on map sheets alone, by guess and by God. That ground out there tends to do its own thing, especially when helped along by the opposing side.

The foolhardy thrust to Jetertown truly finished the battalion, grinding it down to the last nub. With the thirty or so effectives left, the troops might be able to defend the trains. Tomorrow morning marked the end of this search and attack phase, another cease-fire, an AAR period, and curtains for the Bulldogs. With hundreds of dead bodies planted on Hunger Hill and in and around Jetertown, the battalion commander expected JRTC to impose one of two options, equally unpalatable. First, the O/Cs could let things ride, and let the battalion keep flailing away, fighting future fights shorthanded until recovery occurred, if it ever did. Alternatively, and even worse, the O/Cs might simply rejuvenate all of the missing casualties. They did that now and then, for National Guard battalions, for hopeless basket cases, for losers. Bolger wanted to solve this mess himself. But he did not know how.

Brigade saved the Bulldogs, aided by the wisdom of Cmd. Sgt. Maj. Mark Ripka. The battalion needed a miracle, a *deus ex machina* to set all things right. They got the next best thing—Capt. J. D. Compeggi and his paratroopers of Team Tank, Company D of the 3-73d Armor. Cut loose at last by Colonel Donald, the pugnacious Compeggi thundered south cross-country. His mission, of course, revolved around pulling out the Bulldog dead, and Compeggi's guys included the engineers and equipment to bust holes in mined roads. The tanks pulled into the 1-327th trains around 2100, an undeniably welcome sight.

Going though Jetertown again, of course, looked pretty scary even with Sheridan light tanks. Here the battalion's senior NCO offered the key insight that made it all work. Mark Ripka, already killed once and recycled, wounded once and treated, bothered to check a map. He noticed a trail not yet used in all the frontal battering to date.

"Why not go straight across, due west? Then turn south," he suggested. "Approach the Company B perimeter from the west. After we do that, then punch down to Jetertown and get out today's losses." It made sense, an indirect approach. The S2, Captain Blackdeer, estimated that the few CLF still in zone would likely be covering Jetertown. They must be exhausted too. A fast night run appeared like a good bet.

Matt Bounds, the S5, asked to accompany Compeggi's mission of mercy. He wanted to see if he could get a truce in Jetertown, a suggestion passed to him by a helpful civil affairs O/C. It seemed worth a try. Bolger assented.

After some hasty planning in the crowded, gamey TOC tents, Compeggi's column of tanks, with the Bulldogs' string of Humvees interspersed, pushed out at 2300. Excepting two Cold Steel sentries mistakenly wounded by tank main-gun fire as the force exited friendly lines, the mission ran superbly.[30] Unopposed, the convoy passed over the stream on this novel route, and reached Hunger Hill about an hour after midnight. The airborne tankers and the infantrymen in the Humvees scrambled into the underbrush. Supervised by Command Sergeant Major Ripka and the tireless Alfredo Mycue, the men physically cleaned off Hunger Hill, carrying the bodies down the wooded slope one after another, a human conveyor belt of simulated woe. It took hours, but by daybreak big J. D. Compeggi roared into the battalion's LZ, bearing with him every casualty from the bogus BSP.

The landing zone sprang alive at daybreak. As Compeggi arrived, two Chinooks churned brown dust, waiting on the ground to pick up the precious cargo outbound. Brigade pumped Chinooks and Blackhawks into the battalion LZ right up until the box froze at 0900, beginning the change of mission and AAR procedures. In this way, if no other, the battalion did business well. They fought for and brought back their own buddies, like Screaming Eagles, like disciplined soldiers, like Americans—like men.

This moral victory offered little solace to the bone-weary Bulldogs. To take out 74 members of the CLF, the battalion sustained 143 dead and 285 wounded, 118 of whom died untreated. The kill ratio came to a mediocre 5.7 Americans lost for each guerrilla bagged, not embarrassing, but nothing to inspire bragging, either. Compared to other JRTC performances, at least the battalion killed a lot of CLF.

But how they paid for this thin achievement! The butcher's balance sheet appalled. A battalion with 388 men lost 428, a horrific 110 percent rate of loss.[31] Just as heartbreaking, the CLF still dominated the region around Jetertown. The Bulldogs hunted the tigers, found them, and bled for it, all for nothing.

As was his style, Dan Bolger took full responsibility for the numbing catastrophe. Tired, begrimed, outfoxed and outfought, Bolger stood up and faced his crestfallen leaders as O/Cs concluded the sobering battalion AAR. Echoing the words of Robert E. Lee at Gettysburg, Bolger spoke clearly: "It is all my fault."[32] Indeed it was.

Notes

The epigraph comes from Marty Kufus, "When Private Hendrix Kissed the Sky," *Command* (November–December 1989), 54–56. Jimi Hendrix served in the 101st Airborne Division from 1960 to 1962, departing on a medical discharge due to injuries incurred during a parachute jump. Many Hendrix biographers, including Kufus, believe the airborne experience deeply influenced the musician. For more on Hendrix as a Screaming Eagle, see Michael Herr, *Dispatches* (New York: Avon Books, 1978), 38, 181.

1. U.S., Department of the Army, Headquarters, Joint Readiness Training Center, "Situation Template vs. Fire Support," *1-327 IN Rotation 94-10 LIC AAR* (Ft. Polk, La.: HQ, JRTC, 20 September 1994), 34.

2. Lt. Col. Lloyd W. Mills, USA, *JRTC 94-07: A Commander's Perspective* (Ft. Campbell, Ky.: HQ, 3d Battalion, 327th Infantry Regiment, 24 June 1994), 1–2.

3. U.S., Department of the Army, *FM 7-20: The Infantry Battalion* (Washington, D.C.: U.S. Govt. Printing Office, 6 April 1992), 3-19 to 3-22.

4. U.S., Department of the Army, 101st Airborne Division (Air Assault), *Air Assault Battle Note #18: Search and Attack Operations* (Ft. Campbell, Ky.: HQ, 101st Airborne Division [Air Assault], 17 February 1993), B-1 and C-1.

5. Paddy Griffith, *Forward into Battle* (Chichester, U.K.: Antony Bird Publications, Ltd., 1981), 125. Griffith served on the faculty at the Royal Military Academy, Sandhurst.

6. HQ, JRTC, "Combat Power at ISB," *1-327 IN Rotation 94-10 LIC AAR*, 22.

7. U.S., Department of the Army, Headquarters, Joint Readiness Training Center, "Company A," *1-327 IN Rotation 94-10 Pausex AAR* (Ft. Polk, La.: HQ, JRTC, 17 September 1994), 9.

8. Malcom McConnell, "Betrayal in Somalia," *Reader's Digest* (April 1994), 65–67.

9. U.S., 9 Department of the Army, Headquarters, Joint Readiness

Training Center, *1st Brigade, 101st Airborne Division (AASLT) Rotation 94-10, First AAR* (Ft. Polk, La.: HQ, JRTC, 16 September 1994), 8–9, 16, 37.

10. HQ, JRTC, "1-327 Minefield BDA" and "Company D," *1-327 IN Rotation 94-10 Pausex AAR*, 7, 10.

11. U.S., Department of the Army, Headquarters, 1st Brigade, 101st Airborne Division (Air Assault), *JRTC Handbook* (Ft. Campbell, Ky.: HQ, 1st Brigade, 101st Airborne Division [Air Assault], 1995), 23.

12. HQ, JRTC, "Battle for the STP 16 Sep 94," *1-327 IN Rotation 94-10 LIC AAR*, 30.

13. Sun-tzu, *The Art of War*, trans. Brig. Gen. Samuel Griffith, USMC, ret. (London: Oxford University Press, 1963), 84.

14. U.S., Department of the Army, Headquarters, Joint Readiness Training Center, *Take Home Package Training After-Action Report: 101st Airborne Division, 1st Bn 327th INF Rotation 94-10* (Ft. Polk, La.: HQ, JRTC, 26 September 1994), 25-B, 26-B, 43-B, 44-B.

15. Ibid., 2-B.

16. HQ, JRTC, "Medical Platoon," *1-327 IN Rotation 94-10 Pausex AAR*, 8.

17. HQ, JRTC, *Take Home Package 1-327 INF Rotation 94-10*, 2-B to 3-B.

18. HQ, "Minefield Map," JRTC, *1-327 IN Rotation 94-10 LIC AAR*, 44.

19. The classic study of all this is Col. S.L.A. Marshall, USAR, *The Soldier's Load and the Mobility of a Nation* (Arlington, Va.: Association of the U.S. Army, 1950; reprint ed., Quantico, Va.; Marine Corps Association, 1980), 70, 72. Marshall argued that a ground soldier's load should not ever exceed a third of his body weight.

20. U.S., Department of the Army, Headquarters, 1st Battalion, 327th Infantry Regiment, *TF 1-327 After-Action Report, JRTC 94-10* (Ft. Campbell, Ky.: HQ, 1st Battalion, 327th Infantry Regiment, 17 October 1994), 3.

21. HQ, JRTC, "Battle for the STP 17 Sep 94," *1-327 IN Rotation 94-10 LIC AAR*, 31.

22. HQ, JRTC, "Deception BSP," *1-327 IN Rotation 94-10 LIC AAR*, 12.

23. HQ, JRTC, "Fratricide," *1-327 IN Rotation 94-10 LIC AAR*, 64.

24. U.S., Department of the Army, Headquarters, 1st Battalion, 509th Parachute Infantry Regiment, "Deception Operations," *JRTC 94-10 OPFOR Laydown* (Ft. Polk, La.: Headquarters, 1st Battalion, 509th Parachute Infantry Regiment), 4. The CLF built their false BSP around their real STP (supply transfer point), a locale where stocks brought in by helicopter get separated for hauling by truck, all-terrain vehicle, or human transport. That gave the right look to the area, while allowing anything of value to escape immediately upon contact with the Americans. The true BSP for 94-10 lay in the Rakkasan area, well east of the Fullerton flight strip.

25. HQ, JRTC, *Take Home Package 1-327 INF Rotation 94-10*, 2-B, 25-B.

26. HQ, JRTC, "1-327 IN Clears Route Pontiac," *1-327 IN Rotation 94-10 LIC AAR*, 43.

27. HQ, JRTC, "Fratricide," *1-327 IN Rotation 94-10 LIC AAR*, 64.

28. HQ, 1-327th Infantry, *TF 1-327 After Action Report, JRTC 94-10*, 2–3.

29. HQ, JRTC, "Minefield Map," *1-327 IN Rotation 94-10 LIC AAR*, 44.

30. HQ, JRTC, "Successes" and "Fratricide," *1-327 IN Rotation 94-10 LIC AAR*, 14, 65.

31. HQ, JRTC, "Task Force BDA," *1-327 IN Rotation 94-10 LIC AAR*, 7A.

32. Douglas Southall Freeman, *R. E. Lee*, vol. 3 (New York: Charles Scribner's Sons, 1934–35), 130.

Chapter 5

Defense

"Well, thank God I don't know what it is to lose a battle, but certainly nothing can be more painful than to gain one with the loss of so many of one's friends."

—The Duke of Wellington

In an ideal training construct, the 1st Battalion, 327th Infantry Regiment, deserved a breather, time to get reorganized and put things back together after their drubbing at the hands of the remorseless CLF. Yet war is never fair, guerrilla wars less so than most. Cutthroat hostiles grant no respite, and neither does the JRTC. With the Bulldogs crumpled like yesterday's tinfoil and the Rakkasans almost as ill-used, JRTC turned up the heat. They introduced the Atlantican People's Revolutionary Army (PRA), threatening a regimental-scale armored onslaught by dawn on 23 September, about sixty hours hence. The rattled 1st Brigade, brought to its collective knees by 1,779 casualties, staggered on, moving to establish a defense around the Fullerton FLS to block a PRA drive from south to north.[1]

Brigade envisioned the main PRA attack in the east, in Rakkasan land, precisely where those worthies conducted their search and attack operations. The better road ran through that side. West of the Fullerton runway, the brigade S2 analysts opined that the PRA regiment might throw some kind of supporting effort into the trackless swamps, trying to skirt along the few low north-running ridges. That side went to the wrecked Bulldog task force, an easier job for the weaker of the two air assault battalions. In reserve, Capt. J. D. Compeggi's Team Tank waited, ready to swing east or west to blunt the enemy's major drive. Brigade envisioned stacking up the bad guys in rough terrain reinforced by mines and obstacles, then flaying the stalled PRA columns with fires of all types, from rifles to A-10A Warthog tank-killing jets.

The earlier the slaughter began, the better. South of the infantry battalion tandem, the 3-101st Aviation Apaches owned the brigade security area. They would kill whatever showed up down there, hopefully stripping out about half the OPFOR armor before it closed with the rifle platoons dug in on either side of the big open area surrounding the Fullerton FLS. Then, when the opponent's second echelon rolled up, the Apaches expected to rip into that, too. As they went about their business, the Apaches should be able to confirm the true deployment of the enemy 61st Motorized Infantry Regiment. Sometimes the PRA did not follow the S2 predictions, and did strange things, like attacking through the bad turf instead of barreling up the faster routes.

In general, though, the PRA stuck to a pretty rigid template. A regiment like the 61st did things by the book, unlike those damnable CLF. Though a tough foe, and often victorious, everyone preferred to mix it up with the PRA. You knew what they would try. Or at least everybody thought they did.

A PRA attack followed the same formula, with only the most minor variations. Brigade estimated that the PRA regiment would strike at dawn on 23 September. About forty-eight hours earlier, the forecast saw Atlantican special forces and CLF recon teams (another cost of losing the search and attack phase) active in the sector, trying to pinpoint U.S. forces. By thirty-six hours from attack time, last light on 21 September, divisional recon parties from the 6th Motorized Infantry Division would move through American lines, proofing routes and gathering terrain data, the sort of thing Dan Bolger's men did not do before blundering south toward Jetertown on 19 September. The day before the assault, hostile air activity promised to be vigorous, both to observe and disrupt U.S. forces as they built their defensive works. All of these preliminaries merely set the table for the arrival of the 61st Motorized Infantry Regiment.

Just after sunset on 22 September, regimental recon troops could be expected to come calling, with the task of verifying the final routes selected for the main attack the next morning. By midnight two dismounted battalions would be moving in sector, ready to break open barriers and defeat U.S. platoons trying to block the enemy advance. These huge infiltration forces often closed to within a hundred meters of unwary Americans squatting in their fighting positions. Within the last hour before dawn, as the PRA foot infantry waited nearby, the enemy would unleash a hurricane barrage of artillery, rockets, and mortars, designed to fix the U. S. riflemen in their holes. When this tumult lifted, the PRA dismounts would race forward, killing the stunned Americans in their collapsed bunkers.

And then, with the sun peeping above the treeline, the tanks would come roaring into battle, skittering through the forests in twos and threes to avoid Apache Hellfire shots and TOW wire-guided missiles. Unlike the Fort Irwin OPFOR, the JRTC motorized formations never came out to mass in the open. In fact, the vast Fullerton field might well be the quietest place on post the morning the PRA struck. Rather than roll through the meadows, the PRA tankers would stay under tree cover, avoiding deadly U.S. Army aviation and Air Force jets. Thus protected, aiming right for the gaps ripped by the artillery barrage and their foot soldiers' work, the tanks and armored infantry vehicles would squirt through, heading into the vulnerable brigade rear areas.[2] A second wave would follow within the hour, finishing off the victory.

You might think that since every U.S. brigade knew what was coming, they could stop it. But like Babe Ruth calling his home run shot, the PRA displayed nothing but contempt for its opposition. Rotation after rotation, the PRA stuck to the same pattern, and with the consistency of the Sultan of Swat tearing the cover off the ball, Polk's armored OPFOR shattered brigade after brigade. Indeed, Col. Jim Donald himself watched his defenses collapse only a few months earlier, during JRTC 94-07. He did not want to revisit that sorry scene.

In trying to cope with the standard enemy attack template, one other idea deserved consideration. The PRA shared one characteristic with their CLF pals. They avoided strength; they flowed to weakness. Brigade might discount trafficability over in the sludge west of Fullerton, ceding it all to the prostrate Bulldogs. But to the PRA, a less obvious axis guarded by a gutted battalion looked a lot like an invitation.

Going down hard on the search and attack put the 1st of the 327th in an unenviable position as the PRA loomed along the border. With more than two hundred men out of action as they ran through the drudgery of the JRTC replacement mill, the Bulldogs faced the prospect of beginning their defense at half-strength. The final platoon live fire, this time levied against Company C's 1st Platoon, did not help. Company A's 1st Platoon remained attached to

---

Task Force 1-327 Infantry
21 September 1994

Company A(-)
HQ/FIST
Mortars (2 x 60-mm)
2d Platoon/A
3d Platoon/A

Company B
HQ/FIST
Mortars (2 x 60mm)
1st Platoon/B
2d Platoon/B
3d Platoon/B
Stinger Team 2

Company C
HQ/FIST
Mortars (2 x 60mm)
1st Platoon/C
2d Platoon/C

Company D (-)
HQ
3d Platoon/D
4th Platoon D (-)
5th Platoon/D
Scout Platoon
FCT 1
Stinger Team 1

Task Force Control
Mortar Platoon (4 x 81mm)
Main CP/Combat Trains
   ATLS
   Sec/4th Platoon/D
   Team Golf
   Stinger Team 3
Field Trains
Engineer Platoon

Detachments
1st Platoon/A to 3-101st Aviation
1st and 2d Platoons/D to 3-101st Aviation
3d Platoon/C to Team Tank
1st Platoon/C to Live Fire (20–21 September)

Strengths (with attachments)

Company A:	53
Company B:	101
Company C:	58
Company D:	72
Mortar Platoon:	27
Main CP/Combat Trains:	70
Field Trains:	44
Engineer Platoon:	19
TF 1-327 Infantry Total:	444

Key to Abbreviations/Terms
ATLS: Advanced Trauma Lifesaving Team
CP: Command Post
FCT: Fire Control Team (Navy/Marine)
FIST: Fire Support Team (Army)
HQ: Headquarters
Team Golf: S5, civil affairs team,
    loudspeaker team, and
    counterintelligence agent

Starting strengths; casualties not included

the Apache aviation battalion. As a topper, brigade subtracted more detachments from what they designated their supporting effort, plucking out another rifle platoon to join Team Tank and two Maddog gun truck platoons to go forward into the security area with the Apache battalion.

In compensation, the battalion received its sorely missed engineer platoon and the equally welcome Capt. Willie Utroska, bringing with him three refurbished platoons of Company D. This, then, comprised the task force: Company B back to full strength; Company D with three of five armed Humvee platoons, and a pair of two-platoon rifle companies; pugnacious Company A; and flaccid Company C, with the latter temporarily down to one platoon while awaiting the return of the live-fire element. While nominally 56 men stronger than during the previous operation, the battalion actually faced a deficit in the only category that really mattered, trigger-pulling riflemen. Even with every replacement restored, the battalion would put only 212 rifle company soldiers on the line. It wasn't much, and unless very well-handled, probably not enough.

Like the biblical poor, what little the Bulldogs had was being taken from them, sapped by conditions. Dehydrated, limited to a single MRE a day by the nonexistent supply chain, the soldiers stumbled along in a haze of exhaustion, a fatigue deepened by the pointless, failed search and attack phase. All their labors to date availed very little. Now, simply to get into place to defend, the battalion faced an eight- to ten-kilometer diagonal movement from the southeast to the northwest of the brigade sector. A chess piece or map icon can perform such an evolution in a trice. But beaten, tired men, moving at night across rough terrain and over mined dirt roads—well, that takes time. And given the imminent entry of the PRA, Bolger's battalion had damn little of that to spare.

The move happened, after a fashion, with much cursing, confusion, and milling. The battalion's few remaining riflemen helicoptered into their new defensive area by last light on 20 September, to be joined eventually by their resurrected comrades. Those ruled dead or wounded at Hunger Hill and Jetertown processed through the JRTC replacement channels, arriving in small clots throughout the night of 20–21 September. Had Bolger not insisted on recovering their bodies, his task force would have defended without them. With them, maybe the battalion had a slim chance.

The truck convoys, masterminded by the same Capt. Mike Delgado who blundered into the Jetertown minefields that first wet night, proceeded slowly toward the new sector. Mines claimed two trucks en route, but compared to the slaughter inflicted earlier, and alongside the arrival of three-fifths of Company D back from the grave, these losses seemed small indeed. The entire mauled battalion coalesced in its new area, west of Fullerton FLS, on the gentle grassy slopes of Hill 109 north of Smith Villa. The CLF in the neighborhood—and they were there, watching—did not interfere.

With the men in place, or nearly so, the mission clear, and a little over two days available to get ready, it fell to Lieutenant Colonel Bolger to decide how to use what he had, to accomplish what he must. The battalion commander never bought brigade's conjecture that the main PRA thrust menaced the Rakkasans. No, 1st of the 327th, bedraggled and ill-used, shoveled onto unfamiliar terrain, beckoned the foe to come hither. Bolger felt certain that the opposition would rise to that opportunity, with or without the brigade S2's approval.

The battalion commander knew how he wanted to fight this one as soon as he received the brigade order. To beat a major combined arms PRA attack, Bolger needed to break the enemy's artillery-infantry-tank teamwork, to take away some of those pieces and thus slow and weaken the hostile juggernaut. Digging in and stopping the full Atlantican battering ram head-to-head simply would not work. Tanks make short work of riflemen, even if those riflemen wear the Screaming Eagle patch of the 101st Airborne. Steel is seldom impressed by élan. It would take more than guts to win this one.

Here, the OPFOR tendencies helped in the equation. The whole PRA attack focused on getting their tanks and armored fighting vehicles north to Artillery Road. The barrage and the dismounted attacks merely opened holes. Since the bad guys hit in a tight, rapid-fire sequence, artillery barrage, then dismounts, then tanks, Dan Bolger conceived a deployment designed to break that neat cycle, to leave the OPFOR fighting vehicles dangling without the help of Atlantican gunners and riflemen, meat for American airpower and J. D. Compeggi's Sheridan tanks.

Where best to do this job? A map reconnaissance clearly showed the best place to stall the enemy armor. Between Hill 109 and Smith Villa wandered a nameless creek, a sluggish, wriggling slash of muddy water and soft mud that guaranteed stuck tracked vehicles by the gross. Without some terrain improvement, like gravel-bedded fording sites, a PRA advance through Bulldog land seemed destined to end right there.

Of course, someone had dumped stones in the creekbed, and Bolger knew it. He had heard stories about that, and did not doubt that this little waterway, too, had undergone enhancement. The JRTC OP-FOR often did such things at Fort Polk. After all, it was their post. It seemed like cheating, but in reality, someone like the CLF would certainly do that, and more, to make straight the paths of their redeemers. No matter—the creek might have some passage lanes, but overall, it still constituted an obstacle. Find those gravel fords, though, and you could find where the PRA armor must go. And that also indicated where their infantry hoped to clean out gaps, and where the enemy howitzers wanted to blow away defenders.

Holding the creek fords, then, had to be done. The battalion might dig in and die right there. That, however, amounted to the old head-cracking match, albeit on better turf, but with the same likely results: lots of dead Americans and an Atlantican breakthrough. The enemy could always pile up enough strength to bull through. Weary as he was, Bolger knew better than to try such an obvious approach. To beat these people, you had to even the odds, to remove some of the opponent's advantages.

What could the Bulldogs take out of the PRA mix? Well, the tanks feared only land mines and aggressive rifle troopers popping AT4 shaped-charge rockets, the current single shot throwaway successor to the World War II bazooka. The bastards would never come out in the open for a decent TOW shot, ditto for the execrable M47 Dragon wire-guided missile. To be honest, the best things to kill tanks were Apache choppers, the U.S. Air Force, and the Sheridan company, none of them owned by 1-327th Infantry. All the mines and AT4s on Earth might kill a few and break the rest into penny packets, but stopping them cold just wasn't in the cards. No use wasting too much effort on it, thought the commander.

How about the enemy dismounts? Here, prospects brightened considerably. For one thing, the Bulldogs possessed the right talents and toys to compete in a rifle and machine gun fight. For another, the PRA dismounts were not the nasty CLF quartets from hell. These OPFOR fought in company-strength columns. They moved with utter disregard for U.S. security measures, largely because none typically existed. What if the Bulldogs could catch these guys hanging around just outside friendly lines, then rip them a new one? That seemed possible, as long as the Americans stayed active, up and out of their holes.

And the hostile artillery? Defeating the PRA gunners involved using their preplanned fires against them. Drawing on the findings of their waves of recon parties passing through the area, the OPFOR locked in their firing schedule hours before the main attack, exactly as one might expect of people adhering to the old Soviet Army mindset.[3] The artillery intended to blast away the U.S. infantry covering those key creek crossings. Bolger decided to show the PRA exactly where to fire, and then not be there. The Bulldogs had to be where the artillery was not, and that involved use of believable deception positions.

Thus emerged the scheme, a defense in depth keyed to fooling the enemy reconnaissance troops. To the south, Company D and the Scout Platoon would screen in the battalion security area to kill as many OPFOR reconnaissance forces as they could. By nightfall on 22 September, about when the PRA regimental recon passed through, Company D would withdraw to backstop the main battle area, ready to plug breakthroughs on the creek line with mobile .50-caliber and 40mm automatic grenade launcher fires. The Scouts, assisted by an ANGLICO team, would stay behind to call indirect fires on second echelon enemy forces.

In the main battle area, tank trafficability ranged from good on the fringe of the vast Fullerton FLS clearing to sloppy in the middle to virtually impassable in the swampy west, along the brigade's boundary. The gravest threat seemed to be a power punch right inside the treeline fronting the landing strip. Accordingly, Bolger put his strongest force athwart that avenue. He wanted all three rifle companies defending in the creekbed, with B (three platoons), A (two platoons), and C (one platoon, later two) aligned from east to west. While they would locate and mine all gravel fords, all three companies would not dig in back there. Rather, they were directed to dig full-scale company battle positions, complete with wire and some mines, on the ridge marked by Smith Villa. Nothing phony here; in fact, the companies would defend these locales in strength until just after dusk on 22 September, then pull back to the creek. As they did, the lieutenant colonel wanted the companies to leave behind forward observers to call fire on the PRA as they arrived to assault the vacant emplacements. This deception defensive belt was planned to attract hostile artillery fire and ball up the enemy infantry, too. Shorn of their assistants, the tanks would hit the mined fords alone. Some might squirt through, but it would not be a formed force, just leakers.

As usual, Bolger kept no reserve. What was the point? This thing would work or break based on the deception effort, and a platoon or so held back could hardly affect that. The plan took risk, but it was risk based upon a pretty good knowledge of the foe's patterns. After all, these OPFOR fought like the ones Bolger knew from a dozen years before at the Fort Irwin NTC. Compared to the fuzzy thinking about the CLF that dogged the earlier search and attack phase, this design represented real progress.

And yet, a good idea does not a victory make. Thoughts must become deeds, and quickly, too. With a clear head, or at least some confidence from success, Bolger would have issued his orders and got on with it. Instead, befogged by lack of sleep, tortured by the humiliation during the search and attack operation, and laden with too much good advice from the O/Cs, seniors, and subordinates, Bolger elected to resort to the tried and true means of what the Army calls C^2, command and control. None of that stuff helped much to unscrew the debacle that swirled around Jetertown over the past five days. In trying to make his C^2 work better for the defense, Lt. Col. Dan Bolger very nearly lost this battle too.

Nobody had a C^2 system to fix back in the bad old days before the Industrial Revolution introduced soldiers to the benefits of modern managerial techniques. Command rested solely with those in charge, the sergeants, captains, colonels, and generals. Staffs, such as they were, amounted to a cluster of relatives, retainers, batmen, and hangers-on, supplemented by the occasional technical expert on siege gunnery, bridging, or horseflesh. These worthies took messages and, after a fashion, handled details of supply and paperwork. The thought of such glorified clerks and errand boys making decisions or actually running the battles and campaigns would have struck Wellington, Napoleon, or Frederick the Great, not to mention Julius Caesar or Genghis Khan, as preposterous, downright laughable, about as sensible as permitting the football team water boys and ball girls to cook up the plays. This nonprocess remained remarkably constant over time. Historian Martin van Creveld rightly dubbed the long stretch from the Neolithic Era to the time of Napoleon the "Stone Age of Command."[4] It is also sometimes called the era of the Great Captains.

History rings with their names, those brilliant paladins who boldly took charge and led their men to stirring victories. Hannibal, Caesar, Attila the Hun, Genghis Khan, Saladin, Gustavus Adolphus, Frederick the Great, Napoleon, and Wellington loom large in every story of these times. As the ever-observant Carl von Clausewitz noted, success in war called forth the same kind of genius as success in architecture, philosophy, or poetry.[5] These men enjoyed that "inner light," that coup d'oeil, that "grip" that allowed them to size up matters rapidly and rightly. The Duke of Wellington, struggling to explain how he won his fights, said it thusly: "There is a curious thing one feels sometimes. When you are considering a subject, suddenly a whole train of reasoning comes before you like a flash of lightning. You see it all. . . ."[6] In his own small, shrunken way, Dan Bolger had felt this same spark, admittedly far fainter, when he concocted his deceptive defensive array. A good commander just knows what to do and does it.

That has been and remains true enough for the greats, the Wellingtons and Napoleons. Yet men of that caliber rarely occur, any more than one might expect every painter to be Leonardo da Vinci or every hitter Babe Ruth. What of the lesser men, the time servers and mediocrities, not to forget the outright dolts? What do they use to get the job done?

Before the mid-nineteenth century, they didn't. It should come as no surprise that those who lack the inner light cast about for help. Up through the American Civil War, the average leaders, and especially the militarily challenged set, found comfort in a gathering of key subordinates known as a council of war. Famous councils of war occurred in the Allied camp prior to Austerlitz in 1805 (the Allies lost) and among the Union generals at Gettysburg in 1863 (they won). Painters who favor martial subjects delight in depicting such gatherings of the chieftains, and diarists recognize that these sessions neatly synthesize opposing views, so records of these meetings are not lacking.

Councils of war follow a certain protocol. All present enjoy the right to speak, to propose plans of action or inaction. Then the assembly votes, bound to the outcome. Of course, the overall commander reserves the authority to overrule the council of war, but since he takes the rap if things go sour, most weaker generals and colonels prefer the comfort of majority opinion. Better to hang together than swing alone!

War by committee, like most everything else done this way, tends to result in a certain sameness. While often an effective curb on an outright idiot—although the true incompetents often lack even the sense to defer to a council of war—doing things the same old way has a cost in combat. Napoleon put it this way:

> The effect of discussions, making a show of talent, and calling councils of war will be what the effect of these things has been in every age: they will end in the adoption of the most pusillanimous or (if the expression be preferred) the most prudent measures, which in war are almost uniformly the worst that can be adopted.[7]

Better to trust in genius, suggests Napoleon, a good recommendation if one can guarantee a surfeit of brilliant commanders. Leave it to the Germans, afflicted with plenty of noble fools, to devise a workaround. Reeling from the batterings suffered at the hands of Napoleon, often groaning under the misapprehensions of the altogether less than great successors of Frederick cast up by the Hohenzollern dynasty, the Germans essentially mandated a professional council of war. This general staff consisted of life-long soldiers schooled in how to win battles. While they did consider gathering intelligence and placed a great premium on terrain studies and historical cases, the Germans mainly worked through skillful use of logistics, matters not subject to the vagaries of Clausewitzian genius but more susceptible to the manipulation of sound industrial management and smart accounting, both conveniently emerging in the nascent Germany of the mid-1800s. It is no accident that the key sections of Helmuth von Moltke's great general staff sprang from the Army's railway office.[8] While not exactly guaranteeing inspiration, the German general staff approach developed a predictable range of outcomes in time and space, allowing various sprigs of nobility to choose from plans that at least matched reality. This method gave the Prussians and their German associates smashing victories over the overmatched Danes in 1864, the befuddled Austrians in 1866, and finally, the arrogant, disorganized French in 1870–71. Considering war as the only important test of the methodology, the general staff system clearly passed muster. Of course, handing a selection of feasible plans to the likes of Kaiser Wilhelm II or Adolf Hitler guarantees nothing, unpleasant truths forced on the Germans in two failed world wars.

Early in this century, our United States Army, like its continental European allies and rivals, adopted much of the German system as our own. With the progress of industry and science in America, this transformation appears inevitable from our vantage. And yet, lacking a requirement to prop up untutored nobles, traditionally favoring professional education and advancement by proven merit, one wonders why the United States jumped so quickly on the Berlin bandwagon. But in armies, as in any other branch of fashion, one sometimes follows the crowd.

More amazing has been our adherence to these measures over time, although militaries seldom give up even a bad idea if it has become ingrained. In the nine decades since the adoption of the German system, we have refined our doctrinal edifice to create the processes familiar to Dan Bolger and his key leaders. Although Uncle Sam's legions added computers and satellite communications to the stew, the recipe remains very much like the original. Dwight D. Eisenhower, Omar N. Bradley, or William C. Westmoreland would recognize and be comfortable with today's methods, so little have they altered in spirit and, indeed, in form. For the same reason, George S. Patton, Matthew B. Ridgway, and Creighton Abrams would certainly bridle in disappointment to see how much we trust in form and process, and how little we grant to substance and genius.

Business, science, and the arts long ago left nineteenth-century techniques behind. Not so the U.S. Army, at least in this crucial area. In truth, the present command and control system, if practiced as the field manuals suggest, amounts to a permanent council of war, meeting around the clock to strangle innovation in planning, purposely built to lose track of the ongoing fight in the bargain, and then compounding matters by binding the commander to an overly large, overly vulnerable command post. One can make the Army C^2 procedures work, in the same vein as one can shove a rhinoceros through a keyhole given a large enough pile driver. But, in both cases, the results aren't pretty.

Planning founders on the rocks of the Deliberate Decision-Making Process (DDMP), a virtual Robert's Rules of Order for councils of war. Intended to create designs for battle, the DDMP is described in official Army literature as "very difficult and time-consuming."[9] With the entire battalion staff present, led by the XO, the boys plod through a series of painful discussions to analyze their mission, figure out what to do about it, and then estimate which solution will work best. Meanwhile, the commander carries out the same torturous drill, acting as a check on his staff officers and NCOs.

At various precribed intervals, the staff prepares elaborate presentations, complete with charts and diagrams à la Ross Perot, telling their commander and each other about certain analyses, proposed courses of action, and decisions recommended. In the culminating brief of briefs, the commander gets to pick one of three possible courses of action. Armed with documentation and charts, the staff kindly steers him toward the best of what lies behind three doors, like Monty Hall on the old *Let's Make a Deal* show guiding a somewhat clueless contestant toward a nice consolation prize. The guys necessarily spend a lot of time looking at maps inside the command post. Looking at real ground, your own soldiers, or, God forbid, the enemy, does not appear on the scope. Army doctrine recognizes that sometimes heat, cold, and badniks can affect this stately minuet. "In extreme situations," warn the experts, "the staff must be prepared to brief the commander without the use of visual aids." [10] Well, as Sherman said, war is hell.

With or without those handy visual aids, the DDMP assures comprehensive work in volume. The massive tomes that barf forth from all of this often run to a half inch in thickness and cover everything from the laser pulse codes for the smart bombs to how many socks to pack. Each mission developed by the DDMP, in theory, comes packaged and tied, a miniature Operation Overlord all ready to execute. It's wonderful stuff when done correctly. It just takes too long to get it.

"You can ask me for anything you like, except time," thundered the perpetually impatient Bonaparte, who certainly knew the value of the unforgiving minute. Unfortunately, the DDMP takes an inordinate amount of time, a challenge admitted by those who pen Army field manuals. Divisions expect forty-eight hours to get out an order, which translates to some thirty-two hours at brigade and about twenty-one hours at the battalion echelon, as each layer uses a third of available time. In air assault operations, the norm for 101st Airborne formations like 1st of the 327th, brigades prefer a ninety-six-hour planning window, with sixty-four hours reserved for the battalions. To put these leisurely paces into perspective, Patton warned his Third Army divisions to expect, at most, twelve hours from mission receipt to execution, with four hours the standard for battalions. But then again, Patton directed that army-level orders "should not exceed a page and a half of typewritten text" with "the back of the page used for a sketch map." [11] Not exactly DDMP, of course, but it was fast, effective, and, sad to say, all too unique to the Third Army.

The Army knows that the DDMP is too damn slow. To speed the plow, the folks at Leavenworth's Command and General Staff College have recommended some shortcuts. Yet even in this, they could not give up the dead hand of the approved format. The thinkers devised two quicker types of DDMP, differing principally in considering two, or one, potential courses of action, respectively. [12] The fastest version of the DDMP takes ten hours, yet deletes nothing. It's akin to playing the "Minute Waltz" at 78 RPM. You get the same old song, only faster.

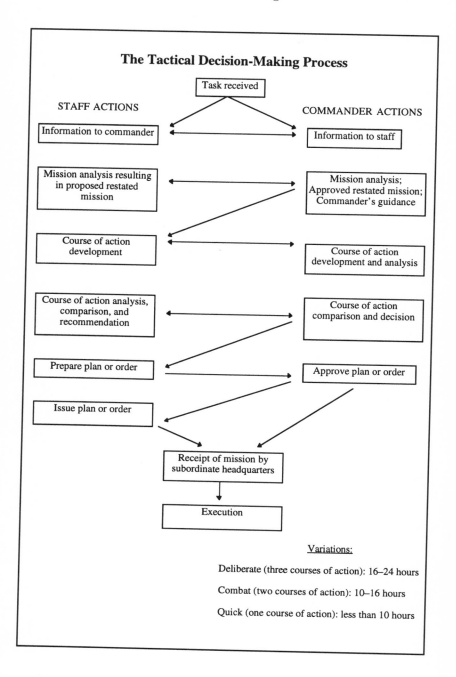

The Tactical Decision-Making Process

Task received

STAFF ACTIONS

COMMANDER ACTIONS

Information to commander

Information to staff

Mission analysis resulting in proposed restated mission

Mission analysis; Approved restated mission; Commander's guidance

Course of action development

Course of action development and analysis

Course of action analysis, comparison, and recommendation

Course of action comparison and decision

Prepare plan or order

Approve plan or order

Issue plan or order

Receipt of mission by subordinate headquarters

Execution

Variations:

Deliberate (three courses of action): 16–24 hours

Combat (two courses of action): 10–16 hours

Quick (one course of action): less than 10 hours

Painful as the DDMP can be, its real danger involves tying up the commander and his staff while the fighting proceeds unabated around them. The thing becomes so all-consuming that JRTC O/Cs have actually witnessed battalion command posts ignoring major engagements to complete one of the briefings. This in a nutshell points to the real danger with mucking around so much with making decisions. After all, what good does it do to concoct the perfect plan and yet have no battalion left to execute it? The Bulldogs had done this when they turned from Company B's struggle in the BSP to begin staging for the proposed Maddox Homestead raid.

Along with generating plans, a command post must *operate*, tracking the battle as it occurs. The book envisions a nice cluster of radios, maps, tents, and vehicles, all smoothly functioning under the tutelage of a "battle captain," an officer from the S3 section who has already led a company and can keep the TOC running while the commander, XO, and S3 attend the orders at brigade or run around the area visiting line companies, the trains, and other points of interest. At any time, a quick call to the TOC allows the commander, or in fact anybody on the battalion radio circuits, to call in and check the location and status of friendly and enemy forces, call for supporting fires, or arrange for resupply. This routine staff supervision garners little ink in the field manuals compared to the DDMP. Even so, it is vitally important, far more so than making plans. Patton thought that creating an order amounted to only 5 percent of the affair. The other 95 percent involved supervising the execution—in short, operating.[13]

Here the 1st of the 327th faltered, at best. The two designated battle captains, Capt. Mike Delgado and 2d Lt. Tom Doughty, shared exactly no experience running a TOC. Delgado was an assistant S3 who typically handled training scheduling and resources, and had yet to command a company. Doughty, Dirk Blackdeer's assistant S2, knew a lot about intelligence matters but nothing about battalion operations. Each man coordinated a shift that included NCOs and junior enlisted men dealing with S3 issues, S2 actions, fire support (in its artillery, mortar, Air Force, and Navy/Marine flavors), logistics (S4) and personnel (S1), air defense, and combat engineers. As the manuals suggested, Delgado and Doughty hoped to track the battle, coordinate minor everyday actions, and keep everyone informed, with each shift on for twelve hours. They held court in front of a bank of radios, seated among map boards and wall charts hung on the sides of three square canvas frame tents, each about the size of a backyard garden tool shed. The TOC had all the right pieces.

This nifty concept degenerated in practice. Once it finally motored into the box, the TOC proved to be virtually immobile, because when it moved, there was no sure way designated to track the battle. Worse, setting up and tearing down the SICPS (standard integrated command post system) tents and rerigging radios often took hours, especially at night. The two shifts disintegrated as the staff convened and reconvened to do the DDMP drill, tried to move the tents, or reacted to enemy probes on the perimeter. Finally, and this really hit at the heart of the issue, Delgado and Doughty were boys sent to do the jobs of men. Uncertain as to how companies worked, let alone battalions, these hardworking young officers could no more anticipate a developing crisis or crank up a sensible order than our favorite football team's water boy could direct the two-minute drill. The Bulldog TOC featured the same cast of earnest errand boys as Wellington's staff at Waterloo, but they were expected to behave like von Moltke's general staff at Koeniggratz. It simply would not be.

Groping for information, its shifts thoroughly muddled by moves and by planning, the TOC became little more than a meeting place. Its droning radio operators wrote down messages, but nobody really understood their significance. The destruction of a truck of valuable antitank mines received the same attention as the nightly report that all weapons had been accounted present. The battle captains nodded, short on sleep and steeped in confusion and frustration, uncertain what to do other than ask for guidance. Young soldiers wrote it all down. Sometimes it even got posted on the maps and charts. But in general, nothing got done unless one of the majors or the lieutenant colonel became interested. The companies could never be sure what the TOC was doing about the problems out on the line. Getting nothing but a bored pfc. on the radio did not do much for confidence, either.

The XO, S3, or battalion commander tended to be present in the TOC, with Bill Phelps awake in the day and Jim Laufenburg up at night, although this sort of evolved, and often both majors were up. Sleep debts grew. As a result, the onset of the defense found both of the battalion's field grade experts at the end of their tethers. Dan Bolger was not much better. But without a strong battle captain, and with some planning almost always at hand, the two majors and their commander hardly entertained any options. If only training back at Fort Campbell had revealed this glaring weakness! It had, but Bolger and company had chosen not to notice. Now it stared them in the face, unsolved and probably unsolvable.[14]

The 1st of the 327th TOC might have been a poor excuse for a command post, despite having all the proper items and men. Bad as it was at operating, its survivability promised to be even more problematic. Slow to move, obvious with its unique SICPS tents and forest of radio antennas and parked Humvees, the TOC offered a wonderful opportunity to both the CLF and the PRA. Bolger accentuated this by siting his command post on the western edge of the Hill 109 opening, in the most predictable place imaginable (and imagination had surely broken down by this juncture).

On this C^2 system, with its staff preoccupied by DDMP, its TOC ineffectual and hardly survivable, Dan Bolger placed the fate of his battalion. He could have dictated the order, or even written it himself, on the night of 20 September. Instead, he allowed the DDMP process to play out until late afternoon the next day, even as his command post team lost visibility on the vital movements of land mines, replacements, and ammunition, and his company commanders sat in the woods, awaiting the word. The opposing forces, naturally, stayed all too much right on schedule.

Everything on the night of 20–21 September took more time than it should. The TOC finally reached its new position by 0300, but it took until well after sunrise for the slow-moving soldiers to erect the "L" of tents that formed its core. Dragging with exhaustion, the staff gathered to bang away at the DDMP, a procedure they could execute within four hours when fresh. This time, even with plenty of guidance from Bolger, it took forever to make up the charts, to check the hostile template, and to prepare the written orders. The staff knew exactly what their commander wanted to do, and yet in their numbed

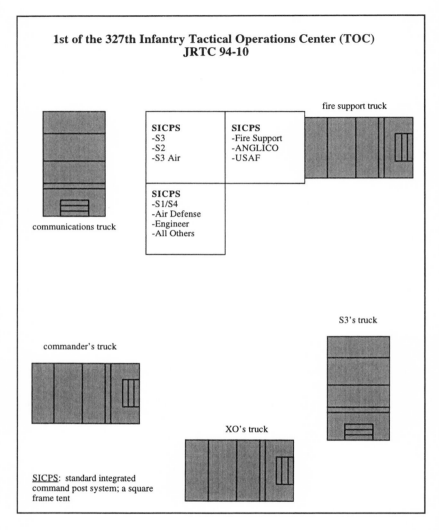

1st of the 327th Infantry Tactical Operations Center (TOC)
JRTC 94-10

fire support truck

SICPS
-S3
-S2
-S3 Air

SICPS
-Fire Support
-ANGLICO
-USAF

SICPS
-S1/S4
-Air Defense
-Engineer
-All Others

communications truck

S3's truck

commander's truck

XO's truck

SICPS: standard integrated
command post system; a square
frame tent

state, and his, all partners ran through the DDMP cycle by rote, even
though it did not apply. Even as the dull hours passed and the staff
abused each other, the men lost sight of the fact that with regard to
shaping this fight, the decision had already been made.

Indeed, although nobody but Dan Bolger knew the entire outline,
execution commenced. As the hot sun rose, helicopters began de-

livering mines, wire, and wood for bunkers to the battalion's false positions to the south, where Command Sergeant Major Ripka and the company first sergeants began to build the deception belt. Even as the engineers and the senior NCOs started work, none of them understood why they were doing all of it. Ripka knew why, of course, but even he was not precisely straight. The soldiers out front comprehended even less, and most assumed it was merely more madness from the same lieutenant colonel who had afflicted them with team rucks and Hunger Hill.

One thing not done might have prevented this distressing lack of "the word." Bolger might have told his staff just what to produce for an order, then spent the day walking the ground with his commanders. Instead, incredibly for a man who knew better, he sat at the TOC, watching the staff make charts.

Oh, he did some other things, too, none of them of any real value, but the kind of activities that serve to pass the time. Bolger gave an interview to JRTC's press corps, an imposition foisted on every battalion commander, and a few company commanders, during each rotation. Made up of real print and electronic journalists, the JRTC media receive coaching from O/Cs to permit these representatives of the fourth estate to ask questions worthy of *60 Minutes,* the "Have you stopped beating your wife" variety sometimes favored by aggressive reporters these days. Bolger turned on his reservoir of charm and did quite well, as befitted the former speechwriter for the U.S. Army Chief of Staff.

That dignitary, too, arrived unbidden late in the day on 21 September, adding his presence to the press to distract Bolger from his command duties. The chief spent a pleasant half hour at the battalion TOC, exchanging views with his former assistant, and commenting on the real-world intervention into Haiti, a major operation proceeding while Bolger and friends dealt with these sham troubles in Cortina. While the lieutenant colonel appreciated this kind gesture by the Army's most senior general, it all took more time.

The company commanders eventually received their orders, and as night fell Bolger departed by helicopter for the 1st Brigade TOC, to back-brief his defense plan to Col. Jim Donald. This fit into the machinery of the brigade-level DDMP, along with a walk-through rehearsal, with commanders hopping about a scaled terrain board in what looked for all the world like human chess. Bad enough that the Army's preferred planning process chained the commander to his CP; in its later phases, the endless "Do you get it?" briefings, it pulled in subordinates as well. The 1st Brigade trusted in the DDMP and played it to the hilt. That night it sucked Bolger away for four precious hours.

Behind the battalion commander, he left his two majors to coordinate both the delivery of the thousands of mines necessary to choke up the creek crossings, and the returning soldiers necessary to fight and win there. The companies knew their jobs, and they found the gravel-bed fords as predicted. Now all they needed were the means to stop the bad guys. If only it had not taken all day to get started!

Now the insidious DDMP took its ultimate toll. As worn out from generating briefing charts as they might have been from moving mines and replacements into sector, the staff turned affairs over to a skeleton night crew. Most of the primary staff officers settled down. Both majors went to sleep. For all, it seemed a well-deserved and long-delayed rest.

When Bolger returned from brigade around 2200, he found 2d Lt. Tom Doughty, the S4, Capt. Ted Donnelly, and a few junior radio operators on duty in the TOC. Over a hundred replacement soldiers, almost all valuable riflemen, remained lost in the shuffle. Nor did anyone know when or where the battalion might expect its critical heliborne mine packages. Not that it mattered; no mine distribution or barrier plan existed. Company D, out on the screen line to the south, was off the radio net. They might well be in contact with PRA recon forces. To Bolger's concerned inquiries, he received shrugs and wide eyes.

Experience at Fort Irwin's NTC convinced Bolger that this could not be allowed to pass. Without mines and replacement troops present by daylight, the creek would not get blocked, as it would take all day to accomplish that task. That would barely be in time, because the battalion expected to fight the PRA the very next night. Things could not wait until daybreak to sort out. Time's winged chariot gathered speed, about to run over the plodding Bulldogs.

Not if Dan Bolger could help it. Tired though he was, this situation cried out for extraordinary efforts. Most subordinates would consider Dan Bolger a reasonable man, considerate of subordinates, unlikely to lash out at someone who made a mistake. Usually, reality mirrored that image. But now, with sands running too damn quickly through the glass, the battalion commander drew on his fire and steel. He summoned his staff in no uncertain terms, violating noise discipline by a wide margin. The O/Cs in the TOC backed out, unwilling to watch this angry scene.

Despite this volcanic eruption, Bolger wasted little time blaming his key staffers for finding things adrift. Recriminations solved nothing, and this hour cried for answers. There had already been blather enough for one day, and everyone knew it. Once the staff arrived, the commander turned to Jim Laufenburg, directing the XO to find the absent land mines and uncork the personnel replacement bottleneck.

Getting mines demanded more than radio calls. Ted Donnelly led this effort, heading out into the night to bring in a succession of helicopters that began slinging in barrier materials after midnight. Brigade eventually dispatched over two thousand mines to the 1st of the 327th. Amazingly, less than half arrived in the landing zones near Smith Villa. Misguided Chinook crews dumped the rest near Carnis Village, among other places.[15]

Personnel also came, but this took more trouble. The S1, even more uncertain than usual, tried to sort out the stalled flow of men. Due to a pittance of records on previous losses, this failed. Laufenburg ended up doing that task himself, working with each company to figure out who was in the field, then backtracking to guess who was not. Those names, submitted through brigade, allowed the JRTC to process the replacement troops previously hung up in the innards of the personnel engine. Within hours, choppers started to carry in these sorely needed fighting men.

With the XO gainfully employed, the battalion commander assigned other key tasks to his second Leavenworth man, Bill Phelps, the S3. Bill was told to find out about Company D's screen. Perhaps more important for the overall defense, Bolger wanted Phelps to make up a real barrier plan, a duty the S3 had mistakenly unloaded on the young second lieutenant engineer. That junior officer, as one might expect, wallowed in confusion, unclear as to what to do. When the mines dropped out of the sky, the battalion needed a concept to distribute these to the companies.

It took about an hour, but Tom Doughty finally achieved communications with Capt. Willie Utroska and Company D. As Bolger suspected, Utroska's gun Humvees were in contact with PRA recon vehicles and dismounts. This action sputtered throughout the night, with both sides hitting and moving. By daybreak, the Maddogs accounted for two BRDM scout trucks and six OPFOR, but this came at the price of two friendly gunships and four casualties. Some of the PRA recon got through, but not all of it.[16]

Even as the TOC regained communications with the Maddogs, Bill Phelps applied his orderly mind to create a battalion barrier plan. His thorough sorting served to drive the companies' work in the morning. Dirk Blackdeer helped by confirming the grid coordinates of the eight stone-bottom crossing sites found by the rifle companies. It took multiple calls to tired radio operators to get the right data. Companies B and A each dealt with three fords. Chris Forbes and his suspect Company C watched two. By sunrise, the mines were en route to the companies.

Bolger assisted in all of this, ensuring through multiple calls to brigade and his companies that his own sense of urgency pervaded the task force. It did. At daybreak on 22 September, the staff could cut back and rest, trying vainly to get those mythical shifts working. Except for Company D, the other letter companies stored up some rest. Watered and fed from (at last) reliable supply lines, with the Maddog screen intact and the deception positions almost complete, the battalion at last appeared to be on course to complete its preparations, then to fight and win. The dawn of another warm, clear day promised good things for the Bulldogs.

Dan Bolger sensed that the worst was over. The battalion staff had overcome its lethargy, and so the 1st of the 327th as a whole began to overcome theirs. Having catnapped for a few hours, the battalion commander set off to inspect the lines, to see firsthand the creek fords and false emplacements his mind had conceived a day and a half be-

fore. With all the focus on stopping the Atlantican regulars, the Bulldog soldiers long ago forgot the CLF guerrillas. Bolger certainly gave
them no thought that busy dawn. But the insurgents were still there,
watching for an opportunity to act. Dan Bolger gave it to them.

   The battalion commander walked the main defensive trace in his
typical style, rifle in hand, radio on his back, and alone. Alfredo Mycue's Bushmasters labored within a few hundred meters of the TOC.
Bolger found them and the engineers installing mines by the gross
in the three improved crossings in Company B's sector. Bolger and
his S2, Dirk Blackdeer, agreed that Alfredo and his men blocked the
best mounted avenue. This route looked certain to feature the Atlantican main effort. Company B, with three platoons and a hell of
a score to settle after Hunger Hill, faced a very tough fight.
   The young riflemen and grenadiers seemed up to the challenge,
and spirits appeared high. The battalion and company commanders
checked every position, ensuring that the Bushmaster infantry truly

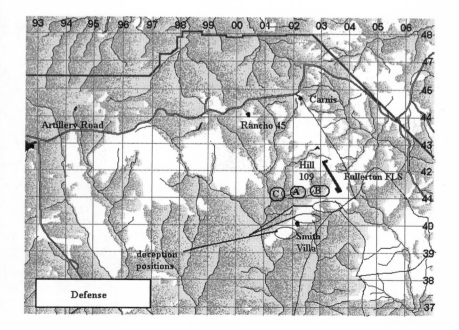

covered the fateful creekbed fords. This meant placing rifle squads right down in the slop and water, and ruled out by-the-book bunkers with sandbagged roofs to keep out shell fragments. The things would be awash if the men even tried to build them. So they did not try.

That suited Dan Bolger just fine. Excavating bunkers and sitting in them gave up an offensive spirit, the hunting and ambush mentalities that characterize good light infantry. When you turned dirt, you fixed yourself in position, doing half the opposition's job for him. It all amounted to bad business for guys whose only armor entailed ceramic Kevlar helmets and cloth battle-dress uniforms. Once the enemy found you, he could keep pouring in shot and shell until you evaporated or went mad. That explains why Patton snorted, "When you dig a foxhole, you dig your grave!"[17] Short on time, determined to plant mines, not men, Bolger's troops did not dig holes along their main line.

Now emplacements existed, all right, rather nice ones, to be honest. Thanks to Cmd. Sgt. Maj. Mark Ripka, the first sergeants, some hardworking engineer earth-moving equipment teams, and most of the battalion's infantry, the deception positions out front bristled with bunkers, trenches, twisting strands of spiraling concertina wire, and a few strips of land mines in key sites. Each company placed a pair of forward observers in the stoutest, most carefully camouflaged fighting holes, where they would stay to direct mortar and artillery salvos against OPFOR infantry who breached into these dummy defense works. The rest of the Americans intended, of course, to withdraw back at last light to set up to fight a mobile ambush battle in the creek bottom.

If Bolger guessed right, the preplanned PRA artillery and rocket barrage would hit unoccupied foxholes, and the dispersed squads in the creek undergrowth had no need for bunkers. But if Bolger guessed wrong . . . well, he was paid to get it right. Unfortunately, the lieutenant colonel's record so far on this JRTC rotation hardly inspired confidence. But the commander stuck to his plan.

Satisfied after a few hours picking through Company B's efforts, Bolger moved cross-country through a thicket to find Capt. Drew Felix and his Abus. They had drawn a tangled mess of a sector, split by three graveled ford lanes. As with the Bushmasters, Drew's men expected to fight a mobile, stalking engagement in the dense undergrowth, right in the marshy creek. With only two platoons, one out front holding the fake position, the Abus probably lacked the manpower to place, fuse, and bury several hundred mines in the three isolated crossings. Bolger knew that Company C, with its live-fire platoon still not returned, needed engineer help to get anything done at all. Here surfaced another penalty for screwing around so long on 21 September.

Bolger called the TOC on the radio, raising MSgt. Ed Bauerle, the forceful operations NCO. "Get every TOC soldier you can down to the Abu sector," ordered Bolger. "You're going to become sappers."

Bauerle, well aware that the battalion depended upon M21 antitank mines to stymie the PRA armor, answered gruffly: "Roger, out." By the time the day ended, the TOC radio operators, NCOs, and officers claimed credit for laying 300 M21 antitank mines and 72 M16A1 antipersonnel mines. To put this in perspective, the engineers laid some 292 mines in Company B's sector. The TOC soldiers' performance as stand-in engineers definitely helped the battalion more than their fumbling attempts to plan and operate as a command post.[18]

A two-hour survey of Drew Felix's work assured the battalion commander that the Abus, aided by Bauerle's TOC sappers, would be ready when the OPFOR came that night. Bolger exited the Abu position heading south, to talk to some of the men manning the deception positions. The day grew hotter, and the commander sweated freely as he walked briskly among the wire entanglements and two-man fighting holes stretching across the front east of Smith Villa.

One of the soldiers Bolger spoke to, Pfc. John Davis, told the lieutenant colonel an interesting story. Apparently, during the previous night's wave of Chinook sling-load deliveries, several pallets of mines and wire ended up in Smith Villa. Davis witnessed the tireless S5, 1st Lt. Matt Bounds, at work. Borrowing a security squad from the Abus, Matt entered the hacienda yard and approached the cowering inhabitants. The battalion S5 not only talked the six civilians into giving the supplies back, he also convinced them to evacuate the area. In return, the people told Matt and his Company A escorts to watch out; the CLF guerrillas had two four-man teams in the western end of the creekbed. Davis related this information with a shrug. "I haven't seen any CLF, sir," he ended.

No CLF; that sounded encouraging. So did the rest of Davis's vignette. Brother Matt Bounds, Mr. Initiative, was out doing good as usual—that made Bolger smile. *If only we backed him so well in Jetertown . . . Well, tonight might even up for all of that.* Bolger thanked Private First Class Davis and wished him luck in the upcoming firefight. Then the commander stretched, wiped the sweat out of his eyes, and headed west, toward Company C's false defensive works.

But Company C was not there. Indeed, with only a single platoon, Capt. Chris Forbes had only a squad patrol out in the half-finished breastworks and small mine-belts south of the creek. The rest of Company C, if you could call this tiny band a company, totaled about twenty-five men. The troops clustered near one of the stone-based fords, unloading M21 mines, waiting on 1st Platoon to come back from its live fire. Those men were late.

About five minutes after he walked away from Private First Class Davis, Bolger saw an unmanned outpost, the yellowish dirt bright in the greenery. A hundred meters to the northeast was a very small finger of water, a rivulet marked by tall, leafy ferns and a thorny wall of brush. A vehicle had crossed this ditch, and Bolger headed toward that opening.

He never made it. Two shots rang out from the lieutenant colonel's rear, and as he spun around, he saw a soldier, a rifleman, kneeling at the base of a tall pine tree. The dull, faded, hospital-green uniform and floppy hat left no doubt. This guy was CLF. Bolger slid behind a flimsy tree and brought his own rifle up, fingering the safety catch. But his adversary had the drop on him. As the battalion commander squeezed his trigger, the foe fired again. Bolger's MILES beeper went off. He had been hit.

"Sir, take your helmet off and show me your casualty card," said Capt. Jerry Henderson, the O/C who silently walked with Bolger on his tour of the front lines. Bolger handed the O/C a small brown envelope. Henderson opened it. The thing contained what looked like a black-and-white playing card. One side showed a man's body with an *X* on the left arm, plus the letter *W*. The other side had instructions, telling Bolger he remained conscious and could walk and talk, although he had been shot in the left forearm. The *W* stood for "walking wounded." Bolger had twenty-four hours to reach an aid station or be decreed dead due to untreated wounds.

Of course, that depended on the tender mercies of this young CLF sergeant, whose eyes widened considerably when he saw Bolger's rank insignia. Now this promised a three-day pass. The sergeant took Bolger's rifle and radio, and then marched the helmetless officer off into captivity.

About the only thing the Bulldog commander did right was zero-ize his complicated AN/PRC-119 frequency-hopping radio. This took a flick of his supposedly good wrist, reaching over his shoulder and giving a good yank and twist to a very prominent knob sticking up off the top of the transceiver box. Bolger did that little drill the instant his MILES went off. Throwing the zero-izing switch lobotomized the radio's cryptographic brain in one neat swipe. The Army designed it that way, for precisely this circumstance.

Bolger's host prodded him into the underbrush along the fern gully, stepping lightly along the dribbling brook. The undergrowth grew oppressively thick and low, and the men crouched to move along the tiny waterway. A second CLF soldier, a private, glided up soundlessly to Bolger's rear, materializing like a wraith from the foliage. Within five minutes the trio popped into a clearing about the size of a suburban patio. Four hammocks, two of them occupied, hung off the pine trees framing the opening. "Nice catch, Sergeant Jackson," said one of the lounging guerrillas.

The clearing looked like a "boys only" clubhouse run by fourth graders. Candy wrappers, paperback books, MRE trash, and sports and girlie magazines lay all over the place, intermixed with bulging rucksacks. Sergeant Jackson dumped Bolger's radio in the middle of all of this, motioned the commander to sit down at the base of a big tree, and brought all of his men into a tight knot around Bolger's dead radio.

"Bigfoot knows we've got a battalion commander here in the Spiderweb," said one of the privates. The man held up the handset of an elderly AN/PRC-77 radio, an unsecured, sole frequency relic of the Vietnam period. Bolger guessed "Bigfoot" must be the OPFOR commander, and "Spiderweb" signified his present location, in the center of all of these stream junctions and underbrush.

The CLF sergeant grunted. "Great, man. Does anybody know how to work a SINCGARS?"

Nobody answered that one. The men took turns jabbing buttons and playing with the newfangled radio, not realizing that Bolger's zero-ization rendered their efforts pointless. One private ambled over and took Bolger's map and notebook. He gave the latter back, unable to find anything interesting. The insurgent kept the map. Bolger said nothing, but inwardly he salvaged another very small bit of pleasure from the lost map. Soon to be whisked away to PRA headquarters, that map showed only one set of positions—the fakes.

Bolger noticed a CLF rifle within arm's reach, loaded and ready. Careful to use only his allegedly good right hand, Bolger lunged for the weapon. Swinging it up onto the crook of his left arm, Bolger shot six times at very close range. All four CLF beepers went off.

"Aw, no . . ." groaned the man who searched Bolger.

The O/C, Captain Henderson, shook his head. "No, not allowed," he ruled. "Nice try, though. Death or wounding of key leaders can only be resolved by the chief of the JRTC operations group."

"So if I was a private, that would have counted?" Bolger asked.

"Yes, sir. But you aren't a private," Henderson finished. "The ops group will send out instructions on you later. But, sir, for now, just sit here, shut up, and play the game, will you?"

Henderson rekeyed the CLF quartet. Sergeant Jackson told Henderson that he bound and gagged Bolger, and produced cord and rags sufficient to do the job. Thankfully for Bolger, they simulated this procedure. All weapons were moved well out of the prisoner's reach. That was not simulated.

And in this manner the four guerrillas, the lieutenant colonel, and the O/C passed another warm afternoon at Fort Polk. Bolger dozed fitfully, his fatigue taking a toll broken by the spikes of hot embarassment. Around 1700, Henderson shook the nodding senior officer.

"Come on, sir. We're going to reinsert you. Follow me."

Bolger said nothing, but gathered his radio and weapon and headed out, leaving the quartet at the Spiderweb. Within a hundred meters he could hear tools clinking and several young men talking. It must be 1st Platoon, Company C, arrived at last, but unknowingly within earshot of the Spiderweb.

As they broke out of the marshy jungle and walked up toward Smith Villa, Bolger asked Jerry Henderson a question. "You've been here three years. You follow the commanders. Has any other commander ever been captured?"

The captain shook his head. "Never heard of it, sir." He said nothing else.[19]

Bolger suspected as much. Great, wasn't it? Hunger Hill–type massacres happened routinely at JRTC. But getting captured? Here was an embarrassing distinction Bolger could have done without.

There was no time to dwell on that kind of stuff. Tonight the Bulldogs expected to host the PRA. Bolger's thoughts and energies belonged there. A victory, he knew, might not wipe out the shame of being stupid. But it would help.

Dan Bolger's return to the living and uncaptured came with one string attached. The commander could not discuss his captors' activities or location, even though he now knew precisely how to find the Spiderweb. Still, one cannot undo memory, and Bolger wondered to himself why the CLF camped so close to Company C. That wasn't a very good avenue for armor. *Too swampy,* thought the battalion commander.

Bolger reached the TOC site, but no TOC tentage stood. Indeed, the bustling activity indicated that the 1st of the 327th command post vehicles would soon be on their way to a new location. Obviously, nobody was sitting around wringing hands waiting for dad. These guys intended to move out.

Jim Laufenburg had decided this, convinced by evidence that something bad had happened to Lieutenant Colonel Bolger. If the CLF roamed the woods, as Bolger's demise proved likely, why offer them a juicy target like the battalion CP? Sure that the OPFOR knew their location, Jim packed up the TOC and lined up its trucks, headed north out of the enemy's likely line of march.

Moving the TOC offered only part of Laufenburg's solution to commanding the upcoming battle. To direct the close fight, Bill

Phelps, Dirk Blackdeer, and fire support officer Capt. Mike Temple planned to use the battalion commander's Humvee with its two long-range radios and set up a tactical command post just behind Company B, where all supposed they might see the bulk of the PRA tanks.

This C² business made sense, but it only pulled a veneer of central order over a plan implementing itself. Aided by TOC men and engineers working feverishly, all mines were in and fused. With night approaching, Company D readied its platoons to withdraw from the forward security area to its backstop battle positions. The rifle companies also prepared to evacuate their phony emplacements and get into the creekbed. Left behind, a few snugly buried and hidden forward observers waited in the dummy emplacements, awaiting hostile dismounted infantry.

During these final adjustments, as Dan Bolger resumed command of his battalion task force, Company C experienced another in its seemingly endless series of mishaps. This mixed-up company redefined the term *snakebit*. Checking his men, Capt. Chris Forbes blundered into his own minefield and "died."

In no position to criticize, ex-prisoner Bolger sighed knowingly. He appointed Capt. Ted Donnelly, the S4, to replace poor Forbes. Ted promptly hit a friendly minefield, too, and joined the casualty list.[20] Well, at least Cold Steel's mines worked. Bolger let 1st Lt. Chris Santos, the XO, take charge. Hopefully, for the sake of Company C, the Atlantican attack would go elsewhere.

Of course, accordingly to the usual perverse logic of JRTC, the onslaught went smack into Cold Steel's thinly held lines. Chris Santos had a very interesting morning, all right.

Bolger and his Tac team slumped quietly around their vehicle during the night, waiting for news of the great Atlantican attack. The brigade nets crackled with Apache reports of recon vehicles seen and engaged. No sightings of walking OPFOR infantry came in. The Bulldog companies waited in the creekbed, with a few artillery observers still out front in the unheld deception emplacements. Somewhere out there, enemy infantry columns, guided by the local CLF, drew closer. The 1st of the 327th needed to wait until those hostiles closed into the false main battle area, destined to become a slaughter pen.

Brigade S2 analysts confidently stuck to their preliminary forecast, arguing for the major PRA stroke to the east. Dirk Blackdeer just as assuredly disagreed. "They're coming this way, sir," he told Bolger. Bill Phelps thought so too.

As the sky grayed at last, about 0610, flashes and booms to the south announced that, indeed, someone was coming, heralded by a firestorm. Bolger and his men watched the southern forest, south of the creek, light up steadily, with a nearly continual stretch of throaty cracks echoing through the trees. Guided by O/Cs, firemarker groups simulated the delivery of hundreds of 122mm rounds, scores of 152mm shells, and dozens of 122mm rockets. The fireworks lasted a half hour, ushering in what promised to be a pretty exciting dawn.

Good as JRTC is, its replication falters in depicting massed fire-power. Hundreds of artillery burst simulators, each about as strong as a really big firecracker, do not do justice to the mayhem such a pounding can deliver. A layer of sandbags on a piece of plywood, which passes for overhead cover in many American units, would never stop a direct hit from an 82mm mortar, let alone the greater impacts inflicted by actual artillery. If not crushed outright by direct hits, weak bunkers do not long endure the larger hot fragments and explosive blast waves of a real Soviet-style rolling barrage. To play this out, JRTC observer/controllers use probability tables and assess losses.

In this case, they assessed nothing, because the evil stuff exploded over empty foxholes and unmanned trenches. The few camouflaged, covered U.S. observers in the area rode it all out, waiting for the enemy infantry sure to follow. As the barrage came to an end, one final set of blasts sounded from the former TOC area, the only target engaged outside of the deception belt. Good thing Jim Laufenburg moved the command post, thought Bolger.

"Be where the artillery is not," said Bill Phelps. Well, so far, that part worked.

"Bulldog 6, this is Bushmaster 6," came Alfredo Mycue's voice. "My element forward reports fifty or more dismounts in the false positions, coming through the wire, over."

"Roger. Engage, out," responded Lieutenant Colonel Bolger laconically.

Company B's mortars began firing. Bolger and his Tac partners heard the rounds popping out to the south, among the fake emplacements. God, those PRA people must be surprised.

"Bulldog 6, this is Bushmaster 6. Cannot tell the casualties, but we are hurting them," offered Mycue. "They're stalled in the tree line south of the creek, over."

Now Bolger heard firing to the west, not far away.

"Abu, sir," suggested Phelps. The commander nodded.

Drew Felix came on the net. He, too, confronted OPFOR infantry, a lot of it, to his front. His mortars opened fire as well.

Bolger checked his watch. It showed 0650. The PRA dismounts usually punched right through, bringing in the tanks on their heels. But that was not happening this morning. Every minute's delay favored the Americans.

Company C reported nothing so far.

On the brigade net, the Apache pilots sighted fifteen armored vehicles moving north through the Bulldog sector. They would be in the false positions within ten minutes. In the clear morning light, the AH-64As counted kills in ones and twos as the OPFOR vehicles twisted and slithered among the tall trees, like elusive trout slipping along a rocky river bottom.

To the east, the Rakkasans, who had not taken much artillery fire, saw only three vehicles and no infantry.[21] Evidently, Dirk saw the truth, that the PRA main body must be going to the west, but the brigade S2 continued to tell Colonel Donald otherwise. Donald hesitated, a bit unsure, awaiting better reports.

Bolger knew, though, that he and his men had attracted the whole thing, the enemy Sunday punch. While the 1st of the 327th dodged the artillery, and hurt the enemy infantry, at some point, a foe willing to take losses—and this one was more than willing—could mass up and break the creek line.

"Bulldog 6, this is Abu 6, over," called Drew Felix.

Bolger answered. The officer heard gunfire to the west, in the Abu thickets. And now, ominously, he heard the roar of diesel engines. Tanks and their running mates, he knew. Could Abu hold?

"We are under heavy attack at the center crossing," said Felix with eerie calmness. A few empty seconds went by. "I think we're going to lose it, over," the captain concluded.

In those few words Felix summarized a brutal round of gunplay flickering around the middle of his three crossings. Skilled PRA marksmen and bold Abu riflemen traded shots. The Abus kept sniping at the enemy engineers who raced forward to clear the mines so carefully laid by Master Sergeant Bauerle and the TOC types. A T-62 tank appeared just behind the frantic PRA infantry, its machine gun sparking.

Felix tried to shift something to back up his melting platoon. With only two understrength platoons at hand, he boldly committed the other one to assist its battered counterpart. The PRA infantry traded even up in a grim exchange. When the smoke cleared ten minutes later, about 0710, all 53 Abus lay dead or wounded.[22] Two T-62s sat with lights blinking, knocked out by AT-4 shots. Three BMP troop carriers, however, squirted through, tailed by a ZSU 23-4 self-propelled antiaircraft gun.

Company B stood by, largely unengaged, its mortars having savaged the infantry column to their front. That same force then smashed into and overran the Abus, sacrificing itself in the process. Now a few vehicles were through the main defenses, headed for Artillery Road. But where had the rest of the PRA gone? An enemy infantry column and the rest of the armor remained at large.

At 0715, this powerful contingent showed up in front of 1st Lt. Chris Santos and his Cold Steel soldiers. Not much had gone right for Company C, but in this close-range knife fight, the men showed an edge previously unseen. With cool young Santos calling the signals, the riflemen, 1st Platoon under SSgt. C. R. Judd and 2d platoon working for 2d Lt. Mike Martel, rose from the creekbed and stopped the enemy advance. The firing barked and swelled. Passing right near the Spiderweb, the rest of the PRA armor pulled into sight, ready to push through once supporting engineers cleared the creekbed crossway.

"Bulldog 6, this is Cold Steel 5, over."

Bolger responded: "This is Bulldog 6, over."

"This is Cold Steel 5," continued Chris Santos. "We have ten T-62s, five BMPs, and a lot of infantry trying to get through the western ford, over."

Bolger checked his map. These crazy PRA guys really wanted to cross the swampiest ground, didn't they? That would take time, and make them big, fat targets.

Bolger could afford to swing firepower to support Cold Steel. Company B had held. Company A sold itself dearly, but was gone. Even now, Willie Utroska and Company D scrambled to catch the BMPs rolling north through the shattered Abu defenses. Now the fight, and Bolger's attention, shifted to Company C.

"Sir, we have A-10 jets and Apaches on station," said Mike Temple. Sure enough, the roar of jet engines and the whopping of rotor blades underscored Temple's comment.[23]

"Cold Steel 5, this is Bulldog 6," said Bolger. "How about some air, over?"

"Roger, that will work, over," Santos replied.

With that 2d Lt. Tom Everritt, Company C's fire support officer, proceeded to administer a clinic on the use of close air support and Army attack aviation. Everritt brought in the A-10A Warthogs[24] four times, interspersing Apache runs and artillery fires each time the ungainly Air Force jets pulled away. Cold Steel riflemen picked off milling PRA infantry. Two tanks, trying to find an unmined path across the creek, bellied into the mud and became hopelessly mired. Chris Santos and his men poured it on these unlucky tankers, killing them all and polishing off their trapped fighting vehicles too. The fight took out half of Company C's strength, but those left closed the door for good.

All of this concentrated fury cost the Atlanticans dearly, five tanks, four BMPs, and some fifty infantrymen. The very attempt, in this relatively impassable spot, reflected PRA frustrations to the east, and dismay at gaining no benefit from their usually effective preassault artillery barrage. Slowly, spitting final shots, the remaining OPFOR infantry and the rest of the combat vehicles pulled back, their thrust defeated.

Unable to get through Company C and Tom Everritt's aerial killers, the PRA went back to the devastated Abu sector, smack in the center of the strained American line. They crunched through unopposed and headed north, the last of the PRA vehicles to hit the U.S. forces. These armored vehicles included the second echelon armor, which had run into the back end of the stalled first echelon as the PRA tried to break through Company C.

The rest of the PRA infantry, having finally sprung loose a significant armored force, now turned on relatively unscathed Company B, striking them hard on the western flank once secured by Company A. Alfredo Mycue's Bushmasters fought back, with both sides dueling to the death. Casualties ran up on both sides, but in the end, the attrited Bushmasters held on.

The Tac crew, Bolger included, participated in this vicious firefight. All four of them fell, killed or wounded, but not before taking out a share of the PRA flanking element that caught them just behind Company B's main lines. Not that it mattered; the battle ended not long after Bolger and his advisors went down. As these dead men could talk, they wondered openly who had finally won the bloody battle, if an engagement carried at such cost can be called a victory.

To the north, Capt. Willie Utroska of the Bulldogs' Company D and Capt. J. D. Compeggi, commander of Company D, 3d of the 73d Armor, cooperated to bottle up and finish off the ones that got away from the rifle companies. Compeggi, the brigade reserve, had no authority to commit his Sheridan tanks. Unbelievably, the brigade S2 people still claimed that the attack that sliced up 1st of the 327th might not be the main enemy attack. Compeggi thought otherwise. Using an agreed-upon special radio channel, he heard from Utroska that targets were en route. Not one to wait for orders, Compeggi launched his company. The speedy 82d Airborne Sheridans caught their OPFOR cousins and killed them without pity, accounting for six of the leakers.

Only ten of thirty-four armored vehicles, five tanks and five BMPs, survived to dribble, singly and in pairs, onto Artillery Road. They arrived like blown horses after a broken cavalry charge, without infantry, their artillery tubes eliminated by counterbattery fires. Certainly from a brigade perspective, this equaled a victory.

On its way north, the ZSU 23-4 overran the TOC site and hosed it down, killing or wounding twenty-six soldiers, including Jim Laufenburg. Coupled with the annihilation of the tactical CP, the loss of the TOC completed the destruction of the bulk of the battalion's C^2 apparatus. These losses exerted no influence on the outcome of the battle one way or the other. Given the staff's ineptitude earlier, however, and their commander's initially poor sense of urgency, abetted by the ludicrous prisoner episode, it all constituted just desserts.

Alfredo Mycue assumed temporary command of the ravaged, but triumphant, Bulldog battalion.

The O/Cs hated it, every damn bit of it. The after-action reviews at all levels skewered the plan as bizarre and overly risky, the preparatory effort as disjointed and only partly completed, and the execution as valiant but foredoomed to heavy casualties. In the brigade AAR, the senior O/C deigned to use the term *success,* a favor not granted at the harsh, negative battalion AAR. Whatever the battalion accomplished, things had been done "the wrong way."

And yet, although messy, the defense worked. The deception plan obviated the PRA artillery as completely as if it never existed. Company A and Company C both waged gutsy fights, and Tom Everritt's application of air-delivered fires deserved a lot of praise. The battalion inflicted a whopping 141 casualties for a cost of 278 friendlies, a very respectable 1 to 1.9 ratio, well ahead of the bellwether 1 enemy to 3 U.S. ratio that delineated a winning kill rate at JRTC. Additionally, battalion efforts accounted for seven tanks, four BMPs, and four recon vehicles.[25]

So the O/Cs disapproved. So what? Bolger did not work for them. Colonel Donald appreciated the results. More important, the men of the battalion's rank and file knew that they had done some pretty good fighting. The lesson in all of this was not lost on Dan Bolger. Learning might be winning at JRTC. But here, as in real war, winning trumped learning.

Notes

The epigraph is quoted in Elizabeth Longford, *Wellington: The Years of the Sword* (New York: Harper and Row, Publishers, 1969), 485. The Duke grew fond of this pithy quote, sometimes rendering it as "Nothing except a battle lost can be half so melancholy as a battle won" or, as Wellington wrote a month after the battle of Waterloo, "Next to a battle lost, the greatest misery is a battle gained." In all variants, the core idea remains intact.

1. U.S., Department of the Army, Headquarters, Joint Readiness Training Center, "BLUFOR Personnel BDA," *1st Brigade, 101st Airborne Division (AASLT), Rotation 94-10, Third AAR* (Ft. Polk, La.: HQ, JRTC, 24 September 1994).

2. U.S., Department of the Army, Headquarters, 1st Brigade, 101st Airborne Division (Air Assault), *JRTC Handbook* (Ft. Campbell, Ky.: HQ, 1st Brigade, 101st Airborne Division [Air Assault], 1995), 28–30.

3. David C. Isby, *Weapons and Tactics of the Soviet Army* (New York: Jane's Publishing, Inc., 1988), 226–30.

4. Martin van Creveld, *Command in War* (Cambridge, Mass.: Harvard University Press, 1985), 17–18.

5. Carl von Clausewitz, *On War,* trans. and ed. by Michael Howard and Peter Paret (Princeton, N.J.: Princeton University Press, 1976), 100.

6. John Keegan, *The Mask of Command* (New York: Viking Penguin, Inc., 1987), 136.

7. Napoleon Bonaparte, *Military Maxims of Napoleon,* trans. and ed. by Brig. Gen. Thomas R. Phillips, USA (Harrisburg, Pa.: Stackpole Books, 1985), 427. Thomas J. "Stonewall" Jackson routinely carried Napoleon's *Maxims* with him, and quoted its tenets regularly.

8. Van Creveld, *Command in War,* 110–11, 150–51.

9. U.S., Department of the Army, Center for Army Lessons Learned, *CALL Newsletter 95-12: Tactical Decision Making* (Ft. Leavenworth, Kans.: Center for Army Lessons Learned, December 1995), I-5.

10. Ibid., IV-3.

11. Napoleon is quoted in U.S., Department of the Army, Center

for Army Lessons Learned, *CALL Newsletter 93-3: The Battalion and Brigade Battle Staff* (Ft. Leavenworth, Kans.: Center for Army Lessons Learned, July 1993), 9. For a model divisional planning cycle, see U.S., Department of the Army, *Student Text 100-6: Tactical Standing Operating Procedures* (Ft. Leavenworth, Kans.: Command and General Staff College, 1989). With regard to the preferred air assault planning sequence, see U.S., Department of the Army, Headquarters, 2d Brigade, 101st Airborne Division (Air Assault), "Brigade Air Assault Timeline Requirements" in *Air Assault Planning* (Ft. Campbell, Ky.: HQ, 2d Brigade, 101st Airborne Division [Air Assault], 6 November 1996), 78. To check Third Army planning figures, see Gen. George S. Patton, Jr., *War As I Knew It* (New York: Pyramid Books, 1970), 301, 307, 344.

12. CALL, *Tactical Decision Making*, p. I-5. Notably, the U.S. Army cautions those who seek to avoid the DDMP rigamarole by trying the two faster procedures mentioned. "There are no major differences between the two abbreviated processes and the DDMP," warns the Leavenworth faculty.

13. Patton, *War As I Knew It*, 307–08.

14. U.S., Department of the Army, Joint Readiness Training Center, *Take Home Package: 1st Battalion, 327th Infantry, Rotation 94-10* (Ft. Polk, La.: HQ, JRTC, 26 September 1994), 6-B, 7-B.

15. U.S., Department of the Army, Joint Readiness Training Center, *1st Battalion, 327th Infantry, Rotation 94-10 Defense AAR* (Ft. Polk, La.: HQ, JRTC, 23 September 1994), 31; U.S., Department of the Army, Joint Readiness Training Center, *1st Brigade, 101st Airborne Division (Air Assault), Rotation 94-10 Third AAR* (Ft. Polk. La.: HQ, JRTC, 24 September 1994), 57. Brigade dispatched 2,137 mines to 1-327th Infantry. Records show 954 arrived.

16. JRTC, *1st Battalion, 327th Infantry, Rotation 94-10 Defense AAR*, 8, 12.

17. Porter B. Williamson, *General Patton's Principles* (Tucson, Ariz.: Management and Systems Consultants, Inc., 1988), 134. Williamson served as a junior staff officer with Patton during the early months of World War II.

18. JRTC, *1st Battalion, 327th Infantry, Rotation 94-10 Defense AAR*, 31; JRTC, *1st Brigade, 101st Airborne Division (Air Assault), Rotation 94-10 Third AAR*, 57.

19. JRTC, *1st Battalion, 327th Infantry Rotation 94-10 Defense AAR*, 27. During the battalion commander's captivity, a Company C patrol passed within 50 meters of the enemy hiding spot in the Spiderweb.

20. JRTC, *1st Battalion, 327th Infantry Rotation 94-10 Defense AAR*, 84–85.

21. JRTC, *1st Brigade, 101st Airborne Division (Air Assault), Rotation 94-10 Third AAR*, 36.

22. JRTC, *1st Battalion, 327th Infantry Rotation 94-10 Defense AAR*, 7–8. Company A's 1st Platoon remained attached to the 3d Battalion, 101st Aviation Regiment.

23. JRTC, *1st Brigade, 101st Airborne Division (Air Assault), Rotation 94-10 Third AAR*, 37. Apaches and A-10A jets killed 71% of all vehicles hit during the battle, many south of the 1st of the 327th Infantry's sector.

24. The A-10A Thunderbolt II, nicknamed "the Warthog," carries a massive 30mm Gatling-type multibarrelled automatic cannon, firing baby-bottle-size slugs made of depleted uranium, the heaviest naturally occurring metal. The Warthog can also carry Maverick guided missiles and general-purpose bombs, both laser-guided and "dumb." See Michael Skinner, *USAFE* (Novato, Calif.: Presidio Press, 1983), 73.

25. JRTC, *1st Battalion, 327th Infantry Rotation 94-10 Defense AAR*, 7–8.

Chapter 6

Deliberate Attack (I)

> "I do not have to tell you who won the war. You know our artillery did."
>
> —Gen. George S. Patton, Jr.

The Bulldogs' sloppy, expensive triumph in the defense created some of the same problems as the earlier failure in search and attack operations. Once again, the battalion dealt with hundreds of casualties, a company gone (in this case, the Abus), and many key leaders out of action. Meanwhile, every platoon and squad cried out for ammunition, water, and food. Reorganizing and refitting, along with time-consuming AARs, devoured the rest of 23 September. The logistics effort persisted into the next day, too.

In one absolutely imperative and long-overdue decision, Lieutenant Colonel Bolger ordered MSgt. Ed Bauerle to quit the ineffectual TOC and go to Company C, to take over immediately as first sergeant. Rifle companies rise or fall based on their NCOs, and Company C had fallen far enough to demand immediate action. The actual first sergeant, like too many of the battalion's soldiers, remained at Fort Campbell, doing something other than his job. An acting first shirt did not cut it, especially in the unending pressure cooker of JRTC. So Bolger sent in the best man he had, and the TOC be damned.

Big Ed Bauerle proved to be just the tonic for Cold Steel soldiers. His entry into the prostrate company resembled the opening scenes of the movie *Patton*. Bauerle reintroduced his new charges to such quaint Regular Army customs as discipline and leadership by example. They grumbled, but the privates did as he said, because at last these men felt a firm hand at the tiller. For the first time since entering the box, the good leaders in the company felt like things were looking up. Capt. Chris Forbes especially appreciated Bauerle's coming. Forbes contributed nothing to his unit's defensive triumph and all too much to its irrelevance during counterinsurgency operations. Saddled with several weak subordinates, himself increasingly uncertain, Chris Forbes wanted help. Bauerle delivered. He arrived just in time to supervise the cleanup after his new company's head-to-head stand in the swamp.

For Bauerle and the rest, it could have been worse, much worse. This time, the concentrated nature of the 1st of the 327th deployment allowed for relatively easy extraction of the dead and wounded. Only 25 died before evacuation, less than 14 percent of those wounded, and a big improvement compared to the medevac breakdowns that dogged the unsuccessful sweeps near Jetertown.[1] For the same reason, ammunition, water, and food reached the tired rifle companies without any serious delays. These developments dramatically increased morale. Spirits rose markedly as the troops regarded the numerous PRA dead and the clots of destroyed hostile vehicles. Also, in line with the time-honored tradition of American defensive victories from Monmouth to Gettysburg to Bastogne, the victors clearly retained possession of the field.

None expected to stay there, of course. The usual JRTC pattern followed a defense with an attack, and Rotation 94-10 continued to adhere to the classic outline. The 1st of the 327th's final mission for this visit to Fort Polk involved what the doctrine writers called a *deliberate* attack. To a man, this appealed to the air assault soldiers. No more CLF, and no more defense—instead, going after conventional OPFOR in a fixed position. That seemed more like it.

Just finding and smacking targets, as done during search and attack operations, made for *hasty* attacks, the old find, fix, and finish act. Most infantry action in the latter half of this century, and a good bit before our time, sputters along in this style, hunters and hunted on the loose, the constant squad and platoon probing and poking that comprises what men like Washington and Clausewitz labeled *petit guerre* ("little war"), the "war of posts." Any American who ever walked through the Vietnam highlands, the Korean Demilitarized

Zone, the streets of Port-au-Prince, or the hills of Bosnia knows this kind of nerve-racking fighting only too well. It is the CLF's brand of war, preferred by most of America's adversaries.

As an Army, we prefer the other choice, the stand-up deliberate attack. In contrast to bushwhacking odd lots of guerrillas, a deliberate attack entails detailed planning, careful reconnaissance, and massive use of all available fire support. Here we send bullets, not men, and we do it all in a very big way, as big as we can.[2] This is war the way we like it, dropping the big hammer right on those nefarious badniks, smashing them to powder. Ask the Iraqis what it's like to be on the receiving end of this awesome, earth-shaking kind of war. No wonder most of them quit outright.

When the average American citizen thinks of U.S. Army fighting, he pictures a deliberate attack. Most Hollywood depictions of ground combat show these kinds of set-piece battles, and for good reason. They fit the format so well. Deliberate attacks have a beginning, a middle, and an end, just like any other kind of movie. The "big show" always starts with preliminary briefings and reconnoitering, allowing screenwriters to introduce characters and set the scene. The fighting ends with men surveying the scene, summing up the battle's relevance to the meaning of life, the universe, and everything. And, best of all, in the middle of one of these screen gems, at the climax, a deliberate attack allows for good old Tinseltown spectacle, a cast of thousands, a Cecil B. DeMille eruption of fireworks and charges and massed vehicles, planes, and men, all choreographed to stirring martial music. You can recite the appropriate titles, but *Gettysburg*, *The Longest Day*, and *A Bridge Too Far* come to mind.

Even the Vietnam experience, almost pure search and attack patrol actions in real life, succumbs in Hollywood to the tastes of American audiences. Think about the base camp assault in *The Green Berets*, the air cavalry raid in *Apocalypse Now*, or even the whole plot of *Hamburger Hill*. That last one supposedly told the story of a pointless, horrific ten-day hill fight in 1969, and the movie has some of that. But in the end, our 101st Airborne boys kill the evil Commies and plant the flag, all in the old style.[3] Ah, the deliberate attack, how we love it!

Like most soldiers, Dan Bolger loved it too. He knew that, compared to the no-win counterinsurgent sweeps or the face-beating administered by the PRA armored juggernaut, heading out by helicopter to finish off a cornered foe suggested a much easier task. So despite his unhappiness with the conduct, if not the outcome, of the defense, he looked forward to a straightforward attack, minus all of those civilians and the needling Cortinian Liberation Force. This time, he could send bullets, not men. And he fully intended to do so.

The end of the defensive AARs on the evening of 23 September segued into the presentation of 1st Brigade's order. The brigade planned to air assault north, into the Peason Ridge training grounds, to destroy the heart of the dug-in 526th Mechanized Infantry Battalion, down to one reinforced company backed by eight BMPs, six T-62 tanks, and four 82mm mortars. The enemy seemed to be split into three major bunches: a mechanized platoon and battalion command post on what brigade called Objective Lee, a mechanized rifle company on Objective Rakkasan, and an armored reserve somewhere between these two goose eggs. Pinpointing opposing forces within Lee and Rakkasan required pretty good reconnaissance, and finding that hidden armored reserve also necessitated a lot of luck. Brigade timed its attack to begin with touchdown of its air assault commencing at 2100 on 25 September.

The brigade concept showed all the subtlety of getting bashed in the forehead with a brick. Bolger's Bulldogs received the mission to destroy the command post at Objective Lee, presumably the easier of the two. The 3d of the 187th, lightly engaged in the defense and not really badly bloodied since the initial landings, drew the dug-in mech company somewhere in Objective Rakkasan, a "death star" of mines, wire, and bunkers, with a couple tanks and BMPs intermixed just for fun. Protecting the air assault pickup zones around the Fullerton FLS fell to the Sheridans of Team Tank and both infantry battalions' antiarmor companies.

Brigade offered no attempt at deception, nor did the planners really care how each battalion skinned its particular polecat. Brigade merely expected to deliver each battalion to its target, with 1st of the 327th leading to knock out the hostile C^2 post. Other than that bit of sequencing, and the guarantee of plenty of reinforcing firepower, the fight wholly devolved on the two battalions.

You might ask why 1st Brigade did not try something more clever, like massing both battalions on one of the two objectives, or bring-ing the tanks north by ground to take out the other, or, indeed, any-thing a little less frontal and stark. With a single battalion commit-ted, the Objective Rakkasan mission certainly appeared to bear a bit too much resemblance to 3-187th Infantry's gory role at Hamburger Hill back in 1969.[4] No matter how skillfully they did it, and the Rakkasans would surely do it well, this one was bound to hurt. Brigade probably gave the 3d of the 187th too much to do.

The Bulldogs, on the other hand, seemed underemployed. A few good scouts with a radio tied into big guns could erase any battalion TOC, even if the bad guys entrenched pretty well. Using a whole bat-talion resembled killing a mouse with a cannon. On the other hand, perhaps by this point in the rotation, Col. Jim Donald lacked confi-dence that Bolger and his men could handle anything more difficult. In any event, Objective Lee went to the 1st Battalion, 327th Infantry.

Working up a plan came much easier this time, even though the battalion commander and his staff appeased the O/C community by sticking to a broad outline of the dreaded Deliberate Decision-Mak-ing Process. Bolger never trusted that painful formula for a council of war—less so than ever after the botched defense orders process—but his key subordinates knew no other. So hobbled, they played by the house rules.

Dan Bolger knew what to do. His plan might be summed up in Uncle Sam's favorite military phrase: Send a bullet, not a man. De-termine the precise location of the objective, then blow the hell out of it. That would do it, all right.

Finding the objective fell to the Scout Platoon. Brigade wanted to insert them nearly forty-eight hours early, on the night of 23–24 September, but Bolger talked Colonel Donald out of this idea. His scouts needed to know where they were going, and why. He slated their insertion into Peason Ridge for the night of 24–25 September. The Rakkasans elected to put in their scouts as brigade proposed, almost two nights early. They died without finding the dug-in PRA mech company, a shortcoming that proved very expensive.

Bolger insisted that the 1st of the 327th scouts, the Tigers, stay alive long enough to locate the true coordinates of the hostile command

Task Force 1-327 Infantry
25 September 1994

Company A(-)
HQ/FIST
Mortars (2 x 60mm)
1st Platoon/A
3d Platoon/A

Company B
HQ/FIST
Mortars (2 x 60mm)
1st Platoon/B
2d Platoon/B
3d Platoon/B

Company C
HQ/FIST
Mortars (2 x 60mm)
1st Platoon/C
2d Platoon/C
3d Platoon/C
5th Platoon/D
    ATLS
      Stinger Team 2
Team Golf

Company D (-)
HQ
1st Platoon/D
2d Platoon/D
3d Platoon/D
4th Platoon D
Stinger Team 1

Task Force Control
Scout Platoon
    FCT 1
Mortar Platoon (4 x 81mm)
Main CP/Combat Trains
    Stinger Team 3
Field Trains

Detachments
2d Platoon/A to 3-101st Aviation

STRENGTHS (with attachments)

Company A:	57
Company B:	95
Company C:	98
Company D:	63
Mortar Platoon:	26
Main CP/Combat Trains:	56
Field Trains:	44
Scout Platoon:	17

TF 1-327 Infantry Total: 456

Starting strengths; casualties not included

Key to Abbreviations/Terms
ATLS: Advanced Trauma Lifesaving Team
CP: Command Post
FCT: Fire Control Team (Navy/Marine)
FIST: Fire Support Team (Army)
HQ: Headquarters
Team Golf: S5, civil affairs team,
      loudspeaker team, and
      counterintelligence agent

post, then call down Armageddon. A Navy/Marine spotter team joined the Tigers to help with that part. If the scouts did their job, Objective Lee would not be there when the battalion landed.

But suppose the scouts went the way of all flesh, as they had before the landings at Jetertown? In that case, finding the 526th PRA battalion's command post became a job for the lead rifle company. Once they made contact with the OPFOR platoon in the wire ring around that enemy battalion TOC, Bolger wanted his Bulldog infantry to back off and start the rain of fire. In this way, if only one man with a radio got near enough to see Objective Lee, the battalion could accomplish its mission.

Of course, getting to Peason Ridge meant another air assault, and a quick look at the allocated aircraft ruled out most of Company D's armed Humvees. Bolger planned to bring in all three rifle companies, the mortar platoon, the medical truck, and a single Maddog gunship platoon. The Tac team would fly in and walk, minus any vehicles.

This left Capt. Willie Utroska's Company D (-), the combat trains (less most of the medics), and Maj. Jim Laufenburg with the TOC free to secure and run the Rakkasan pickup zone, a little additional duty levied on the 1-327th Infantry by brigade planners growing nervous about the 3-187th's daunting mission. To permit all Rakkasans to fly in and join the fight, Jim Laufenburg and the Bulldogs would launch the other battalion's air assault, hooking up vehicles and cargo slings, marshaling troops and loads, and coordinating the grand ballet of helicopters coming and going in the night. With the CLF still very much at large, the Rakkasan departure fields out on the rolling Fullerton prairie cried out for strong security measures. Willie Utroska and his armed Humvee contingent inherited that thankless job.

Sending the Bulldogs on their way fell to 1st Lt. Dave Bair, the S3 Air. He suggested, and Bolger approved, a do-it-yourself pickup zone to be manned just prior to the arrival of the aircraft. Until then, the battalion expected to stay in its defensive positions along the creek south of Hill 109.

Bolger and Bair also agreed that this air assault, and all others from here on out, demanded one good battalion landing zone, a really well-defined clear patch that the fliers would not change or miss. Nobody wanted to go through that Blackbird-Bluebird foolishness again, trying to use an LZ for each company and ending up with a mishmash. Separate company LZs often turned a heliborne assault into a parachute landing, with small bands of frustrated men stumbling and cursing through field and stream, looking for each other rather than the enemy. Better to show up in force, thought Bolger. One big battalion LZ worked fine, with an alternate in the event the enemy strongly contested the primary.

The 101st Airborne Division leadership preached landing on or near the objective with all guns blazing. Open areas on Objective Lee definitely allowed for that, but Bolger thought otherwise. Air assault forces proved most vulnerable on the LZ, so why land right on top of aroused hostiles itching to kill you? Why not land unmolested a short way off, a few kilometers out? That way, you could get your men on the ground in one piece, assemble into some kind of order, and move out to find the ever-elusive enemy by some means other than getting shot. With Bolger's thinking about identifying the enemy CP and destroying it by fires, rather than infantry assault, landing offset made a lot of sense.

It also gravely complicated the PRA's problem, because while a small force easily protected open fields adjacent to its position, guarding all the pastures and meadows in a five-kilometer radius seemed pretty unlikely. Unable to be everywhere, an enemy dealing with this dilemma usually kept everything right around the main position, a logical solution that perfectly satisfied Dan Bolger. With the enemy conveniently fixed, all that remained was verifying his location, then dumping in a steady stream of high explosives and hot metal.

Reliance on destructive bombardment enjoys an undeservedly poor reputation among many. German panzer grenadiers, Chinese mortar-men, Viet Cong machine gunners, and Iraqi Republican Guardsmen all disparaged the Yankee propensity to send things, not men. And in case after case, from Monte Cassino to Heartbreak Ridge to Hamburger Hill, firepower alone did not suffice to liquidate determined foes. The tonnage of munitions expended in combat by U.S. forces seems largely wasted, to read the usual accounts.

Of course, prisoners in warm interrogation tents, former foes penning their postwar memoirs, and archly critical journalists, as well as some know-it-all historians, forget that American firepower has been pretty damned effective, thank you. During World War II, artillery killed and wounded 60 percent of all those who fell. American ground barrages, even without the weight of naval gunnery and aerial bombing lumped in, proved to be the most lethal of all. Some estimates credit U.S. gunners with 75 percent of all ground casualties inflicted by Americans during the campaigns of 1941–45.[5] It's messy, but it works. And all our enemies know it, hate it, and fear it.

Why, then, do so many knock the U.S. Army for its infatuation with firepower? To our less lavishly equipped foes, it must seem that we do not fight fairly. In the words of defense analyst and former artilleryman Jim Dunnigan, "Artillery is a rich man's weapon,"[6] and Americans can afford to use it in all its forms, from 60mm mortars up to massive air-delivered blockbusters. By one U.S. Army estimate, it took 340 shells to kill a single Vietnamese Communist soldier during that ugly war, a pretty prodigal expenditure by any measurement. For those who would blame that high number on the innate inefficiencies of chasing elusive insurgents, consider that in the constricted Anzio beach fighting of 1944, with a trench warfare deadlock in progress, it took 200 cannon rounds to eliminate a German.[7] The approved U.S. Army artillery firing tables very much reflect these highly pessimistic realities, calling for lots of metal and cordite invested for not much return. Your tax dollars at work, of course.

This kind of arithmetic argued against trusting too much in firepower. With some forty Atlanticans expected in and around the command post at Objective Lee, Dan Bolger might easily expend eight thousand notional shells, or more, plastering the likely target area. That bullets not men stuff goes only so far, especially in pretend warfare. The Bulldogs had to cook up something better than that, and their commander knew it.

The alternative to dumping explosives centered on ensuring accuracy. In truth, you can destroy just about any command post bunker with one solitary 105mm round—if you can get a good observer in close to adjust fire. Seeing the enemy, "eyes on target" as the troops call it, renders all of those cannoneer balance sheets null and void. Only steel and concrete bastions can withstand modern ordnance. Few field fortifications have a chance, once you drop a screaming shell through the dirt, log, and sandbag roof.

This is easier said than done, because miscreants, especially stationary ones, try not to be seen, and prefer not to wait around while the skies open up and deliver government-issue lightning. So, as in the search and attack scenario, everything hinges on finding the bad guys, then getting the howitzer rounds onto the chosen target. When it works, you get precision firing: Panama City in 1989, an AC-130H Spectre punching single 105mm shots through the roof of the *Commandancia* without scratching the paint on cars parked across the street. When it fails, you get a a bloody stewpot: Monte Cassino in 1944, you blow up the abbey, you blow up the village, you blow up the mountaintop, but you don't blow up the hidden, dug-in Germans.[8]

Cassino represented what might well happen when the indirect fire system failed, and why those nasty firing tables allotted hundreds of rounds to be certain of actually killing anything aside from unlucky flora and fauna. By definition, indirect fire means that the shooter cannot see his intended target, and so relies on a detached onlooker, a forward observer (or Air Force forward air controller, or Navy/Marine fire control team) to do the seeing, to act as eyes. Aside from his mortars, a worthy quarter of the Bulldogs' aggregate firepower, Bolger controlled only those folks, the observers, a third of the problem. The other two thirds, the guns and the brains to aim them, belonged to others.

Everyone likes to focus on the shooting irons, but in fact, the deadliness of American military firepower rests far more in the brains that translate observer sensations into hard firing data. Today, some of these observations may be done by laser range-finders and precision-location devices pinging off a satellite constellation, but regardless of how the eyes report in, it falls to a bunch of smart guys to sort it all out. In the artillery or mortars, this constitutes the FDC, the fire direction center. Shipboard gunnery employs a similar cell. Here, skilled crews use calculators and firing charts to send shells from over here to an unseen target way over there. Simple trigonometry and geometry can get you close, but to avoid using up those eight thousand rounds, FDCs also factor in adjustments for shell type, wind, ambient air temperature, humidity, barrel droop, relative altitude, powder temperature, and a host of other tweaks, all designed to close the gap between one and eight thousand. But the best way to get effect on target still revolves around a skilled observer who knows his business. Accuracy depends upon eyes on target.

Getting close enough to see what you are shooting at without becoming part of the beaten zone demands a practical knowledge of explosive characteristics for the bewildering panoply of killing items that comprise U.S. firepower. By doctrine, observers tag anything within six hundred meters of friendlies as "danger close."[9] A nice safety touch, this practice ignores two truths of ground war. First, terrain and weather rarely give you a reliable view of the enemy past a hundred meters, let alone six times that distance, especially in an overgrown semitropical morass like Fort Polk. Second, and even more unnerving, nothing except certain outlandish fuel air explosives affect anything out to six hundred meters from ground zero. To see your work, to tell if the shot pierced the bunker top in question, you must get really close to the bursting radius of the rounds. Often, especially in combat, zealous forward observers get too close. Sometimes it works, but now and then the odds catch up with young men who play chicken with shrieking metal.

To help forward observers resolve that potentially fatal dilemma, the Army teaches a technique called echelonment of fire. It follows a simple rule: Fire big stuff first. In theory, a force approaching a dug-in enemy uses big, inaccurate weapons early, then substitutes smaller, more precise armament as the range closes. Done correctly, a ground assault column can follow right on the heels of an endless curtain of shot and shell, not unlike the old World War I rolling barrage.[10] The 1st of the 327th planned to carry out this method at Objective Lee if the scouts failed to solve their problem for them.

The scouts did not fail. Their success in completing the battalion's mission in less than twenty-four hours stands as a shining example of that first pillar of U.S. Army practice, expending things, not soldiers. It fully justified Bolger's reluctance to send in his Tigers without preparations simply to comply with a preprinted brigade time schedule.

Minimum Safe Distances for Explosive Ordnance

450 meters	
400 meters	————————— 127mm naval gun (410 meters)
350 meters	
300 meters	
250 meters	
200 meters	————————— Maverick missile/Mk82 bomb/Hydra-70 rocket (220 meters)
	————————— cluster bomb unit (195 meters)
150 meters	
100 meters	————————— Hellfire missile (100 meters)
50 meters	————————— 155mm howitzer/30mm cannon (50 meters)
	————————— 81mm mortar/105mm howitzer (35 meters)
	————————— 60mm mortar (28 meters)

Enemy

Sending the scouts in at all risked seventeen lives and the loss of surprise for the deliberate attack. Operating well beyond the radius of the SINCGARS radios, the Tigers depended upon calls to passing aircraft from the Apache battalion and the Navy/Marine ANGLICO pair's high-frequency radio sets. If the scouts took casualties or came under heavy attack, brigade would have to extract them using aviation assets. The 1st Battalion, 327th Infantry, had no hope of get-

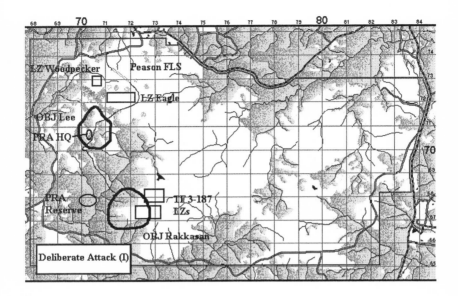

ting to them on the ground, at least not in time to do anything except fight for their corpses.

Before midnight on 24 September, as they flew north aboard two blacked-out UH-60L choppers, SSgt. Kirk Mayfield and his fifteen men knew their job. Working in three teams, the Tigers intended to pinpoint the true site of the 526th PRA Mechanized Battalion's TOC. The brigade order specified a six-digit grid coordinate, but that only represented a guess, and nobody had eight thousand projectiles to invest to ensure that close would be good enough. In previous JRTC rotations, as in real combat, that preliminary position sometimes turned out to be a kilometer off, an intentional bit of friction tossed in by the Fort Polk scenario developers just to keep the Americans on their toes. Objective Lee was a pretty big area, and a forty-odd-man OPFOR headquarters element could really get hidden in there. Mayfield and his scouts aimed to find their quarry.

Battalions often give their scouts too many missions, but here, Dan Bolger and Bill Phelps showed prudence. The Tigers typically received one task only, focused on one place. In this case, the task was obvious. Bolger appended the ANGLICO twosome to the platoon and issued concise guidance: "If you find it, kill it with fires." Mayfield fully understood how much rode on his work.

Along with Mayfield flew one other man, also key to this mission. Platoon leader 1st Lt. Mark Lawry took his scout platoon through the NEO and defense missions while platoon sergeant Kirk Mayfield stayed near the Bulldog TOC, acting as a liaison and communications base. Tonight, the roles reversed. Lawry would return to the 1st of the 327th assembly area and stand by near the battalion headquarters, ready to speak for his scouts and their interests regardless of what else transpired to distract the Bulldogs. The Tigers called this role the "guardian angel."

With Tigers and guardian angel aboard, the two Blackhawk aircraft popped up together, tilting at an absurd angle, then pancaked to the ground in unison. The UH-60Ls settled in a broad clearing fronted by waving slash pines. This nondescript spit of clearing, LZ Woodpecker, lay between Peason's flight strip and the presumed location of the enemy command post. The scouts scrambled off the birds within thirty seconds, vanishing into the treeline. Overhead, droning AH-64A Apaches flew cover for Mayfield's teams. The PRA did not react.

After a ten-minute security halt to adjust to this stretch of woods and weeds, the scouts split into three teams. Each moved off slowly on its own path, destined to occupy three preselected vantage points that purported to offer a glimpse of the 526th Mech Battalion's buried command post. Among the gear carried, the heavy ANGLICO shore-to-ship radio set loomed large in both bulk and importance. When one or more of the Tiger elements found the heart of Objective Lee, that naval communications device would serve to finish off the unwary Atlantican battalion CP with a few volleys of destroyer gunnery.

The scouts walked slowly, bent low under heavy rucksacks. Unlike a line infantryman, a scout does not enjoy the option of a light load. Dumped into forbidding badlands, the understrength little scout platoon, eighteen strong if fully manned, must carry everything it needs. So Kirk Mayfield and his men humped along, groaning under the weight of awkward radio transceivers, spare antennas, compact but weighty batteries, extra water in collapsible 5-quart blivets, and enough ammunition to break contact and pull back to an extraction LZ. Paying attention while laden with a hundred pounds of war gear took a lot of practice, and special men.

Scouts, you see, represent the lowest order of true special forces, men picked and trained to work behind enemy lines, or, if you prefer to acknowledge today's wars without fronts, to penetrate denied territory and report back. Above the scouts, further up the ziggurat of elite recon forces, stood divisional long-range surveillance detachments (LRSD, known in Vietnam as long-range reconnaissance patrols, LRRPs), corps long-range surveillance companies (LRSC), the 75th Ranger Regiment's regimental surveillance detachment (RSD), and finally, at the very pinnacle, the greatest of them all, the squadrons of the Intelligence Support Activity (ISA), who scouted for the black-garbed shooters of Delta Force, 1st Special Forces Operational Detachment—Delta, America's premier counterterrorists.[11] All of these groups shared one mission: Find the enemy. Killing the foe fell to other forces and other means.

The 1st of the 327th's scouts, many of them Ranger School graduates, consistently trained to work in four- to five-man teams at or beyond the extreme range of communications. Their reconnaissance mission necessitated men with patience and attention to detail, soldiers who could lay for hours in the rain and then notice when one branch moved the wrong way. Of course, the same schools that produced scouts also produced the highly aggressive door-kickers and life-takers who populate the Rangers, Green Berets, and Delta. Although both go deep into the dark territory, scouts do not equal shooters. Not being detected drove the scouting function.

Mayfield understood this, and to a lesser extent, so did his platoon leader, Mark Lawry. Their men were learning, because the previous battalion leadership used them as a raiding force, as hit-and-run killers. Now the game involved a long stay on deadly ground, with maximum effort devoted to not being seen. Old habits die hard, though, and all that Ranger indoctrination does not fade away overnight. As they picked their three separate ways south, some of the soldiers in each team longed to shoot, not snoop. The PRA afforded them that opportunity.

At 0712 the next morning, the 2d Squad ran up on an Atlantican observation post, two PRA troopers talking behind a big hardwood tree, inside what looked like a deer-stand encrusted with vines and leaves. Perfect scouts would have pulled back and watched. Not quite so perfect, the men of the Tiger 2 element opened fire. The OPFOR shot back. One bad guy fell, but so did two scouts. Worse, now the enemy knew they had company.

With his leader down, command of 2d Squad passed to Pfc. Perry A. Hoffman, whose crack shooting allowed his two partners to pull out their wounded sergeant and his radioman. Hoffman recognized exactly what he had just hit. A static little OP like that meant the 526th CP must be very close. Hoffman called Staff Sergeant Mayfield and reported his contact and his estimate.

At the same time Hoffman hit the OP to the southwest of the suspected command post perimeter, Sgt. Eric S. Freeborg and one of his 3d Squad mates slowly crawled through the tall grass along the eastern grove of thin, stunted pine trees. The other pair of scouts waited in a nearby draw. At 0825, a PRA four-man patrol hit Freeborg's stay-behind team. Another vicious exchange boiled up, then died. Both scouts were hit, but an enemy also went down. Freeborg remained undetected. The PRA began to move around in response to the American activity on both sides of their perimeter.

That motion, which increased over the next half hour, enabled Freeborg to pinpoint the 526th Mechanized Battalion's command bunker complex. Watching and listening, Freeborg crept across an enemy bivouac site and settled into a thicket within a hundred meters of the opposition's TOC. By 0915 he was sure that he had it. Freeborg clearly saw the mound of a central position with long antennas protruding. Around it, butted against tree trunks, squatted an oval ring of eight fighting positions with overhead cover. A tall stack of concertina wire ran around the entire circle. Men with weapons moved purposefully around inside the wire, clearly alarmed by reports from the two firefights. This must be it.

Freeborg set his radio to whisper mode and began transmitting to Staff Sergeant Mayfield, who owned the bigger radios that could talk back to brigade and battalion and, just as important, the naval gunfire spotters who could take care of this whole issue right now. The report went into just enough detail, and passed a precise grid coordinate, accurate to within ten meters, for the OPFOR command post. Just as the sergeant completed his message, but before Mayfield could answer, a roving PRA pair found Freeborg. With two shots, they killed him and his buddy. Freeborg dumped his radio fill and laid back, out of the fight.

The enemy thought that this destroyed the Tigers just outside their wire. After all, the PRA knew American scouts ran in three squads, and the three contacts so far seemed to indicate that Atlantican vigilance had done in all three with minimal harm to the security platoon. This complacency almost immediately received its just reward.

Mayfield did not hesitate. Ordering his ANGLICO men to move to adjust fire on the target, he called into the sky, trying to attract an Apache section. He made voice contact with an OH-58C Kiowa observation helicopter crew by 0931, and relayed Freeborg's news. Then he called in the gunships.

By 0938 two AH-64A Apaches identified and began attacking the PRA battalion headquarters. Loosing simulated 30mm rounds and four pods of 70mm folding-fin rockets, the aircraft slaughtered a mortar crew and destroyed the tube, knocked out a BMP fighting vehicle, and toasted three BRDM armored recon trucks.[12] The enemy, caught in the open as he moved to police up the 1st of the 327th scouts, offered feeble resistance. Even more awful pounding followed.

Under cover of the rampaging helicopters, two Marine Corps spotters settled in just north of the target and called on their high-frequency sets, establishing communications with a notional guided missile destroyer, the USS *John Hancock* (DD-981), sailing some twenty kilometers to the south. In response to the Marines' description and target data, a real destroyer like *Hancock* would swivel its two Mk45 127mm (5-inch) single-cannon automated gun turrets into line with the designated impact points. Elevating tubes, mechanized loaders select high explosive, variable-time fused (HE-VT), ram one round into each breech, and stand by. The JRTC controller office playing the ship told the Marines the guns onboard stood ready to adjust on target. The observers waited until the Apaches peeled off, then ordered: "One round per mount, commence firing."

Two ranging shots, one per turret, supposedly sped toward Objective Lee. Replicated by fire-marker personnel with blast simulators, the HE-VT projectiles smacked squarely inside the wire. That looked good enough. The lead ANGLICO man growled: "Salvo firing, forty per mount, commence firing."

Arcing out of the barking cannons at one round every second and a half, eighty pretend HE-VT shells came screaming into Objective Lee.[13] The firemarkers and O/Cs went wild, dropping explosive devices and slaying the trapped PRA. They faithfully reproduced the aftermath, if not the ear-shattering, earthquaking arrival, of eighty more HE-VT 127mm naval shells. Built to clean off the upperworks of Soviet cruisers or turn a *Kiev*-class carrier's flight deck into a *flambé*, the 5-inchers made hash of the small PRA perimeter. Here was accurate firepower; bullets, not men, pounded right onto target; a nail hit squarely by an anvil.

By 1130 the OPFOR had lost their entire TOC staff, a total of eighteen men, plus the two killed by the scouts and those wiped out in blown vehicles by the relentless Apaches. The 526th commander, who survived by the skin of his teeth, elected to extract his remaining twenty-six men and one 82mm mortar, and add them to his armored reserve hidden near Objective Rakkasan. That afternoon, the PRA evacuated Objective Lee. At the cost of six men, Kirk Mayfield's Tigers accomplished the mission of the 1st Battalion, 327th Infantry.[14]

If the Bulldogs succeeded brilliantly at sending a bullet, not a man, they failed rather badly in adhering to the other practice of the U.S. Army, shaping tactics to match the situation on the ground. By noon on 25 September, Dan Bolger and Bill Phelps knew that Staff Sergeant Mayfield and his men had utterly destroyed Objective Lee. The brigade staff, including Colonel Donald, knew it too. And yet the Bulldogs and 1st Brigade continued right along with their plan to attack Objective Lee, a place that no longer existed.

Why? Aside from obstinacy and perverse logic, two legitimate reasons stand out. In the first place, the battalion commander could not be certain that whatever the scouts assailed really formed the enemy command post. After all, these CLF bastards showed an inordinate flair for fake positions, and even the Bulldogs had tried them with some positive results. No, like the biblical doubting Thomas, Bolger wanted to stick his hands in the shell craters and poke the trashed antennas with his boot. Then he would believe. Brigade agreed with this caution, for the same reasons. You just never knew about the PRA or the CLF.

Well, actually, Bolger and friends knew only too much about the CLF, the second reason the battalion missed the significance of the Tigers' efforts near Lee. The wily rebels had resurfaced like bad bile in the throat, determined to torment the 1st of the 327th as they prepared for their deliberate attack. Insurgent snipings and mortar strikes created a mounting series of bloody distractions, making it hard to focus on events up in Peason and only too easy to deal with the guerrillas right here in front. That suited the OPFOR perfectly.

Unmolested by the quiescent Bulldogs, who practiced and prepared to attack Objective Lee as if the Americans remained safely in their home training ground at Fort Campbell, the CLF hit and hit hard. Late on the afternoon of 24 September, long after the battalion staff issued their crisp, simple order for the mission up north, twelve rounds of 82mm fire landed near the TOC, killing five, wounding eight, and destroying three Humvees. A repeat that night caught six more men and two more Humvees still hanging around that known target area. Bolger's almost immobile TOC, with its three square tents and fleet of Humvees, ended up in a ditch off to the north. Nobody dared run the generators, and the radios stayed on whisper mode as the scouts inserted up near Peason FLS.

The next day, the same CLF mortar scored again, killing fourteen and wounding twenty-three Bushmasters as the meticulous Alfredo Mycue rehearsed his company's breach of a wire obstacle. The men made the mistake of coming out into the open on Hill 109, and the CLF gunners answered with sixty rounds. This brought to fifty-six the number of battalion casualties suffered in the assembly area, just waiting to attack.[15]

Proper security patrols and outposts would have prevented all this. A healthy series of platoon-scale search and attack sweeps might have cured it even at this late hour. Instead, too far along and too untrained to solve the nagging CLF problem, Bolger pulled the plug. He moved his men out to their pickup zones early. Maybe the CLF observers lacked the sense, or the freedom, to follow. Chased from their assembly area like scalded rats, the battalion plunged through the creekbed, across their old deception positions, and out into the woodline bordering the Fullerton FLS open area. In a final insult, the Abu guide, just in front of Dan Bolger and his Tactical CP crew, stepped on one of his own mines as he led the sweating soldiers out of their former defensive lines.[16] What a night this promised to be!

For Maj. Jim Laufenburg and his PZ force, for Capt. Willie Utroska's Maddogs of Company D, and for Capt. Ronz Sarvis at the field trains, the harbingers of OPFOR activity proved only too true. The night of 25–26 September featured a battle royal on the outskirts of the Rakkasan PZs and in the brigade's field trains assemblage. Things got so confused that the O/Cs never made a valid assessment of just what happened. It served as the last hurrah of the unbowed, thoroughly defiant CLF, but at least it let Willie's gun trucks administer a few licks, even if they did not truly "count."

The battle that counted happened to the north, after a completely uneventful air assault unaffected by anything more than blowing dust. Bolger's men thumped down in LZ Eagle, with Capt. Chris Forbes and Company C leading to secure the initial landings and provide a secure base for reinforcement or casualty evacuation. Forbes inherited a Humvee gun truck platoon from Company D, as well as the medics, Team Golf, and effective control of the battalion's 81mm mortars, a bunch little heard from on this whole JRTC exercise.[17] Well, tonight they could remedy that. Objective Lee shone as a mortar-man's dream, rife with chances to shoot high explosive, white phosphorus, and illumination flares.

Learning from the circus down near Jetertown, Chris designated his XO, the tireless 1st Lt. Chris Santos, to control inbound birds. As a result, LZ Eagle ran very smoothly, although one errant Chinook insisted on landing, rather hard, up near the Peason FLS. The Cold Steel soldiers, responding to the firm hand and solid example of 1st Sgt. Ed Bauerle, did their part well. When OPFOR mortarmen peppered the LZ, a Cold Steel patrol took out the shadowing observer team, effectively silencing the hostile gun. Perhaps Bolger had guessed right, and with Bauerle's help, Forbes might shape up.

Expedited by Cold Steel's work, actions on the LZ went fairly well. Capt. Drew Felix and his Abus, with 1st Platoon returned from the aviators and 2d Platoon sacrificed to the same role, took the lead as the battalion formed to attack Objective Lee. Drew's job was to find the place.

It fell to Alfredo Mycue and Company B to breach through the wire and destroy the objective. Since the CP appeared to be small, the Bushmasters allocated a platoon to direct fire support, a platoon to breach, and a platoon to assault through. Even allowing for the CLF-inspired carnage that afternoon, Mycue thought he could do the job.

As Bolger and his rifle companies moved toward Objective Lee, SSgt. Kirk Mayfield arrived out of the darkness, slipping out of a curtain of ferns like a gray apparition. "We've blown it away, sir," he said in a low voice. "The enemy is gone."

Beside the battalion commander, Drew Felix hesitated. Now what, Bolger?

The lieutenant colonel did not waver. "We go as planned. We have to be sure."

The Abus headed out, a long Ranger file shimmering in the starlight and the glow of the crescent moon. Off to the south, gunfire erupted. While it changed pitch and intensity, it persisted for a long time. "The Rakkasans," muttered Maj. Bill Phelps. "Sounds like they're catching it."

Indeed, the 3d of the 187th followed the usual 101st Airborne formula and landed in multiple LZs, right among the enemy's position. They found an aroused PRA mechanized company only too happy to see them. The resultant running fight ebbed and swelled all night long, consuming hundreds of good men as the Rakkasans tried to bull through the wire. The 3d of the 187th underwent a brutal flensing. How different it might have been if their 1st of the 327th friends raced south to help them, to appear unexpectedly on an open Atlantican flank.

The Bulldogs, though, did not turn from their preprogrammed course. Haunted by the memory of the deceptive BSP, the Abus pressed on. They passed the abandoned shell of the BMP, and the remnants of fighting positions. Movement went carefully, at a dawdling pace, just to be certain.

Mayfield ranged ahead of the ponderous column, verifying once more that nothing lived on the destroyed CP site. Among the mapboards, broken antenna pieces, and other debris on site, the scout NCO listed four AN/GRA-39 remote radio speakers. These boxy items, known in TOCs throughout the U.S. Army as "angry 39s," went with the older generation of single-frequency unencrypted radios still used by the JRTC OPFOR. Angry 39s allowed signalmen to put up a radio and antenna hundreds of meters from a command post, then run wire to the AN/GRA-39 speakers. A soldier in the TOC talked and heard normally on the angry 39, but the high-powered radio, with its blaring electronic signature, sat far enough away that if it attracted unfriendly firepower, the CP would likely escape. Finding these particular pieces of hardware reliably identified the place as a real TOC, as surely as finding golden arches indicated a McDonald's hamburger stand.

Word of angry 39s just about confirmed the issue, but to be doubly certain, Bolger vectored his scout platoon sergeant south to the original brigade location stated in the operation order. Mayfield fired a single 81mm illumination round to light his way. He and his Tigers saw nothing. Meanwhile, the brigade net crackled with mayhem as the Rakkasans fought on alone.

By midnight, the battalion consolidated on the bald hill overlooking the enemy CP, with Abu on the top and the Bushmasters of Company B to the northwest, blocking a draw. Abu's prominence, a bit of key terrain, allowed anyone on it to call fires on any likely CP sites. Not surprisingly, earlier that morning, the ANGLICO Marines used a corner of that same hill to smash up the 526th TOC. Now Drew Felix and his men employed the small knoll as a bed of ease, the final stop en route to the end of this JRTC sojourn. Sunrise meant "endex," end of exercise, the conclusion of tactical play for Rotation 94-10. With Objective Lee well in hand, the Abus, and indeed the entire battalion, leaned forward, anticipating that happy hour. Turning south, leaving behind this meaningless ground to march to the aid of the Rakkasans, never even came up.

An hour went by. Midnight came and went. The clock crawled toward 0100, and the battalion sat on its hill and waited. Nothing happened near Lee. Objective Rakkasan kept cooking away down south. The Bulldog soldiers, settling into glassy-eyed stupor, ignored it.

At 0050, an Apache pilot excitedly called over the brigade net. "Bastogne TOC," he said, "this is Widowmaker 23. I have two BRDMs moving near Peason FLS. Engaging, out." A few minutes later the soldiers around Objective Lee heard the dull booms of explosive simulators. The Apache certainly hit something.

By rights, Widowmaker 23 needed to clear his fires with Lieutenant Colonel Bolger. Instead, he shot first and asked questions later, a bad choice. The pilot's targets turned out to be two Maddog Humvees, in fact, the two set down by the misguided CH-47D that plopped onto the Peason Ridge airstrip. The overeager Apache driver compounded his fellow fliers' initial error, fatally so. Six Americans died and two fell wounded, with both trucks totally trashed.[18] Chris Forbes and his people recovered these unfortunates.

The PRA commander finally noticed the battalion hanging around near his wrecked command post. Just after 0100, he committed the leftovers of the security platoon, twenty-six strong with a single mortar. These OPFOR soldiers received one task: Kill Americans. Separating into four-man teams, the PRA troopers metamorphosed into CLF guerrillas. Back in their familiar role, they proceeded to teach yet another painful lesson about security.

One foursome infiltrated quietly into the sedentary Abu perimeter. Just after 0120, sixteen 82mm rounds stitched across the hilltop, knocking down Abu troops like bowling pins. Casualties ran up to more than twenty, among them Captain Felix. From the west, out of the ruins of the abandoned command post, a white flashlight beam clicked on. It served to cue OPFOR riflemen who lacked night-vision goggles but knew how to hit where they aimed. The flat crack of blank 5.56mm shots sounded, all coming from outside the perimeter. Then the light went off.

"Medic . . . medic . . ." Bolger and the Tac officers heard the Abu soldiers rasping the dreaded request in low voices. The white light came on again, followed by more shots. More Abu troops fell. Alarmed by the mounting counterattack, Bolger began to call for Captain Mycue's Company B to move in from the west, to flush out the flashlight man and his CLF comrades. The Bushmasters stirred, but moved sluggishly, as if in a nightmare.

Then an unfamiliar voice came over the battalion command net: "Bushmaster 6, this is Abu 6, over." It wasn't Drew Felix. Obviously, the CLF now had a SINCGARS radio, already conveniently tuned to the right frequency hopset. That promised nothing good.

In a better-disciplined and better-trained battalion, the men of 1st of the 327th would have made short work of the enemy quartets stinging them from the woodline and snaking through the sievelike U.S. perimeter. Had the Abus and Bushmasters used the night-sight technology provided at great expense by Uncle Sam, the American infantry could hardly have missed the PRA riflemen stumbling through the underbrush. An AN/PVS-7B goggle device, used with an AN/PAQ-4B laser designator properly hooked on the barrel of an individual weapon, allowed a U.S. shooter to hit wherever he placed his dot of laser light. Both rifle companies had seventy of these highly accurate night firing sets. Unfortunately, the Abus used only twenty-three, and only six of these correctly. Company B's numbers were better, but not by much.[19] The opposition took full advantage of the American lapses and cavorted aggressively around and among the passive, unseeing Bulldog lines.

Over the next few hours, in the dark drag of time before the sky grayed to herald another morning in Cortina, this brand of sniping and scrapping sputtered and flared. The 1st of the 327th soldiery, intermixed with their aggressive foes, held their ground or moved feebly about the hilltop. American mortars and artillery sat impotent, idled by the opposition's intentional closure to belt-buckle range. Steered by the intermittent illumination and darkenings of the OP-FOR's white flashlight, bold teams of enemy riflemen darted to and fro. They rambled at will. Gradually, by pairs and trios, enemy firing whittled away most of Company A, then a platoon or so of Company B. American return firing, sparse and inaccurate, took out only a few tormentors.

The battalion commander and his Tac men went down last, emulating George Custer at his futile 1876 stand at the Little Big Horn. With dawn a half hour hence, fifty-two of fifty-seven Abus down, and Company B unable to work its way past dead-eye PRA rifle teams to reach the knoll, Bolger committed his own people to the fray.[20] So far, the lieutenant colonel and his associates urged on Company B and monitored the unremitting purgatory of Company A, neither with much effect. A kilometer-plus to the northeast, Company C, steadied by Bauerle and a rejuvenated Chris Forbes, handily brushed aside a PRA element that endeavored to close on LZ Eagle. But Bolger and his Tac claimed no credit for that positive event. Their fight lay here, within spitting distance of the dismounted command post crew. Well, they carried rifles, didn't they?

The enemy trooper with the white light assisted the Tac's foray. He switched on, hunting the last of the Abus. At a nod from his commander, Bill Phelps, the best shot in the Tac with several confirmed kills to his credit this rotation, swung wide around. He rapidly flanked Mr. Flashlight from the southeast. Dirk Blackdeer, former rifle platoon leader turned intelligence officer, went along as the S3's wingman. Their rifles barked, yellow flashes in the night.

Seeing that, the lieutenant colonel opened fire. Aping Bolger, six more rifle-armed staff officers reared up from the tall grass and shot too. The enemy light went out, but the Tac soldiers had their goggles on. They stayed with their work, scanning and shooting methodically.

Four PRA men, one the light-bearer, turned in shock, their buzzers sounding. Preoccupied with rummaging through the pockets and pouches of an untidy row of Company A's casualties, the hostile quartet never saw the their demise coming, let alone from a flank and the rear at once. Why, it simply wasn't American! Bolger heard the OPFOR soldiers cursing bitterly.

The firing stopped abruptly. A minute crawled by, then two. Bolger could still see the newly inflicted enemy casualties laying unchecked. But the rest of the hill lay silent now. All the other PRA seemed to melt away, their light out in more ways than one. A slight breeze rustled the leaves overhead. Or was someone moving out there?

Yes, that sound must be men picking through brush. *Not ours,* thought the commander. Bolger motioned his excited partners into a muddy hollow scooped out beneath an abandoned ton-and-a-half water trailer parked incongruously off in the southwest scrub line that framed the embattled hill crest. Together, heads barely above the thick grass, they watched Phelps and Blackdeer disappear in the direction of the 526th PRA Mechanized Battalion's blasted command bunker. Another five minutes passed. Then, two shots sounded, close together, and the buzzers trilled.

Then noise, heavy rustling, and right atop them, as if born from the belly of the green water tank, three enemy gunmen loomed. They fired together, ripping three-round bursts from their M16A2s, shouting "Close kill! Close kill!" A passionless O/C aimed his controller gun, squeezed, and put paid to the feisty Bulldog Tac. That did it.

Bolger's MILES harness sounded its alarm. Sighing, the tired commander fished up his MILES casualty card. This one read "KIA." Dead again, the battalion commander reached into his radio backpack and slowly pulled out a poncho liner. Settling into the dewy grass, useless and dejected, Bolger slid swiftly into dreamless slumber in the predawn twilight. Exhausted, the lieutenant colonel missed the crescendo of firing around daybreak that marked the Rakkasan's bloody denoument to the south. Neither Bolger nor his battalion had the capability to do a damn thing about it.

Sunup brought the formal end of JRTC Rotation 94-10. For the Bulldogs, this sour ending to the battalion's deliberate attack saw 203 American casualties sustained in return for a paltry 23 Atlanticans knocked out on and near Objective Lee.[21] Admittedly, O/C record-keeping must have erred in favor of the enemy. The numbers do not reflect the PRA vehicle crewmen who died in the Apache runs or the losses suffered in the confused melee on Abu's hill, let alone those enemy dropped near LZ Eagle or, for that matter, back in the Fullerton area courtesy of Captain Utoska's Maddog gunships and Capt. Ronz Sarvis's steady headquarters troops. All the Bulldogs hit, of course, made the final butcher's roll. Even if all 46 enemy in the area died in battle, the battalion paid a very steep cost to accomplish its mission on Objective Lee.

Despite the price, after all, the battalion carried out its assigned task, largely thanks to Dan Bolger's trust in his scouts, their brilliant execution on the ground, and the fine effects achieved by well-directed supporting fires. That said, as wonderfully as the scouts did business, the rest of the 1st of the 327th's pointless, and ultimately gory, nonmaneuvering defied explanation. Even allowing for the battalion commander's understandable reluctance to believe in the effects of preassault fires in view of the JRTC OPFOR's love of trick positions, the confirmation of the CP's destruction by midnight should have spurred action. Rather, paralysis ensued. By all rights, by common sense and any military logic, Bolger should have marched to the sound of the guns, to succor the Rakkasans and help complete the 1st Brigade mission. Instead, his objective a torched dry hole, Bolger and his men sat and waited for a counterattack, then obligingly absorbed it in the most unpleasant possible fashion.

In this rough style, JRTC Rotation 94-10 concluded. In reviewing the scoreboard, Bolger's men acknowledged a clear defeat in the search and attack phase. Nobody argued with that judgment, although the noncombatant evacuation correctly counted as a nicely executed opening gambit and ameliorated some of the embarrassment inflicted by the unyielding CLF. Despite this bitter failure in the opening round, the battalion recovered, and accomplished their defense and deliberate attack missions, albeit at the awful toll of 909 men. Bolger's mistakes and his men's training and tactical lapses used up twice the battalion's average field strength in less than two weeks, hardly comforting. On the other hand, the Bulldogs chewed up 238 hostiles, no mean number by JRTC standards. The battalion came to Cortina to fight, and they certainly did so.[22] But expertise did not keep pace with aggressiveness. As a result, the 1st of the 327th's OPFOR kills exacted too high a price in friendlies.

On the four-tier scale of unofficial JRTC evaluation—kill ratio, mission success, going the distance, and just "learning"—the 1st of the 327th landed somewhere in the null zone between steps two and three. They succeeded at two of three missions, but the battalion's kill ratio earned few kudos. Still, 94-10 featured an especially difficult scenario, with more civilians, more enemy, and more curve balls than the average trip to Fort Polk, all very much a tribute to Col. Jim Donald's JRTC-experienced brigade headquarters, and very much a trial for the Bulldogs and the Rakkasans along for this wild ride. With the exception of the final mission, the Bulldogs drew the majority of the tougher assignments in an already challenging exercise. Many battalions did a lot worse under easier conditions.

The performance of the 1st Battalion, 327th Infantry Regiment, ranked as, well . . . okay, maybe a few hairlines above average. No objective observer could deny the battalion's hard edge and guts in the face of adversity, and the O/Cs formally acclaimed the organization's motivation, toughness, discipline, and quality leadership.[23] Left unstated, but equally obvious, lingered one critical question: With such a promising base to build on, why didn't they do better?

It fell to Dan Bolger, his officers, and his NCOs to wrestle with that reality, and its sobering implications for future combat when and if the battalion deployed in earnest. Those 909 dead and wounded, the men who lay untended for days on Hunger Hill, the bodies stacked like cordwood near Objective Lee, demanded a wholesale reevaluation of how the 1st of the 327th trained and fought. Himself twice shot and once ignominiously captured, outthought and outfought near Jetertown by the Cortinian insurgency, Bolger certainly owned every personal incentive to apply his full energies to doing better, a lot better. Many battalions and battalion commanders learn a great deal at JRTC, but not very many do anything about it. With the test over, and another unlikely for years, leaders tend to declare victory, accentuate the positive, and move on to other matters.

Not so the Bulldogs—Dan Bolger would not have it. In the 101st Airborne, wars and rumors of the same daily threatened to call the 1st of the 327th to act. They dared not ignore all that went wrong, nor could they let slip that which went right. Bolger guessed that he and his men might get a chance to demonstrate their new, highly improved battalion task force in the Middle East, Asia, or Latin America, in some hellhole *du jour*. Instead, Bolger's Bulldogs got another crack at the CLF. This time, they were ready.

Notes

The epigraph is quoted in Russell F. Weigley, *History of the United States Army* (Bloomington, Ind.: Indiana University Press, 1984), 474.

1. U.S., Department of the Army, Joint Readiness Training Center, *1st Battalion, 327th Infantry Rotation 94-10 Defense AAR* (Ft. Polk, La.: Headquarters, Joint Readiness Training Center, 23 September 1994), 7. Records showed that of 285 soldiers wounded during search and attack operations, 118 died untreated, a grim 41%.

2. U.S., Department of the Army, *FM 7-20: The Infantry Battalion* (Washington, D.C.: U.S. Govt. Printing Office, 1992), 3-25 to 3-28.

3. Lt. Col. Michael Lee Manning, USA, ret., *Vietnam at the Movies* (New York: Fawcett Columbine, 1994), 240. This excellent study of how our entertainment industry deals with warfare offers numerous insights as to why war movies tend to be so similar in appearance, regardless of subject.

4. Samuel Lipsman, Edward Doyle, et al., *The Vietnam Experience*, 25 vols. (Boston: Boston Publishing Co., 1981–1988), *Fighting for Time* (1983), 17–23. The 3d Battalion, 187th Infantry bore the brunt of the fighting at Hamburger Hill.

5. Russell F. Weigley, *Eisenhower's Lieutenants* (Bloomington Ind.: Indiana University Press, 1981), 28; Capt. Michael D. Doubler, USA, *Busting the Bocage: American Combined Arms Operations in France, 6 June–31 July 1944* (Ft. Leavenworth, Kans.: Combat Studies Institute, 1988), 29; James F. Dunnigan, *How to Make War* (New York: William Morrow and Co., Inc., 1988), 97.

6. Dunnigan, *How to Make War*, 97.

7. Samuel Lipsman, Edward Doyle, et al., *The Vietnam Experience*, 25 vols. (Boston: Boston Publishing Co., 1981–1988), Edgar C. Doleman et. al., *Tools of War* (1984), 48.

8. For Panama City, see Philip D. Chinnery, *Any Time, Any Place* (Annapolis, Md.: Naval Institute Press, 1994), 246–47; for Cassino, see Lt. Col. Carlo d'Este, USA, ret., *Fatal Decision* (New York: Harper-Collins Publishers, 1991, 258–61.

9. U.S., Department of the Army, Headquarters, 101st Airborne Division (Air Assault) Artillery, *Fire Support Handbook* (Ft. Campbell, Ky.: HQ, 101st Airborne Division [Air Assault] Artillery, 1995), 2-1.

10. U.S., Department of the Army, Joint Readiness Training Center, *1st Battalion, 327th Infantry Rotation 94-10 Attack AAR* (Ft. Polk, La.: Headquarters, Joint Readiness Training Center, 26 September 1994), 47–48.

11. For a discussion of these various reconnaissance forces, see U.S. Department of the Army, *FM 7-85 Ranger Unit Operations* (Washington, D.C.: U.S. Govt. Printing Office, 1987), 2-2; U.S., Department of the Army, Headquarters, U.S. Army Infantry School, *FM 7-93 Long-Range Surveillance Unit Operations* (Ft. Benning, Ga.: U.S. Army Infantry School, 1986), 1-4, 1-5; Terry Griswold and D. M. Giangreco, *Delta* (Osceola, Wis.: Motorbooks International, 1992), 64.

12. U.S., Department of the Army, Joint Readiness Training Center, *1st Battalion, 327th Infantry Rotation 94-10 Attack AAR* (Ft. Polk, La.: Headquarters, Joint Readiness Training Center, 26 September 1994), 14D.

13. U.S., Department of the Army, Headquarters, 101st Airborne Division (Air Assault) Artillery, *Fire Support Handbook* (Ft. Campbell, Ky.: HQ, 101st Airborne Division [Air Assault] Artillery, 1995), 2-3; Michael Skinner, *USN* (Novato, Calif.: Presidio Press, 1986), 51, 61.

14. U.S., Department of the Army, Joint Readiness Training Center, *1st Battalion, 327th Infantry Rotation 94-10 Attack AAR* (Ft. Polk, La.: Headquarters, Joint Readiness Training Center, 26 September 1994), 14D, 32, 34, 63.

15. Ibid., 16–17.

16. Ibid., 22.

17. The mortar platoon's minimal contribution reflected five days spent searching for a lost pair of AN/PVS-5 night-vision goggles. The platoon lost the set while shooting in support of platoon live fires on 17 September. The mortarmen missed the second half of the search and attack operation and the entire defense.

18. U.S., Department of the Army, Joint Readiness Training Center, *1st Battalion, 327th Infantry Rotation 94-10 Attack AAR* (Ft. Polk, La.: Headquarters, Joint Readiness Training Center, 26 September 1994), 64.

19. U.S., Department of the Army, Joint Readiness Training Center, *1st Battalion, 327th Infantry Rotation 94-10 Defense AAR* (Ft. Polk, La.: Headquarters, Joint Readiness Training Center, 23 September 1994), 25. Night-vision usage figures for the deliberate attack, although not separately recorded, were even lower than those seen during the defense.

20. U.S., Department of the Army, Joint Readiness Training Center, *1st Battalion, 327th Infantry Rotation 94-10 Attack AAR* (Ft. Polk, La.: Headquarters, Joint Readiness Training Center, 26 September 1994), 14C.

21. Ibid., 14C, 14D. The observer/controller community agreed that their data on the enemy should have reflected higher losses, but that numbers became hard to calculate in the confusion of multiple night battles.

22. Ibid., 14B. During JRTC 94-07, the 3d Battalion, 327th Infantry Regiment racked up what Ft. Polk and Ft. Campbell officials later described as the best record achieved to date at the training center. They killed 242 OPFOR for the loss of 426 Americans. See Lt. Col. Lloyd W. Mills, *JRTC 94-07: A Commander's Perspective* (Ft. Campbell, Ky.: Headquarters, 3d Battalion, 327th Infantry Regiment, 24 June 1994), 1.

23. U.S., Department of the Army, Headquarters, Joint Readiness Training Center, *Training After-Action Report: 1st Battalion, 327th Infantry, JRTC Rotation 94-10* (Ft. Polk, La.: HQ, JRTC, 26 September 1994), 1-B, 3-B.

Entering a one-room shack, a soldier hesitates in the "fatal funnel." Additionally, the soldier does not have positive control of his M-16A2 rifle/M-203 grenade launcher dual-purpose weapon. This is a demonstration of how *not* to do it.

During JRTC 95-07, a UH-60L Blackhawk from 5th Battalion, 101st Aviation prepares to land at a field refueling point. Note the winglets on the helicopter, which can carry extended range fuel tanks and armament.

Obeying the 9th Commandment, a soldier cleans his 5.56-mm M-16A2 rifle. To allow cleaning, he has removed the MILES weapons transmitter. Like every friendly and enemy soldier and civilian role player in the JRTC maneuver box, he wears rows of laser detectors on his helmet and on his torso.

An M-119 105-mm howitzer crew fires in support of a live fire exercise associated with JRTC 95-07.

Soldiers of 2-327th Infantry get "the word" during JRTC 95-07. To the left, an O/C (wearing a patrol cap) watches the lieutenant explain his platoon's mission. The platoon leader employs a terrain model to help his men understand where they will soon fight.

A posed picture, taken at Fort Campbell, Kentucky, shows a soldier manning an M-2HB .50 caliber heavy machine gun mounted on a Humvee. The weapon is not loaded or MILES-equipped. Company D, 1-327th Infantry employed twenty similar gun trucks in JRTCs 94-10 and 95-07.

An AH-64A Apache attack helicopter climbs above the trees. The aircraft carries 70-mm rockets outboard and Hellfire missiles inboard, one of many possible combinations of wing stores.

Caught in the act of firing, a live Stinger surface to air missile leaves its throwaway launch tube. The shooter is a civilian contractor (note the old-style helmet and flak vest).

A U.S. Air Force C-130H Hercules turboprop transport taxies slowly along a dirt flight landing strip. The big C-130s bring in vital reinforcements and supplies to initial entry forces like the 101st Airborne.

The AN/TPQ37 Firefinder radar system, along with its smaller cousin, the Q-36, tracks inbound artillery, rocket, and mortar projectiles. The Firefinder section then computes the origin point of the rounds, and the U.S. artillery responds to destroy the enemy shooters. One Q36 radar section participated in JRTCs 94-10 and 95-07.

Along with carrying supplies and vehicles on slings, the CH-47D Chinook can carry up to 33 combat-equipped troops. Here, a mortar crew moves toward their designated aircraft.

Hitting 'em high and hitting 'em low, a pair of AH-64A Apaches work with a U.S. Air Force A-10A Thunderbolt II ("Warthog") to finish off a hostile armored force in a simulated battle at JRTC.

A pair of CH-47D Chinooks deliver two Company D armed Humvees at JRTC. Once the crew releases the slings from the hooks, the aircraft will reposition a safe distance away and unload the crew.

An Avenger air defense truck engages a hostile aircraft. Mated to a Humvee, the Avenger features two quad-tube Stinger launchers and a .50 caliber machine gun, all slaved to a superb thermal detection system capable of day or night fire control. The Avenger can be carried into battle under a CH-47D Chinook helicopter.

A UH-60L Blackhawk helicopter carries an M-119 105-mm howitzer, a British design battle-tested in the 1982 Falklands War. Batteries can reposition rapidly by this means.

Screaming Eagle riflemen and sappers work their way through a concertina wire entanglement during live fire training at Fort Campbell.

This visually altered M551 Sheridan light tank plays a T-62 type at JRTC. The original Russian version mounts a 115mm main gun.

While one CLF soldier stands watch, three other plot their next move. The four-man team is the basic guerrilla fighting force at JRTC.

Forced to defend, several CLF soldiers wait for action. Their low, camouflaged positions are hard to find from the air and on the ground.

Moving fast, a pair of CLF insurgents go into action along a road somewhere in Cortina.

Winning
JRTC 95-07
May 1995

Americans love a winner and will not tolerate a loser. Americans play to win all the time. I wouldn't give a hoot in hell for a man who lost and laughed.

—Gen. George S. Patton, Jr.

Chapter 7

Earth Pigs

Lieutenant Colonel Raspeguy, veteran of Dien Bien Phu: "I'd like France to have two armies: one for display, with lovely guns, tanks, little soldiers, fanfares, staffs, distinguished and doddering generals, and dear little regimental officers who would be deeply concerned over their general's bowel movements or their colonel's piles, an army that would be shown for a modest fee on every fairground in the country.

"The other would be the real one, composed entirely of young enthusiasts in camouflage battledress, who would not be put on display but from whom impossible efforts would be demanded, and to whom all sorts of tricks would be taught. That's the army in which I should like to fight."

Colonel Mestreville, veteran of Verdun: "You're heading for a lot of trouble."

Lieutenant Colonel Raspeguy: "That's as may be, but at least I shall have courted it deliberately; in fact, I'm going to start courting it right away."

—Jean Larteguy
The Centurions

Unlike actual war, a visit to the Joint Readiness Training Center allows you to get killed, indeed, slaughtered by the hundreds, and live to learn from your mistakes. That underlies the observer/controller mantra that, at Fort Polk, learning is winning. Because the U.S. Army saw fit to move this segment of its personnel at the pace of 15 percent monthly, a battalion like the 1st of the 327th started forgetting pretty quickly, both as a group and as individuals. Many who stayed inherited new postings, changing from line to staff or from fighting to supporting, thereby rendering their JRTC experience somewhat difficult to apply.

That phenomenon explained why most soldiers, especially leaders, remembered only the highlights from their JRTC trips. Everybody told you what went right, and bragged on those battles where the OPFOR knuckled under. The screw-ups and fiascos, like Hunger Hill or Bolger's capture, conveniently drifted out of the collective consciousness. Young men dwell on positive, upbeat experiences, and forget about failures—young soldiers, doubly so.

Here, the 1st Battalion, 327th Infantry Regiment, acted differently. Initially, Dan Bolger bent to the usual tendencies, even encouraging his subordinates to believe that the Bulldogs' successes far outweighed their defeats.[1] Within a month after JRTC 94-10, the commander grew uncomfortable with this happy talk. Feeling good contributed only slightly toward success in combat, and who could be certain that a real foe would be less able than the tough CLF? To win in war, you must *be* good. Nobody cares how you feel about it, particularly the dead.

More than nine hundred JRTC 94-10 casualties, and the crystal-clear understanding of who and what caused them, pushed Bolger to act decisively. And act he did. Encouraged by his subordinates, especially Cmd. Sgt. Maj. Mark Ripka, the lieutenant colonel commenced a massive overhaul of the battalion's practices. In turn, the organization developed much more effective tactics, built a team of leaders and soldiers capable of fighting under these new concepts, and created a unique C^2 system to ensure that the battalion headquarters made a positive contribution to every encounter. In taking these steps, many quite painful, the Bulldogs transformed themselves from also-rans to winners.

Defeating Third World insurgents and terrorists, the types replicated by the wily CLF, necessitated a shift in tactics. Drawing on bitter experiences in 94-10, Dan Bolger and his key subordinates understood that more of the same would not work. The safe answer meant just doing the standard stuff better, but that promised only an incremental improvement in battle results. The smart answer required Bolger and company to do things differently, to adapt to this damn CLF enemy and his Cortinian haunts. The 1st of the 327th would certainly do as much in war. Spurred by Bolger, learning how to best a JRTC-style foe became the battalion's burning goal.

Thanks to 94-10, the Bulldogs knew their enemy and knew themselves. One basic fact of life dominated everything. In a direct firefight, all matters being equal, the battalion could count on losing a minimum of three Americans for every OPFOR soldier that dropped. The bad guys just shot better with MILES; they did it every day, and practice makes perfect. Unable ever to equal this amount of concentrated emphasis on MILES marksmanship, Bolger's men had to accept the realities of the JRTC direct fire engagement. The real art depended upon the battalion's ability to use other means to level those 3:1 odds. Namely, the Bulldogs must fight smarter.

From this basic and obvious premise sprang a new way of fighting. It evolved over the months after JRTC 94-10, a combination of bottom-up initiatives and top-down ideas. The 1st of the 327th eventually codified the major points of this approach as the Ten Commandments for JRTC. That title did not arise by accident. Dan Bolger said it best at their issue: "Treat these like they've just come down from Sinai." As with the original Ten Commandments, compliance was not optional.[2]

Intended for every private soldier, these simple rules became ingrained in the battalion's rankers over many training exercises during the harsh winter of 1994–95. Eventually, this decalogue could be found posted all over the battalion, in orderly rooms, in barracks, in the motor pool, and even in latrines. Pocket versions, the size of calling cards, went to every single man. The soldiers read it, understood it, and lived it. Like Communist guerrillas indoctrinated with the true faith, the Bulldogs believed.

Each commandment reflected another facet in a coordinated effort designed to defeat the Cortinian Liberation Front. But as with the real thing, the biggest one came first.

Ten Commandments for JRTC

1. Kill the enemy.

2. Win over the civilians.

3. Act on contact—secure flanks/rear—squads fix, platoons attack—always a 90-degree bold flank.

4. If you fight somewhere, don't stop there—move out.

5. Never lose contact with our dead and wounded—no Hunger Hills!

6. Security is a must, moving or sitting—front, flank, and rear.

7. Major roads are off-limits; make combat trails to be where mines are not.

8. Night-vision gogles are worn in head/helmet mounts.

9. Daily duties: zero weapons, maintain weapon/commo, hasty fighting position at halts, "safe" when not shooting.

10. Live and fight light—Earth Pigs.

1. Kill the enemy. Now, that seems pretty obvious, but at JRTC, the obvious has a way of slipping out of sight in the heat, the underbrush, and the lengthening U.S. casualty list. Indeed, between dredging up battalion supply points, clearing heavily mined routes, evacuating the dead and wounded, hugging the local civilians, and merely keeping up with all the friendly men and equipment wandering around the play box, things became a mite confused. Up to their buttocks in angry alligators, commanders often forgot that they came to drain the swamp.

All fancy wordsmithery aside, infantry units can do two things: kill bad guys or control key ground. You can dress it up, attach titles like "noncombatant evacuation" or "deliberate attack," but it always comes down to destruction or control. When riflemen receive a mission, they need to get a clear focus on either the enemy force or critical terrain. Only one can be done well, so which takes precedence? This question dogged the battalion during JRTC 94-10. Especially at the fake BSP around Hunger Hill, but also on the contested route to Jetertown and on bloody Objective Lee, the Bulldogs chose both answers, and so chose neither. The OPFOR then resolved the dilemma the hard way.

For those afflicted by this issue, the doctrinal ilk pointed to a small portion of the traditional five-paragraph field order, the little header on paragraph 3, "Execution," labeled "Commander's Intent." Supposedly, in the chaos of battle, with everything else forgotten or superseded, this jewel of insight would shine like a beacon, telling the men What to Do. Okay—that made some sense. Unfortunately, the various Army schools then each churned out different guidance on what constituted a statement of commander's intent. During the 1980s, the curia at Fort Leavenworth's staff college settled on three components: purpose (why), method (how), and endstate (what does success look like?), with the latter expressed in terms of the enemy, friendly forces, and terrain.[3] This ensured the death of many innocent groves of trees as would-be Clausewitzes labored to belch forth three-page, single-spaced manifestos that amounted to a commander's regurgitation of the entire operation order, even though the intent allegedly existed as a subset of same. Chances seemed slight that a captain, let alone a corporal, could make something from this drivel. Patton's warning not to dictate *how* to carry out missions went unheeded. As for telling you What to Do when all else failed . . . well, forget it.

With this in mind, Dan Bolger invented the First Commandment. "Kill the enemy" became the default setting for the battalion under all circumstances. Just as Lord Nelson once said, "No captain can do very wrong if he places his ship alongside that of an enemy,"[4] so Bolger exhorted his men to seek and slay the CLF. Those miscreants lived on the fat of their little patrol bases, stole U.S. items as needed, and knew that the Atlantican invasion loomed within days. Finding supply stocks or command posts, the "Ps" (BSP, CSP, PSP, CP), meant nothing to the CLF. Therefore, messing with the Ps meant nothing to the 1st of the 327th. No, food pallets, ammunition cans, water jugs, and the like never threatened anybody. Bolger and his men put their emphasis on wiping out CLF riflemen, mortars, and SA-14s, the stuff that could kill you.[5]

Every man understood the intent to kill the enemy. Observer/controllers and field manual writers might wag their heads in smug disapproval, but the battalion's dictum certainly did the job. In three words, vs. three paragraphs or, God help us, three pages, the battalion knew What to Do. In the absence of orders or communications, the Bulldogs would look for the CLF and take them out. With a definite purpose, it only remained to fill in the details. The other nine commandments did that.

2. Win over the civilians. To kill the CLF, you must find them. Like all guerrillas, these fish swam in the sea of the populace. Skilled in gathering information, aided by their Leesville Urban Group (LUG) cadres, the CLF dominated the villages and, in the process, gathered lots of knowledge about the U.S. forces and their dispositions. The accepted figure of the civilian contribution to the CLF reconnaissance effort hovered around 60 percent.[6] Since each settlement always included a LUG cell, a U.S. S2 looking for the enemy knew exactly where to start.

Thanks to the battalion's successful RAMP system of training for rules of engagement, Bolger felt confident about sending his troops into the villages. He fully intended to secure Cortina's little towns, pamper the people with food and water, and then crank them for intelligence. This promised to blind the CLF, cut them from their support infrastructure, and provide valuable targeting data to direct the 1st of the 327th's operations. Whatever else happened, the Bulldogs planned to go into town and stay there, allowing the S5 and his Team Golf cronies to do their thing. Perhaps the loss of their populated base might urge the CLF to fight. If so, the First Commandment applied.

3. Act on contact—secure flanks/rear—squads fix/platoons attack—always a 90-degree bold flank. Killing the badniks and pumping the locals all sounded great, but how did the Bulldogs expect to even those steep odds that characterized the MILES gunfight? In Bolger's opinion, U.S. battle drills must be just as decisive as the infamous OPFOR three-step. To even the odds, the 1st of the 327th did not permit squad attacks. That way, no isolated six to nine men could be minced by a CLF quartet.

The bold flank, a wide swing to the side, became mandatory. Coupled with flankers and trailers keeping watch, a bold flanking element necessarily broke the CLF's favorite box technique and imperiled enemy baited traps. It changed the guerrillas' battlefield geometry from a tight, rehearsed drill to an unexpected two-direction fight. This novel brand of disruption tended to affect OPFOR shooting prowess, and thereby leveled the playing field.

For extra fun, the Bulldogs resorted to the American predeliction to send a bullet, not a man. They learned to add supporting fires to the stewpot. In search and attack operations, the Americans decided to plot a goodly number of artillery and mortar targets, about one per grid square. When the battalion's forces found the CLF, the leaders could call in the preplanned target one grid square over, known as a "Quickdraw."[7] Once the rounds landed, it would take only a few short minutes to creep them into the right area. Quickdraw put fires down immediately on an open CLF flank; the insurgents had no way of knowing exactly who called the rounds, and would start looking for concealed U.S. forward observers or other approaching forces. These Quickdraw shots might not kill many CLF, but they certainly added to hostile distress. And once again, they shook up that normally rock-steady MILES marksmanship.

In all of this, the most important aspect involved doing something immediately—acting, not reacting. The enemy very much feared this sort of speedy battle drill. One CLF officer observed, "If we see a leader take a knee and call on the radio, we know we'll win. If he's running and talking, we're in trouble."[8] Trouble for the CLF suited the Bulldogs just fine. They commenced drilling and training accordingly.

4. If you fight somewhere, don't stop there—move out. A corollary of killing the enemy, this stricture worked to obviate the OPFOR tendency to call in mortars on those American units that hung around too long cleaning up their messes. This applied in spades if the battle transpired around a BSP or a CP, always pretargeted by the OPFOR. Since the 1st of the 327th had no desire to monkey around with caches, these would be either destroyed by fire, used for circle-back ambushes, or, if it made sense, ignored. In any case, nobody would be hanging around to retain terrain.

5. Never lose contact with our dead and wounded—no Hunger Hills! Americans do not abandon their casualties. At JRTC, that meant being careful not to crawl out on a limb and cut yourself off, as in the ugly imbroglio that became Hunger Hill. Because the MILES training environment recycled the "dead," losing touch with them soon resulted in no men to continue the fight. Keeping a guaranteed vehicular route to every force, a trail unbroken by Fort Polk's deep, impassable creeks, offered the best way to get casualties out. Blowing this off or trusting in somebody else—brigade, the aviators, the medical people—had failed in JRTC 94-10. It would fail in war.

To solve this conundrum, it required a commitment by the entire battalion to account for and recover casualties quickly. Bolger and his leaders made that commitment. The Bulldogs learned not to outrun their evacuation system. In doing so, they cured their supply ills, too.

6. Security is a must, moving or sitting—front, flank, and rear. Army doctrine preaches this continually, and just as continually, everyone does otherwise. In combat and at JRTC, the costs of screwing this up mount steadily, with the CLF just as steadily assailing U.S. flanks and rear elements. The idea of surrounding a formation in motion or at rest with a screen is nothing new, but it is rarely done well. Stung badly during 94-10, Bolger insisted on solving the security problem. He directed that buddy teams or even fire teams with radios be used, to make contact first at least a hundred meters out from the main body. Once the battalion learned how to secure itself, no CLF foursome would approach unseen and unmolested.

7. Major roads are off-limits; make combat trails to be where mines are not. The carnage along the road to Jetertown convinced Bolger and his subordinates that mined roads constituted known CLF kill zones. If so, why go there? Throughout JRTC 94-10, the battalion's soldiers watched O/C Humvees and firemarker vehicles putter easily off-road, bouncing over the wooded ridges and across and around the creekbeds and ravines. Even having seen this, the 1st of the 327th lemmings kept flogging away at the roadbed, all at great cost. It made about as much sense as Ambrose Burnside's idiotic insistence on crossing knee-deep Antietam Creek over a stone bridge during the 1862 battle.[9] Avoiding roads equaled avoiding mines. That became the rule among the Bulldogs.

8. Night-vision goggles are worn in head/helmet mounts. The AN/PVS-7B night-vision devices came with a head clamp replete with straps that wrapped around the skull and hard plastic holders that pressed into the flesh. The damn thing resembled a medieval torture implement. Left to their own preferences, troops chose not to wear that. Instead, they suspended their goggles around their necks, picking them up like opera glasses to see when they so chose. This tied up a hand, and you cannot shoot anything but a pistol one-handed, at least not anywhere east of Hollywood. Also troubling, the lift and look method naturally left men most of the time without enhanced vision in the darkness. And that played the game on CLF terms.

The insurgents lacked these night sights, and so hated to deal with any unit that used them religiously. Tied in with a properly mounted AN/PAQ-4 laser pointer, the U.S. goggles allowed a rifleman to see targets, lase them, and hit them with a single shot. Of course, when the Americans left their night goggles dangling, they gave up this advantage, and the typical exchange rate applied. Few units had the discipline to endure the pain and wear their goggles correctly. The 1st of the 327th elected to tolerate the discomfort and do it right.

9. Daily duties: zero weapons, maintain weapon/commo, hasty fighting position at halts, "safe" when not shooting. The leaders may think great thoughts, but in the end, the men must perform. To kill the foe, each man had to be ready. The MILES transmitters demanded daily attention, tinkering with aim-points and changing out batteries, tasks never neglected by the dead-eyes of the CLF. Additionally, without being told, men needed to know what to do during lulls. Good soldiers take up positions ready to fight when they halt, in case the OPFOR comes calling. They watch where they stick their rifle barrels, and do not lightly click their loaded firearms off "safe." They clean weapons and change out radio batteries, too. And when they get tired and start letting things slide, their sergeants put a size-11 up their backsides as necessary. Killing the enemy begins right here, with being ready. The battalion did this poorly at JRTC 94-10. The next time would be different, vowed Command Sergeant Major Ripka and his corps of NCOs.

10. Live and fight light—Earth Pigs. What does the well-dressed infantryman wear into the JRTC maneuver box? Many units paid little attention to this subject, and carried in most everything out of a gnawing suspicion that the supply system appeared doomed to go awry. Well, that happened, but the rucksacks also took their toll. Rifle squads staggered under the burden of massive loads. The CLF, stripped to the minimum and subsisting from hidden caches, ran rings around most plodding American columns.

The 1st of the 327th fared only a bit better than the norm. The supply system broke down as usual, and the team rucksacks tried on JRTC 94-10 did not work out, even though most of the men enjoyed freedom from the oppressive weight of overstuffed backpacks. But as always, the CLF proved significantly more nimble, and better supplied. To beat this whole problem, the battalion devised a three-fold solution.

First, the battalion ditched the book's combat trains, with its ponderous fuel truck, wrecker, ammo wagons, and superfluous administrative/logistics center (ALOC), yet another command post on the loose, in this case ensnaring the S1 and S4. It its place, the Bulldogs substituted a lean Landing Zone Support Team (LZST) of a few medical and supply Humvees, configured to pick up and drop off air-delivered men and supplies, then go cross-country to extract casualties or deliver water, food, and ammunition.[10] Aside from this clutch of designated logistics trucks, the battalion also added water, ammunition, and food stores to each of the few Humvees that Bolger actually planned to allow into the combat zone. But that only made up insurance. Under the impetus of a hard-core support platoon leader—and the battalion owned one—the LZST really had the ball for sustaining the force. Like the proverbial postman, neither rain, nor snow, nor gloom of night, let alone the CLF, would stay these couriers from the swift completion of their appointed rounds.

Next, the battalion took a leaf from the guerrillas' book, and issued a buttpack to every man. Two decades ago, every U.S. Army soldier wore a buttpack, just as most mothers and students do today. Unfortunately, generals and post sergeants major disliked these unkempt little items, with their often-dribbling straps and unseemly bulges just atop an area of the anatomy better left unnoticed. So buttpacks went away. In the 101st Airborne, they were expressly outlawed. A flimsy little camouflage backpack, shaped like a kid's bookbag and about as sturdy, came into use. It stunk. When senior NCOs finally raised a hue and cry so great that the commanding general took notice, he reversed the ban on buttpacks. His only condition required the use of the newly minted nylon models, not the Vietnam-era canvas bags. Of course, the general made his concession in the sure knowledge that it would be Fiscal Year 2000, if ever, before the U.S. Army issued the new nylon buttpacks. Meanwhile, rucksacks and those pathetic little bookbags remained the order of the day.

Not so in the 1st of the 327th; here, an energetic new S4 outfoxed the supply system. Scrolling through the entire Department of Defense database, the tireless 1st Lt. Craig Doane located an untapped stockpile of nylon buttpacks at the Philadelphia Navy Yard, of all places. Submitting a wholly lawful request, Craig procured some seven hundred of these things before U.S. Marine Corps supply officers slammed the lid on this joint service venture. With these buttpacks, every man in the 1st of the 327th carried a few necessities, and the team rucks went away. The Bulldogs' trimmed load precisely matched that of the CLF, with the exception of the Kevlar helmet mandated for the Americans. Bolger and his men never asked permission or advertised their good fortune. One day, they just suited up. Oh, and by the way, they did ensure the excess straps got tied off neatly.[11]

With the LZST and buttpacks in place, the final piece of the puzzle came from within. The men of the battalion learned to be hard. They found out how to do without, no easy task for members of the richest army on Earth. Soldiers grew to expect a single MRE per day, watched their ammunition expenditure, and sucked up water off every truck that went by. Everybody, from the lieutenant colonel down to the lowliest new private, lived exactly the same, close to the dirt. Dan Bolger himself coined the term for this primitive lifestyle: Earth Pigs. It is often said that you need not train to be miserable. Bolger and his troops rejected that conventional wisdom, all in a quest to make their enemies even more miserable.

These ten rules, then, built the battalion's fighting mindset, and tied together every man in the organization. The focus on killing the enemy integrated everything, and the rest made killing easier. Above all, the Ten Commandments reflected practice, not gassy theory or doctrinal dogma. Killing is blue-collar work, and the Ten Commandments offer blue-collar common sense. Getting the right men to execute this approach, and the CLF, came next.

With regard to personnel quality in the ranks, the battalion was almost there already. The JRTC 94-10 After-Action Report penned by the O/Cs had plenty of good to say about the skill and will of the private soldiers.[12] Assigned to puny six-man squads and weakened two-squad platoons, many privates and pfcs. did the work of two or three men through the rotation. These youths marched through swamps and over wooded ridges, day and night, often burdened by the inert carcasses of comrades ruled dead and wounded. Beleaguered by CLF gunmen, they shot as true as they could. Struggling in the heat, short on water, lacking certain knowledge of what to do next, the men pressed on, hour after weary hour. Few victories marked their tired paths. Average men, even average soldiers, might well have quit, and who could blame them? Yet these were not ordinary folk, but Regulars, picked volunteers, chosen air assault infantrymen, wearing the symbol and traditions of the 101st Airborne Screaming Eagle on their left shoulder. Even had a few wanted to give up, to stop trying, the shades of Normandy, Bastogne, and Vietnam would never permit it, nor would their ranker friends beside them. The nineteen- and twenty-year-olds who formed the fighting edge of the 1st of the 327th were better than that.

Better they may be, but too many of their tentative, careless leaders, including Dan Bolger, had not seized the advantage promised by these fit, able young men. Robert E. Lee said it so well in 1863,

"There never were such men in an army before. They will go anywhere and do anything if properly led. But there is the difficulty—
proper commanders—where can they be obtained?"[13] The Army of
Northern Virginia lost the battle of Gettysburg, and the war, trying
to answer Lee's plaintive question.

Where indeed to find leaders worthy of tough young infantrymen?
Actually, the Joint Readiness Training Center helped in the search.
You could, in fact, find some pretty good leaders in the crucible of
the maneuver box. Pressures and pain also allowed the weaklings to
show themselves. While it seemed dangerous to heap too much
praise based upon the results of gussied-up laser tag encounters, so
too was it unhealthy to keep faith with those who broke under the
stresses of command at JRTC. If you folded in the face of the CLF,
an imaginary enemy shooting blanks and laser beams, how could you
ever hold up in a real firefight?

For the 1st of the 327th, JRTC 94-10 showcased some weak
sergeants and a few less capable officers, men holding jobs by virtue
of seniority or good humor but unfit to inspire soldiers going in
harm's way. Making honest mistakes, even serious ones, was okay in
the battalion, as long as the leaders learned and did not commit the
same goofs over and over. Tactics abound in miscalculation and fal-
tering, even under the best of circumstances. The chaos of combat
ensured that.

The failures that attracted the battalion commander's interest
went well beyond wrong guesses made in the heat of an ambush. Officers and NCOs could try and fall short, as long as they led by example, displayed integrity, and exhibited the basic competence that
men in the 101st Airborne grew to expect from their chain of command. Sergeants unable to take the physical pounding of field conditions, staff officers who shaded the truth, kind hearts unwilling to
enforce discipline on exhausted foot soldiers—these men lost the
confidence of their young charges, and hence, of Dan Bolger too.

Confronted with the daily possibility of deploying into combat, the
battalion commander acted to shore up his chain of command. The
consequent moves happened without rancor, but without pity, either.
In this determined purge of those found lacking, Bolger gave little
thought to mere seniority. "We're running a fighting battalion, not

the post office," he told his men. Guided by Mark Ripka's knowing eye, the battalion focused its reshufflings on one key group: the platoon sergeants.

Most wars, but certainly nasty guerilla wars, will be won or lost at the platoon level. The battalion's Third Commandment acknowledged as much. In the U.S. Army, infantry platoons consist almost wholly of new men, including their assigned lieutenant, should they be lucky enough to have one. On paper, the squad leaders appear as staff sergeants with a decade in harness. In reality, squad leaders tend to be sergeants or very junior staff sergeants, most with considerably less than ten years of service. Only the platoon sergeant, a senior staff sergeant or sergeant first class, has done the jobs that now occupy his men. The rookie lieutenant is not all that helpful, as he amounts to a highly trained, exceptionally bright private, at least in terms of experience. It's a given that you can easily run a platoon without a platoon leader, but no sane soldier in the American Army would dream of carrying on without a platoon sergeant. He, and he alone, will ensure a platoon is disciplined and trained to fight and win.

Of the twenty platoon sergeants allocated to the 1st Battalion, 327th Infantry during JRTC 94-10, twelve required outright replacement in the aftermath. Some of this came from natural attrition, but the hard hands of Bolger and Ripka could be felt. New blood came to four of the six HHC platoons, one in Company A, two in Company B, all three in hapless Company C, and a pair in Company D. In every case, the new platoon sergeant proved to be younger, smarter, more physically fit, and a lot more demanding on his soldiers.

While these platoon sergeant changes represented the most critical alterations to the battalion's leadership slate, other adjustments occurred too. What else could you expect with that breakneck 15 percent personnel turnover engine still roaring away? Every company and the staff accommodated new faces. As with the platoon sergeants, many of the new men came from a better caliber than their predecessors. No weaklings applied; none were taken.

Company A, the tough-minded Abus, saw the least change of the rifle units. Drew Felix and Scott Craig kept their posts as commander and first sergeant, and all three platoons maintained their NCO chain intact, with one exception. A very steady, highly experienced senior squad leader, a Ranger just like the sergeant first class he replaced, took over 1st Platoon. New lieutenants, eager but wet behind the ears, filled out the fighting platoons. The Abus did well enough during 94-10, exhibiting considerable toughness and determination, definitely reflections on Captain Felix and his senior sergeants. Combining this solid foundation with the kind of fighting style described in the Ten Commandments, the battalion counted on an even better performance in the future.

In Company B, former S4 Ted Donnelly succeeded to command. His arrival brought some much-needed decentralization to the Bushmasters, and did it without a drop in standards. All three rifle platoons absorbed some degree of new leadership, but the knowing minds of 1st Sgt. Gerald Eubank and Sfc. Charles W. Lipke continued to set the right tone for training and tactics. In the persons of 2d Lt. Lance Oskey and 2d Lt. John Hall, the Bushmasters benefited from two unusually talented young officers, both more than capable of fighting independently. Blessed with this extraordinary chain of command, Company B continued to be the rock of the battalion.

If two rifle companies gave little concern following some key platoon sergeant swaps and routine assignments, Company C still gave considerable pause. To be fair, Capt. Chris Forbes probably should have been selling shoes by then. The company under Forbes placed about fifth out of three. An undisciplined mob prior to Forbes's arrival in March 1994, matters seemed little improved six months later during JRTC 94-10. Maybe things would never get better.

And yet, not everything engendered pessimism. Under the able 1st Lt. Chris Santos, the company did its job in the defense. Nor could folks overlook the positive influence of 1st Sgt. Ed Bauerle, whose initial efforts put some backbone in the outfit during the final mission of JRTC 94-10. Companies cannot press-gang their own men, and the Cold Steel bunch degenerated over years. Fixing the unit necessarily took time.

The sergeant major and battalion commander knew this, and did not ignore it. As they did with Bauerle, the battalion leadership handpicked the NCOs sent to Company C. Within months, 1st Sgt.

Bauerle enjoyed the backing of an extremely sound and tough cadre of platoon sergeants. Together, they reinstituted Regular Army discipline. Spurred by these uncompromising men, Cold Steel began to demonstrate real proficiency, and a degree of pride.

Still, the biggest question concerned Forbes himself. Few officers gave evidence of as much promise as Chris Forbes. His infectuous enthusiasm, unconventional thinking, and genuine love of soldiers all marked him as a far better infantry captain than indicated by his sorry record in JRTC 94-10. Dan Bolger had once judged Chris Forbes to be the best commander in the battalion—*potentially*. That reservoir of innate ability granted Forbes a rare boon in the 1st of the 327th, an opportunity to redeem himself following a consistent, unremitting, long-term sequence of failures, with JRTC as the capper. But Capt. Chris Forbes earned a second look because Bolger knew in his gut that this officer could, indeed must, do better.

That acknowledged, when, if ever, would this driven young man realize his immense potential? With his company rebuilt around superb sergeants, no excuses remained. Given Bolger's intolerance for repeat offenders, Forbes knew that he had one more chance. He did not intend to blow it.

Unlike the rifle companies, it appeared difficult to judge the JRTC performance of the armed Humvee troopers of Company D. Gutted by odd task organization decisions at brigade, the Maddogs hardly ever made a contribution proportionate to their 50 percent share of the battalion's organic firepower. Their best engagement, the huge melee on the final night, did not "count." So ruled the O/Cs.

Now the Maddogs reported to Capt. Mike Delgado, formerly an extra officer in the S3 section, an erstwhile "battle captain" whose major experiences on JRTC 94-10 included wrong turns with the TOC convoy and becoming a casualty. This did not auger well for the new commander of a mounted force. On the plus side, Delgado brought in a good knowledge base from his previous tour with the defunct 9th Infantry Division (Motorized), akin to a divisional-strength version of Company D. In the new battalion fighting style, Delgado's company assumed the escort role for the LZST, an unglamorous light cavalry tasking pregnant with many evil little scraps and counterambushes.

Much of the time, Company D expected to be protecting elements of Headquarters Company. Although Capt. Ronz Sarvis remained, 1st Sgt. Jordan L. Jeffcoat departed, going to take over the brigade headquarters company. In line with the intensive work to strengthen platoon leadership, five of HHC's six subordinate units went to a new officer, a new NCO, or both. Only the medics stood pat.

In the supply and service components, Sarvis made some improvements. This clearly showed in the Support Platoon. Given its pivotal place in the new battalion scheme, its leaders must necessarily be first-rate fighters and sustainers. The platoon went to a truly dynamic duo, 1st Lt. Matt Moore and SSgt. Maurice Dean Wood. Moore, a former Abu with stamina and ingenuity enough for a half-dozen lieutenants, treated his role as LZST chief as a hunting license. Wood felt likewise. It became a matter of honor for Moore and Wood that the companies could count on getting supplies in and casualties out. If a good number of CLF died trying to impede those missions, very well.

The two fighting platoons, scouts and mortars, each made course corrections. Although Mark Lawry continued to lead the Tigers, Sfc. Charles McKamey moved over from the Bushmasters to work as Lawry's deputy. Certainly hard enough and more than clever, this pair probably liked to mix it up too much. Look but don't shoot defines the scout ethos, and both Lawry and McKamey definitely hailed from the shooter family. The Tigers might bear some extra guiding, but nobody doubted their warrior spirit.

In the Mortar Platoon, 1st Lt. Chris Santos stepped in, determined to make this powerful unit live up to its capacity to deliver some 25 percent of the battalion's assigned firepower. He designated a junior sergeant, Reid K. Spencer, as his second-in-command, an unusual decision fully supported by the battalion commander and sergeant major. Santos and Spencer set very compelling personal examples, and their men responded with new zeal and efficiency. Next time, the mortars would make the enemy pay.

The rest of HHC comprised the battalion headquarters, an organ that did not distinguish itself all that much during JRTC 94-10. With one exception, the staff officers evidenced no personal failings that marked them for transfer. Rather, all but a single swapout reflected scheduled transitions. Even so, these fresh faces profited from joining a staff that ran quite differently from the group that attempted to guide the Bulldogs through 94-10.

The new breed included a different second-in-command, Maj. Steve Roberts. Roberts came in from a lengthy stint as the 1st Brigade S4, and Bolger knew him well from their previous service together in the 101st Airborne Division's G3 Operations section. Practical, taciturn, and bluntly honest, Roberts lacked Jim Laufenburg's dash and charisma, but made up for it with tenacity. The Bulldogs never received that much payoff from Laufenburg's sterling credentials, mainly due to serious flaws in the battalion's C^2 structure. The far less flashy Roberts, nurtured under what emerged as a radically different system, eventually contributed a tremendous amount to the 1st of the 327th.

The battalion's other major, Bill Phelps, stayed on the team. Like Bolger, Phelps yearned for rematch at Fort Polk. He, too, had some scores to settle. His S3 conglomerate, which incorporated the S2, S3 Air, S5, plus all the attachment leaders, made some noteworthy shifts, all pointing toward killing bad guys with greater effect. Dirk Blackdeer and his perceptive assistant, 2d Lt. Tom Doughty, stayed the course in the S2 arena, both substantially wiser about the wiles of the CLF and their ilk. Brigade snatched up 1st Lt. Dave Bair to be their S3 Air, and the irrepressible 1st Lt. Matt Bounds succeeded him. In the unauthorized but exceedingly useful S5 billet, 1st Lt. Ken Leeds, just graduated from Ranger School, assumed control of the battalion's civil-military operations. He bore a major responsibility for carrying out the Second Commandment, winning hearts, minds, and a crystalline picture of where insurgents chose to hide. These fine officers, and the rest, buoyed Phelps's confidence. He knew his stable owned some real thoroughbreds.

While evolution in the right direction characterized the S3 world, the S1 met his fate under less than happy circumstances. More suited to be an aide-de-camp than a battlefield adjutant, this unlucky first lieutenant submitted his resignation from the Army about ten minutes prior to being removed from his duties. Although a West Pointer and plenty smart, the officer never gave evidence of the fire and determination that marked his peers, men like Dave Bair, Matt

Bounds, Matt Moore, and Chris Santos. Lance Bailey, who turned out to be the best lieutenant in the battalion, succeeded to the un-enviable title of S1. During JRTC 94-10, Lance ran the battalion's rear detachment, and did it well. His attention to detail garnered special notice. With the precision of a Cray computer, Bailey could juggle a thousand different balls, not drop one, and tell you the size, color, and position of each one at any given time. Simultaneously, he might calmly shoot a hole in a bad guy three hundred meters away, then bring in a medevac chopper, all on about an hour's sleep. Next time, Lance Bailey planned to be in the box alongside the rest of the Bulldogs.

So, too, would the singularly adept new S4, 1st Lt. Craig Doane. Doane demonstrated his talent immediately in his unorthodox pro-curement of Marine Corps buttpacks, and that only proved to be a small sample of this man's vision, intelligence, and energy. Once con-sidered a bit too far outside the approved mold, Craig had been shipped off to the division protocol office before Bolger assumed command of the 1st of the 327th. Dan Bolger recognized Doane's worth and brought him back to replace Ted Donnelly as the battal-ion S4. Grateful for release from pushing cookies and seating the commanding general's garden parties, Craig Doane attacked his job like Patton racing for Bastogne. He did not look back, and neither did the battalion's soldiers, finally furnished with the assurance of adequate supplies.

Thus Bailey tracked people and Doane found material goods, and it all hooked into the companies through the good offices of 1st Lt. Matt Moore, hell-for-leather commander of the LZST. This coupling of unusual leaders and unique methods mended a broken limb from 94-10 and, in doing it, reinforced the battalion's new way of war. The revitalized platoons, these born-again Earth Pigs, counted on bat-talion to provide. Thanks to the LZST and its talented leadership, the battalion did so.

With proper officers and NCOs properly placed, the 1st of the 327th chain of command handily resolved one last nagging person-nel issue. During JRTC 94-10, the battalion left behind several dozen troubled soldiers, disciplinary, physical, and motivation breakdowns allowed to relax in comfort back at Fort Campbell while the shorthanded Bulldogs labored in Cortina. The less capable leaders of that time knew no preferable solution.

The steel-eyed crew that succeeded to power showed no such misplaced tolerance. Spurred by Bolger and Ripka, the companies cleaned house among the privates. Caught hot on a drug test? Overweight and unable to solve it? Can't get through Air Assault School after multiple attempts? Thinking about suicide? Missing mommy? The excuses mattered little. An air assault infantry battalion will do anything to protect and succor their own, but first, you must be willing to pay the price to belong. As in all units, a few lacked the manhood to measure up.

With their lieutenant colonel's blessing, the battalion's hardened platoon sergeantry applied the same remedy as the 75th Ranger Regiment and other elite organizations: meet standards or move out. Those who tried but lacked skill received a grace period, and plenty of coaching, to get square. Most did. Those few who gave up out of hand often found themselves headed out of the battalion, and the U.S. Army, before the sun went down. Over the months after 94-10, the battalion led the 101st Airborne Division in adverse separations from the Army.[14] While this trend lasted, it raised a few eyebrows, but it also galvanized a band of brothers who "knew the deal," and understood the expected standards, including the Ten Commandments.

During the months that the Bulldogs shook out their deadwood, the leaders relearned the virtues of what baseball general managers know as "addition by subtraction." Stated simply, a bad man kept infects others. A hole infects nothing. Moreover, a gap made demands a fill, and chances are the replacement will be sound. The more openings you create, the better your chances to bring in good men. Keeping trouble and sloth only spawns more trouble and sloth. The 1st of the 327th unloaded theirs, and gathered more good men for their efforts. As a result, rifle companies began going to the field with over one hundred soldiers. Platoons expanded to their mandated three squads. The rear detachment shrunk down pretty near that intractable 15 percent of folks coming and going, the price of being in the contemporary U.S. Army. In every sense, the fat went away.

With more effective tactics and a stronger chain of command directing a greater number of able troops, the battalion needed one more reform. In many ways, this one looked to be the most essential of them all. Throughout JRTC 94-10, the battalion's command and control system faltered and wheezed, adding little and taking much. Assigning and reassigning people only went so far to cure that disease. The book prescribed a bigger TOC and more training in the Deliberate Decision-Making Process, another way of saying more of the same. Instead, perhaps impressed by the virtues of addition by subtraction, Dan Bolger tried another tack with his rather traditional C^2 construct. He got rid of it.

The Bulldogs abandoned the TOC and the DDMP with both eyes open. While the battalion's departure from typical processes soon horrified the JRTC O/Cs and alarmed the battalion's superiors, this seemingly radical solution made quite a bit of sense. It came to Dan Bolger in a single flash one afternoon in December 1994, after he sat through an order for a divisional computer wargame. The interminable slideshow transpired in a tent complex the size of a small hangar that advertised itself as the division's TOC. Whatever those scenes portended, they did not point to any method of operating, planning, or surviving suited for war. Hadn't JRTC 94-10 taught the battalion commander that same hard lesson?

Fixing operations, the tracking of execution, came first, because doing far outstripped planning in importance. To be honest, the battalion TOC never made a single positive contribution to tactical operations at JRTC, except in two minor aspects—as a way-station for the battalion's senior leaders and a gathering place for operation orders. In furnishing these ephemeral advantages, the TOC ensnared Bolger and his key staff, absorbed valuable time and resources in movement and erection, and encouraged business as usual. Well, business as usual ended up with an obviously mixed outcome at JRTC 94-10.

The answer to this debacle did not come from a field manual, but it did spring from those known doctrinal enthusiasts, the O/Cs. In their final report on the 1st of the 327th, they admitted that "the Tac successfully controlled the battle." [15] Impressed by this observation, Bolger checked the results of other rotations. Consistently, the small tactical CPs, often dismounted, outperformed the much more robust TOC tent clusters.[16] Why?

The secret of an effective command post depended on who ran it, not its physical plant, the number of radios, or the degree of training of the clerks. Since the most experienced officers in the battalion—the S2, the S3, and the commander himself—manned the Tac, naturally this first-string outdid a TOC run by privates, lieutenants, and the occasional junior captain. The "battle captain" concept espoused by Army doctrine envisioned two former company commanders, one per twelve-hour shift, holding the fort at the TOC.[17] In reality, battalions made do with battle lieutenants, often second lieutenants, trying to watch the fight, inform higher, and coordinate routine actions, all with less than a year of service under their belts. It just could not work.

One may argue that such malassignment offers good training for young staff officers, if you consider flapping like a beached carp to be a form of training. No matter how smart, few men with five or less years of duty, all below the company level, can truly master battalion and higher tactics. These junior officers may know how to execute missions, but they will not know what is important about an ongoing flurry of radio traffic, when something is going haywire, or when to intervene to affect these matters. No field manual explained that stuff. Knowing what to do took experience and training.

The Army seems to know that, which may explain why a battalion has two majors. In the Gulf War, battalion commanders routinely designated their XO and S3, Leavenworth-schooled majors, as TOC-meisters and battle captains. Brigades used their lieutenant colonel XOs and major S3s. At the divisional echelon, a pair of brigadier generals alternately took the conn.[18] Few actual captains, let alone lieutenants, played battle captain in the shooting war. That about says it all.

Mindful of these ideas, Dan Bolger reorganized his CP into two shifts, each headed by a major. Along with their staff college graduate chiefs, these squad-size Tac teams each included an S2 officer, a fire support officer or NCO, an Air Force officer or NCO, an AN-GLICO officer or NCO, and the S1 or S4, cross-trained to handle all logistics and personnel functions. The S5, S3 Air, air defender, and

1st of the 327th Infantry Tactical Command Post (TAC)
JRTC 95-07

S2/S3 truck

fire support truck

—S3
—S2
—S1/S4

—Fire Support
—ANGLICO
—USAF

S3's truck

Outside
—S3 Air
—S5
—Air Defense
—Engineer
—All Others

Black Tac
—S3
—S2
—S1
—FSO
—ANGLICO
—TACP

Gold Tac
—XO
—Assistant S2
—S4
—Fire Support NCO
—ANGLICO
—TACP

White Teams
—Co A NCO/RTO
—Co B NCO/RTO
—Co C NCO/RTO
—Co D NCO/RTO

Tac functions:
• supervise operations *or*
• plan future operations *or*
• run a pickup zone (PZ)

Concept: One Tac will be on duty, one off during normal operations. Both Tacs are on duty during air assaults (one flies, one runs the PZ) or during a planning cycle.

White Team functions:
• report positions/strengths
• independent reporting channel
• free up company commanders

Concept: White Teams allow company commanders to run their companies while still ensuring clear reports to battalion.

engineer plugged in as needed, leaving them free to carry out their more vital roles as actual field leaders. The battalion commander might hang with either Tac, or launch forward on his own as the situation dictated.[19]

Stuffed into two cargo Humvees (one for fire supporters, one for the rest) or walking with radios, either of the Tacs had the ability to track the battle. Eschewing tentage, radio operators, chart posters, and drivers, these tiny elements looked like any other cargo trucks in the battalion when mounted, and any other rifle squad when on foot with M16A2s in hand. That neatly solved the survivability problem, the TOC displacement problem, and a whole host of other standard CP ills. Best of all, when you called "Bulldog Tac," you talked directly to the decision makers. Bolger had excised all the middlemen.

In stripping down to these Tacs, known as Gold Tac (under Steve Roberts) and Black Tac (under Bill Phelps), the battalion freed up a dozen junior NCOs and privates, the bright S2/S3 types who used to try to run the old TOC.[20] In garrison, these men arranged for training resources, scheduled schools, and performed routine security clearance checks for the companies. These Fort Campbell functions had to be done, so the battalion dared not release the soldiers back to the line units as extra bodies.

With the shift to Tac teams, however, these quality soldiers had no real job in the CP. Unwilling to let this talent go to waste, Lieutenant Colonel Bolger knew what to do. It always seemed noteworthy that while a unit may not be able to find its own butt, let alone its accurate position or manpower roll-up, the O/Cs seem to know everything. It isn't magic, either. It flows naturally from the fact that O/Cs stand apart from the outfit they accompany. Detached and therefore objective, they see and record without becoming too much a part of the experiment.

So reasoning, the Bulldog battalion commander elected to designate his own unencumbered observers. He organized what historian Martin van Creveld calls a "directed telescope," a reliable means for the commander to see events beyond his immediate purview. Napoleon Bonaparte with his Corps of Guides, Field Marshal Bernard Law Montgomery and his Phantom service, and General

George S. Patton, Jr., and his 3rd Cavalry Group, among others, used similar means.[21] They worked, too, for the same reasons O/Cs do so well at tracking things. When all you must do is watch and report what you see, you get good at it.

Accordingly, Dan Bolger created four White Teams, one per letter company. Each pair packed a SINCGARS radio and a PLGR, a Position Locator Ground Receiver, a satellite navigation device capable of pinpointing its bearer's place on the globe within a few meters. They also carried rifles, to protect themselves and to blend in.

Educated in the rudiments of the usual battalion missions, present at orders groups, these duos shadowed the company commanders and kept battalion informed. White Teams provided routine location and strength reports, collected and sent casualty lists, and generally described what they saw.[22] These detached watchers moved with the company headquarters, doing as they did. By sending status and position data on a regular basis, White Teams left the company commanders free to run their units rather than deliver play-by-play to the battalion headquarters.

With a new structure in place dedicated to operating, planning was reduced to its actual degree of importance, about 5 percent by Patton's reckoning. Either Tac could crank out a battle plan in about an hour, less if necessary.[23] Rather than plowing through the sludge of the DDMP, Bolger and his Tac buddies stuck to three framing questions. What do we want to do? What does the enemy want to do? How do we beat him? That little formula produced handwritten matrix orders, with tasks and purposes specified for each subunit. Copies came via carbon paper. It was simple, but quick and effective. The word definitely went out.

Pushed by the experienced majors and the principal staffers, a Tac rapidly generated a 70 percent solution while the other Tac continued to run the current fight. This prevented the usual TOC paralysis that accompanied planning. Some responsible first team always kept their eyes on the ongoing mission.

Chucking the DDMP put the final piece in place for the battalion. In the 1st of the 327th, one Tac team could do four things: operate, plan, rest, or move. Both Tacs were up and running during the few hours necessary for the battalion to plan an operation, do an air assault, or move the Tac. Otherwise, one bunch stayed down, recharging their mental batteries.

An air assault really amounted to the ultimate test for the Gold, Black, and White teams. While the directed telescope pairs accompanied their assigned rifle and antiarmor forces into the box, one Tac team flew in to take charge. The other laid out and supervised the pickup zone, then came forward on the final flights or by ground convoy. The battalion tried their new techniques in a January 1995 force-on-force exercise in the back forty at Fort Campbell. The novel methods succeeded handily.

Even as the Bulldogs learned their Ten Commandments, completed personnel transitions, and reinvented their approach to battalion C^2, the powers that run the U.S. Army approved a change to the approved JRTC rotation slate. The 10th Mountain Division, veterans of Somalia and then Haiti, backed out of their May 1995 slot at Fort Polk. Those guys had definitely validated their skills with real bullets. Now JRTC had an opening, and solicited customers.

The 101st Airborne Division volunteered, and JRTC and the other higher authorities agreed. That done, the division tapped good old 1st Brigade for JRTC 95-07. Among others, the brigade selected the 1st of the 327th to participate. From the battalion commander on down, all vowed that this time, things would be different.

Notes

The section epigraph comes from Martin Blumenson, ed., *The Patton Papers* (Boston: Houghton Mifflin Co., 1974), vol. II. 1940–1945, 457. A slightly modified version can be found in the motion picture version of Patton's life, and another in Lt. Col. Carlo d' Este, USA, ret., *Patton: A Genius for War* (New York: HarperCollins Publishers, 1995).

The epigraph comes from Jean Larteguy, *The Centurions,* trans. Ian Fielding (New York: Avon Books, 1963), 266.

1. Lt. Col. Daniel P. Bolger, USA, *JRTC 94-10 Results* (Ft. Campbell, Ky.: HQ, 1st Battalion, 327th Infantry Regiment, 10 October 1994), 1-2. Intended to inform all ranks of the commander's assessment of the recently completed JRTC training, this brief summary of the battalion's achievements during Rotation 94-10 clearly called the NEO, defense, and deliberate attack missions successful, and noted other accomplishments. It did describe the search and attack failure in detail, but other than that, the tone definitely inflated what went right and ignored much of what did not.

2. U.S., Department of the Army, Headquarters, 1st Battalion, 327th Infantry Regiment, *Victory in Cortina* (Ft. Campbell, Ky.: HQ, 1st Battalion, 327th Infantry Regiment, 28 February 1995), 3. This presentation to platoon sergeants and above introduced and explained the Ten Commandments for JRTC.

3. U. S., Department of the Army, Headquarters, Joint Readiness Training Center, "Intent," *Leadership Training Program: Commanders' Seminar* (Ft. Polk, La.: HQ, JRTC, March 1995). This one-page excerpt lists a variety of distinct descriptions of commander's intent, drawn from eight separate field manuals.

4. John Keegan, *The Price of Admiralty* (New York: Viking Penguin, Inc., 1989), 58.

5. Lt. Col. Daniel French, USA, "Joint Readiness Training Center OPFOR Observations," *CALL News from the Front* (January–February 1995), 1.

6. Ibid., 2.

7. U.S., Department of the Army, Headquarters, 2d Battalion,

320th Field Artillery, *Clearance of Fires* (Ft. Campbell, Ky.: Headquarters, 2d Battalion, 320th Field Artillery, 10 March 1995), 2, 8. The Quickdraw technique was invented by Lt. Col. Mark T. Kimmitt, the commander of the 2d Battalion, 320th Field Artillery from 1993–95, and a veteran of three JRTC rotations, including 94-10 and 95-07.

8. HQ, 1st Battalion, 327th Infantry, *Winning in Cortina*, 7. This quote came from a JRTC OPFOR company commander.

9. Bruce Catton, *Bruce Catton's Civil War: Three Volumes in One* (New York: Fairfax Press, 1984), 179–83.

10. U.S., Department of the Army, Headquarters, 1st Battalion, 327th Infantry Regiment, *Tactical Standing Operating Procedures* (Ft. Campbell, Ky.: HQ, 1st Battalion, 327th Infantry Regiment, 1 March 1995), 24.

11. The 1st of the 327th's unusual channel for buttpack procurement did not work for other organizations. As a result, the buttpack became a signature item for the Bulldog battalion. In 1995, if you saw a 101st Airborne soldier wearing a buttpack, you could be sure he hailed from the 1st Battalion, 327th Infantry Regiment.

12. U.S., Department of the Army, Headquarters, Joint Readiness Training Center, *Training After-Action Report: 1st Battalion, 327th Infantry, JRTC 94-10* (Ft. Polk, La.: HQ, JRTC, 26 September 1994), 1-B, 3-B.

13. Douglas S. Freeman, *R. E. Lee*, vol. 3 (New York: Charles Scribner's Sons, (1935), 16.

14. In the volunteer military, the chain of command possesses broad powers to remove soldiers from active duty for inefficiency or minor misconduct. For a list of eighteen kinds of administrative discharges, all within the purview of Army commanders, see U.S., Department of the Army, The Judge Advocate General's School, *Senior Officers Legal Orientation: Administrative and Civil Law* (Charlottesville, Va.: The Judge Advocate General's School, April 1994), 3-A-5 to 3-A-8.

15. HQ, JRTC, *Training After-Action Report: 1st Battalion, 327th Infantry, JRTC 94-10*, 4-B.

16. BDM Management Services Corporation, *JRTC Training Study: Battle Tracking in Brigade and Battalion Tactical Operations Centers* (Ft. Polk, La.: BDM, December 1993), I-2, I-3. Compared to TOCs, and in absolute terms, tactical CPs received very high marks in this study.

17. U.S., Department of the Army, Center for Army Lessons Learned, *CALL Newsletter 95-07: Tactical Operations Center* (Ft. Leavenworth, Kans.: Center for Army Lessons Learned, May 1995), III-2. This document explains the role of the battle captain.

18. U.S., Department of the Army, Headquarters, Training and Doctrine Command, *TRADOC Pamphlet 525-100-1: Leadership and Command on the Battlefield* (Ft. Monroe, Va.: HQ, TRADOC, 1992), 24–25.

19. HQ, 1st Battalion, 327th Infantry Regiment, *TACSOP*, 15.

20. The colors black, gold, and white come from the 101st Airborne Division shoulder patch.

21. Martin van Creveld, *Command in War* (Cambridge, Mass.: Harvard University, 1985), 75, 191, 272.

22. HQ, 1st Battalion, 327th Infantry Regiment, *TACSOP*, 15.

23. Ibid., 17, 19A, 19B.

Chapter 8

Air Assault

"Death from above."

—Traditional Airborne Motto

Airborne! That single word conjures stirring images: a night sky droning with a stream of big transport aircraft dark against a thin bank of scudding clouds, thousands of parachute canopies blossoming like evil mushrooms under a furtive moon, the grunts and curses of men hitting hard dirt, and the spattering of small-arms fire as an enemy awakes to find the skies and ground alive with determined paratroopers bent on mayhem. If the nineteenth century lionized the cavalryman, the mid and late twentieth century swoons to the romance of the paratrooper. Whether the All-Americans tearing up the German rear area in Normandy, the French paras stalking guerrillas in the mountains of Algeria, or the British Red Devils taking snowy hills at bayonet-point in the Falklands, the paratrooper stands supreme. He claims the mantle of the last single-combat warrior, arriving out of the blackness above like an avenging demigod. Airborne!

But paratroops are only half of the story. Right from the start, air assault forces made up the rest of the airborne idea. This explains why the 101st persists in calling itself "airborne," much to the annoyance of the 82d Airborne Division, which has gained sole proponency for conventional parachute operations. Today's 101st builds on the heritage of those units that went into battle in small aircraft. Presently, such assault birds equal helicopters. But in the 1940s, air assault forces used gliders.

Every state that organized parachute troops also developed glider elements to complement the jumpers. The Soviet Russians played with gliders before World War II, but it took the Nazi Germans to put gliders to large-scale military use. In the Low Countries in 1940 and on the island of Crete in 1941, Luftwaffe glider craft slid silently into numerous landing zones. Whereas paratroopers land in a scattered jumble, some giving new meaning to the title *Gone with the Wind*, air assault forces land in formed small units, ready to fight, and carrying heavier weaponry than those who parachute into battle. German glidermen took the fortress of Eban Emael in Belgium in a textbook example of how silent wings can deliver attackers right atop their objective. In 1944, the British repeated this coup de main by seizing a key river crossing, later christened Pegasus Bridge, in a glider-borne insertion that kicked off the D-Day invasion. Gliders played a major role in every major Allied airborne operation in 1943–45.[1]

Aside from the tactical advantages of this kind of air assault, glider warfare seemed to offer all the benefits of parachute operations without the investment in selective recruitment standards and specialized training. The U.S. Army bought this "airborne on the cheap" argument with few questions. Accordingly, glider regiments like the 327th Infantry did not get the pick of the manpower, nor did they undergo any particularly rigorous training. Denied unique uniform items and extra incentive pay, but afforded the opportunity to court death in motorless, flimsy wooden contraptions, the glider riders joked bitterly. One mock recruiting poster, replete with photos of junked gliders, urged rookies onward: "Join the glider troops! No flight pay. No jump pay. But never a dull moment!"[2]

Crashing into hedgerows and orchards certainly guaranteed excitement, a little too much for the senior airborne leaders. In the 1944 Normandy Invasion airborne generals like Matt Ridgway, Maxwell Taylor, and Jim Gavin fearlessly jumped into action under the silk.Only one general, Don Pratt of the 101st Airborne, actually rode to battle in a glider. Not surprisingly, he died in a crack-up.[3]

Such occupational hazards typified glider warfare. True, the wooden craft brought intact squads and platoons into combat. They also plunked down field artillery, antitank guns, jeeps, and engineer equipment. On the other hand, with only one chance to get it right on uncertain LZs, the damn gliders tended to flop down all over the place, off target and in the rough. In the process they skipped, skidded, shed wings, and shattered. To add to the horror show, heavy onboard loads often broke loose and rattled around or even punched through the flimsy carriers, randomly crushing and mangling help-less men. Worst of all, once a glider landed, that was it. The ticket only worked one way.

Because of these factors, not to mention relative shortages of trans-port planes, glider assaults tended to feature artillery and heavy gear, not infantry. The 327th, for example, made one glider assault in its history, slipping into Holland on the second day of Operation Market-Garden. This venture used four hundred and fifty gliders. Of course, twenty-two splattered into the Dutch polders with ugly casu-alties. Some two hundred suffered substantial damage.[4] So much for the regiment's glorious glider heritage.

Gliders passed unlamented after the end of World War II, but the air assault concept lived on. In Korea, French Algeria, and in the early years of the U.S. war in Vietnam, helicopters took over the old glider role. Landing whole units together in wild terrain, Army air-mobile tactics evolved to become the centerpiece of the 1965–73 ground war against the CLF's prototypes, the Viet Cong. Like glid-ers, the rotary-wing aircraft offered many of the advantages of a mass jump, again without the costs in extensive preliminary training and elite recruitment. Unlike the gliders, however, choppers steered right to the LZ, or at least tried to do that. And best of all, helicopters could wave off a hot LZ, or come back to extract troops in trouble. No en-gineless glider ever did that.

Airmobility built on the vision of Lt. Gen. Hamilton Howze and his aviation-minded study group, and the pioneering work of the 11th Air Assault Division. The 11th, drawing on the heritage of the 11th Airborne but manned by line infantry battalions, perfected the new air-ground tactics made possible by the new UH-1 Hueys with their powerful turbine engines. After running rings around con-ventional units in stateside maneuvers, this outfit deployed to Viet-nam in 1965 as the 1st Cavalry Division (Airmobile). Their big black and yellow patch, cavalry swagger, and unique fighting ethos paced the growing war in Southeast Asia. Eventually, the Army organized a second airmobile division around the battle-tested 101st Airborne. When the war ended, the 1st Cavalry became an armored formation. The airmobile tradition, with its glider connection, passed to the Screaming Eagles.[5]

In doing so, the propenency for this brand of warfare returned to its airborne heritage, which, to be honest, perfected it. For the first time since the glider troops organized, the U.S. Army acknowledged that these kinds of forces, too, required extraordinary recruitment and specialized training. At the behest of Maj. Gen. Sidney Berry, in 1974 the 101st Airborne designated itself "air assault." Berry commenced to issue the badge of the same name to graduates of the division's demanding ten-day Air Assault School. The school consciously resembled the Army Airborne School's Basic Parachutist Course at Fort Benning, Georgia. The badge, too, took its design from the paratrooper's silver wings, substituting a bow-on view of a Huey for the inflated parachute found in the center of the older award. Berry ditched the Nam-era term *airmobility,* with its connotation that anyone could do it. Airmobility conjured up thoughts of a flying bus. Air assault, though, signaled picked men, trained for forced entry, marked by aggressiveness, and inspired by an indomitable will to fight.[6] And the Screaming Eagles intended to fight, all right.

Throughout the 1970s and 1980s, the 101st Airborne refined air assault tactics to accommodate modernized aircraft like the UH-60L Blackhawk troop ship and the AH-64A Apache attack bird. By 1991, the division had the capability to land an entire brigade ninety miles behind enemy lines—then pick it up and do it again the next night.[7] In the Gulf War that year, during the hundred-hour Coalition ground offensive, the Screaming Eagles plunked down all three brigades to block the Iraqi retreat from Kuwait.

At the cease-fire, division troops fought across a wide arc that spanned the entire left flank of Gen. Norman Schwarzkopf's great armored wheel, with air assault brigade concentrations stretching for some three hundred miles, linked together by roving bands of deadly AH-64A Apaches. If you superimposed this pattern on a map of the eastern United States, the division's operations ranged from the suburbs of Washington, D.C., to the boroughs of New York City. That's a hell of a footprint. Not only did the Screaming Eagles go deep and wide, they also went for the enemy jugular. Saddam Hussein's forces particularly feared the brigade that seized the Euphrates River causeways less than one hundred miles—one more night's work—from Baghdad. For a few hours the division stood poised to descend on the Iraqi capital. But American political leaders thought otherwise. The one hundred-hour blitz never gave way to what 101st Airborne planners wistfully dubbed the "Baghdad Sequel."[8] The division's Gulf War ended on the Euphrates, a long, long way from Normandy, Holland, and Bastogne, and especially, Vietnam.

The war against Iraq validated modern air assault operations and made the 101st Airborne the hottest property in the Army inventory. Want raw combat power? The division matched any armored division thanks to its horde of Apaches. Need infantry? No light infantry division had more, or better. Is is important to get there fast? The division could move out in eighteen hours, just like the 82d Airborne. The four-star commanders responsible for America's regional commitments wanted the 101st for various missions. The generals and admirals vied for priority on the country's, and indeed the world's, only air assault division. And at JRTC, Fort Campbell, and elsewhere, the Screaming Eagles kept training, trying to live up to their awesome reputation.

All of this meant absolutely nothing to the bad guys out there, including their stateside training analogues, the Cortinian Liberation Force. They had no night-flying choppers. The only tech they knew was low. Yet they feared not. If JRTC 94-10 proved anything, it underlined the lessons of Vietnam, Lebanon, and Somalia: Smart insurgents could beat America's best, even the 101st Airborne. To paraphrase the old line—with a slight twist—the CLF smirked and hummed: What have you done to me lately?

The guerrillas might have been wiser to consider history. Commenting on his American opponents after their poor showing at Kasserine Pass in 1943, German Field Marshal Erwin Rommel granted that, although slow starters, the Americans seemed to be quick and avid learners.[9] These Bulldogs, these Earth Pigs, had definitely learned. On JRTC Rotation 95-07, they administered the lessons.

As always for the 101st Airborne, everything at JRTC started with a massive forced entry operation. The Fullerton Flight Landing Strip again took center stage, beckoning the 1st Brigade into Cortina.

Like 94-10, the brigade envisioned an all-night operation, staging from the England Air Park. The forces that did not fly planned to drive in on Artillery Road, the standard course. After the insertion ended, the brigade proposed to begin search and attack in zone, scouring the same terrain that damn near broke the organization in September 1994.

There the breakers waited, hiding, biding their time for the rematch. Like the 1st Brigade, the CLF 91st Assault Battalion consisted of many veterans of the previous encounter. They knew what a 101st Airborne air assault looked like, having seen the 1st Brigade in May and September 1994, the 2d Brigade in November, and the 3d Brigade in March 1995. Polishing up their marksmanship, camouflaging their spiderholes, Fort Polk's resident henchmen anticipated the usual brigade-scale landing, done according to the tested recipe. The CLF response would see a fair helping of gore on at least one of the landing zones, then death and immolation along the convoy route. When the Americans began to search and attack, the Cortinian hostiles plotted big kills near their supply points and minefields. So it went, time after time.

This rotation, though, the CLF got it wrong. The judgment errors started before the first American entered the play box. Caught maldeployed at the outset, the insurgents never really recovered. Even though they eventually introduced the blackshirts from the seldom-seen PRA Special Operations Forces, it did not help. The opening U.S. blow set the tone.

The air assault that kicked off JRTC 95-07 lends itself to detailed analysis. This one came pretty near to being a model mission, especially measured by its impressive effects. In almost every respect, 1st Brigade did it right. How did they do it?

Success started with a new commander open to different ways of thinking. Although the rest of the chain of command and the staff stayed more or less intact, Col. Jim Donald finally left his beloved 1st Brigade. Everybody recognized Donald as a 101st Airborne man to his bones, a reputation cemented by his Gulf War duty as an air assault infantry battalion commander and three pretty much successful JRTC rotations as a brigade commander. If air assault expertise really existed, Jim Donald had it. So his men figured.

Others thought so, too, and after a brief stint on the Army Staff, the authorities made Donald a brigadier general. This new guy, though, made you wonder.

A Marine rifleman in Vietnam, Col. Jack Donovan's record as an officer centered on long service in the 82d Airborne Division, culminating in company command and assignment as a battalion S3 as a captain, a rare appointment indicative of this officer's talents. As a lieutenant colonel, Donovan commanded the battalion that ran the Mountain Ranger Camp for the Ranger Training Brigade. About halfway through this tour, he received a cryptic telephone call that abruptly terminated his Ranger command and sent him back to Vietnam. Hand-picked by the U.S. Army's senior leadership, Jack Donovan formed and commanded Detachment 2 (Vietnam), Joint Task Force—Full Accounting a multiservice team dedicated to resolving missing-in-action cases. His brilliant work in that unpleasant and unforgiving assignment earned him command of a brigade.[10]

Unlike Colonel Donald, Donovan never served a day in the 101st Airborne before he took the colors in December 1994. Old-timers and insiders wagged their heads, certain that this former enlisted jarhead, an 82d Airborne product, looked like trouble. After all, ignoring that Ranger Camp or that Hanoi lash-up, he never commanded a line battalion, did he? Surely JRTC 95-07 portended trouble for such a neophyte. Whatever he did know, the smart money at Fort Campbell whispered that Col. Jack Donovan didn't know "the real deal" about the 101st Airborne.

Donovan did not. And that proved to be his greatest strength. Unbound by the way things always were done, Jack Donovan dared to be different. While this approach made many subordinate battalion commanders uncomfortable, it suited Lt. Col. Dan Bolger perfectly. The more Donovan deviated from the norm, the more Bolger liked it. The CLF felt otherwise, of course.

The 1st Brigade's 13 May 1995 air assault looked quite different from any previous similar operations. Even so, it shared a lot of traits with every other brigade air assault. For one thing, the mission required seizure of the Fullerton airstrip, then destruction of the CLF in zone; no noncombatant evacuation distractions affected this one. The opponents remained the tricky, deadly CLF guerrillas, with their

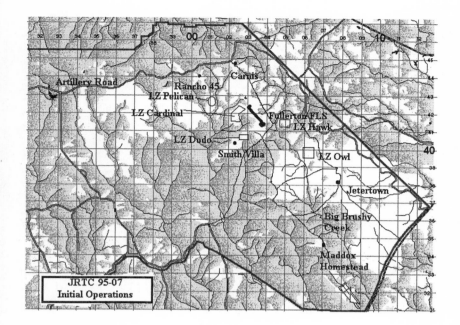

JRTC 95-07
Initial Operations

conventional PRA pals not far removed. And the terrain—whew! That same hideous pastiche awaited: swamps, slash pines, red clay ridges and choking dust, dotted with depressing clapboard villages full of sullen Cortinians and hidden insurgent sympathizers. The May weather mirrored the September weather almost day for day. Yes, indeed, the brigade had been to this party before.

The Always First team drew on the same basic troop list brought to 94-10. Aside from Colonel Donovan's crucial new influence on the mix, two other significant changes deserve note. First, the 3-187th Infantry gave way to one of the 1st Brigade's habitual organizations, the 2d Battalion, 327th Infantry Regiment, radio call sign "No Slack." Task Force No Slack went to JRTC 94-07 a year before, and so enjoyed about the same relative experience level as 1-327th. They, too, had made some adjustments since the earlier visit, although nothing as sweeping as what happened in the Bulldog battalion.

The other new entry in the brigade batting order came from Fort Lewis, Washington, home of the 3d Brigade, 2d Infantry Division.

Commanding Team Animal, built around Company A, 1st Battalion, 32d Armor, Capt. Ken Blakely delivered a heavy punch to complement the lightly armed air assault people. Blakely's bunch included two tank platoons, each with four mighty M1A1 Abrams tanks, seventy-ton monsters sporting 120mm main guns and enough armor to shrug off almost anything the CLF or PRA might throw at them. Along with the tanks came two platoons of mechanized infantry, riding to combat in M2A2 Bradley infantry fighting vehicles, twenty-seven-ton armored track-layers, every one packing a turreted 25mm autocannon. Finally, Team Animal's armored engineers ensured mobility, bringing explosive mine-breaching systems to the fray.[11] When Team Animal rolled, bad guys sat up and paid attention.

Other than the No Slack battalion and Team Animal, all the other usual suspects gathered. The 1st of the 327th, born-again Earth Pigs, under new management, TOC-less, itched to start killing the CLF. The 2d of the 320th Field Artillery prepared to deliver indirect fires in volume. Attack aviators of 3-101 Aviation and lifters of 5-101 Aviation came together, providing flying guns and winged steeds for the men of the Always First brigade. Finally, the 426th Forward Support Battalion again endeavored to feed the maw of Mars, sending in the bandages, beans, benzene, and bullets that make air assaults possible. Along with these came the engineer company, the air defense battery, the military intelligence company team, the chemical decontamination and smoke platoon, the military police platoon, and all the rest of the odds and ends. Atop it all squatted the brigade headquarters, with its long-haul satellite communications and its big TOC, posed to spew out orders and overlays. Donovan's tools stood ready.

To understand the exquisite air-ground ballet that becomes an air assault, you must start as Jack Donovan and his staff did, with the framework. An air assault proceeds in five phases: staging, loading, flying, landing, and ground fighting. In a bow to the heritage shared with paratroopers, however, air assault commanders routinely plan their operations in reverse. That is to say, the ground plan drives the landing array, the landing array dictates the flight scheme, the flight scheme affects the loading concept, and the loading concept steers the staging plan. In theory, and by doctrine, the ground combat blueprint assumes absolute primacy. That explains why U.S. Army doctrine on the subject, *FM 90-4*, baldly says: "The ground tactical plan is normally developed first and is the basis from which the other plans are derived." [12]

Now, that sounds good, especially to rifle officers already suspicious of guys who wear flight suits and talk with their hands. But in the 101st Airborne, infantry commanders quickly discovered that they insisted on priority for the ground plan at grave peril to the overall operation. In ideal environs, the green-black choppers swooped down out of the starry skies right on each platoon's final objective, disgorged lightly loaded riflemen, then zipped off. Unfortunately, in this world, miscreants hid deep in the woods, far from open LZs. If the CLF loitered in the treeline along a clearing, they wanted to fight, and licked their chops at the thought of blowing away slowing UH-60Ls, or better, lumbering Chinooks. No, brother, you had better not just slap down your infantry willy-nilly. That is, unless you like to train on medevac.

Getting in, the landing plan, actually drove the air assault train. And why not? After all, this represented the true interface between air crew and grunt, where everything came together. The holy ground tactical plan represented little more than a compromise between where you wanted to go and where the birds could land, and how many might make it in. Just as in parachute operations or amphibious assaults, where to land invariably became the pivotal question. Everything turned on the choice of landing zones.

The attack on Fullerton demonstrated the overwhelming importance of the landing plan. A quick map survey, combined with a glance at aerial photography and comments by the many who had already been there, convinced Donovan and his planners that only three realistic choices existed. The brigade may land on the FLS (inside-out). It might land off the runway (outside-in). Or, it could do both at once (simultaneous). In picking the best landing option, brigade weighed the usual situational factors: mission, enemy, terrain, troops available, and time.

The mission bore a nasty dilemma. Secure terrain or kill the enemy? Usually, brigades split the difference and sent one infantry battalion to grab the FLS and the other to commence slaying the CLF.

Essentially, 1st Brigade did this in JRTC 94-07 and 94-10, with a detour on the latter to police up some trapped American citizens. This time, a chastened 1st Brigade staff, urged on by Dan Bolger among others, realized that if you kill the enemy, you get the FLS anyway. If you take the airstrip, the CLF may charge too high a price for that real estate. Splitting the task merely weakened the killing effort. Brigade concurred with destroying the CLF first. That argued for outside-in, trapping the gomers on the fringe of the FLS clearing and then driving them out in to the open to be slaughtered by bullets, not men, in the grand American tradition.

Enemy issues also pushed the brigade to stay off the FLS. Every other 101st, 82d, and Ranger attack led with boots on the runway, smack on the objective, like the books all said to do. The CLF naturally read those same books, and so aligned multi-barreled DShK antiaircraft guns to sweep the FLS, a killing ground festooned with wire, metal stakes, and mines by the gross. A landing in that death-trap guaranteed mass casualties. Ask the Rakkasans after 94-10. To beat this kind of ring of fire anchored to the FLS, the Americans needed to land on the outskirts and head in.

Terrain allowed for plenty of decent-sized LZs in the Fullerton area. Finding a good LZ meant finding a six-shipper, an opening of about 600 meters by 150 meters, since the Blackhawks tended to fly in groups of four to six aircraft on a brigade air assault.[13] Anything smaller might be too hard to find at night, and risked dribbling in the riflemen one bird at a time. With a good six-helicopter LZ, you could bring in an entire battalion in three minutes, with Chinooks following with trucks and cannons until you ran out of Chinooks to use. Fullerton allowed you to do that in over a dozen spots aside from the big rectangular cutout itself. Outside-in, inside-out, simultaneous; it did not matter from the standpoint of ground. In any event, the CLF could never watch all of these clearings. It only made sense to land where the bad folk were not.

The characteristics and preferences of the U.S. troops on hand pulled at the brigade planners too. The endurance of the pilots on night-vision goggles ran out after about six hours, and each trip from England Air Park into Cortina and back took about an hour and a half. Allowing for screwing around at the pickup zones, form-up time, and refueling, the brigade counted on three turns of twenty Black-hawks and eight Chinooks. That sufficed to insert two infantry bat-talions minus most of their antiarmor companies and vehicles, a how-itzer battery with the AN/TPQ-36 countermortar radar, the brigade Tac CP, an engineer runway clearance team, and a tiny forward lo-gistics element. Everything else had to drive in behind Team Animal, and arrive up to a day later.

Those who lacked firsthand knowledge might argue for extend-ing the fliers' goggle time, pushing the envelope. That kind of thinking ignores the intensity of goggle flying, akin to driving your car at ninety miles an hour down a twisting country road with only the parking lights on and a good swack of oncoming traffic appear-ing unbidden just to keep you honest. Formation flying under gog-gles drains the pilots, literally and figuratively. Going beyond the ap-proved limits really begs for disaster. In a blacked-out flight of six, it only takes a number-four crew with vertigo to ruin everyone's evening, especially the helpless riflemen stacked like cordwood in the cargo bays. The Army normally permits four hours under gog-gles. Aviators in the 101st Airborne have standing permission to waive this to five hours, and six with general officer approval. For JRTC, the approval always comes. But you must be careful.

With this in mind, each infantry battalion expected one lift, plus a few CH-47D sorties. The other Blackhawk and Chinook turns be-longed to the brigade, to use for moving artillery, enginners, the brigade command post, and so on. With a single shot to get in, the infantry commanders faced their own choices: how many landing zones, and where?

The No Slack commander, an experienced lieutenant colonel, did it the usual way, with one LZ per rifle company, all within a few kilo-meters of each other. The 2-327th troops wanted to avoid the FLS, and insisted on coming in away from the airstrip. Combined with three company-size landings, that allowed maximum flexibility.

It also separated the battalion, allowing the CLF to gang up on one company and ring up a horrific body count, as happened to the Rakkasans back in 94-10. Dan Bolger discarded the typical drill of one LZ per company. He directed the entire battalion to go into a single six-shipper. "If we get in cold, we're together. If we get hit, we're together," he said. "But regardless," he went on, "we're together right from the start." The advantage to air assaults, versus parachute assaults, hinged on massing intact units. Bolger thought he could outsmart the CLF by choosing an undefended, or lightly defended, landing zone. Like his No Slack counterpart, he strongly voted for outside-in.

Time, a six-hour block that the brigade staffers expected to pass like summer heat lightning, cemented the brigade's scheme. Committed to killing the CLF first, working from outside-in to avoid the FLS ambush zone, Col. Jack Donovan and his men hit upon the final modification to business as usual. They elected to throw both battalions against the airstrip area, landing on the outer ring and clearing in, then heading off in search and attack. This unconventional game plan focused all brigade efforts on one thing: killing the enemy. The 1st of the 327th understood that task, and welcomed it.

Settling on an outside-in scheme employing both infantry battalions, Donovan sent 2-327th to the north and west, to its three chosen LZs. No Slack inherited the runway proper, but brigade clearly told them to wipe out resistance before monkeying around with the FLS clearance task. The 1-327th men, a supporting effort, looked to the south and west. They chose a single LZ, Hawk, just off the southeast edge of the rectangle of rolling meadow that surrounded the landing strip. Donovan set H-Hour, wheels-down for the main effort, as 2100 on 13 May. He scheduled Bolger and the Bulldogs to come in two hours later. If the brigade commander guessed right, both battalions would land behind two to four evil enemy DShK guns, and catch their crews and the rest of the CLF looking the wrong way.

The ground scheme and its affiliated outside-in landing plan began to lock down the other three moves of the air assault five-step. Next in order, brigade and the aviators cooked up an air movement plan. Although the ground business reflected a common thread between two cultures, this airplane-driving part fell to the men (and a few women) in baggy flight suits. They plotted the shortest possible legs to get from England Air Park to Fort Polk, avoiding populated areas en route; no need to upset the locals more than necessary. Most of the route specified a leisurely altitude, a thousand feet or so, with

some position lights illuminated. But at the Polk reservation boundary, the edge of Cortina, the fun ended. There the formations would
descend sharply to treetop level and pick up the pace. Lining up
from the south, keying on Jetertown (that place again) as a release
point, the pilots planned to break left to the west to drop off No
Slack, or plow due north to unload the Bulldogs. Then up and away,
out to the north, and the choppers would fly back to England for the
next load or refueling. It all fit on a clipboard, a neat matrix of times
and places known as the route card, a subset of a bigger matrix of
times and places called the air movement table.

Dan Bolger and his followers groused about this obsession with
where and when. They sneered at the "bus schedule," but for fliers
trying to merge several six-chopper gaggles in the dead of a muggy
Louisiana night, precise timing and accurate location meant everything. To lag or rush, to wander about the sky or fudge on altitude—
well, that sort of foolishness led to incandescent smash-ups, real fire-
balls with real deaths, not MILES gameplay. Coupled with attempting
to keep tight formation, peering through those damn toilet-paper-
tube night goggles, avoiding mishaps like banging into lone trees or
bouncing into odd LZ holes, and dodging pretend flak and sham SA-
14 missiles, tracking time and location kept the pilots and copilots
hopping. The flight instructors called it task overloading, and
frowned on it. Army aviators in the 101st Airborne got used to it or
turned in their wings. After a hairy night insertion, the fliers often
wrung a pint of sweat out of their dank clothing, regardless of heat
and humidity.

Aviators in the 101st Airborne prided themselves on bringing in
their passengers at plus or minus thirty seconds of the plan, to plus
or minus fifty meters of the designated spot. They usually did it, too,
provided the infantry stayed reasonable about LZ selections. Hunting too many different stops, remembering who had to go where,
begged for Mr. Murphy to exert his baleful influence. The pilots
much preferred Bolger's all-in-one technique.

The air armada assembled for 1st Brigade on 13 May totaled 64
helicopters. The fleet broke into two groups, those on station overhead and those actually going to ground. First among the station-
keepers were the AH-64A Apaches overwatching the LZs in relays of

four, two to the east, and two to the west, well clear of the assault bird flight paths. Off-post, circling in an isolated orbit, a C^2 Blackhawk and its spare prepared to burn fuel boring lazy ellipses in the night sky; the C^2 craft allowed Colonel Donovan to maintain communications with his far-flung forces as the assault went down. In another orbit, one could find the emergency helicopters, the medevac and search and rescue aircraft dedicated to losses caused by MILES or, God forbid, a real accident. Finally, back at England Air Park, brigade left a few ground spares, just in case something did not crank or, even worse, conked out after a turn or two.

In the sense of putting men and gear in the dirt, only twenty-two UH-60Ls and eight CH-47Ds constituted true mission birds. The brigade staff made the most of this amount because they proposed to make three turns. Planners designated each turn as a *lift*. With only three to use, the staffers at brigade got creative trying to milk maximum insertion strength from the equivalent of 66 Blackhawks and 24 Chinooks over a six-hour window. In war, the entire 101st Airborne Division's aviation flotilla would concentrate on moving a single brigade in one lift.[14] But at JRTC, you lived with less, about a third of what you wanted.

For the 13 May mission, brigade sequenced forces in four lifts, shaving six Chinooks and two spare Blackhawks to start with a Lift 0 at 1930, minutes after sunset. This endeavored to put down the Brigade Tactical CP, plus a four-howitzer battery with a Q-36 radar, to ensure coverage for the real landings at 2100. In other 101st Airborne forced entries, like 94-07, previous brigades committed an entire infantry battalion to emplace this offset battery. Donovan elected to let the guns defend themselves.

At 2100, the twenty-two Blackhawks and four Chinooks of Lift 1 expected to land the 2d Battalion, 327th Infantry Regiment in its three company landing zones. Two hours later, that same package, now known as Lift 2, wanted to deliver the Bulldogs to LZ Hawk. A truncated Lift 3, minus those aircraft used to emplace the brigade Tac and the artillery, closed the air assault by bringing in the start of the brigade's engineers, air defense battery, and service support contingent.

A look at the assault into LZ Hawk explains how this comes together between air and ground participants. Working with the avi-

1st Battalion, 327th Infantry Regiment
Air Assault of 13 May 1996

Lift 2   Primary: LZ Hawk Alternate: LZ Owl

Time	Serial	Chalk	Aircraft	Ground Forces
H+2:00 (2300)	1	1-6	6 x UH-60L	102 men (Company A) 9 men (Black Tac) 3 men (Team Golf)
H+2:01 (2301)	2	7-10	4 x UH-60L	76 men (Company C)
H+2:02 (2302)	3	11-16	6 x UH-60L	31 men (Company C) 83 men (Company B)
H+2:04 (2304)	4	17-22	6 x UH-60L	26 men (Company B) 20 men (Team Golf) 4 x armed Humvees
H+2:06 (2306)	5	22-26	4 x CH-47D	10 men (LZST) 20 men (Mortars) 17 men (Scouts) 16 men (FCT Teams) 8 x Humvees

Ground Convoy
Company D (-)   53 men, 28 Humvees (battalion area)
Gold Tac (+):   11 men, 3 Humvees (battalion area)
LZST   11 men, 4 Humvees (battalion area)
Mortars   6 men, 3 Humvees (battalion area)
Field Trains   48 men, 31 Humvees, 9 5-ton trucks (brigade support area)

ators, Dan Bolger's S3 Air, 1st Lt. Matt Bounds, broke out the allocated Lift 2 aircraft. Trying to string together more than six helicopters just did not work. The things flew and landed in trail like ducklings following mama, and more than a half dozen made the choo-choo entirely too long. Accordingly, the lift consisted of four Blackhawk *serials,* each following a single flight lead drawn from one of 5-101st Aviation's two flight companies. The Lift 2 serials, each led by an experienced pilot, included six, four, six, and six Blackhawks respectively. Each aircraft hauled one load, or as the Army termed it, a *chalk.*

Mixing aircraft types was also bad karma, so the Chinooks always made up their own serial, in this case Serial 5. The Chinooks used their own flight lead. Inevitably bearing sling-loaded trucks, the CH-47Ds routinely flew in last. That way, if the LZ went hot with hostile fire, those flying furniture vans could wave off. The nimble Blackhawks at least had a chance to get out of a hornet's nest; the Chinooks, never.

Allocating these airframes to the 1st of the 327th's infantry showed exactly how reality profaned the sanctity of the ground tactical plan. Ideally, each serial would hold a single company, but it did not work that way. The battalion's concerted emphasis on weeding out weaklings did produce addition by subtraction, but at nineteen bodies per ship (leaving a spot for an O/C), the enlarged rifle companies fit less than neatly into the available groups of Blackhawks. Company A and the Tac rode in the six UH-60Ls of Serial 1; most of Company C went in Serial 2. Serial 3 carried the rump of Company C and the bulk of Company B. The rest of Company B flew on Serial 4, along with four Company D trucks and their crews, all assigned to Team Golf. The Chinooks carried four 81mm mortar trucks, the fire support vehicle, a USAF radio Humvee, and two LZST cargo carriers. This delivery flow barely matched any conceivable ground plan, but you could work with it.

Guided by Dirk Blackdeer's read on the CLF and Bill Phelps's wise counsel, Bolger devised a simple assault scheme. He sent Company A due north, Company C west, Company B east, and Team Golf south to set a roadblock between LZ Hawk and the happy citizenry of Jetertown. Men merely needed to head out in the appropriate cardinal direction through the sides of the roughly rectangular landing zone. Blackdeer thought that Company C enjoyed the best chance of killing a DShK, followed by Company A. The rest would simply hit isolated CLF teams—and kill them.

To kill anyone other than yourself, getting off that open LZ comes first. To hell with the thirty minutes allowed by the battalion Mission Training Plan, the Army's grade sheet for such things.[15] Bolger gave his riflemen one minute to sprint to the treeline. Lightly loaded, in Earth Pig ensemble complete with buttpacks, they knew it to be possible. But to tell the truth, Bolger thought LZ Hawk would be cold. That's why he picked it, to get in clean, then work back toward the FLS.

With aircraft apportioned, Bolger tidied up one more detail regarding moving into the box. He organized the rest of his battalion, mostly the Maddogs and Headquarters Company, into two segments. The combat-oriented component readied to go into the box under Capt. Mike Delgado of Company D. All the rest formed a service support herd reporting to Capt. Ronz Sarvis of HHC. Remembering only too well the mine-induced bloodbath incurred during 94-10, Bolger draconically policed the number of trucks permitted forward of the field trains. The air defense lieutenant, the psychological operations team, the U.S. Air Force liaison, and others, including the chaplain, demanded their vehicles. Some grew rather impassioned, and even brought in their superior officers to press their claims. Bolger, who did not take his own Humvee, who carried his own radio and a rifle, showed absolutely no sympathy. The vehicle limits held. Taciturn Maj. Steve Roberts, who brooked no nonsense, took charge of the convoy as it gathered.

Now, Roberts made an excellent ground column commander, because he also supervised the loading plan, assisted by his Gold Tac comrades. They would launch the air assault, then drive into Cortina down Artillery Road. The ambushes and land mines looked grim as ever. Even so, Gold Tac faced an even tougher time on the pickup zone.

By long custom, control of PZs falls to executive officers. The brigade XO, a lieutenant colonel, assumed overall responsibility. The light PZ, which served the UH-60L Blackhawks, fell to No Slack, the main effort battalion. It was easy to run. The much more challenging heavy PZ for Chinooks went to Steve Roberts and the Gold Tac, plus as many ground convoy men as he chose to use.

Roberts chose to use quite a few. The heavy PZ reinvented the concept of friction in war popularized by brother Clausewitz. On the heavy PZ, blacked-out Chinooks hovered over trucks, howitzers, and cargo nets rigged with specially woven sling ropes. Thanks to the CH-47D's flat bottom, the pilots had no ability to see the minuet played out beneath their belly. Instead, a nineteen-year-old crew chief looked out through a square opening called, appropriately, the hell-hole. Wired to the aviators, this young man talked the big twin-rotored bird onto the load.

Two gutsy soldiers waited atop each thing to be slung. Balanced in the darkness on slippery truck tops and spongy cargo nets, without lights to aid them, the pairs watched the big slab cross over them. The dark surface bobbed above them, close enough to touch, with the rotors roaring wind that distorted faces and made it impossible to hear. No, they did this all by sight and touch, except they couldn't see much and the only touch they needed involved slamming metal to metal and then getting the hell out of the way.

One soldier held a static electricity probe, to touch the Chinook's three steel alloy cargo hooks and ground away the charges that built up there. If the probe man missed, the chopper's ration of local lightning might zap the hook man right off the load, and stop his heart in the bargain. So the prober tapped all three hooks with his aluminum tent peg tied to a wooden stick—so much for high-tech.

Then the hook man did his thing, with the great slab heaving and weaving and the rotor wash howling and the crew chief's helmeted head hanging down out of the hellhole watching it all, talking to two fliers trying to be gentle with a machine built for brute force. Hookmen learned not to play around, but to bang their connecting bar down on the dangling hook, like an NBA star stuffing the ball, with authority and finality. That done, and confirmed, the pair scampered off the load and away from the aircraft. The Chinook then picked up and loitered overhead, checking the hang of the external cargo. If all the lines unraveled as designed, if the truck or bag hung level, if the bird felt all right, or as right as a Chinook can feel with a pair of Humvees rocking below it—then the helicopter fell in with its serial and headed out.[16]

Naturally, this process offered plenty of frustrations and more than a few potential fatalities. Tangled sling legs, improper or damaged hookup equipment, goosey flying, or a poorly laid-out PZ all drew one into the black vortex of failure. Truly, however, the biggest variable involved the soldiers working on the PZ. For them, perfect was good enough. Screw-ups might mean maiming or death, and not by MILES, either.

Because the sling-craft had to pick up any passengers before grabbing their accompanying loads, you never hooked your own stuff. The PZ teams from the tagged infantry battalion did all of that for you. They had to get it right with stuff they often saw for the first time on the heavy PZ. Weird engineer equipment, like dozers and excavators, vied with irregular supply and fuel bundles as the worst loads to rig and hook. Often, the people who showed up with the stuff had no idea how to prep it to sling out. Not surprisingly, the customers sometimes showed up for their great adventure with sling items missing or unserviceable.

To get the loads properly rigged and staged for pickup (the fifth step in air assault backward planning doctrine), it helped to start early, preferably in daylight. Show times twelve hours before lift-off were not unheard of. Even that early, Steve Roberts and his people anticipated kicking a substantial number of butts to get everything ready.

In a secure PZ like England Air Park, the PZ-meister carefully aligned all loads. At England, the heavy stuff launched from one of the former runways; the soldiers departed from another, separate hardstand. In staging ahead of time, the chalks dotted the PZ at regular intervals, leaving plenty of room between loads for CH-47Ds on final approach. The UH-60L slingloads waited at one end; those hooked up pretty easily compared to the blind grappling under the damn Chinooks. Follow-on lifts waited in orderly rows, already rigged, on call to move up when the previous chalks flew off.

Rehearsals occupied much of the time between arrival of the chalks and the coming of the aircraft. Designated hooker teams practiced clambering up and down on their loads, and each chalk familiarized itself with where to go and when. Roberts also drilled his men, and the passengers, on what to do if an aircraft did not show, or a load failed to fly and became "frustrated" (an apt appellation, to be sure). Some problems, like twisted sling legs, allowed immediate resolution by a rapid response band of fixers dispatched by

Roberts and the Gold Tac at the PZ CP, their special Tac truck with its bevy of radios. Other crises, like damaged sling gear, missing loads, or broken-down choppers, did not permit immediate cures. In these cases, Roberts turned to a priority list approved by Colonel Donovan. Chalks flew in this order, and no other, if things went south.

While Steve Roberts and his soldiers checked and practiced, the riflemen riding on Blackhawks also lined up, awaiting their rotor-borne conveyances. Again, early arrival, in daylight when possible, equated with proper PZ etiquette. England Air Park let you do so, so the Bulldogs did. As the sun sank on 13 May, hundreds of solemn riflemen lay alongside the abandoned taxiway in neat rows, waiting patiently, the way their like has always waited, before Marathon, Waterloo, Hue City, or a million other long-forgotten skirmishes. The battalion commander, monitoring the various radio nets, noticed that the orderly files looked very much like pictures of dead men in Vietnam, a disturbing image to say the least. Dan Bolger prayed it was not an omen.

That evening, though, all other omens appeared favorable. Colonel Donovan and the 3-101 attack crews cooperated nicely to deceive and badger the OPFOR, pinning their attention neatly to the FLS and its wide, lonely meadow. The brigade commander refused to insert infantry battalion scouts, a decision wholeheartedly agreed to by Bolger and his fellow commander in 2-327th Infantry. As Rocky told Bullwinkle, that trick never works. Scouts lack the radios for going ninety miles deep, nor do they train at pre-D-Day clandestine recon. That belongs to the long-range recon teams held at division and corps, or the special operators.

Instead of relying on the scouts like everyone else, Donovan pinned his hopes on his vigilant Apaches. For three nights these persistent warbirds zigzagged over Cortina, shooting at likely targets. One set of AH-64As definitely tanked a technical vehicle, a pickup truck bearing a .50-caliber machine gun. This kill occurred at the southwest end of the FLS, a perfect spot. Apaches repeatedly buzzed the dirt strip, lending credence to CLF beliefs that the U.S. hoped to land there, like always. It evidently did not dawn on the enemy that the Apaches also filmed, in glorious black and white, all the LZs around Fullerton FLS. The CLF wanted to cover the runway, and did.

The 1st Brigade's air assault upended that smug insurgent view. Although the brigade Tac took it on the chin, landing squarely in a CLF patrol base, every other chalk set down unopposed. No Slack troopers met little resistance to the southwest, but not so on the northwest corner of the FLS. There, a big firefight brewed up as the 2-327th soldiers attempted to push north.

That fight sparked and flared as the Bulldogs landed at 2300. Bolger had outfoxed the CLF this time. They were not there. *So far, so good,* though Lieutenant Colonel Bolger.

Tumbling out of the Blackhawks, flexing leg muscles cramped and crunched by the grating no-seats ride, the soldiers fanned out behind their leaders. True to their orders, the riflemen vacated the cold LZ within a minute. The Abus plunged north, Cold Steel headed west, and the Bushmasters moved to the east to press to the creekbed. By 2305, LZ Hawk again lay empty, awaiting sling-loads.

First came the Blackhawks, four with loads, two without. They dropped and cleared swiftly, on time. Next, almost before the empty UH-60Ls rose from the LZ, the Chinooks appeared, bang on schedule. Stately and slow, the great birds bobbed to a stop, sighed rotorwash, and cut their welcome cargoes, one after another. As each Chinook dropped its sling, it slid sideways and landed. The rear ramps dropped, and out came the passengers.

Those people did not screw around, either. While the CH-47Ds soared away, the men raced to their various trucks, unrigging quickly. Motors cranked out on the dark LZ. In one key development, 1st Lt. Ken Leeds and his Team Golf boarded 2d Lt. Tony Chester's Maddog gunships. With all aboard, Team Golf rumbled off through the sparse woods, paralleling the Jetertown Road, but carefully staying off it in obedience to the Seventh Commandment. They pressed south about a kilometer, halting just shy of an overgrown, abandoned ammunition storage bunker known as Dugout 5. There, unhindered by the CLF, Leeds and Team Golf established a roadblock to troll for civilians attracted to the party in progress around Fullerton.

Led by their commander, the Black Tac dashed into a leafy ditch not far from LZ Hawk.[17] The squad of staffers settled down to watch and listen as the battle developed. The landing had been great, with none of the confusion that marred the LZ near Jetertown nine months ago. This one already felt different. Out on the LZ, the diesel

Humvee engines growled as the trucks bounced away. Matt Moore's strong voice crackled over the net, reporting the LZST in its hide near the Abus, awaiting business.

Every company reported all men in hand and moving to check out the first string of likely enemy positions. Bill Phelps checked in with the White Teams, which sent in PLGR grids for their companies. Gunfire muttered on up in the No Slack area. The brigade radio net sprang to life intermittently, and Bolger reported the code word that meant the Bulldogs had landed intact on a cold LZ. Out there, seventy-three kilometers distant at England Air Park, reliable Steve Roberts and his men no doubt plugged away to get Lift 3 on its way. They would be into the box by this time tomorrow, thought Bolger, if all went well.

If all went well; that same refrain, the prayer of the rifleman in a strange land. Landing unopposed surely seemed nice enough, but in the long run, so what? The game here involved dealing with the CLF. They'd be here sooner or later, Bolger knew. Dirk Blackdeer, his teeth white in his camouflaged visage, voiced his commander's thoughts for him. He whispered that it would not be long before somebody hit something.

On cue, somebody did hit something. Four bangs sounded from up in Abu land, followed by eight more. "It must be a mortar, and not one of ours," Bolger said to Phelps.

Drew Felix sent nothing, and calls for Abu 6 went unanswered. This boded ill, for certain. Lance Bailey, the S1, tried White Team A.

Six more explosions sounded.

"Bulldog Tac, this is White Alpha," came the voice. "We have at least twelve down from enemy mortar fire. Company dispersing. Commander is down. Abu 5 is in charge, over."

So at least one White Team earned their pay tonight.[18] That minor validation of one of the battalion's unusual C² methods gave meager comfort with the Abus getting hammered. Would 1st Lt. Scott Schoner, the XO, have the sense to go after the CLF observer sure to be in visual range? Or would the Abus sit there and get pounded, as happened all too often in 94-10?

Schoner came over the air himself to answer that. "Bulldog 6, this is Abu 5. We're after two CLF trying to break contact to our north. Our Abu 26 is on him, over."

"Abu 5, this is Bulldog 6," answered Bolger. "Don't get suckered, over."

"Bulldog 6, Abu 5. We won't, over."

With that, Schoner and his men went to work. At the same time, 1st Sgt. Scott D. Craig began moving his dead and wounded back to LZ Hawk, aided by Matt Moore's LZST. The casualties added up to eighteen men. The CLF appeared to get away without loss, a bad start for the battalion.

And yet, this bloody nose featured several big differences from last time. The medevac system was working already; Lance Bailey already had a by-name casualty list and brigade had sent in a medevac chopper.[19] The Abus kept pressing, doggedly hunting for the enemy outpost that called in the fires. With their night-vision goggles in use, Company A wanted revenge, and gave no sign of stopping short. That gave Bolger heart.

The next contacts happened right as dawn grayed the eastern horizon. They, too, differed greatly from past experience. Men of Cold Steel's 2d Platoon, having spent two hours creeping patiently into range, leaped from the foliage to surprise a dug-in enemy DShK and five guerrillas. Led by 2d Lt. Mike Martel and the pugnacious SSgt. J. E. Ferebee, one of Mark Ripka's new breed of platoon sergeants, the men found the camouflaged DShK at night by relying on a flank patrol. Guided by this recon team, the platoon silently deployed while the bored CLF dozed unaware. With all ready, Martel and Ferebee struck.

Every guerrilla died. Return fire took out twelve of Martel and Ferebee's Cold Steel soldiers. But one of the enemy's two DShKs lay destroyed, its crew finished off, rather nicely, too. Captain Chris Forbes and Cold Steel had done their part. The south edge of Fullerton had been swept clean.

To the north, the Abus, too, tasted CLF blood. Personally led by Scott Schoner, Company A's 2d Platoon caught four guerrillas clustered around a bunker, a false DShK emplacement. The CLF were only too real, and tried to break contact. Abu's bold flank and a 60mm mortar round down the throat ended that hostile maneuver before it started. One CLF man got away, but three lay dead. The Abus lost none on their side. Thus the Americans achieved their sweet vengeance. Two of the dead admitted that they directed the deadly barrage near LZ Hawk. More important, Schoner's determined push north had cleared the entire eastern treeline fronting Fullerton FLS.[20]

After sunup, with Cmd. Sgt. Maj. Mark Ripka walking point, Bolger and the Black Tac moved to a thicket near Company C. Linking up with the fire support section's radio truck, the Tac soldiers went to work not far from the south rim of the Fullerton opening. So far, Dirk Blackdeer counted eight CLF dead against 1st Lt. Lance Bailey's roster of thirty U.S. casualties, not all that impressive. But if you culled out the mortar losses, the exchange stood at eight CLF to twelve Americans. That sounded better, didn't it?

Dirk Blackdeer, as a good S2 must, gave an opinion that deflated any particular optimism among the operators. "We've embarrassed them, sir," Dirk noted. "But now comes the hard part, their fight."

Their fight indeed—didn't Bolger know it! The lieutenant colonel nodded to his S2, silent, pensive. Search and attack came next. The preliminaries were over. The main event beckoned.

Notes

The epigraph is one of the many phrases associated with U.S. airborne forces. Among the many occasions in which this saying occurs in fact and fiction, it can be seen painted on the nose of an air cavalry helicopter in the motion picture *Apocalypse Now*.

1. Maj. Gerard M. Devlin, USA, ret., *Paratrooper!* (New York: St. Martin's Press, Inc., 1979), 45, 101–07, 401.

2. Clay Blair, *Ridgway's Paratroopers* (New York: The Dial Press, 1985), 54.

3. Devlin, *Paratrooper!*, 404–05.

4. Cornelius Ryan, *A Bridge Too Far* (New York: Popular Library, 1974), 366. Brig. Gen. Anthony C. McAuliffe, the 101st Airborne Division artillery commander who later gained fame at Bastogne, rode into Holland in a glider. On landing after a typically hair-raising flight, he told Maj. Gen. Maxwell Taylor that from now on, he would rather jump than glide.

5. Capt. Shelby L. Stanton, USA, ret., *Anatomy of a Division: The 1st Cav in Vietnam* (Novato, Calif.: Presidio Press, 1987), 15–43, 45–67, 250–51.

6. Patrick H. F. Allen, *Screaming Eagles* (London: The Hamlyn Publishing Group, Ltd., 1990), 19–20, 27.

7. U.S., Department of the Army, Headquarters, 101st Airborne Division (Air Assault), *How We Fight* (Ft. Campbell, Ky.: HQ, 101st Airborne Division [Air Assault], 1995), 19.

8. Ibid., 26; Col. Thomas Taylor, UAR, ret., *Lightning in the Storm* (New York: Hippocrene Books, Inc., 1994), 264–65.

9. B. H. Liddell Hart, ed., *The Rommel Papers* (New York: Harcourt, Brace & Co., 1953), 407.

10. U.S., Department of the Army, Headquarters, 1st Brigade, 101st Airborne Division (Air Assault), *Change of Command Ceremony* (Ft. Campbell, Ky.: HQ, 1st Brigade, 101st Airborne Division [Air Assault], 2 December 1994), 3.

11. The men of the 1st of the 32d Armor refer to themselves as "the King's Own," an odd title that caused British, Australian, and

Canadian observers at JRTC to scratch their Commonwealth noggins. In fact, the "king" in this appellation is none other than Elvis Presley, the late King of Rock 'n' Roll. Elvis served in the Scout Platoon of 1-32d Armor in the late 1950s. For an entertaining look at this interlude, see Col. William J. Taylor, Jr., USA, ret., *Elvis in the Army* (Novato, Calif.: Presidio Press, 1995).

12. U.S., Department of the Army, *FM 90-4: Air Assault Operations* (Washington, D.C.: U.S. Govt. Printing Office, 1987), 3-1.

13. A UH-60L needs a circle of 100 meters at night. A CH-47D needs 150 meters, and they fly in groups of four or less. See U.S., Department of the Army, Headquarters, 101st Airborne Division (Air Assault), *Air Assault Handbook* (Ft. Campbell, Ky.: The Air Assault School, 1990), 1-42, 1-43.

14. U.S., Department of the Army, Headquarters, 101st Airborne Division (Air Assault), *Command Report: 101st Airborne Division (Air Assault), Operations Desert Shield/Desert Storm, 2 August 1990 through 1 May 1991* (Ft. Campbell, KY.: HQ, 101st Airborne Division [Air Assault], 1 July 1991), 50. In the Gulf War, the initial air assault employed 66 Blackhawks and 30 Chinooks, each making three turns, to insert the 1st Brigade.

15. U.S., Department of the Army, *ARTEP 7-20-MTP: Mission Training Plan for the Infantry Battalion* (Washington, D.C.: U.S. Govt. Printing Office, 1988), 5-76.

16. U.S., Department of the Army, Headquarters, 101st Airborne Division (Air Assault), *Air Assault Battle Note #20: Sling Load Operations* (Ft. Campbell, Ky.: HQ, 101st Airborne Division [Air Assault], 18 September 1992), E-1 to E-2.

17. The Tac soldiers later discovered that their pleasant patch of plants consisted of poison ivy, with predictable results for all concerned.

18. U.S., Department of the Army, Headquarters, 1st Battalion, 327th Infantry Regiment, *TF 1-327 SigActs* (Ft. Polk, La.: Tactical CP, 1st Battalion, 327th Infantry Regiment, 14–19 May 1995), 2.

19. Although several en route aerial ambulances diverted to the growing battle in the No Slack zone, help came about 0230. Out of assets, Col. Donovan finally aided the 1st of the 327th by sending in

his own command and control chopper to extract the badly wounded.

20. HQ, 1st Battalion, 327th Infantry Regiment, *TF 1-327 SigActs,* 4, 6, 7.

Chapter 9

Search and Attack (II)

> There are in Europe many good generals, but they see too many things at once. I see only one thing, namely the enemy's main body. I try to crush it, confident that secondary matters will then settle themselves.
>
> —Napoleon Bonaparte

The echoing howl of four turboprop engines announced the arrival of the first C-130H Hercules transport plane on the red-brown dirt of Fullerton FLS. This landing formally marked the conclusion of the 1st Brigade's air assault, mission accomplished.[1] Aside from the eighteen Abu soldiers laid low by OPFOR mortar-men, the CLF inflicted nothing approaching mass casualties. Outmaneuvered and surprised throughout the 1st Brigade zone, the enemy lost two DShKs and another armed technical vehicle, plus some twenty men, all for nothing. Swiftly shorn of its battered defenders, Fullerton airstrip dropped neatly into 1st Brigade's hands. The brigade commenced building up its supply trains, emplacing artillery batteries and installing a large, dug-in command post, all adding to a loose perimeter forming around the FLS.

The pace of operations slowed noticeably on both sides as the CLF withdrew and the Americans slowly expanded their areas of dominance. In JRTC 94-10, Bolger's impatience at this juncture sent his companies out beyond the radius of the 1st of the 327th's logistics, a fatal error. This time, the companies moved very deliberately as they waited for Maj. Steve Roberts and the ground convoy, the guarantors of resupply. In the hot light of day, the riflemen found plenty to do in the underbrush all around LZ Hawk. As Dan Bolger told them back at England Air Park, "Search and attack starts the minute we hit the ground." So it had.

In search and attack operations, Americans like Bolger stuck to the find/fix/finish formula. In the Vietnam era, perhaps in recognition that the other side might impose its own views, the infantry knew this jingle as find/fix/*fight*/finish.[2] How many Fs in the equation really didn't matter. How to do it, though, demanded command interest.

In Bolger's view, how you proceeded depended on what you knew about the enemy. A true guerrilla, faithful to the Maoist creed, stood up and fought only if he expected to win. Otherwise, the bad guys hid: "Enemy advances, we retreat." So finding the guerrillas paced everything. And that took a long, long time, and a lot of effort, especially when the gringos needed a while simply to get acclimated to a Third World pleasure spot like Cortina.

The book, and even practice in Vietnam and at JRTC, ignored the necessity for a dedicated, large-scale finding effort with boots on the ground, sending men, not bullets (horrors!). Instead, doctrinal inertia pushed battalions to rely on electronic sniffers, aerial spottings, and sneaky little pathfinder and LRSD patrols to pinpoint the insurgents in their secret lairs. Higher headquarters, which had enough staff analysts to know all, would amalgamate and boil these nuggets into the truth, then issue a "go" order to the fighting battalion. For its part, each battalion kept a big reserve, perhaps the majority of the outfit, waiting on a leash, straining to lash out when a juicy enemy concentration turned up. The 101st Airborne's helicopters gave special impetus to this technique, known in Vietnam as an "Eagle Flight." Of course, the bad guys would have to cooperate by congregating to create a lucrative target near a decent landing zone, then stand like tethered goats while the Americans sharpened, aimed, and swung the lethal blade. It sounded tempting, and indulged the usual U.S. love of technology, in this case, rotary-wing aircraft. Hell, the Eagle Flight unit might even live in comfort, drinking beer at some firebase while awaiting the call to arms.

The only problem with the Eagle Flight technique involved the enemy, who refused to stage such battles, either in Vietnam or Cortina. Over the years in Southeast Asia, with real bullets, the People's Army of Vietnam occasionally got caught napping or elected to make a stand. But in the aggregate, most U.S. sweeps to count "sure kills" became walks in the sun, many Eagle Flights hopped into dry holes, and too many quick-strike raids strode boldly into enemy traps, now and then with high losses.[3] As the inheritors of the Viet Cong mantle, the CLF, too, chose not to assemble to be bashed. When they gathered, it was to inflict harm on an isolated U.S. unit, as at Hunger Hill.

To beat an opponent moving in four-man fire teams, mortar crews, and SA-14 elements, finding required saturation patrolling. Each enemy foursome represented a thread in the tapestry, and it only made sense to start here, with one's own means, rather than make some leap of faith into God knew what. This war of posts, a succession of small actions, of snipings and ambuscades, proceeded through the find/fix/finish sequence in minutes, not hours, and did so with the forces at hand.

Thus the Ten Commandments intimated that each Bulldog platoon must have the capacity to find, fix, and finish any OPFOR quartet. The Third Commandment mandated holding the OPFOR with the engaged squad and executing a bold flanking action with the platoon, a simple concept. To make it work, the Bulldogs found it useful to develop a hunting formation, an array built for tracking and killing. Usually, U.S. infantry meandered along in a loose column or, even worse, the much overused Ranger file, an annoying and dangerous resort to follow-the-leader. During JRTC 94-10, as in real combat, that expedient, sloppy movement formation only pleased the enemy.

Encouraged by Sfc. Charles W. Lipke, platoon sergeant of 2d Platoon, Company B, and a veteran of the Hunger Hill debacle, rifle platoons adopted an open-order V formation that bore its originator's name. Lipke, an educated Ranger, another graduate of wily Jim Dubik's 5-14th Infantry school of light infantry tactics, knew well that his proposed method represented a throwback to tactics pioneered by the Chinese People's Liberation Army. Known as "one point/two sides," the Chinese system emphasized holding with one element and bold enveloping action with the rest. In Korea, Chinese platoons used one point/two sides to snap up isolated U.S. outposts and patrols.[4] Now, 1st of the 327th planned to use one guerrilla army's means to defeat another.

Why did Mao Zedong's armies favor one point/two sides? Perhaps the V imagery appealed to some Taoist fascination with triangles. But while that sort of abstraction may have sparked Lin Piao to cook it up, one point/two sides became popular because it worked. Japanese, Nationalist Chinese, and Americans all learned to dread its nasty simplicity. Fighting from the V does demand practice, but

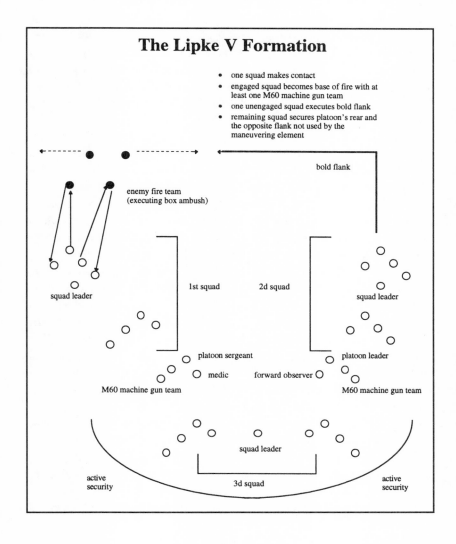

The Lipke V Formation

- one squad makes contact
- engaged squad becomes base of fire with at least one M60 machine gun team
- one unengaged squad executes bold flank
- remaining squad secures platoon's rear and the opposite flank not used by the maneuvering element

bold flank

enemy fire team
(executing box ambush)

squad leader

1st squad   2d squad   squad leader

platoon sergeant   platoon leader

medic   forward observer

M60 machine gun team   M60 machine gun team

squad leader

active
security   3d squad   active
security

if the rude peasant boys of Hunan figured it out, so too would the young Americans with Lipke and Bolger. A platoon sweeping in a Lipke V could engage hostiles instantly in any direction—by definition, two of three points of this lethal triangle always stood ready to maneuver. By spreading out, by shifting instantly into the attack, platoons thwarted the favorite CLF drills, especially the box. Coupled with good MILES marksmanship, the Lipke V broke the mystical power of the OPFOR three-step.

The Lipke V represented the platoon-level solution to CLF battle drills and shooting skill, and incidently underscored the battalion's shrewd investment in quality platoon sergeants. But for Lipke and his fellows to V around Cortina, they needed some backup. The first step in this effort fell to U.S. fire support, the only kind of reinforcement available that moved faster than fleeting CLF teams. Before a platoon moved out, its leadership plotted on-call Quickdraw targets in every grid square. If the CLF appeared, the V maneuvered and popped a preplanned target on the bad guys' open flank, about a kilometer away. Once the rounds impacted, the Americans speedily crept in the fires to get effects. As an added bonus, in the JRTC game world, the automatic introduction of indirect fires swiftly brought the Fort Polk marking teams into the area, thus cutting down unnecessary delays. Quickdraw firing did not hit that many CLF, but it screwed them up, and scared them, and made them look over their shoulders rather than at their American targets.

To ensure that the CLF did not reply to the Quickdraw shot with their own mortars, Lipke and his brother platoon sergeants taught their top marksmen to pick off the CLF radioman, usually the leader, found in each quartet. By capping the radio operator early on, the insurgency's normally superb 82mm mortars did not join the fight. To assist in slaying OPFOR radiomen, the battalion issued commercial-grade telescopic sights, two per rifle squad.[5] And before the Bulldogs deployed, they practiced all of this: the Lipke V, the Quickdraw calls, and sniping radio guys.

Tying together the nine industrious rifle platoons busily driving their Vs across the wooded countryside, the battalion imposed a deliberate clearance regimen that kept the companies in proximity, never more than a few grid squares distant from each other. A com-

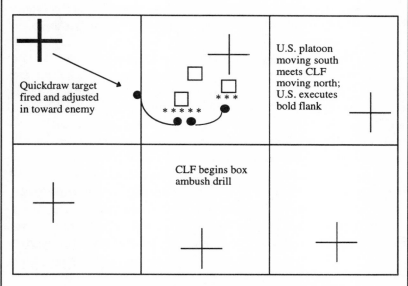

U.S. Search and Attack Tactics
Actions on Contact

Quickdraw target fired and adjusted in toward enemy

U.S. platoon moving south meets CLF moving north; U.S. executes bold flank

CLF begins box ambush drill

<u>1st Battalion, 327th Infantry Regiment, Actions on Contact</u>

1. Initiate or return fire on contact; squad in contact becomes base of fire.
2. Execute bold flank with trail squad.
3. Call in Quickdraw target on the opposite side of the flanking squad.
4. Adjust Quickdraw fires onto enemy.
5. Kill the enemy.

pany's platoons worked right around the same area, within the 3,500-meter radius of the 60mm mortars. Each company kept a definite ground line of communication (water and ammo in, casualties out), an endless web of capillaries weaving through the pines and around the ravines, leading back to the brigade trains at Fullerton FLS. Matt Moore, LZST leader, dubbed this network the "Ho Chi Minh Trail." Company D's Maddog gunship Humvees kept it open.

So the battalion sallied out to meet and destroy the CLF, intent on beating the bush and taking down the foe a team at a time. The men focused on the hostile shooters, cleaning out grid squares like remorseless exterminators popping rats. Each firefight, each encounter, threw up scraps of information. Together, slowly, slowly, these bits and pieces coalesced into a mosaic, and the face of the enemy emerged. To see that face meant fighting, killing to see. Commandment One applied all the way.

Along with dead and wounded, every encounter produced information to be studied. Field manuals prod commanders to draw up lists of key data wanted from subordinate units, the inputs into the master control cell that enable a budding Napoleon to experience lightning flashes of insight, stick pins into the right parts of the map, and issue orders for deft maneuvers that catch the enemy unawares. Things to know include Priority Intelligence Requirements (PIR), Information Requirements (IR), Essential Elements of Friendly Information (EEFI), and Commander's Critical Information Requirements (CCIR).[6] In short, know everything. Troopers stuck in mud up to their knees, getting shot at now and then, do not get around to sending in the travelogues implied by this approach. In fact, you rarely get much of anything. Reporting is always bad. Sometimes, it's worse.

As with the other raw points (the TOC, commander's intent), Bolger went for a simple and clever solution. The White Teams sufficed to track friendly status and locations, and they had the objectivity, and a PLGR, to do so. To give focus to all hands, White Teams, chain of command, medics, and riflemen, Bolger drew up a very short list, the absolute essentials. Convinced himself that the Army's habitual stream of PIR, IR, EEFI, and CCIR equaled so much B.S., the lieutenant colonel canonized his version with those familiar soldierly letters. The battalion's information requirements rested on the acronym B^2S^2: blowers, bleeders, shooters, and sitters. Blowers were minefields, American and OPFOR. Bleeders referred to casualties: Americans to evacuate, and hostiles to tote up the blood count. Shooters, of course, constituted the battalion's prime targets. And as for sitters, the siren-song Ps: the CPs, PSPs, the CSP, or the famous BSP. Well, you had to keep a handle on them, maybe to facilitate

B^2S^2

- Blowers
    —mines (U.S., enemy, or unknown)

- Bleeders
    —U.S. casualties
    — enemy casualties

- Shooters
    —mortars
    —SA-14 air defense missile launchers
    —enemy fire teams
    —enemy air defense guns
    —enemy combat vehicles

- Sitters (the "Ps")
    —platoon, company, and battalion supply points
    —platoon, company, and battalion command posts

    When soldiers find these, they report in accordance with
    SALT (size, activity, location, and time).

some more finding or killing, or perhaps to blow away with artillery
or demolitions when the spirit moved you. Just as every man in 1st
of the 327th knew their commander's intent—kill the enemy—all the
soldiers remembered B^2S^2, and reported on these matters, thereby
facilitating more killing. And so, the battalion tac teams had their
battle tracking system, just like that.

Where to look? Frankly, LZ Hawk would do. Now, of course—
bowing to the dictates of Chairman Mao—Dan Bolger, Dirk Blackdeer, and Bill Phelps sensed from the outset that the miserable hamlet of Jetertown must figure in the battalion's operations at some
point. Guerrillas depended on the people, and the CLF certainly
did. The good old Eagle Flight approach argued for skipping down

there now, immediately, by air. But that would leave a force on its own down in Indian country, dependent on heliborne resupply that Dan Bolger did not own. Additionally, the ground around LZ Hawk teemed with information to be fought for and understood. The battalion had a lot of finding to do, days of it, before they could make a legitimate lunge for Jetertown, its civilians, and what they knew. That move, when it happened, should serve to put a stake through the heart of the CLF in zone, fixing them for good in every sense of the word. But finding came first.

The battalion organized for search and attack by dividing the ground into areas, each a few kilometers across. Each company received its own plot to comb, with Company C to the west and south of LZ Hawk, Company A to the northeast, and Company B to the southeast. On the Jetertown Road between Cold Steel and Bushmaster, Ken Leeds, Team Golf, and his armed guards held court, looking for civil traffic heading up toward Carnis Village.

Two other elements worked on the outskirts of the battalion footprint. To the northeast, across the deep creek that bounded the Abu area, the Marines and sailors of the ANGLICO fire control teams scouted for enemies, specifically an 82mm mortar believed to be squatting up there across the waterway. Through a special radio system, these elite forward observers talked to JRTC personnel simulating the warships USS *Hancock* and USS *Spruance*. Should the CLF mortarmen poke up their heads, the ANGLICO fully intended to blow them away with naval gunfire. But the area across that creek looked pretty empty and unused.

The other independent unit, the battalion scouts, moved one area ahead of Company B, trying to pinpoint a possible enemy patrol base for destruction. An Air Force forward air controller stalked along with the Tigers, ready to bring in the blue-suiters if anything interesting turned up. By 1109, not far from LZ Owl, the battalion's unused alternate landing zone, the scouts brushed a CLF team, with two enemies killed and three Tigers hit. This tangle near the earthen mound called Dugout 5 pricked what turned out to be a sizable CLF scab around that landmark. Nobody knew that yet, however.

Task Force 1-327 Infantry
14 May 1995

Company A(-)	Company B	Company C
HQ/FIST	HQ/FIST	HQ/FIST
Mortars (2 x 60mm)	Mortars (2 x 60mm)	Mortars (2 x 60mm)
1st Platoon/A	1st Platoon/B	1st Platoon/C
2d Platoon/A	2d Platoon/B	2d Platoon/C
3d Platoon/A	3d Platoon/B	3d Platoon/C
White Team A	White Team B	White Team C
		LLVI Team

Company D (-)
HQ
1st Platoon/D
2d Platoon/D
3d Platoon/D
4th Platoon/D
Engineer Platoon
White Team D
Stinger Team 1

Task Force Control
Scout Platoon
FCT 3 & 4
Mortar Platoon (4 x 81mm)
     Stinger Team 2
Team Golf
     5th Platoon/D
     Stinger Team 3
Gold Tac/Black Tac
LZST (with ATLS)
Field Trains

Detachments
none

STRENGTHS (with attachments)

Company A:	102
Company B:	109
Company C:	107
Company D:	53
Scout Platoon:	17
FCT Teams:	16
Mortar Platoon:	26
Team Golf:	23
Gold Tac/Black Tac:	20
LZST:	21
Field Trains:	48

TF 1-327 Infantry Total   542

Starting strengths; casualties not included

Key to Abbreviations/Terms
ATLS: Advanced Trauma Lifesaving Team
CP: Command Post
FCT: Fire Control Team (Navy/Marine)
FIST: Fire Support Team (Army)
HQ: headquarters
LLVI: low-level voice intercept
LZST: Landing Zone Support Team
Team Golf: S5, civil affairs team,
loudspeaker team, and
counterintelligence agent

The brush at Dugout 5 brought in Capt. Ted Donnelly and Company B, men who had seen no action all night and all morning and did not care for that one bit. Moving with customary speed, the Bushmasters killed one of the remaining CLF and captured the other. The Bushmasters then began policing up the injured scouts for extraction.[7] Across the road, Capt. Chris Forbes's rifle platoons patrolled south toward LZ Owl itself. Perhaps Forbes flushed the CLF who met the scouts and Company B.

Donnelly's soldiers passed their captive to the nearby Team Golf roadblock. There, motoring back through the woods via a branch of the expanding Ho Chi Minh Trail, a pair of Maddog Humvees evacuated the prisoner to brigade, a task accomplished by the early afternoon. That ended the fighting for a few hours. The CLF melted into the shade, temporarily withdrawing from the painful field.

That felt like a very good idea, come to think of it. Rising heat and humidity, unseasonably high for May even in Louisiana, took its own toll on 1-327th Infantry soldiers. The adrenaline of the air assault and the initial engagements dwindled, giving way to a grow-

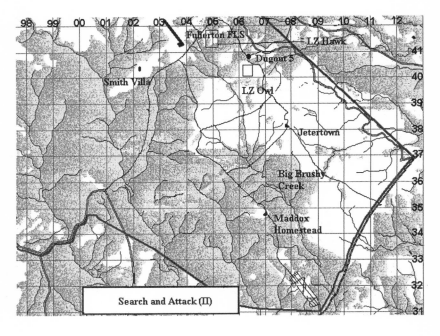

Search and Attack (II)

ing languor as the sun blazed in a cloudless, infantry-blue sky. Most of the men had been awake for more than thirty-six hours, the last eighteen pretty stressful and physically demanding. The sergeants pushed, and the officers pulled, but everyone felt the weight of that hot, sticky afternoon. At the Black Tac, reports dried up like drizzle on a hot sidewalk.

Then, predictably, almost inevitably, tired eyes began seeing things. Over in No Slack territory, several units sighted Atlantican tanks on the flight landing strip. That unexpected news kicked off a flurry of copycat reports from throughout the brigade. One of the 1st of the 327th's Navy/Marine FCT outfits added to the mess by reporting an enemy BRDM recon vehicle probing around east of the creek, a few hundred meters east of Company A. Brigade scrambled Apaches and cranked newly arrived howitzers onto these phantom armor spottings.[8] But nothing came of any of this shadow-boxing.

Company D rolled in about this time. In keeping with the mood, they had their own strange tale to tell. The column showed up under its XO, 1st Lt. Rich Basher, bearing two wounded and the scars of an ambush in Carnis Village. With Capt. Mike Delgado in front, the lead platoon bulled blindly into the jumble of sheds and tar-paper shacks that amounted to Carnis. Hidden insurgent gunmen immediately tagged the unlucky Delgado, and the fracas ended only when 1st Lt. Craig Doane of the Gold Tac Team popped an AT-4 rocket (simulated) into the cantina. That structure erupted with a feigned secondary explosion, evidence that the proprietors served stuff a lot stronger than alcohol from time to time. Doane's quick response allowed Delgado's men to extract their stricken commander, his wounded driver, and their allegedly damaged Humvee from the dusty main street of Carnis.

The rest of the company, with its accompanying headquarters and LZST elements, stopped outside of town, halted by 1st Sgt. Ronald Morgan. That experienced NCO found a passable trail which skirted the little rat nest of a village, and thus avoided the ambush. They arrived unscathed.

Mike Delgado's detour through Carnis violated Commandment Seven, common sense, and a warning from First Sergeant Morgan. While Morgan led the bulk of the Maddogs around Carnis, Delgado plunged in anyway, and paid for it.[9] Embarrassed but chastened, the captain underwent evacuation to the rear to churn through the limbo of the JRTC personnel mill. The episode underlined the battalion's insistence on staying off the main roads in Cortina.

With the Maddogs, the rest of the LZST, and the Gold Tac present and intact, Bolger moved his command post away from LZ Hawk and north into the Abu area. The Black Tac truck, visually identical to the cargo Humvees used by Company D and HHC, halted inside a rough ring created by the Maddogs' four platoons of gun trucks. Any hostile intruders trying to get at the Tac first had to pick it out from all the like vehicles, then get through Company D's circle of automatic weapons, ground patrols, and early-warning outposts. The Maddogs and LZST also launched from this cluster to run the Ho Chi Minh trail and service the rifle companies.

After a very still afternoon, all three companies made one more round of contacts prior to sundown. Company A, with Drew Felix back at the helm, found a cache of fuel cans stashed along the streambed east of the FLS. Perhaps the CLF used this fuel to heat their false gun position thermal markers, designed to confuse Apaches. The undisturbed foliage around the cans also led Felix and his riflemen to guess that the items might have been left behind by a previous rotation. The company established an ambush for the night, just in case the guerrillas swung by to reclaim their goods.

The other two fights flared around Dugout 5, the mossy, cavernous old bunker near LZ Owl. Company C hit two CLF teams, one at 1643 and another at 1800. Aggressive and confident, Capt. Forbes went after the hostiles with Quickdraw fires and dramatic platoon flanking maneuvers, killing two for no loss.[10] A glance at the Tac's laptop situation map showed two more red dots around Dugout 5.

Why was the CLF hovering around Dugout 5? Dirk Blackdeer wondered about that, but as yet, he had no firm answer. He recommended leaving the scouts, 1st Lt. Mark Lawry and his Tigers, overwatching the landmark. Maybe the next day would clarify the picture.

That did it for the night, except for a female picked up at 2122 by Team Golf at their roadblock. This confused civilian, the second to walk north from Jetertown, told 1st Lt. Ken Leeds that the CLF held her family hostage, along with all her neighbors in the miserable hamlet. After conveying the news to Maj. Steve Roberts and his Gold Tac team holding down the night shift, the Maddog roadwatch crew bundled the woman off to the brigade detainee pen.[11] Nobody in the Tac CP knew exactly what to make of her complaints, but Tom Doughty, the Gold Tac S2 officer, offered a trenchant observation: "We'll be going to Jetertown soon, I think."

Doughty was right. But first, the battalion had a few more appointments in the wilderness between LZ Hawk and LZ Owl. The fifteenth of May dawned hot and muggy; even the official U.S. Air Force weather report, issued at 0447 local, used the depressing term *steamy* to warn everyone what to expect. The numbers looked bad: 92 degrees, 92 percent humidity, and no rain in sight. The day matched those predictions only too well.

The long, grinding marches through the underbrush, coupled with a restless night, made the companies thirsty, and therefore sluggish. The men needed water. Like the British regiments in India, the Bulldogs learned that "when it comes to slaughter, you will do your work on water, an' you'll lick the bloomin' boots of him that's got it."[12] Matt Moore and his support Humvees already topped off all the canteens the previous night, but the dry-throated riflemen quickly gulped that down. Now, as the fiery sun rose, the LZST and its Maddog consorts again puttered along the ruts and across the smashed trees of the Ho Chi Minh trail, delivering another round of precious drink to energize the soldiers. That unanticipated resupply took all morning.

The companies' slow start left the initiative to the CLF, and the gomers took it. Enemy teams began probing the rifle company security screens within hours after daybreak. Nothing came of that business. The company patrols and outposts proved vigilant while their sweating fellows drew water. Unwilling to test these active measures, the CLF turned elsewhere.

Here, the hostiles found weakness, and tore into it. An incursion against the Scout Platoon's perimeter near LZ Owl sparked a running engagement that lasted all morning. By its end, all but five scouts lay dead. The bill included the Tigers' platoon leader and platoon sergeant. In return, the aggressive but poor-shooting scouts killed only one CLF guerrilla, a pathetic 12:1 exchange.[13] At least the scouts kept the CLF entertained, and made it clear that the area around LZ Owl still teemed with OPFOR.

The demise of the scouts encouraged the Black Tac crew, back on duty, to push two companies that way as soon as they could move. To the east, Ted Donnelly got ready to lead Company B toward the CLF activity near Dugout 5; attack choppers waited to launch on his call if anything interesting cropped up. West of the road, a refreshingly reliable Company C would move toward LZ Owl. Only Company A hung back near LZ Hawk, essentially uncommitted. The Abus had cleared out the entire eastern treeline on Fullerton FLS with no real contact since the first few hours in country. Now they took water and a little ammunition and waited for orders.

The Abus did not have long to wait. Just before noon, 1st Brigade called to say that they had lost all communications with the four-man low-level voice intercept (LLVI) team that accompanied 1st of the 327th into the box. Military intelligence doctrine recommended moving these kinds of collection teams hither and yon to suck enemy transmissions out of the ether, and LLVI teams had a bad habit of reporting only to the brigade S2, and not to the commander whose area they traversed. Whereas Dan Bolger could, and did, direct placement of his engineeers and air defenders, he lacked the authority to do so with the LLVI people.[14] Seeking lines of bearing and triangulation with brother LLVI assets, they moved in obedience to a captain looking at a map in the brigade command post. Yes, the LLVI moved in mysterious ways, and this time, like most times, they marched right into a CLF trap.

This independent foursome had struck out to the southwest of Company C, pushing into the Y formed by the juncture of two creeks just west of LZ Hawk. There, in the splendid isolation demanded by military intelligence, something ate them. Well, Capt. Chris Forbes and Company C lay near enough to do something about it. If they found a viable stream crossing, one good enough for the LZST Humvees, Forbes and the Cold Steel soldiers stood to catch the bad guys that took out the LLVI.

In consultation with Dirk Blackdeer, Bill Phelps considered the situation. The battalion commander was gone, sucked into an after-action review for the initial air assault. During JRTC 94-10, this same period saw the commitment that became the Hunger Hill disaster. A lesser man might hesitate to act with his commander gone, and thereby add a wasted afternoon to a wasted morning. But Bill Phelps knew better than that. The intent remained to kill the enemy—Commandment One—and the battalion had done damn little of that today. Phelps chose to kick-start matters. On his firm orders, Company A assumed the task to clear out LZ Owl. Phelps told Company C to sweep through the Y-stream area and destroy the CLF that took out the LLVI.

When Bolger returned from his brigade-level AAR, he found everyone fully engaged. To the west, Cold Steel located the LLVI "corpses" and the remnants of a CLF patrol base to boot, replete with candy wrappers, sunflower seed bags, and four water cans. After helping themselves to the water, Forbes's men continued searching, slopping through the swampy low ground and tangled undergrowth. At 1608, right before Bolger reached the Tac, Company C cornered three CLF soldiers. Using rifle scopes, the Cold Steel troops took down all three at over a hundred meters. Sharpshooting Pfc. John W. Gregory accounted for two himself. One of the guerrillas turned out to be a lieutenant, and their maps and frequency cards greatly interested the intelligence chain.[15] It took all afternoon, but Forbes and his men had avenged the death of the LLVI team.

Meanwhile, Ted Donnelly and his Bushmasters endured a frustrating afternoon. An errant Apache sprayed a platoon of unlucky Americans not far from Dugout 5. The newly minted female pilot, one of the Army's first women to drive an Apache, mistook a JRTC field cameraman for an OPFOR SA-14 gunner. She shot first and asked questions later, and three Bushmasters fell.[16]

Such incidents characterize combat, and always have. Known as amicide, misadventure, friendly fire, blue-on-blue, own goal, or, most commonly, fratricide, these mistakes represent what happens when young men with lethal tools have at it. Bullets and shells do not discriminate, and tired, confused men screw up. Fratricide results, the blood debt attached to Murphy's Law, the brutal cost of the Clausewitzian friction that hobbles one's own forces. Estimates of fratricide deaths and wounds range from 2 percent to 20 percent of all combat casualties, depending on the circumstances. This dirty secret of warfare received special attention in the Gulf War, where the mercifully light U.S. losses included thirty-five killed and sixty-seven injured by U.S. weaponry. Stung by news media criticism and determined to take care of its own, the U.S. Army has since spotlighted the issue. Every fratricide at JRTC generates a formal investigation. Investigators attributed the event on 15 May to lack of proper direct fire control measures, misidentification of the target by the flier answering to Blue Max 23, and inaccurate reporting.[17]

Now that neatly ties off the issue, implying that it could have been prevented by taking certain prudent steps, by checking this or asking that, by looking twice more before leaping. In the same way, diligent Federal Aviation Administration investigators can always figure out how metal fatigue and a wrong switch setting may bring an airliner screaming to earth. Much of the industrialized world's safety investigation bureaucracy represents *post hoc ergo propter hoc* (after this, therefore because of this) reasoning run riot. Investigators tend to imply that accidents like fratricide can be prevented. Sometimes they can.

And yet . . . and yet, just how careful can you be, and still kill the enemy? Those not quick are soon dead. If that JRTC camera operator had been an SA-14 shooter, and Blue Max 23 hesitated, some other wiseguy would have scored her dead, remarking on her slow trigger finger. In a world of hurtling machines, split-second decisions, and hot bullets moving faster than the speed of sound, you cannot have it both ways. It is notable that every single fratricide incident at JRTC burps up a full-blown investigation. A cock-up like Hunger Hill never leads to a witch-hunt. This is a dangerous trend, focusing overly much on what appears to be, sadly, an irreducible risk of war. The JRTC powers might do well to heed the British commander in the Falklands War, then-RAdm. Sandy Woodward, who warned: "The essentially bureaucratic peacetime mind will, for the sake of avoiding a single Blue-on-Blue, cause Blue-on-Red (hitting the enemy) to cease!"[18] Woodward has it right. Bolger agreed with Woodward, and did not overreact to the Apache error or any other fratricide cases. Commandment One continued to rule.

Ted Donnelly and his men shook off the Apache imbroglio. By 1725, lasting until sunset, 2d Lt. Lance Oskey and Sfc. Rory Malloy led 1st Platoon into the wilderness overlooking the Dugout 5 intersection. They made contact with three different CLF teams. The ensuing clashes sparked into the early evening, and as the desperate insurgents maneuvered to escape the Lipke Vs, even 1st Sgt. Gerald S. Eubank and his headquarters men participated. When the dust cleared, the Bushmasters had taken out seven more CLF, recovered some of the dead Tigers of the Scout Platoon, and controlled Dugout 5. Three wounded Americans paid for this encounter.[19]

To the west, Company A, still unengaged, force-marched south to get into position overlooking LZ Owl, their area for the morrow. Company C fell in behind them, well satisfied with their engagements. The Navy/Marine FCT men, now acting as battalion scouts, laagered with Company B for the night to refit. Before day broke, the FCT would cross into the virgin area south of Dugout 5 and east of the Jetertown Road, looking for CLF. Company B expected to follow the superb Marine forward observers. Team Golf's roadblock, now just behind the advanced pickets of the neighboring rifle companies, kept checking civilians enroute from Jetertown to Carnis; bad news from the south got worse with every interview. Finally, laden with water and ammunition, First Lieutenant Moore's tireless LZST waited for sunset, which would cover their off-road drive to succor the weary riflemen.

All expected to get rest tonight, for Dan Bolger and his leaders had discovered something interesting about the rhythm of the Cortinian theater. Lacking sophisticated night sights, the CLF preferred to fight in the day, when their marksmanship paid off. That suited the Bulldogs, as it proved impossible to find hidden guerrillas at night, particularly quartets stashed in nasty, overgrown streambeds. Rather than beating themselves senseless all night, both sides carried out resupply and went to sleep.

So far, the 1st of the 327th could be pretty proud of their work. The battalion held the initiative, despite a glacial start on the morning of the 15th. The Americans created some two thirds of all contacts, quite a departure from the pattern throughout the rest of the brigade area of operations.[20] The Bulldogs kill ratio ran just over 1:1, impressive by JRTC standards. Most important, the battalion was operating, getting the job done. The troops ate and drank, casualties and prisoners were extracted, and the Tac and White Teams kept track of it all. Slowly but surely, the battalion squeegeed the CLF away from the Fullerton FLS. The enemy had been found and killed. Jetertown awaited.

The call to go to Jetertown came just after another blazing noon on 16 May. At brigade, Col. Jack Donovan decided to relieve the embattled hamlet, to wrest it from CLF control and allow the World Endeavor charitable group[21] to deliver much-needed humanitarian aid. Donovan made his decision under some pressure from his senior commanders, impatient to expand the airhead a little faster. While the opening air assault received praise as the best in JRTC his-

1st Battalion, 327th Infantry Regiment Contacts

Date	U.S. Initiated	CLF Initiated	% Initiated by U.S.
13 May	0	1	0%
14 May	6	2	75%
15 May	7	4	64%
16 May	5	3	63%
17 May	3	2	60%
18 May	3	2	60%
19 May	11	3	79%
20 May	1	0	100%
TOTAL	36	17	63%

tory, and things had gone well enough in Bulldog land, there had been problems elsewhere. In the most serious development Company B, 2d of the 327th, and Team Animal had gotten into a horrendous donnybrook in and around Smith Villa, to the tune of 107 casualties in return for 34 CLF—Hunger Hill revisited, and with the same crippling effects on that American battalion.[22]

Thankfully uninterested in the "Ps," Donovan looked to Bolger's 1st of the 327th to fix the CLF by grabbing Jetertown. He gave the lieutenant colonel Capt. Ken Blakely and Team Animal, with its fleet of tanks and other armored vehicles. The brigade commander also gave 1-327th priority of fires, plus enough Chinooks to ferry in a rifle company. "Get that aid convoy into Jetertown," the colonel told his battalion commander.[23]

Jetertown, thought Bolger. *Once more it came down to that clutch of hovels.* Bolger did not want to go there, let alone go there now. But the CLF was holding the town in at least platoon strength, daring the Americans to attack. The enemy hoped to create another Smith Villa, another Hunger Hill.

Bolger thought otherwise. By the time he and his Maddog escort returned to his CP, he had a good idea of what to do. While his Black Tac awoke Maj. Steve Roberts and the Gold Tac to run the war, Bolger and his inner circle, Blackdeer and Phelps, plotted. Nobody suggested the DDMP, a concept now regarded by this staff as antiquated as divination from the entrails of fowl. Indeed, the Gold Tac and the bulk of the staff kept running the ongoing battle, including relocating the Maddog/LZST/Tac wagon train to the pine stand south of LZ Owl.

Killing proceeded apace. The Abus killed one foeman near LZ Owl, then used mortars to take out two more. The fighting FCT surprised four guerrillas and slew them, losing one of their own. And at the end of the day, Company B added four more to the bag, losing two wounded in a gun battle involving 2d Lt. John Hall and Sfc. Charles W. Lipke's 2d Platoon. Operations proceeded while the commander concocted his plan.[24] The battalion issued its order at 2200, near LZ Owl.

Bolger went for speed, stealth, simplicity, and a very big foot. Commencing before dawn, at 0415, the battalion would isolate Jetertown, with Company A to the west and Company C to the east, both emplaced on key terrain overlooking the town. The goal here involved moving the two kilometers so swiftly as to be in position by daybreak. In this, the battalion attempted to steal a march on the CLF.

Trapping the opposition in town or barring them from entry in one swift stroke, the predawn cordon took advantage of a demonstrated enemy tendency detected by Dan Bolger and confirmed by Dirk Blackdeer's analysis. The CLF liked to sleep in, an inevitable consequence of relying on decentralized little teams led by corporals and lieutenants with somewhat casual body clocks. Guerrillas often rose about 0800 or so, spent the morning reconnoitering, passed the heat of the day resting, and then hit likely U.S. targets in the late afternoon. Bolger christened this stretch from 1500–1900 as "OPFOR Happy Hour," and the badniks proved to be reliable customers. With that preferred schedule, the enemy left the morning to the U.S. infantry, to let those type-A morning people batter themselves stupid sweeping to and fro. Until now, the guerrillas had not found it necessary to rouse themselves before sunup to shoot Americans. *Fine,* Bolger figured. *We'll give them a wake-up, all right.*

At 0700, Team Animal would reach Dugout 5, pick up Team Golf, and begin its rumble toward town. Bolger gave Ken Blakely full freedom to go off-road, or to enter Jetertown from any direction. "Get Team Golf in, Ken," the battalion commander said.

Once the tanks established Team Golf, 1st Lt. Ken Leeds expected to start winning hearts and minds the old-fashioned way. His bag of tricks included medics, a chaplain, civil affairs advisors, loudspeakers with propaganda tapes, a water buffalo full of ice, and, incredibly, hot food. With this, the battalion consciously wanted to feed the people of Jetertown better than its own troops. The riflemen knew how to subsist on water and an MRE a day. Civilians do not. But civilians with full bellies remember everything. Humanitarian urges constituted at best a secondary interest for Dan Bolger. The lieutenant colonel wanted hard intelligence, and was willing to pay for it in a big way.

Now, the doctrinal approach frowns on feeding the locals. It raises expectations too much, and they grow dependent on the U.S. soldiers. Don't promise or deliver anything, warn the experts. Ignoring this, and heeding Mao Zedong, who has a substantially better track record in guerrilla combat, Bolger told Leeds to do whatever it took to make the Jetertown inhabitants happy. Then, with the locals belching in content, the Team Golf counterintelligence specialist could start mining for gold.

To protect this main effort, this ultimate finding foray, Bolger planned to insert Capt. Chris Forbes and Company C via four CH-47D Chinooks. Rotoring right into town, the Cold Steel men planned to guard the settlement against all comers. In doing so, Forbes's soldiers depended on the confidence born in RAMP training. They knew how to handle civilians, and how to sort out friends from foes. Their arrival served to free Team Animal to return to Fullerton, and to release the other two rifle companies to continue to search and attack, Abus to the east, Bushmasters to the west. Forbes and his soldiers prepared to stay put, to protect the villagers by active patrolling in the nearby woods.[25] As in the NEO to Jetertown that opened JRTC 94-10, the 1st of the 327th leaned on extensive practical drills using the simplified RAMP rules of engagement.

The O/Cs, even unorthodox Dubik disciple Lt. Col. Mace Crowe, anticipated a debacle. When the brief orders group ended at around 2240, Crowe pulled Bolger aside. "This can't possibly work, you know. There's not time to synchronize everything."

Synchronization, huh? There was an O/C buzzword for you. Shrouded by the densely humid darkness, Bolger stared past the senior O/C. The Bulldog commander squared his shoulders and smiled grimly. No time to synchronize, Crowe cautioned. *No, Mace, we only have time to do it.* You synchronize watches, not men, and never warfare. Combat has its own chaotic pace, and you don't reign in the dogs of war. You cry havoc, and let those suckers run. And let the enemy beware.

The Jetertown mission went off perfectly. Without a shot fired, the 1st of the 327th grabbed the town, punched the tanks through, and commenced making friends. No CLF interfered; they had not been in Jetertown after all, and now found their way blocked by powerful rifle forces. The World Endeavor convoy masters drove unchecked into a secure, safe, happy village, and then made it out without incident. Captain Chris Forbes and his Cold Steel soldiers flew in by Chinook, plopping into the same LZ that allowed 1st of the 327th to carry out its NEO back during JRTC 94-10. This time, the battalion, represented by Company C, came to stay. Forbes's men fanned out, thereby freeing the other companies to get back to search and attack operations.

Happy townspeople almost overwhelmed Team Golf's busy counterintelligence agent. By late morning, Team Golf provided the entire enemy minefield and mine cache overlay, complete with detailed descriptions of the sites. Captain Mike Delgado and his attached engineers swiftly rode out, simulated demolitions in hand. Working systematically, Delgado and 2d Lt. Shad Reynolds of the 326th Engineers blew up six different caches. Drawn in by civilian tips, they also destroyed an unattended platoon supply point (PSP), some twelve other hidden stocks of ammunition and the like in the vicinity of Dugout 5. As of late afternoon, the Jetertown road stood wholly clear of mines, all without any U.S. losses.[26]

The Maddogs and sappers' good work partially made up for a sorry spectacle north of Jetertown, when one OPFOR fire team successfully hit the seam between companies A and B on the Jetertown Road. Finding little U.S. security around both companies' headquarters and supply teams, and the LZST trucks halted in the middle doing a water run, the CLF went to work. Six Bushmasters and three Abus succumbed in the first five minutes, with no effective return fire. If this went on . . .

It didn't. The LZST, under the pugnacious 1st Lt. Matt Moore, tore into the enemy. American rifles barked, and Moore brought up his two escort gun trucks to add to the firing line. The alert Maddog gunners, erect in their Humvee cupolas, opened up with big .50-caliber machine guns. They took down two CLF, and the other duo ran away. Thus ended an eight-minute melee.[27]

Nobody knew it, but that amounted to the CLF's last gasp, their final Parthian shot. With the town and its populace completely under U.S. control, the insurgency grew increasingly fragmented. For the first time at JRTC, the 1st of the 327th began to see signs of flagging CLF morale. On the night of the seventeenth, an insurgent surrendered to a patrol from 3d Platoon, Company C. When questioned by 1st Lt. Jason Henneke and Sfc. Jeffrey England, the CLF man showed his empty canteens. "I've had it," he said.[28] By concentrating on killing the enemy forces, culminating in taking the town, the Bulldogs had also overrun and thereby eliminated the CLF supply network.

Following a pause in the exercise for a series of field AARs, the battalion continued to operate on 18 May. The Lipke Vs pressed on despite a warm, heavy rain that began about midday. Company B swept the meadows and treelines east of Jetertown, the same area occupied by the battalion trains during JRTC 94-10. About 1500, two Bushmaster platoons—1st under Lance Oskey and Rory Malloy, and 3d under 2d Lt. Bill Burnard and Sfc. William Shook—swept ahead, while 2d Platoon trailed. Burnard's riflemen saw what looked like a sleeping guerrilla. They crept forward to check it out.

Oskey's bunch also saw the prostrate form, plus five more hostiles, all snug in their ponchos, literally caught sleeping. The light rain pattered on the bushes and leaves as the Americans deployed. Both platoons opened fire, killing every enemy instantly. Two more CLF sprang up from a nearby thicket and raced away.

When Malloy and his riflemen checked the enemy dead, they discovered that these sleepers were OPFOR mortar-men. Although the 82mm tube did not surface, the maps, call signs, and radio frequency cards proved a sufficient bounty.[29] Ted Donnelly vowed to find the actual mortar.

At the same time, Company A carefully crossed Big Brushy Creek to reconnoiter Hunger Hill. Company patrols had heard generator noises in that haunted ground, so Drew Felix sent a small team across a ford to pinpoint the target. Led by 2d Lt. Matt Fine and SSgt. Richard E. Thomas, 1st Platoon soldiers combed slowly over the thinly wooded slope that rose west of the waterway. At 1721, they fired in several barrages of artillery. The generator noise ceased. Not stopping to count coup, Fine and Thomas recrossed the creek. They had killed something, and exorcised some ghosts, too.

Also on the eighteenth, watchful Maddog sentries near LZ Owl captured one of the rebels' most elusive members, a Leesville Urban Group operative, a LUG. Tipped off by Team Golf's cornucopia of intelligence garnered from the Jetertown populace, First Sergeant

Morgan and his security team quickly identified a suspicious civilian who approached LZ Owl. The imposter claimed to be Mr. Steve Roberts, coincidentally the same name as the 1st of the 327th XO, but in JRTC lore, a citizen of Jetertown killed days before by CLF terrorism. Because Morgan knew that this Roberts must be bogus, he clapped the LUG, his partner, and their truck under guard. The whole package went to brigade shortly thereafter.[30] Few visiting units intercept a member of the Leesville Urban Group, but the Maddogs had done it.

Although the guerrillas bent on the seventeenth and eighteenth, they broke on the nineteenth of May. That day, a bloody one for the CLF, belonged to Company C and Chris Forbes. In a series of twelve contacts, Cold Steel platoons flushed out and killed thirteen opposition troops. One, an enemy lieutenant, provided yet another radio frequency card. While First Sergeant Bauerle listened in and passed information, Forbes directed mortar fire and Apache gunships to waylay the hapless CLF moving to attack Company C. The battalion's 81mm mortar platoon, already in on numerous kills with the other companies, rang up three on two separate occasions.

The captured radio also gave advance notice of a CLF air assault, with an enemy foursome trying to land in Jetertown. It appeared they hoped to stage a massacre, to blow away innocent civilians and undermine support for the hamlet's Yankee benefactors. Instead, while orchestrating the ground fight, Forbes passed the word to the 1st of the 327th's attached air defense platoon. The Stinger gunners of Battery A, 2-44th Air Defense, thrilled to have something to shoot at, potted the bug-nosed Mi-2 almost as soon as it came into range. When it fluttered down, Cold Steel ringed the "wreckage." When those aboard refused to give up, riflemen killed the surprised passengers of the Soviet-made chopper.

The fighting flared until nightfall, with some seven Cold Steel soldiers hit in the succession of clashes.[31] As the sun went down, though, the shooting died away. Dan Bolger spent the night as he had spent the day, on the ground in Jetertown, rifle in hand, looking to shoot a badnik. He never got the chance. His men had already done that for him.

The Abus operated south and west, the Bushmasters north and east, both without any contacts. Mike Delgado's Maddogs waited back near LZ Owl, launching their convoys as necessary. The LZST made its night rounds, and Steve Roberts (the U.S. soldier version) and his Gold Tac men monitored another silent graveyard shift under a swelling silver moon. The Scout Platoon, finally all back from the dead, hid in the tall grass near Maddox Homestead to the southwest.

Brigade wanted the Bulldogs to go there next, even though the settlement officially belonged to the 2d of the 327th. Something definitely seemed to be brewing at Maddox, or even farther to the west. An enemy transport dropped paratroopers out that way on the morning of the nineteenth, and Apache pilots reported seeing men in black uniforms—Atlantican Special Operations Forces (SOF). What did that portend?

Bolger could only guess. The morning brought one more exchange of fire, then a halt. The first phase AARs took up the rest of that day, and they were good indeed. But the battalion commander did not forget those black-suited guys up to mischief out there. They, too, demanded some killing be done.

Killing had been done all right, throughout the 1st Brigade. Naturally, the opponents had gotten in their licks too. While the Bulldogs carried out their sweeps near Jetertown, the No Slack battalion bore the brunt of OPFOR ire, notably a chemical strike on their large, well-appointed TOC and the immolation of a rifle company helicoptered into a detached LZ ten kilometers away, out to the north. The overall scoreboard read 1,261 Americans lost against 196 CLF eliminated, a respectable 6.4 to 1 ratio.[32] It also amounted to some 500 less casualties than the brigade took during JRTC 94-10, even though this time the search and attack phase lasted eight days rather than five.

The 1st of the 327th far exceeded JRTC standards for performance against the CLF. For the cost of 159 men, the battalion inflicted 109 CLF casualties, a 1.5:1 ratio, better even than that achieved by the brilliant Lloyd Mills and his 3-327th troopers on JRTC 94-07 the previous year.[33] The 1-327th men did that without causing any civilian casualties, without ever suffering a single attack against the miniscule battalion CP, without enduring any OPFOR mortar fire after the first night, and without losing a single supply vehicle to mines. The battalion evacuated every casualty and accounted for every man and all equipment. Bulldog soldiers ran Jetertown and had crossed Hunger Hill with impunity. They dominated the entire eastern side of the Fullerton box, and the CLF knew it.

Everything had not gone perfectly, but, clearly, this time the battalion came ready to fight. The enemy definitely knew it. Whereas some portions of the brigade longed for the break marked by the After-Action Reports, the 1st of the 327th wanted more blood. As might be expected, the Atlantican SOF soon obliged.

Notes

The epigraph is quoted in David G. Chandler, *The Campaigns of Napoleon* (New York: The Macmillan Company, 1966), 141.

1. U.S., Department of the Army, Headquarters, 1st Battalion, 327th Infantry Regiment, *TF 1-327 SigActs Log* (Ft. Polk, La.: Tactical CP, 1st Battalion, 327th Infantry Regiment, 14–19 May 1995), 8. This record of significant actions, kept by the active Tac, shows the first C-130 landing at 1100 local on 14 May 1995.

2. U.S., Department of the Army, FM 7-20: *The Infantry Battalion* (Washington, D.C.: U.S. Govt. Printing Office, 1992), 3-20, 3-21. For the idea in its Vietnam context, see Lt. Gen. Phillip B. Davidson, USA, ret., *Vietnam at War* (Novato, Calif.: Presidio Press, 1988), 363.

3. Lt. Col. Andrew F. Krepinevich, Jr., USA, *The Army and Vietnam* (Baltimore, Md.: The Johns Hopkins University Press, 1986), 190–93.

4. Stephen B. Patrick, "The East Is Red," *Strategy & Tactics* (January/February 1974), 14. The Chinese preference for one point/two sides evolved into a stereotype; the PLA used it at all echelons from platoon to division, and sometimes even at army level.

5. Like the buttpacks, the scopes showed the diligence and ingenuity of 1/Lt. Craig Doane, the S4. The O/Cs tried to disallow these store-bought items, but Doane produced a properly signed and stamped table of organization modification document. The Bulldogs kept their rifle scopes.

6. Department of the Army, FM 7-20: *The Infantry Battalion,* 2-26.

7. HQ, 1st Battalion, 327th Infantry Regiment, *TF 1-327 SigActs Log,* 12.

8. The mystery tanks may have been garbled reports of the arrival of Team Animal's U.S. combat vehicles.

9. HQ, 1st Battalion, 327th Infantry Regiment, *TF 1-327 SigActs Log,* 12–13.

10. U.S., Department of the Army, Headquarters, Joint Readiness Training Center, *1st Battalion, 327th Infantry Regiment, Rotation 95-07: Pausex* (Ft. Polk, La.: HQ, JRTC, 18 May 1995), 47. Of note, the O/Cs critiqued Company C for not maneuvering more platoons into each

skirmish. This comment rings a bit hollow, as the company handily dealt with each enemy element. Some O/Cs prefer to see things that conform to the field manuals, even when other methods work just as well, or better.

11. Ibid., 48.

12. Rudyard Kipling, "Gunga Din," in *The Portable Kipling*, ed. Irving Howe (New York: The Viking Press, 1982), 615.

13. U.S., Department of the Army, Headquarters, Joint Readiness Training Center, *1st Battalion, 327th Infantry Regiment, Take Home Package, Training After-Action Report: Rotation 95-07* (Ft. Polk, La.: HQ, JRTC, 25 May 1995), 67-B.

14. Department of the Army, *FM 7-20: The Infantry Battalion*, 1-4, 7-21 to 7-23. Infantry battalions normally receive full authority over interrogators, ground radars, and ground sensor teams. Low-level voice intercept elements may work in battalion zones, but they report to brigade and move on brigade orders.

15. U.S., Department of the Army, Headquarters, Joint Readiness Training Center, *1st Battalion, 327th Infantry Regiment, Rotation 95-07: AAR* (Ft. Polk, La.: HQ, JRTC, 20 May 1995), 28–29.

16. HQ, 1st Battalion, 327th Infantry Regiment, *TF 1-327 SigActs Log*, 21.

17. Some 24% of American Gulf War casualties came due to fratricide. See Rick Atkinson, *Crusade* (New York: Houghton Mifflin Co., 1993), 314–317. For the specifics of Blue Max 23's ill-fated gun run, see HQ, JRTC, *1st Battalion, 327th Infantry Regiment, Rotation 95-07: AAR*, 81.

18. Adm. Sir John "Sandy" Woodward, RN, with Patrick Robinson, *One Hundred Days* (Annapolis, Md.: Naval Institute Press, 1992), 317.

19. HQ, 1st Battalion, 327th Infantry Regiment, *TF 1-327 SigActs Log*, 22–23.

20. Overall, the 1st Brigade initiated 22% of all contacts (87 of 398). See U.S., Department of the Army, Headquarters, Joint Readiness Training Center, "Momentum," *1st Brigade, 101st Airborne Division (Air Assault), Rotation 95-07: AAR* (Ft. Polk, La.: HQ, JRTC, 21 May 1995), 27. The other infantry battalion, 2-327th, created 32% of its contacts (15 of 47). See U.S., Department of the Army, Headquarters, Joint Readiness Training Center, *2nd Battalion, 327th In-*

fantry Regiment, Rotation 95-07: AAR (Ft. Polk, La.: HQ, JRTC, 20 May 1995), 14.

21. This invented nongovernmental organization mimicked the actions of such real air groups as CARE, *Médicins sans Frontières* (Doctors Without Borders), and World Vision. On occasion, actual aid workers participate in JRTC rotations, playing themselves.

22. HQ, JRTC, *2nd Battalion, 327th Infantry Regiment, Rotation 95-07: AAR*, 14, 36.

23. U.S., Department of the Army, Headquarters, 1st Brigade, 101st Airborne Division (Air Assault), *FRAGO 95-05-30* (Ft. Polk, La.: HQ, 1st Brigade, 101st Airborne Division [Air Assault], 16 May 1995), 1-2. A FRAGO is a fragmentary order, a change or addition to a current operation order.

24. HQ, 1st Battalion, 327th Infantry Regiment, *TF 1-327 SigActs Log*, 30, 33–34.

25. HQ, JRTC, *1st Battalion, 327th Infantry Regiment, Rotation 95-07: AAR*, 32–33.

26. Ibid., 37.

27. HQ, 1st Battalion, 327th Infantry Regiment, *TF 1-327 SigActs Log*, 37–39.

28. Ibid., 40. Questioning by Capt. Dirk Blackdeer back near LZ Owl determined that, indeed, the prisoner voluntarily gave himself up. It was not some kind of scenario play.

29. HQ, JRTC, *1st Battalion, 327th Infantry Regiment, Rotation 95-07: AAR*, 37–38.

30. HQ, 1st Battalion, 327th Infantry Regiment, *TF 1-327 SigActs Log*, 42.

31. U.S., Department of the Army, Headquarters, Joint Readiness Training Center, *JRTC Rotation 95-07: Scenario Laydown* (Ft. Polk, La.: HQ, JRTC, 30 March 1996), 42; HQ, 1st Battalion, 327th Infantry Regiment, TF 1-327 *SigActs Log*, 47–51.

32. HQ, JRTC, "Friendly Casualties by Type Weapon System", *1st Brigade, 101st Airborne Division (Air Assault), Rotation 95-07: AAR*, 13; U.S., Department of the Army, Headquarters, 1st Battalion, 509th Parachute Infantry Regiment, "Friendly BDA by Role-Play Unit," slide prepared 25 May 1995.

33. HQ, 1-509th Infantry, "Friendly BDA By Role-Play Unit;" HQ,

JRTC, *1st Battalion, 327th Infantry Regiment, Rotation 95-07: AAR,* 8–9. The 3d Battalion, 327th Infantry Regiment, generally acknowledged as one of the most successful outfits to visit JRTC, killed 74 and lost 152 during search and attack operations, a fine 1:2 ratio. See Lt. Col. Lloyd W. Mills, USA, *JRTC 94-07: A Commander's Perspective* (HQ, 3d Battalion, 327th Infantry Regiment, 24 June 1994), 1.

Chapter 10
Deliberate Attack (II)

Find out where your enemy is. Get at him as soon as you can. Strike him as hard as you can and as soon as you can, and keep moving on.

—Gen. Ulysses S. Grant

With the CLF 91st Assault Battalion depleted by its exertions and hounded by the relentless pressure of 1st Brigade, the enemy high command elected to raise the stakes. Normally, at this stage of the war, the JRTC OPFOR resorted to tanks, heavy artillery, and the commitment of motorized infantry formations. This time, though, the opposing forces chose the stiletto rather than the bludgeon. Drawing on a company borrowed from the U.S. Army's best infantry, the 75th Ranger Regiment, the moguls of Fort Polk conjured up a nightmare, dressed in black and armed to the teeth.

The Screaming Eagles saw them come in under the silk, dozens of elite SOF troopers spilling into the warm skies over Cortina south of the Americans' forward outposts, safely beyond the reach of U.S. Stinger antiaircraft missilery. As the nineteenth of May faded into the twentieth, numerous reports of black-garbed soldiers confirmed the worst. The 2d Company, 10th Battalion, 142d Airborne Brigade, had entered the exercise box, bringing with them an extra ration of ferocity and a toybox full of unusual armaments.

The men in black represented the same sort of elite warriors who once made up the Soviet Union's *spetsnaz* (special purpose) brigades, and who still populate the swollen special forces ranks of Cuba and North Korea. In those kinds of states, and so in their mythical analogue Atlantica, SOF fulfill not only the same kind of deep reconnaissance, partisan liaison, and direct action tasks as in western armies, but also act as politically reliable stiffeners and final arbiters

315

for unpopular regimes. More heavily salted with long-term professionals than the almost completely conscripted ranks of the motor-rifle battalions, indoctrinated for independence of mind in societies known for ruthless conformity, this category of SOF always enjoys priority on training and weaponry. When dictatorships care enough, they send their very best. So it has gone in Angola, Ethiopia, Nicaragua, Lebanon, and Afghanistan.

Now that special breed of enemy joined the war in Cortina. The high command sent in its SOF with one purpose: to kill Americans, and in doing so, to reinvigorate the flagging Cortinian Liberation Front. Like the Vietnamese Communist sapper troops, Uncle Ho's lethal answer to Uncle Sam's waves of B-52 Stratofortress heavy bombers, the 142d Airborne's black legion brought appropriate tools for their duties.[1] Despite plenty of JRTC experience over the past few years, 101st Airborne soldiers had not seen these SOF-peculiar implements, nor felt their harsh stings. Introduced specifically to even the odds against the American intervention forces, and thus buy time to rebuild the shattered CLF, the Atlantican 142d Airborne company came to play with three new instruments: the as-Saqr 30, the Type-63, and the RBS-70.

The as-Saqr 30 (Hawk 30), a four-barreled 122mm rocket launcher built in Egypt, hardly qualifies as a wonder weapon. First shown in 1988, looking for all the world like a rack of four long water pipes on a two-wheel trailer, this brute has about as much high technology as a monkey-wrench, and about as many moving parts. It does, however, display some characteristics that make it dear to Atlantican blackshirts. The launcher can fire its four projectiles, each with a forty-pound warhead, some thirty-six kilometers, far beyond the range of American 155mm and 105mm howitzers endeavoring to answer back. The as-Saqr also outreaches the envelope of the AN/TPQ-36 counterfire radar.[2] The as-Saqr is accurate enough to hit area targets, and mobile enough to be gone when Apache gunships scramble to find the damn thing. The Atlantican SOF company brought one as-Saqr 30 to the party.

As a companion to the as-Saqr 30, the enemy also deployed a single Type-63 multiple rocket launcher. Of Chinese manufacture, the venerable Type-63 fired twelve 107mm rockets out to eight-and-a-half kilometers. Unlike the as-Saqr, the Type-63 had much to fear from the Americans' all-seeing Q-36 radar and its affiliated artillery pieces. After every volley, the Type-63 gunners had to pack up their rack on its trailer mount, hook it to a truck, and drive like hell. If they hung around more than a minute or so, the U.S. counterfire would erase them. Despite this drawback, the Type-63 did vomit a dozen twenty-pound rounds in seconds, plastering targets with more than a third again as much firepower as the otherwise preferable as-Saqr 30.[3] If carefully placed, and used in tandem with the longer shooting as-Saqr, the elderly Type-63 might inflict a lot of destruction against aircraft laagers and supply dumps.

To shield these killer rocket launchers from American aviation, the Atlantican leadership provided state-of-the-art air defense missile systems, the Swedish-made RBS70, also called the Robot 70, built by the famous Bofors Corporation. Carried in three one-man packs, the stand, sight, and missile can be assembled in two minutes or less. Built expressly to defeat rotary-wing aircraft, a RBS70 can down a chopper out to six kilometers and up to almost ten thousand feet, a lethal pattern that compares favorably to the U.S. Stinger. The RBS70 differs from the Stinger, and indeed most short-range anti-aircraft missiles, in that it tracks its target based on a laser pulse. The gunner merely marks his prey, aligns his missile, and lets fly. The RBS70's microchips and sensors do the rest. Because of its unusual guidance system, the RBS70 cannot be spoofed by the heat dampers and flares employed to distract conventional heat-seekers.[4] An opponent looking for leverage against the AH-64A Apache could not choose a better weapon. The enemy SOF included two RBS70 teams, each with a single launcher and plenty of reloads.

Unfamiliar with the as-Saqr, the Type-63, and the RBS70, the 1st Brigade's intelligence community fell back on the usual ploy of uncertain analysts. They exaggerated. To hear the line issuing from the innards of 1st Brigade's well-staffed TOC, you might believe that the Fuehrer had just thrown in the equivalent of the V-1 Buzz Bomb, the V-2 ballistic missile, and the Me-262 fighter jet, plus the Iraqi Scud, the atomic bomb, the death ray, and the thing that ate Cincinnati. Two rather unremarkable towed rocket launchers and a good, if somewhat unusual, surface-to-air missile gained reputations out of all proportion to their actual battlefield capacities. When smart OP-FOR rocketeers battered the static, sprawling brigade trains near Fullerton, then swatted down two Apaches trying to do something about it, the brigade S2 people, at least, felt satisfied. They had warned everybody, by God.

Well, this bunch of evil Atlanticans called for action, and so 1st Brigade's follow-on mission crystallized, a deliberate attack to eradicate these pesky SOF boys and their wonder weapons. Usually, the shift to fighting Atlantican regulars meant facing a conventional armored component, hard enough, but compared to the exasperating CLF, a dilution of pressure for the U.S. infantry. This time, though, given the extremely high quality of Atlantica's SOF teams, the 101st Airborne soldiers knew there would be no break in the action. The 1st Brigade, especially its Bulldog battalion, had thrashed the CLF. Now those men, and their Ranger buddies, were back in new black suits, rested, rearmed, and longing for vengeance.

The 1st of the 327th prepared to battle the 142d Airborne Brigade because of decisions made long ago and far away, in mid-January 1995, when the Screaming Eagles inherited rotation 95-07. Back then, the generals who ran the 101st Airborne Division consulted with the JRTC commanding general. Together they devised a unique scenario, designed to stress the air assault brigade by having it conduct three attacks in twelve days: the initial FLS seizure, a deliberate attack to destroy OPFOR armor in fixed defenses, and then a finale against the SOF. The first and final operation would include follow-up search and attack segments. Even though it had been a standard phase of every previous Screaming Eagle visit, the defense fell out. The 101st Airborne's commanding general summarized the approved plan neatly as "attack, attack, attack."

Driven by this offensive scenario, the Always First brigade went into Cortina on 13 May. Somewhere around the fifteenth or sixteenth, the 101st Airborne generals made a course correction, and asked the JRTC hierarchy to cancel the middle mission. The senior Screaming Eagles wanted the brigade to carry out an extended search and attack operation, and JRTC honored their desire. Why this occurred is known only to those who made the decision. Speculation in the trenches said that the higher-ups wanted to see a brigade actually finish the struggle against the insurgents, one way or another. Others guessed that the 101st Airborne general officers disdained air assaults aimed at reducing armor-encrusted "death star" field fortifications. Finally, and in light of developing missions out in the real world, a few later observed just how well the altered scenario mirrored 1st Brigade's eventual deployment into an all too similar environment. It may have been one of these, all of these, or simply what the generals wanted to do.

Whatever the reason or reasons, the lengthy counterguerrilla fight represented a departure from the programmed scenario. Had the O/Cs stuck to the script, the war against the CLF would have ended about the 17 May. At that point, the JRTC planners hoped to send 1st Brigade north to Peason Ridge, into the maw of a dug-in mechanized defense network pretty similar to the array that concluded JRTC 94-10. With that battle over for good or ill—probably for ill, given such hard targets—the brigade would fly back to Fort Polk proper, into a newly opened training ground called Zion Hill. There, the JRTC staff desired to pit the 1st Brigade against the dastardly Atlantican SOF and their menagerie of odd shooting irons. That part happened on schedule, beginning on 20 May 1995, when the OPFOR began raining death out of hidden bases in the Zion Hill region.

Taking out the SOF bases in Zion Hill required a brigade air assault. That much seemed obvious. Brigade divined three worthwhile objectives. To the west, at what Col. Jack Donovan's staff called Objective Holland, radio intercepts painted the 2d Company CP, broadcasting to CLF insurgents over a long-haul transmitter. About four kilometers to the east lay the CLF's buried battalion supply point, the holy of holies BSP that never turned up over in Fullerton. Brigade tagged that as Objective Veghel. Nine kilometers more to the east, higher intelligence identified the as-Saqr and Type-63 firing racetrack, centered on an open field, and guarded by both RBS70s. Brigade listed this as Objective Zon.

How to crack it? Donovan's staff drew up a predictable scheme: one battalion against the CP, one against the BSP, and Team Animal driving overland to blot out the rocket launchers, or at least flush

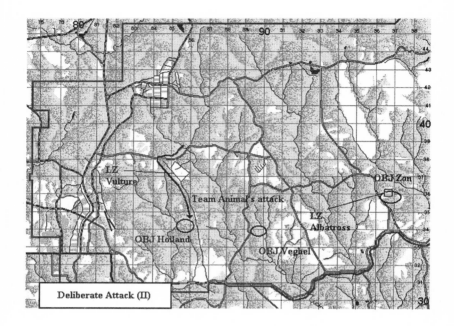

Deliberate Attack (II)

them. That looked pretty safe, and not unlike the 94-10 curtain call. One for you, one for me, and one for him—it had a nice logic to it, even if it only accommodated the opposition.

Donovan rejected the staff proposal out of hand. Instead, he put his finger on the map, right on Zon and its nest of *wunderwaffen*. "We get that first." He stabbed Holland's CP. "Then that." He ignored the BSP. "We'll worry about that later." What about Team Animal? The brigade commander told his men to send the tanks against the CP at Holland, as that would be the 1st Brigade's main effort. If you severed the radio link between the CLF remnants near Fullerton and the SOF in Zion Hills, the as-Saqr and Type-63 lost their ties to their forward observers. Take out the company CP and the rocketmen go blind. And by the way, hit the rocket folks first so that they can't fire up the follow-on waves of helicopters departing from the Fullerton area. Everything focused on killing the command post, cutting off the SOF's head and connections to the CLF. Then, the Always First team could digest the other morsels at their leisure.

With that directive planning guidance, the brigade staff quickly sketched in the details. The supporting effort, 2-327th Infantry, drew Zon and its rocket park, plus an LZ time of 2000 local on 22 May, two hours before the main show. In the big one, brigade gave Objective Holland to Dan Bolger and his Bulldogs, reinforced by Team Animal. The brigade commander set 2200 as H-Hour for the 1st of 327th's landing. Considering the nature of the enemy, Donovan told both battalions to ready themselves for immediate transition to search and attack operations.[5] Since all knew that the exercise ended on the morning of the twenty-fourth, that meant at least another day and night of counterinsurgency sweeps. However it impressed the rest of 1st Brigade, more search and attack sounded fine to Bolger and his Bulldogs.

The 1st of the 327th's order for the deliberate attack on Objective Holland looked a lot like the strike into Objective Lee back in September 1994. Once again, the battalion counted on the Tigers of the Scout Platoon and an attached Navy/Marine FCT to locate and blow away the enemy command post. Ideally, this promised to obviate any need for a full-scale ground attack.

Of course, when you weighed the Tigers' meager contributions to the battalion's operations to date in JRTC 95-07, betting the farm on the Scout Platoon looked kind of shaky. That explained why Maj. Bill Phelps, Capt. Dirk Blackdeer, and their battalion commander created a base plan that assumed no help from the scouts. The Bulldogs selected their usual single LZ. Vulture lay an inconvenient three kilometers north of the objective, unlike three others in close proximity. Bolger knew that the SOF couldn't be everywhere, and probably wouldn't be at LZ Vulture.

From LZ Vulture, a trail ran right down to Objective Holland. On hitting dirt, the Abus would halt in the woods east of the dirt road, with Cold Steel doing the same to the west. Assuming the scouts dead or ineffective, both units prepared to dispatch small patrols to pinpoint the actual heart of the hostile position. Once one or both recon squads located the real Objective Holland, the patrols intended to hunker down. At that event, the rest of the companies planned on moving south, halting at a succession of phase lines to bring in the obligatory fire support: naval gunfire, 155mm, 105mm, 81mm,

Task Force 1-327 Infantry
22 May 1995

Company A(-)
HQ/FIST
Mortars (2 x 60mm)
1st Platoon/A
2d Platoon/A
3d Platoon/A
Engineer Platoon (-)
White Team A

Company B
HQ/FIST
Mortars (2 x 60mm)
1st Platoon/B
2d Platoon/B
3d Platoon/B
Engineer Squad
White Team B
10 x Humvees

Company C
HQ/FIST
Mortars (2 x 60mm)
1st Platoon/C
2d Platoon/C
3d Platoon/C
Engineer Squad
White Team C

Company D (-)
HQ
1st Platoon/D
2d Platoon/D
3d Platoon/D
5th Platoon/D
Engineer Platoon
White Team D
Stinger Team 1

Team Animal (Team A/1-32nd Armor)
HQ/FIST (2 x M1A1 tanks)
Tank Platoon (4 x M1A1 tanks)
Tank Platoon (4 x M1A1 tanks)
Mech Platoon (4 x M2A2 infantry fighting vehicles)
Mech Platoon (4 x M2A2 infantry fighting vehicles)
Armored Engineer Platoon
Team Golf

Task Force Control
Scout Platoon
    FCT 3
Mortar Platoon (4 x 81mm)
    Stinger Team 2
Gold Tac/Black Tac
LZST (with ATLS)
    4th Platoon/D
    Stinger Team 3
Field Trains

Detachments
Team Animal (+) (on order from 1st Brigade)
    1st Platoon/B
    2d Platoon/D

STRENGTHS (with attachments)

Company A:	102
Company B:	109
Company C:	107
Company D:	53
Team Animal:	133
Scout Platoon:	25
Mortar Platoon:	26
Gold Tac/Black Tac:	20
LZST:	37
Field Trains:	48

TF 1-327 Infantry Total: 660

Starting strengths; casualties not included

Key to Abbreviations/Terms
ATLS: Advanced Trauma Lifesaving Team
CP: Command Post
FCT: Fire Control Team (Navy/Marine)
FIST: Fire Support Team (Army)
HQ: headquarters
LLVI: low-level voice intercept
LZST: Landing Zone Support Team
Team Golf: S5, civil affairs team,
        loudspeaker team, and
        counterintelligence agent

and 60mm, echeloned right by the firing tables. As their two brother rifle companies moved south to overwatch Objective Holland, the Bushmasters planned to assemble and get aboard ten cargo Humvees grouped in the treeline east of LZ Vulture. Once Team Animal appeared around 2300, Capt. Ted Donnelly would follow them down to Holland. The battalion counted on Team Animal to crunch over the enemy command post and its defensive outworks, going in from the north and out through the south, spewing fire and brimstone. While Company B hopped off their makeshift transportation to complete the destruction of any SOF still wandering dazed across the objective, Capt. Ken Blakely's tanks endeavored to swoop through a nice Bat-turn, à la the Caped Crusader's nimble jet-powered car, and head back north, mission completed. Then the Bulldogs would settle down to carry out search and attack operations, with Company B to the south, Company C to the west, and Company A to the east.[6] So went the thinking among the Bulldog brain trust.

Even as they choreographed this base plan, with its stately progression of echeloned supporting fire lines and its mailed first climax, the battalion commander and his key staffers also developed a contingency concept in the event the scouts actually located and destroyed the SOF command post prior to the 1st of the 327th's air assault. If that came to pass, the battalion chose to discard all the elaborate supporting fires and slip right into the search and attack. Brigade insisted on making Team Animal swing down through Objective Holland even if the Tigers demolished the command post. To some extent, this reflected 1st Brigade's reluctance to trust a preliminary report that the CP had been liquidated. Like Saint Thomas in the New Testament, brigade wanted to stick their fingers in the wounds, just to be sure. In this case, those fingers weighed seventy tons and spit 120mm depleted-uranium long-rod penetrators.

The 1st of the 327th issued their order early on 21 May, after a short planning session by the Black Tac held during the normal Gold Tac night shift. As the participants learned their roles, it became obvious that the battalion commander must get one thing right. Dan Bolger had to be certain about the condition of Objective Holland. If the Tigers and FCT smashed it, all to the good. If not, the battalion faced a groping search for the real objective, then the methodical application of a storm of steel, admittedly simulated, but essential before Team Animal and Company B entered the wreckage of the enemy SOF position.

Regardless of the version of ground operations that ensued, the battalion air assault stayed consistent. Working with the aviators and brigade headquarters, 1st Lt. Matt Bounds, the Bulldog S3 Air, dreamed up a simple scheme that launched the battalion from LZ Owl and landed it at LZ Vulture. Unfortunately, brigade required all CH-47D loads to fly out of Fullerton FLS, and the battalion's assault package looked almost identical to that used on 13 May. So eight Humvees and fifty-odd men had to make the dangerous trek north to the brigade's FLS, ground zero for those popping away with the as-Saqr and Type-63 multiple rocket launchers.

With a few CLF die-hards still roaming the woods and the OPFOR rocket gunners salivating over likely targets, staging Task Force 1-327 for an air assault mandated a vigorous security posture. The battalion consolidated around LZ Owl, with Company C to the west and north, Company A to the south, and Company B to the east. This repositioning consumed most of the daylight hours of 21 May, and looked to the enemy very much like search and attack operations. That was not an accident.

During the previous rotation, the battalion erred in its poor security efforts while the men prepared for the air assault to Peason Ridge. Enemy stay-behinds inflicted some fifty-six casualties, literally chasing the beleagured 1st of the 327th to their pickup zone. To avoid that this time, the battalion continued to patrol vigorously to keep the badniks well away or, better yet, kill them.

The rifle companies succeeded handsomely in this venture. Ted Donnelly and Company B persisted in beating the bushes east of the Jetertown Road. Having capped the OPFOR 82mm crew and unearthed eight of their stashed piles of rounds, the Bushmasters combed the pinestands trying to find the actual mortar tube. Dan Bolger knew that whether or not Company B found the real implement, their activity clearly smothered enemy mortar firing. Stopping that threat was worth a rifle company. So the Bushmasters trolled on, trudging the woods, cuts, and red dirt hillocks to keep a lid on the furtive CLF mortar-men, wherever they might be.

The only body count came from Company C, a fairly common pattern by now. The Cold Steel men extracted from Jetertown early on 21 May, departing by ground convoy. Upon reaching LZ Owl, they entered the marshy creek to the west and spread out. Within a half hour, the aggressive rifle squads nabbed two Atlantican observers, complete with the usual ebon togs, a radio, nicely marked maps, and a complete operation order. Interrogation and search on the spot revealed these interlopers as men from Company C, 1st Battalion, 75th Ranger Regiment. Introduced to keep tabs on 1st of the 327th, the sullen Rangers instead gave away their unit's entire surveillance network. Three pages of notes from these characters allowed the 1st Brigade to scoop up or kill all of the OPFOR SOF watch teams, leaving only a couple of thirsty, exhausted CLF to keep vigil in the entire Fullerton region.[7] Once more, Company C's heads-up play demonstrated how thoroughly Chris Forbes had reschooled his charges, and indeed himself, over the nine months between their two trips to JRTC.

The coagulation of the battalion around LZ Owl created a lucrative target for the enemy, but Dan Bolger figured his companies' stout patrolling pushed away or zapped the hostile observers, thereby saving his battalion from attrition by indirect fires and random sniping. That was all to the good, and kept LZ Owl free of trouble as the battalion assembled for its flight. Unfortunately, one of the lieutenant colonel's prejudices intervened at this point, coincident with some observer/controller desires to impose a particular training event. Mass casualties resulted, the only legitimate case during the rotation.

The Bulldogs' commander knew his military history, and stayed very current on military threats and trends worldwide. For this reason, Lt. Col. Dan Bolger habitually and consciously disregarded air defense. And why not? Errant Scud rockets aside, the last legitimate air attacks on American troops occurred back in 1945. As their song advertises, nothing can stop the U.S. Air Force, not to mention Navy and Marine Corps air, plus Army choppers. So Bolger did not fear attack from the air.

Of course, in Cortina, attacks from the air came anyway, to exercise the U.S. Army air defense system for training purposes. What enemy this replicated has never been spelled out. The Koreans, Vietnamese, Iraqis, and all the other riff-raff never flew against our ground troops, and the Russians cannot even figure out who is on their team anymore. But because our Army has air defenders, by God, they need a workout, just in case somebody launches an air strike some day. Given that the the entire Army air defense establishment within our fighting divisions consists of variously mounted Stinger missiles, with a whopping five-and-a-half kilometer range, it appears that the U.S. national security apparatus has given up on troop air defense as a waste of manpower, time, money, and all other resources. But like the Federal Helium Reserve, the Bureau of Indian Affairs, or subsidies for mohair, once in place, a chunk of the federal leviathan does not go gently into the good night. The U.S. Army air defenders remain, and JRTC tickles them to make them feel wanted.

The Stinger teams come with their own trucks. Like the little military intelligence parties, Stinger pairs prefer to roam at will across battalion areas of operations. Although dished out to fighting battalions, they also respond to an air defense battery commander, a captain ensconced in the brigade command post. The air defenders demand infantry squads for security, resupply of necessities for them and their Humvees, and access to the TOC for their platoon leader and platoon sergeant to advise the battalion commander on how to frustrate enemy airplanes.

None of this impressed Bolger. He declined to permit the Stinger folks to bring in their trucks, because the CLF so easily captured them as they tooled about in splendid isolation. He ignored the bizarre positioning directives spewing from the air defense battery captain, and of course denied infantry security for the Stinger teams. Bolger knew that the air defenders would be eaten on their own, and so kept them in tight. And Bolger did not run a TOC, and so demanded that his Stinger platoon lieutenant get his butt out and hang with his gunners rather than offering unsolicited and unnecessary advice. Lieutenant Freddie Mack prospered under these conditions during JRTC 94-10. His replacement did not.

The air defenders had their day on 21 May, thanks to the O/Cs. Mindful of Bolger's disdain of air defense, and yearning to see a mass casualty event that the CLF had been unable to cause, the JRTC leadership allowed a ridiculous occurrence at 1715 on 21 May. At that time, a single armed UH-1H OPFOR helicopter flew straight toward the Abus, then dispersed in the sparse woods northwest of Jetertown. Vectored in by luck or, more likely, by the O/Cs, the enemy bird approached nonchalantly above the treetops. It then swung hard to the right, into an orbit. The helicopter made ten lazy circles, ripping the insides out of Company A. Drew Felix again went down, along with forty others.[8] The company responded angrily to its aerial tormentor, delivering a shattering fusillade, but the hostile Huey's MILES harness proved conveniently defective. Well, so be it. The air defense structure had been struck and found wanting. The O/Cs at last got to watch a mass casualty situation develop. And Bolger's obstinate dismissal of conventional Stinger usage now came home to roost.

The medevac process ran like clockwork, much to the surprise of the observer/controllers, who no doubt expected the opposite. Instead, they saw 1st Sgt. Scott D. Craig organize an efficient, protected triage point. Craig shipped out his thirty-one wounded in short order by air ambulances and aboard Matt Moore's LZST trucks. The ten dead also left within an hour or so. By nightfall, the Abus cleaned their sad pickup zone.[9] Throughout this, the rest of the company continued its patrolling, just in case. But the beaten CLF lacked the strength to exploit the air attack.

The air defense lieutenant came racing up to the Tac CP, even as 1st Lt. Lance Bailey finished transmitting the final list of casualties to the 1st Brigade S1. The air defender found Bolger present, and spoke earnestly to the commander. "If we don't get a Stinger down to Jetertown," the young officer moaned, "the same thing is going to happen tomorrow that happened today."[10] The lieutenant demanded that the battalion reoccupy Jetertown in force to get his teams a good firing site. The fact that the happy village and its inhabitants had been ceded back to Cortinian authorities that morning, or that the battalion faced an air assault in twenty-four hours, meant nothing to the air defense officer. With all the certainty of a second lieutenant, the young man insisted on action.

Dan Bolger looked at him. The detached observers of the Abu White Team had already told their battalion commander the sordid details, and the lieutenant colonel knew damn well that another Stinger more or less meant nothing in this sort of affair. As for retaking Jetertown—well, forget it. "You need to defend LZ Owl, and forget about perfect positioning," Bolger growled. "And don't overreact to this one. If we stay dispersed, out hunting, the OPFOR air can't do too much to us."

The next morning, the enemy Huey came back. Again invincible, it overflew the entire Fullerton box, stopping to bang away at the brigade support area, the brigade TOC, 2-327th Infantry, Team Animal, and the FLS proper. Bobbing majestically south, the UH-1H strafed the 2d Platoon of the Bushmasters (three killed, eight wounded) and the Mortar Platoon (three killed, six wounded) and then soared away. Fourteen Stinger teams engaged with no effect, including the one with 1st Lt. Chris Santos's mortarmen.[11] Even had the battalion gone back into Jetertown, none of this could have been prevented, as the OPFOR chopper hit everything before crossing that proposed firing site. Probably, no matter what the battalion did, the killer Huey was destined to survive. Not all of JRTC makes sense or reflects reality.

The air attacks caused sixty-four casualties in the battalion, bad enough. Some kind of strange O/C accounting evidently added another hundred to that butcher's bill, a bit of statistical sleight of hand that never squared with Lance Bailey's scrupulous casualty logs. Since battalion records for the search and attack phase showed nearly 190 killed and wounded, not the 159 officially reported in the AAR, Dan Bolger never pursued the discrepancy. Even with sixty-odd questionable losses courtesy of the Huey from hell and a hundred phantom dead added to the rolls, the overall numbers for the rotation still shook out very much in the 1st of the 327th's favor.[12] The battalion's hard-nosed performance in the Zion Hills mission saw to that.

The Scout Platoon justified their existence the morning of 22 May 1995. Skillfully slithering up to Objective Holland, the Tigers and their Navy/Marine pals brought in dozens of rounds of 127mm naval gunfire on the unsuspecting SOF command post, blowing it to splinters. The men didn't use the right communications channels, sending their messages through the ship rather than through the 1-327th's battalion ANGLICO cell.[13] It did not matter. Objective Holland was history, and Dan Bolger knew it by the afternoon of 22 May.

That activated contingency plan "Hunter," sending the companies straight into search and attack operations. The entire battalion knew the change in orders by liftoff time. Unlike 94-10, the Bulldogs did not stick to the sheet music, but played by ear, listening to the new situation as it developed. The troops readied for more sweeping in Lipke Vs, more hunting, and more kills by ones, twos, and threes.

The air assault that night began quietly, at least for the 1st of the 327th. Dan Bolger and his Black Tac team huddled in the treeline east of Owl, getting ready. They stared in fascination as the No Slack air assault went in right along the western horizon. Through night goggles, you could actually see the waves of Blackhawk choppers swarming around the landing zone, coming and going in their usual fours and sixes. Hundreds of explosive simulators recreated the effects of preparatory fires, and night-capable F/A-18D Hornet attack jets buzzed Objective Zon, lighting the skies to the west with a continuous show of shining afterburners. A steady rumble of cracking and roaring rolled slowly across the dark forests. With their scouts long since compromised and slain to no avail, Task Force 2-327 definitely had a tiger by the tail tonight. The Bulldogs could only watch and wonder.

The radios crackled as the 2d of the 327th plowed right into the heavily defended objective. Their LZ Albatross turned out to be hotter than molten plutonium, to the tune of a hundred-plus men down in the first few minutes. The enraged No Slack troopers tore into the hostile rocketmen and their sentries, killing or wounding all fifty-three in a monumental firefight, the largest of the rotation. The as-Saqr, Type-63, and both RBS70s passed into American hands.[14] All of this happened before the Bulldogs even left LZ Owl.

That launching went off as scheduled, although boiling red dust made landings chancy. Men ran to the birds through choking, billowing clouds of gritty sand. The nasty stuff sparked off the churning helicopter blades, mixing with static electricity to create flashing halos of greenish sparkles running all the way around the spinning rotor disks. It reminded Bolger of mariners' tales of St. Elmo's fire. But neither he nor anyone else had time to admire such phenomena. The men clambered aboard, the doors hissed shut, and the Blackhawks pitched up and away, bound for LZ Vulture.

The landings there went smoothly, putting the battalion on the ground without much trouble. The Abus walked south, and the Bushmasters moved east to await Team Animal. On his own initiative, Ted Donnelly seized two road bridges that looked useful to the tanks' approach. Chris Forbes led Cold Steel across the firebreak of a dirt trail, also heading south toward the ruins of Objective Holland. The LZST came in without incident, as did the 81mm mortars. Far away, the Maddogs under Capt. Delgado called in that the ground convoy had left LZ Owl. So far, so good, thought Bolger, now safely squirrelled into the forest north of Company C.

The Tigers reported in about 2235, telling Maj. Bill Phelps that they had four men left. The rest had been killed by aroused OPFOR survivors following the naval gunfire cannonade. The live scouts still observed Holland, which included two Jetertown-style clapboard, single-story buildings with tar-paper roofs. They noted bodies, abandoned antennas, and no activity.[15] Once Team Animal cranked through there to stir the embers, the scouts could pull back. But for now, Phelps told the Tiger holdouts to hang on.

The movement of Team Animal dragged behind schedule, as Ken Blakely fought through CLF minefields and snipers. None of these proved more than a nuisance, but each cost time. When 2300 came, Team Animal did not. Their radio messages indicated them to be up to two hours away.

The battalion swept slowly forward. The soldiers knew that search and attack worked poorly at night, and that moving forces merely became targets to well-placed stationary observers. Atlantican mortar observers again underscored that truth, catching 1st Lt. Britton Yount's 2d Platoon, Company A, in motion. In two eight-round missions, at 2355 and then 2356, the long-silent 82mm cadres had their way, knocking down a half-dozen Abus before the SOF outpost scuttled off.[16] Drew Felix, seemingly cursed by ill luck, drove his company deeper into the woods, leaving First Sergeant Craig to evacuate those hit.

About an hour later, as 1st Lt. Matt Moore's LZST put the Abu wounded aboard a Chinook medevac bird on LZ Vulture, Team Animal clanked into the zone. The big engines roared, but not so loud as to drown out the drone of the twin-engine CH-47D squatting on the landing zone. Having been oriented by Capt. Ted Donnelly, Blakely's tankers, armored engineers, and Bradley infantrymen bulled south along the firebreak. Although more than two hours late, they expected to be in and out before another hour passed. The enemy, and Mr. Murphy, made things go otherwise.

Blakely's men were in foul spirits. Along with tangling up in more than a dozen point minefields en route, they had lost two Bradley Fighting Vehicles and fourteen men to U.S. naval gunfire called in by a curious Apache pilot. At 0146, near the southern edge of LZ Vulture, the lead tank hit a minefield.

Team Animal responded by battle drill. The vehicles pulled alternately to the right and left, bows facing into the woods. The tank and Bradley carrier just behind the lead vehicle laid down a heavy burst of suppressive machine gun firing. The lead M1A1 Abrams tank began making choking white diesel smoke to screen the breaching attempt. Under cover of all of this, Blakely's engineers ran forward to direct the mine-rolling tank through the open column. Once the engineers picked the breaching lane, the tank with rollers would clear it.

The spasmodic firing fest mowed down six more Abus from poor 2d Platoon, just now recovering from the enemy mortar strike.[17] The shooting also came very near to slapping the Tac team laying prone in a cluster of ferns and bushes. Once again, blue-on-blue took a strip out of the Bulldogs. The tanks never knew they hit anyone, but some good did come out of the fratricide. The Atlantican SOF in the area fled south. Except for tanks blasting through a few more mines, that did it for the night.

As the infantry picked their way southward through the woods, the tanks ran down the firebreak to Objective Holland and found it empty. Their task finished, the armored column turned and departed. A few treads were damaged by landmines, but other than that, Team Animal escaped cleanly, fully ready for more action. For all its noise and firing, the tankers really had no effect on the enemy. They did, though, clean three mine patches off the firebreak, a major help when fighting flared again at daybreak.

Emboldened as the tanks pulled back, the remaining Rangers playing the SOF came out swinging as the sun rose. Capt. Chris Forbes and Company C hit a hornet's nest as their lead platoon approached the two buildings on Objective Holland. Before the commander could stop him, call for supporting fires, or get a look for himself, the impetuous 1st Platoon leader leaped in with both feet. From 0613 to 0652, the black-shirted SOF and the men of Company C fought an engagement that had more in common with Little Round Top than a modern contest between well-trained light infantry.

Battle drills collapsed among the tall hardwoods flanking the clearing that featured the two wooden buildings. Enemy soldiers shot and moved, and Company C's 1st Platoon did likewise. Both sides crossed and recossed the broad lawns around the two shacks. The casualties mounted as the well-zeroed OPFOR popped off round after round with telling effect. Shorn of supporting fires by the lead lieutenant's gusto, this one would be a *mano-a-mano* firefight. The three to one rule began to exert its baleful effects. It was hard to tell, but 1st Sgt. Ed Bauerle thought 1st Platoon might have lost some thirty men, almost all of them, in return for about ten black suits.

In it now whether he liked it or not, Chris Forbes brought up his 3d Platoon under 1st Lt. Jason Henneke and Sfc. Jeff England. Those two cool heads, seeing 1st Platoon in terminal trouble, called in mortar fires from the battalion platoon to seal off the hostile exit. Briefing the men on the run, England swung a squad onto the enemy flank, then hooked the platoon's machine guns into that vantage. They began to chew up the hostiles finishing off 1st Platoon. When the foe wheeled to deal with England, Henneke and the other two rifle squads opened fire with deadly accuracy, from what used to be the enemy front. Eleven SOF fell almost immediately, then another two. That finished off the Atlantican SOF on Objective Holland. Those twenty-three black-uniformed bodies cost Cold Steel forty-six good men.[18] It was the battalion's largest stand-up fight of Rotation 95-07.

Now Team Animal's help really showed. Speeding down the cleared firebreak, thankfully unconcerned with mines, Matt Moore and the LZST began recovering Company C's casualties even as 3d

Platoon's vicious counterattack turned the tide. If the SOF brought in mortar fire on this medical treatment and extraction conglomerate, the enemy might still salvage this battle. But the Bushmasters, marching to the sound of the guns, spiked that hope.

Ted Donnelly's men had never found that offending tube near Jetertown. This time, they found it almost immediately. Pushing south through the battered Abus at first light, Company B pulled up even with Objective Holland, but east of the firebreak, as Company C's fracas crackled to life. As they crested a small ridge, 2d Platoon's point team heard voices, and the sound of ammunition crates opening in the hollow below them. Without asking permission or forgiveness, the lead squad went prone and opened up. At this, Sfc. Charles Lipke and 2d Lt. John Hall pushed their famous V into its designed bold flank. It cost one friendly soldier killed and four wounded, but in ninety seconds, Hall and Lipke captured an 82mm mortar intact, killing its six-man crew.[19] This effectively ended all SOF resistance in the battalion zone.

Some ten SOF remained alive, but fleeting actions in the late afternoon took down five more. Undaunted by their long night motor march, Company D's gunners knocked off two up near LZ Vulture. Those OPFOR, lacking water, tried to waylay a pair of armed Humvees. The brutal return fire killed both would-be ambushers. When the "dead" men met their killers, they expressed amazement. "We didn't know you truck drivers could fight," blurted one embarrassed Ranger. The Maddogs on the scene only smiled at that.

Company C finished off another pair just northeast of Objective Holland, and in this little engagement, Lieutenant Colonel Bolger at last hoped to kill an OPFOR man. But the Cold Steel riflemen were too fast, and the battalion commander's weapon remained unfired on the entire rotation, despite his presence in and around significant skirmishing. *What a contrast with 94-10,* mused Bolger.

Fittingly, the often-battered Abus drew the last blood. After finding the "wrecked" OPFOR radio truck, the Abus took out a lone SA-14 gunner a kilometer south of Objective Holland. That happened at dusk on 23 May.[20]

The next morning, SSgt. James A. Angone caught three black-garbed OPFOR on the trail near Objective Holland. Ordering his

60mm section to direct lay on the trio, he barked orders to the two gun teams. The young men sighted and began "dropping" fake rounds, firing blank M16 rifle bullets down the empty tubes to simulate the distinctive "blook" sound of a mortar firing. The section spit out twenty-four pretend white phosphorus rounds, more than enough to slash and burn the opposition.

Yet, although the fire markers dumped their simulators right on target, the bad guys neither fled nor stopped moving. When Angone crawled up to the lip of the roadbed to figure this out, one of the black-clad men saw him. He turned around, pleading, "We're already dead. And besides, the war is over."

So it was. The JRTC authorities ended the exercise at 0700 on 24 May 1995. This time, the 1st Battalion, 327th Infantry Regiment, knew that they had won. So did the opposing forces. Using their own sweat and CLF blood, the Bulldogs had erased the stain of shame from Rotation 94-10.

Notes

The epigraph is quoted in John Keegan, *The Mask of Command* (New York: The Viking Press, 1987), 194.

1. Lt. Gen. Phillip B. Davidson, USA, ret., *Vietnam at War* (Novato, Calif.: Presidio Press, 1988), 531–33.

2. The as-Saqr 30 is known at JRTC as the SAKR. For a detailed description, see *Jane's Armour and Artillery 1992–93*, ed. Christopher F. Foss, (Alexandria, Va.: Jane's Information Group, Inc., 1992), 719–20. For American counterfire capabilities, see U.S., Department of the Army, Headquarters, Division Artillery, 101st Airborne Division (Air Assault), *Fire Support Handbook* (Ft. Campbell, Ky.: HQ, Division Artillery, 101st Airborne Division [Air Assault], 1995), 2-2, 2-21. The 105mm can shoot 19.5 kilometers; the 155mm reaches out to 30. The AN/TPQ-36 radar tracks incoming rockets out to only 24 kilometers.

3. Foss, *Jane's Armour and Artillery 1992–93*, 708–09.

4. For a detailed description, see *Jane's Land-Based Air Defense 1992–93*, eds. Tony Cullen and Christopher F. Foss (Alexandria, Va.: Jane's Information Group, Inc., 1992), 719–20. Supremely confident in this proven Bofors missile, Sweden will shortly field the RBS90, a greatly enhanced version of the RBS70. Missiles in this series can be found in the arsenals of Argentina, Bahrain, Indonesia, Iran, Pakistan, Tunisia, the United Arab Emirates, and Venezuela.

5. U.S., Department of the Army, Headquarters, 1st Brigade, 101st Airborne Division (Air Assault), *FRAGO 95-07-01* (Ft. Polk, La.: HQ, 1st Brigade, 101st Airborne Division [Air Assault], 20 May 1995), 1-8. A FRAGO is a fragmentary order, a change or addition to a base operation order. The first version, later modified, reflected the staff plan to attack Holland (the CP) and Veghel (the BSP) with infantry battalions at the outset.

6. U.S., Department of the Army, Headquarters, Joint Readiness Training Center, *1st Battalion, 327th Infantry Regiment, Rotation 95-07: AAR* (Ft. Polk, La.: HQ, JRTC, 24 May 1995), 9–11.

7. U.S., Department of the Army, Headquarters, 1st Battalion, 327th Infantry Regiment, *S2 Notes from Enemy Soldiers* (Ft. Polk, La.: HQ, 1st Battalion, 327th Infantry Regiment, 21 May 1995), 1-3.

8. HQ, JRTC, *1st Battalion, 327th Infantry Regiment, Rotation 95-07: AAR*, 25–26.

9. U.S., Department of the Army, Headquarters, Joint Readiness Training Center, *1st Battalion, 327th Infantry Regiment, Take Home Package, Training After-Action Report: Rotation 95-07* (Ft. Polk, La.: HQ, JRTC, 25 May 1995), 33-B.

10. HQ, JRTC, *1st Battalion, 327th Infantry Regiment, Rotation 95-07: AAR*, 24. The battalion senior O/C, Lt. Col. Mace Crowe, put this on a slide titled "Famous Quotes."

11. Ibid., 25.

12. The OPFOR casualty numbers also took time to get resolved. Initially, JRTC gave the 1st of the 327th credit for killing only 41 CLF during search and attack. Research into the actual OPFOR records revealed the true number, 109. See U.S., Department of the Army, Headquarters, 1st Battalion, 509th Parachute Infantry Regiment, "Friendly BDA by Role-Play Unit," slide prepared 25 May 1995.

13. HQ, JRTC, *1st Battalion, 327th Infantry Regiment, Rotation 95-07: AAR*, 42–43, 86.

14. U.S., Department of the Army, Headquarters, Joint Readiness Training Center, *2nd Battalion, 327th Infantry Regiment, Rotation 95-07: AAR* (Ft. Polk, LA.: HQ, JRTC, 24 May 1995), 12, 20–21.

15. HQ, JRTC, *1st Battalion, 327th Infantry Regiment, Rotation 95-07: AAR*, 37. The other scouts, including their platoon leader and platoon sergeant, died unnecessarily when their O/C inadvertently exposed their hide sites. The O/C got up to go to a meeting, and astute OPFOR soldiers followed his trail back to its source, with deadly results. Such things do happen at Fort Polk, but rarely.

16. Ibid., 40.

17. Ibid., 39, 69.

18. HQ, JRTC, *1st Battalion, 327th Infantry Regiment, Take Home Package, Training After-Action Report: Rotation 95-07*, 1, 51-B. The enemy force originally totalled 15 men, built around the company CP, but two four-man teams joined the stand.

19. HQ, JRTC, *1st Battalion, 327th Infantry Regiment, Rotation 95-07: AAR,* 40.

20. Ibid. Abu commander Capt. Drew Felix later became a JRTC O/C, a certain tribute to his demonstrated skill on two rotations.

Epilogue
Rendezvous

I have a rendezvous with Death
at some disputed barricade.

—Alan Seeger

They were burning tires again in Cité Soleil. Sharp, oily, sickening and sweet, reminiscent of the industrialized world so little in evidence otherwise, the unmistakable smell of smoldering steel-belted rubber wafted through the omnipresent miasma. Even among an overpowering smorgasbord of disgusting odors welling up from rotting animal (and sometimes human) flesh, putrifying vegetables, raw sewage awash in the cracked gutters, and belching, unfiltered car exhaust, the stench of tires alight stood out. Welcome to another clear, bright morning in the worst slum in Port-au-Prince, capital city of the Republic of Haiti.

The concepts of slum, Port-au-Prince, and Haiti seem somewhat redundant, but even in conjuring Hell, Dante Alighieri distinguished the lower circles from the higher. Cité Soleil formed rock-bottom, the very dregs of the western hemisphere's poorest country. And here, caught up in the stalled procession of rattletrap Toyotas and colorful "tap tap" taxis laden with chattering Haitians and various livestock, here waited three green U.S. Army Humvees. They looked as out of place as a trio of Corvettes in the Amazon jungle.

Yet the vehicles were very much where they belonged, coming straight down Avenue de Jean-Jacques Dessalines, the widest, straightest thoroughfare in the city, just about paralleling the trace of the filthy harbor, and known to all simply as "JJ."[1] The Americans marking time on JJ, one of seven similar patrol platoons out all night, were en route back to Cougar Base, the defended American compound on the northeastern edge of Port-au-Prince. Usually, JJ offered a relatively free ride. But this morning, as sometimes happened, something had gone wrong a block or so ahead. Smoke rose, good and black. Those burning tires did not ignite themselves.

The little patrol consisted of two armed Humvees, the same brand of hard-topped carriers with machine gun cupolas used by Company D in the 1st of the 327th. These two, however, hailed from the 2d Squadron, 2d Cavalry Regiment, the light cavalry force from Fort Polk that often supplemented the 1-509th Parachute Infantry as an opposing force for JRTC rotations. This was no exercise, but the fourth week of the fourth iteration of U.S. participation in the United Nations Mission in Haiti (UNMIH). Every man aboard carried live ammunition, and for good reason. They had just spent the night cruising the blacked-out, twisting streets of Port-au-Prince. The cavalry lieutenant, riding on the passenger side of the lead truck, did not like what he smelled. The billowing black smoke ahead indicated that this time, the denizens of Cité Soleil meant business, and the eight cavalrymen might not be able to do all that much about it.

The lieutenant's options very much rested on the mettle of the men affiliated with his third Humvee, the one without a top. Between the pair of gunships, that cargo truck sat idling. Around it, spread in a loose perimeter, weapons at the ready, crouched seven riflemen wearing Kevlar helmets covered in United Nations baby blue. They also wore the Screaming Eagle patch on their left upper sleeves. That, and their training and leadership, made them the force of choice to deal with this brewing problem.

Meeting Haitian troublemakers on foot, face-to-face, always fell to the infantry. One of them, SSgt. Brian Cagle, led the squad. Cagle and his men sweated under heavy Kevlar and nylon bulletproof vests, bulking with slabs of extra armor designed to protect them as they rode through Port-au-Prince. Now, with the sun creeping above the eastern hills and the temperature rising, Cagle and his men grew anxious. Having already seen several dead citizens tonight, experienced the usual Friday night voodoo rituals, and visited several quarters of the city frequented by armed thugs, Cagle was ready to get off the street and back to Cougar Base. Now the locals wanted to burn tires and, no doubt, beat up or hack up their rivals. To hell with that, thought Cagle. He walked forward to speak to his patrol leader, the cavalry officer.

The lieutenant had the radio handset in his ear. Someone in the Cougar Base TOC busily jabbered away, telling the young leader what to do, what not to do, and the like. Cagle sighed.

"Sir," he started.

The officer looked up, the radio net blessedly silent at precisely the right instant.

"Yes, Sergeant Cagle?"

"Sir," Cagle continued, "let me take my squad up there. It's only a block and a half. Maybe I can clean it up."

The officer responded slowly, tentatively: "I don't think . . ."

The NCO spoke again, quietly. "Listen, sir, maybe I can make contact with the Bangladeshis. It's in their zone, anyway. At least let me get a look at it."

That didn't seem like too much to ask now, did it? Cavalrymen always reconnoiter, don't they? A few seconds passed.

"Okay, get going," the officer finally mumbled. "I'll get the trucks up in support as soon as I can," he promised. That might work. But SSgt. Cagle did not count on it. He knew he was on his own. Well, he'd been to that dance before.

Brian Cagle hefted his black M16A2 rifle to his left hand, and waved his men to him. In classic Fort Benning style, he explained the plan; no DDMP posturing, either, just the facts, like *Dragnet*. Move to the intersection, check it out, find the Bangladeshis, and, if possible, restore order. Any questions?

The men had none. Every soldier's rifle featured a full magazine, thirty 5.56mm bullets, with another 180 in six other magazines on their web gear. The crowd ahead numbered more than a thousand, easily. We can't kill all of them, not even close, the squad leader knew. Already, the Americans heard the flat crack of gunshots. Great.

"If we want breakfast, let's get going," Cagle offered. That half-jest drew no reply. Rather, the men deployed, three forward, the squad leader centered, and three to the rear. They moved out, padding like an articulated hunting beast, heads and eyeballs scanning all 360 degrees, just in case.

The men threaded their way through the shuddering, idling cars and trucks, past the curious, slim Haitian women balancing wicker baskets on their heads. Two emaciated brown dogs tied to the stump of a lamp post barked and yelped, straining at their rope leashes, trying to get to these strange smelling big men in green camouflage and blue helmets. Cagle's troopers ignored them, watching instead for the telltale flash of a muzzle, searching rooftops for the black nose of a rifle barrel.

One block went past in a few minutes. The crowd grew more dense, but respectfully melted to the sides as the Americans came on, then closed behind them. The Screaming Eagles looked determined, all right, and nobody chose to challenge these gringos. It was a scene from a bygone era, the colonial regulars brassing it out, overawing the indigenous types who could have easily swallowed them whole. But who wanted to eat those first few rasping bullets squeezed off by hard-eyed young men, white, black, and brown, combat soldiers who clearly meant business? Nobody volunteered. Instead, the citizenry of Cité Soleil got out of the way.

As the squad neared the fringe of the choking tire smoke, the point man held up his hand. Cagle nodded. Wordlessly, moving amidst the howl of the crowd and the thrum of idling engines, the Americans spread into a security halt, weapons trained outward, but pointed to the ground. The Haitians right around them stood back, watching, fascinated. The point man jerked his thumb over his right shoulder, indicating an alleyway blocked by a junked vehicle. The top of that might provide a look into the smoky, congested intersection.

Climbing on the rusted, burnt-out pickup truck, Cagle saw the problem. A huge crowd chanted in Creole *patois*, swaying like sports fans. "*L'ennemi, l'ennemi*"—the enemy, they were saying. In the center of an uneven ring, two bedraggled Haitian National Police constables stood back to back, gray uniform shirts soaked with sweat, eyes wide with fear. God only knew what they had done, or not done. Cagle saw clubs in the air, and the glint of machetes, favorite Haitian devices for settling arguments once and for all.

As the staff sergeant backed off the wreck, he heard a crisp call: "I say there, American," came the voice, definitely in Her Most Britannic Majesty's own dialect, Bay of Bengal subdepartment. Cagle turned to his right, facing into the narrow alley.

There before him, impeccably decked out in forest green tropical kit, stood a very dark-skinned middle-aged man not much more than five feet in height, his head crowned with a dark green Russian-style dome helmet. Behind him, drawn up in a four man front, stood at least a hundred stiff, silent little dark-skinned men, dressed the same as their officer, with AK-47s across their chests. The Bangladeshi quick reaction force had obviously arrived. Thank goodness. These guys may be small, but they knew something about busting heads. And there were more than seven of them, too.

"Sir," Cagle commenced, guessing correctly that he spoke to the artillery colonel commanding the dismounted gunners who comprised BANCON, the Bangladesh Contingent in Haiti. "There are two Haitian policemen about to get killed out there."

The Bengali colonel waved his right hand impatiently. "Yes, yes, we know all of that," he chirped. "So,"—he looked right into Cagle's eyes—"what are you going to do about it?"

Cagle's jaw dropped. "Sir?"

The Bengali commander repeated his question in the same annoyed tone. Then he added: "We're not really up to this sort of thing, you know." He gestured, his right hand on a shining leather Tokarev pistol holster, his left sweeping broadly. "After you, American."

A loud shout rose up from the intersection to his back. Cagle whirled to see a hail of stones arc into the open area, no doubt aimed at the poor creatures caught in the ragged circle. Enough screwing around, thought Cagle.

He remembered to call in on his little plastic brick radio: "Foxtrot One-Two, this is Cold Steel Three-One, we're going in, out." He did not wait for a reply. Lives were at stake.

"Let's go." He motioned to his men. They picked up in unison, and waded away from the corner, into the jostling, tightly packed crowd.

Most of the Haitians moved away as soon as the Americans touched them. A young tough shoved back at the right front soldier, and the rifleman calmly jacked his rifle butt into the youth's stomach. That clash caused the people to surge and stumble around the U.S. troops. Arms and hands grasped at Cagle and his men. They swung their rifles, clouting men and women with butts and barrels. *If this goes on, we'll be forced to fix bayonets, then shoot,* thought Cagle. But discipline held, on all sides.

Two more buttstrokes, another few shouts, and the squad broke through. They found three skinny Haitian males with long cane poles smacking at the hapless police officers. A man with a machete raced from the side of the circle opposite Cagle's squad. The lead U.S. trio raised their weapons to their shoulders. The Haitian slowed to a shuffle, the machete still up, waving.

Here we go, thought Cagle. The crowd sucked in its breath with a collective "Ooooh!" The chanting circle stilled.

A beat, then another passed. The taut riflemen did not move a muscle.

The Haitian dropped the machete with a metallic clatter.

"Flex-cuff all four of these guys," Cagle ordered. "And let's get these cops to the aid station."

Two of the Screaming Eagles pulled white plastic strips off their belts and went to work. The crowd stayed, watching, silent.

An air horn sounded, and the crowd parted like the Red Sea struck by Moses. Into the intersection rolled the three green Humvees, armed cav troopers standing in the cupolas of the lead and trail trucks.

"Gentlemen, the cavalry is here," Cagle announced to nobody in particular.[2]

So began Saturday, 25 November 1995, in Port-au-Prince, Haiti. It was another day, one of several equally exciting and many more less so, for SSgt. Brian Cagle and the men of Company C, 1st Battalion, 327th Infantry Regiment, late of JRTC and Fort Campbell, and assigned at that time to UNMIH. A veteran of combat in Panama, Brian Cagle did not think anything much of his little fracas. The Bengali colonel thought otherwise, describing Cagle's venture as "the bravest act" he had ever witnessed. Of such wise displays of courage are victories made.

Brian Cagle's encounter in the Haitian dawn reflected his own considerable talent and character. The way he reacted, though, and the calm discipline shown by this NCO and his men came from training like that conducted at the Joint Readiness Training Center. Indeed, the reason a solitary rifle squad did not hesitate to quell an ugly mob came from the confidence bred in the swamps, forests, and sham villages of JRTC.

Performance at JRTC earned the 1st Brigade the nod for the Haiti mission, even though by rights it probably should have gone to another Screaming Eagle brigade. The hybrid task organization called for 1st Brigade's headquarters company to take charge of a joint (all services) and unified (UN) task force known as JTF Bastogne. Composed of the 2d Squadron, 2d Cavalry Regiment, the 317th Military Police Battalion, with an attached company from the Indian subcontenent, a civil affairs team, a psychological operations section, counterintelligence elements, and an infantry company from Djibouti, Donovan inherited downtown Port-au-Prince, including security for the Presidential Palace. Higher authorities rebuffed the 101st Airborne's requests to do the entire mission with organic troops, but they did assent to letting Donovan reinforce the truck-mounted cavalry with two of his own air assault rifle companies.

Based on JRTC performance, both of those companies might have come from the 1st of the 327th, Ted Donnelly's Company B and Chris Forbes's Company C. But the division leadership shied from so gutting out one infantry battalion. Told to chose his rifle companies from two battalions, Col. Jack Donovan picked Forbes and Company C based on their performance in Jetertown, and Company B from 2-327th, a unit that saw bloody action in and around Smith Villa. This greatly disappointed the Bushmasters, but it left two battalions somewhat capable, rather than hollowing one down to the quick. Leaving no doubt about his preferences, Donovan ceded most of the Haiti trainup for both companies to Lt. Col. Dan Bolger, Cmd. Sgt. Maj. Mark Ripka, and their fellow Bulldogs. Drawing on common JRTC experiences and standards, the difficult six week training regimen well served the riflemen of both companies. They functioned as UN-MIH's elite arm in Port-au-Prince and in missions throughout Haiti.[3]

As it turned out, JTF Bastogne carried out every mission to standard. They secured the Haitian presidential election and transfer of power of December 1995 through February 1996, defused several potential riots and insurrections in Port-au-Prince and the countryside, and protected the U.S. force withdrawal in February–March 1996. Significantly, schooled in RAMP techniques refined at JRTC and retrained by 1-327th Infantry, the Screaming Eagle infantry controlled many, many shooting and crowd violence situations, often at night, and always without killing a single innocent civilian. Just as important, JTF Bastogne sustained no casualties despite ample opportunities to do so. One might argue, and many did, about whether the mission in Haiti accomplished anything much for that destitute nation. But as far as military performance, the Screaming Eagle contingent certainly closed out this round of American intervention in grand style.

The Haiti undertaking validated 1st Brigade's JRTC experience. Nobody knew that better than those men of 1st of the 327th who experienced both the agony of JRTC 94-10 and the triumphs of 95-07, especially Capt. Chris Forbes. His growth as a commander, from nearly useless to absolutely pivotal, demonstrates why JRTC exists. In real combat, Forbes would have been dead, cut down for no good purpose during his first week in action. Worse, his company would have been shredded, scores of men killed and maimed as awful proof that their captain erred. But thanks to JRTC, Chris Forbes stumbled, got up, regrouped along with the rest of his battered battalion, went back into the arena, and cleaned the clock of the unforgiving CLF and their SOF buddies. In that light, success in Haiti followed naturally, just the way the U.S. Army intended. The JRTC did its job, in his case and many, many others, including that of Dan Bolger.

One must be careful in alleging that organizations can learn, especially an outfit as dynamic as a U.S. Army infantry battalion. But even granting that the 1st of the 327th did not truly "learn" collectively, the chain of command certainly absorbed a great deal between the start of JRTC 94-10 and the opening of 95-07. The results speak for themselves. By all four of the usual yardsticks—kill ratio, mission accomplishment, going the distance, and learning—the 1st of the 327th excelled. That did not just happen by itself.

A cursory consideration of what went right on 95-07 might well focus on techniques, tricks, and gadgets: the Ten Commandments, the Lipke-V formation, Quickdraw targeting, contact battle drills, the LZST, the tactical CPs and White Teams, the buttpacks and rifle scopes, RAMP, Team Golf, B^2S^2, the refusal to use the DDMP, the single landing zone tactic, landing off the objective, or the Earth Pig ethos of doing without. Anyone looking at mere procedures misses the major reason the second rotation went differently. Far from being solutions in themselves, the innovations represent indications of the real change in the battalion, the empowering of good junior leaders to do as they saw fit. Leadership by example, not the dead hand of method, marks the true divide between 94-10 and 95-07.

In trusting men over method, the Bulldogs gave way to American military tradition and practice rather than bowing at the shrine of the great amorphous deity Doctrine. If swallowed uncritically, untempered by experience, Doctrine becomes a false god, a Moloch that eats unwary battalions whole. The entire edifice of U.S. Army schools field manuals, observer/controllers, and AARs exists to propagate a myth, to wit, that war can be controlled, friction smoothed away, fog dissipated, the crooked made straight, the hard made easy, if only the pupil will do these three, or thirty, or three hundred things, any one of which is utterly unlikely.

War is chaos. It cannot be harnessed, or bent, or shaped to our whims. Hours spent planning can be swept away by one wrong turn, one unlucky mortar barrage. The clash of men determined to slay each other, war proceeds with all the subtlety and formality of a knife fight. Both sides struggle to enforce their will on parties unwilling to be so forced. The resultant violent collisions defy the efforts of either side to organize them into neat processes.

Burning up hours on the Deliberate Decision-Making Process, coloring in charts in a roomy TOC, or rehearsing intricate maneuvers amounts to spending more and more time solving only a third of the problem, our side. As for the bad guys and the environment, well, they demand their due. And you had better get organized to give it to them your way, or they will take it in theirs.

All of the things the 1st of the 327th did to prepare for JRTC 95-07 put resources, especially time, in the hands of the fighters. To their credit, Dan Bolger, Bill Phelps, and their comrades stripped away anything that did not kill the Fort Polk enemy, or contribute directly to it. The methods developed matched the world of Cortina, the CLF, and the JRTC model, but Bolger would be the first to tell you that these tricks must change as the environment alters. Nothing is carved in stone. Indeed, the forces schooled for Haiti marched with Ten Commandments, too, but theirs began with "Protect the force," more appropriate for their theater of commitment.[4]

Encouraging NCO and junior officer initiative, teaching the same and insisting upon it by force of personal example, the 1st of the 327th chain of command necessarily drew a hard line on those unable to keep pace. Along with his own superb personal example out hunting the CLF, Mark Ripka's greatest role in preparing the battalion for JRTC revolved around his unstinting determination to fill the battalion's platoon sergeant and first sergeant slots with quality senior NCOs. Moving Ed Bauerle to be the first sergeant of Company C near the end of JRTC 94-10 showed the virtue in choosing leaders with the right stuff. Ripka filled every key NCO position with a quality man, thereby providing the key links in the chain that allowed the Bulldogs to trust in each other, not some book-born system. Led by a strong band of sergeantry, the battalion naturally derived nontraditional answers to the usual JRTC problems. Each new method showed the hand of tough, smart noncommissioned officers, in that they were very simple to execute and very hard to defeat.

Task Force 1-327th need not have taken this less traveled route. Not many battalions did. Of course, few benefited from two trips to Fort Polk's JRTC in nine months. For most outfits, it seems easier to go back to your post, crank out some DDMP drills, keep running through live fires, and remember what went right on your excursion to the wilds of Cortina. Any critical look back at JRTC usually relied on the two-inch thick AAR book bequeathed by the O/Cs. Here, the O/Cs expanded on their teaching points from the rotational AAR gatherings. The JRTC leadership stressed systems and processes, mainly because their portfolio denied them the ability to finger weaklings, chuckleheads, units in disarray, quitters, and other such touchy subjects. That degree of personal assessment fell to the organization's chain of command.

The circumscribed JRTC documentation runs two inches thick whether you win or lose, whether you suffer 909 casualties (94-10) or 397 (95-07).[5] Much of it reads the same: weak mission analysis, poor synchronization, inadequate attention to logistics forecasts, incomplete reporting, so on and so forth. If you swoop down on that kind of administrivia, you will not figure out the real key to killing the CLF. It's all fine, but it merely dresses up the rigging without touching the hull.

To get at the essence, you must get beyond the dry catalog of symptoms compiled by the dutiful O/Cs. The core truth makes sense to any student of Sun-tzu, or those conversant with Taoist theory, or even fans of George Lucas's bastardized concept of the Force in *Star Wars*. The winning system is, in fact, no fixed system at all. Get good soldiers, give them the tools, and turn them loose. That's all there is to it.

The 101st Airborne Division (Air Assault) routinely concludes every ceremony with the "Screaming Eagle Song." By long tradition, the band plays this stirring march all the way through, then the soldiers present sing it. The first line also encapsulates the division motto: "We have a rendezvous with destiny."[6] A rendezvous with destiny, a meeting with fate—it's a fitting idea for a division that goes to war on short notice, at very long range, in the black of night, many miles into hostile country. In a few short minutes, a Screaming Eagle moves from relative safety to the ultimate test. Failure means death.

The Joint Readiness Training Center allows soldiers to make their rendezvous with destiny and come back to talk about it. It made the individuals in the 1st Battalion, 327th Infantry Regiment, into better soldiers, challenged every leader to the limit of his competence, and taught all how to fight and win in a thoroughly uncompromising scenario. In an exceedingly volatile and dangerous world that draws them in with damn little warning, America's soldiers will usually be outnumbered and outgunned, just like SSgt. Brian Cagle in Port-au-Prince. In a tense face-off or street gunfight, our men need every advantage, every bit of leverage, and every edge they can get. Fort Polk's JRTC ensures that when the fateful rendezvous comes, our soldiers have the winning edge.

Notes

The epigraph is quoted in John Robert Young, *The French Foreign Legion* (New York: Thames and Hudson, Inc., 1984), 24. Cpl. Alan Seeger, an American, served in the *Régiment de Marche de la Légion Etrangère* (French Foreign Legion Marching Regiment) during World War I. He died in action in July 1916 on the Western front.

1. U.S., Department of the Navy, Marine Corps Intelligence Activity, *Haiti Handbook* (Quantico, Va.: Marine Corps Intelligence Activity, 1993), 2-1. Jean-Jacques Dessalines played a major role in overthrowing French colonial rule in 1804. Characteristically, he then declared himself emperor and ruled as a despot, a depressingly common occurrence in Haitian politics.

2. For basic patrolling procedures and organization, see U.S., Department of Defense, Joint Task Force Dragoon, *Zone V Command Briefing* (Port-au-Prince, Haiti: HQ, 2nd Armored Cavalry Regiment, 1995), 9–13. SSgt. Brian R. Cagle told this story to the author in Haiti on 29 November 1995 and again, at more length, on 21 April 1996. The author went to the site and verified documentary and eyewitness accounts in classified Department of Defense records. An unclassified account, the basis for the description in this text, has been included in Lt. Col. Daniel P. Bolger, USA, "Memorandum for the Commanding General, Subject: Command Visit to Haiti, 27–30 November 1995," 1 December 1995, 1–2.

3. U.S., Department of Defense, Joint Task Force Bastogne, *Haitian Handbook* (Ft. Campbell, Ky.: HQ, 1st Brigade, 101st Airborne Division [Air Assault], 1995), 3–4, 6. This handbook mirrored the brigade's highly successful *JRTC Handbook* in format and content. The brigade's task organization labeled the psychological operations section as MIST (Military Information Support Team), and so sidestepped the unpleasant propaganda and terror connoted in the term "psychological operations."

4. The Haiti forces operated in a peacekeeping milieu less active than the search and attack phase at JRTC, its closest analogue. The challenge in Haiti focused on staying ready for the time when the local versions of the CLF finally made their moves.

5. U.S., Department of the Army, Headquarters, Joint Readiness Training Center, *1st Battalion, 327th Infantry Regiment, Take Home Package, Training After-Action Report: Rotation 94-10*, (Ft. Polk, La.: HQ, JRTC, 27 September 1994); U.S., Department of the Army, Headquarters, Joint Readiness Training Center, *1st Battalion, 327th Infantry Regiment, Take Home Package, Training After-Action Report: Rotation 95-07*, (Ft. Polk, La.: HQ, JRTC, 25 May 1995). Both reports are about 60% the same in content.

6. Patrick H. F. Allen, *Screaming Eagles* (London: Hamlyn Publishing Group, Ltd., 1990), 7. The 101st Airborne's first commander, Maj. Gen. William C. Lee, coined the phrase "rendezvous with destiny."

Appendix

1st Battalion, 327th Infantry Regiment
Commanders, Staff, and Key Leaders

Position	JRTC 94-10	JRTC 95-07
Commander	Lt. Col. D. P. Bolger	Lt. Col. D. P. Bolger
XO	Maj. J. F. Laufenburg	Maj. S. R. Roberts
Cmd Sgt. Maj.	Cmd. Sgt. Maj. M. S. Ripka	Cmd. Sgt. Maj. M. S. Ripka
S1	1st Lt. G. C. Hardewig	1st Lt. L. M. Bailey
S2	Capt. D. C. Blackdeer	Capt. D. C. Blackdeer
Assistant S2	2nd Lt. T. Doughty	2d Lt. T. Doughty
S3	Maj. W. G. Phelps	Maj. W. G. Phelps
S3 Air	1st Lt. H. D. Bair	1st Lt. M. D. Bounds
Assistant S3	Capt. M. D. Delgado	none
Chemical Officer	2nd Lt. J. R. Boyles	2d Lt. J. R. Boyles
S4	Capt. M. E. Donnelly	1st Lt. C. M. Doane
S5	1st Lt. M. D. Bounds	1st Lt. K. Leeds
Chaplain	Capt. N. W. Jones	Capt. J. E. Shaw

Headquarters and Headquarters Company

Commander	Capt. R. L. Sarvis	Capt. R. L. Sarvis
XO	1/Lt. F. R. Prins	1/Lt. R. C. Ackerman
1/Sgt.	1/Sgt. J. L. Jeffcoat	1/Sgt. M. A. Miller
Scout Plt. Ldr.	1/Lt. M. A. Lawry	1/Lt. M. A. Lawry
Scout Plt. Sgt.	S/Sgt. K. A. Mayfield	Sfc. C. M. McKamey
Mortar Plt. Ldr.	1/Lt. D. M. Richey	1/Lt. C. N. Santos
Mortar Plt. Sgt.	Sfc. G. A. Peele	Sgt. R. K. Spencer
Medical Plt. Ldr.	1/Lt. P. C. Sheridan	1/Lt. P. C. Sheridan
Surgeon	Capt. R. Bhatar	Capt. R. T. Ramos
PA	1/Lt. M. A. Bratcher	1/Lt. M. A. Bratcher
Medical Plt. Sgt.	Sfc. R. V. Johnson	Sfc. R. V. Johnson
Support Plt. Ldr.	1/Lt. J. D. Williams	1/Lt. M. R. Moore
Support Plt. Sgt.	S/Sgt. D. S. Ceretti	S/Sgt. M. D. Wood
Maint. Plt. Ldr.	Mr. H. A. Tomlinson	Mr. H. A. Tomlinson
Maint. Plt. Sgt.	Sgt. D. L. Donnelly	S/Sgt. R. C. Bisquera
Commo Plt. Ldr	1/Lt. M. J. McCabe	Capt. J. D. Lee
Commo Plt. Sgt.	Sfc. G. Vanvolkinburg	Sfc. G. Vanvolkinburg

Position	JRTC 94-10	JRTC 95-07
Company A		
Commander	Capt. R. D. Felix	Capt. R. D. Felix
XO	1/Lt. J. J. Berkmeyer	1/Lt. S. Schoner
1/Sgt.	1/Sgt. S. D. Craig	1/Sgt. S. D. Craig
FSO	1/Lt. R. Wang	2/Lt. H. L. LaRock
Mortar Sec. Ldr.	S/Sgt. J. A. Angone	S/Sgt. J. A. Angone
1st Plt. Ldr.	1/Lt. M. R. Moore	2/Lt. M. W. Fine
1st Plt. Sgt.	Sfc. S. D. Louis	S/Sgt. R. G. Thomas
2d Plt. Ldr.	none	1/Lt. J. B. Yount
2d Plt. Sgt.	S/Sgt. D. Brackenbury	S/Sgt. D. Brackenbury
3d Plt. Ldr.	none	1/Lt. C. A. Calvaresi
3d Plt. Sgt.	S/Sgt. M. A. Gerkin	S/Sgt. M. A. Gerkin
Company B		
Commander	Capt. A. J. Mycue	Capt. M. E. Donnelly
XO	1/Lt. P D. Jutras	1/Lt. P. D. Jutras
1/Sgt.	1/Sgt. G. S. Eubank	1/Sgt. G. S. Eubank
FSO	2/Lt. D. H. Grubbs	2/Lt. D. H. Grubbs
Mortar Sec. Ldr.	S/Sgt. J. S. Decker	Sgt. R. M. Streeter
1st Plt. Ldr.	2/Lt. L. D. Oskey	2/Lt. L. D. Oskey
1st Plt. Sgt.	Sfc. C. M. McKamey	Sfc. R. L. Malloy
2d Plt. Ldr.	none	2/Lt. J. W. Hall
2d Plt. Sgt.	Sfc. C. W. Lipke	Sfc. C. W. Lipke
3d Plt. Ldr.	none	2/Lt. W. A. Burnard
3d Plt. Sgt.	Sfc. D. A. Anderson	Sfc. W. J. Shook
Company C		
Commander	Capt. C. S. Forbes	Capt. C. S. Forbes
XO	1/Lt. C. N. Santos	1/Lt. J. Smith
1/Sgt.	Sfc. D. LaRocca	1/Sgt. E. T. Bauerle
FSO	2/Lt. T. Everritt	2/Lt. M. Dyer
Mortar Sec. Ldr.	S/Sgt. J. D. Lee	Sgt. W. C. Clark
1st Plt. Ldr.	none	2/Lt. S. W. Trisler
1st Plt. Sgt.	S/Sgt. C. R. Judd	Sfc. L. D. Primeaux
2d Plt. Ldr.	2/Lt. M. P. Martel	2/Lt. M. P. Martel
2d Plt. Sgt.	S/Sgt. B. E. Blagg	S/Sgt. J. E. Ferebee
3d Plt. Ldr.	none	2/Lt. J. C. Henneke
3d Plt. Sgt.	Sfc. K. A. Willis	Sfc. J. C. England

Position	JRTC 94-10	JRTC 95-07
Company D		
Commander	Capt. W. T. Utroska	Capt. M. D. Delgado
XO	1/Lt. R. A. Williford	1/Lt. R. J. Basher
1/Sgt.	1/Sgt. R. D. Morgan	1/Sgt. R. D. Morgan
1st Plt. Ldr.	none	none
1st Plt. Sgt.	Sfc. E. Edwards	Sfc. E. Edwards
2d Plt. Ldr.	none	none
2d Plt. Sgt.	S/Sgt. W. O. Bailey	Sfc. T. E. Stinnett
3d Plt. Ldr.	none	none
3d Plt. Sgt.	S/Sgt. C. L. Detzel	S/Sgt. C. L. Detzel
4th Plt. Ldr.	none	none
4th Plt. Sgt.	Sfc. J. L. Morales	S/Sgt. C. D. Berry
5th Plt. Ldr.	none	2/Lt. A. Chester
5th Plt. Sgt.	S/Sgt. T. R. Walden	S/Sgt. T. R. Walden

Attachments

FSO	Capt. J. M. Temple	Capt. J. M. Temple
FSNCO	S/Sgt. D. A. Naugle	Sfc. R. J. Smith
ADA Plt. Ldr.	2/Lt. F. A. Mack	2/Lt. A. Dewees
ADA Plt. Sgt.	Sfc. J. Edgar	Sfc. J. Edgar
Engr. Plt. Ldr.	2/Lt. A. M. Speck	2/Lt. S. Reynolds
Engr. Plt. Sgt.	S/Sgt. S. P. Otto	Sfc. G. Combs

1st Battalion, 327th Infantry Regiment

JRTC 94-10 and JRTC 95-07
Simulated Losses Inflicted and Sustained—A Comparison

Rotation 94-10

	Rotational Forces	Opposing Forces	Ratio (U.S./OPFOR)
Search and Attack	428	74	5.7 to 1
Defense	278	141	1.9 to 1
Deliberate Attack	203	23	8.8 to 1
TOTAL	909	238	3.8 to 1

Rotation 95-07

	Rotational Forces	Opposing Forces	Ratio (U.S./OPFOR)
Search and Attack	159	109	1.5 to 1
Deliberate Attack	238	52	4.6 to 1
TOTAL	397	161	2.5 to 1

Index